DONOR-CENTERED LEADERSHIP

What it takes to build a high performance fundraising team

PENELOPE BURK

CYGNUS APPLIED RESEARCH, INC.
UNITED STATES | CANADA | UNITED KINGDOM

Donor-Centered Leadership
Penelope Burk

© 2013 by Penelope Burk

Publisher: Cygnus Applied Research, Inc.
Editor-in-Chief: Ingrid Lawrie

Printer: Friesens Corporation Printed in Canada

First printing, April 2013

ISBN: 978-0-9687978-3-9

To order direct from the publisher, please contact Cygnus Applied Research, Inc.

In the United States:
444 N Michigan Ave.,
12th Floor
Chicago, IL 60611
t. (800) 263 0267

In Canada:
69 John Street South
Suite 410
Hamilton, ON L8N 2B9
t. (800) 263 0267

email: cygnus@cygresearch.com
www.cygresearch.com

DONOR-CENTERED LEADERSHIP

The research with fundraisers, chief executive officers, board members and donors which forms the basis of *Donor-Centered Leadership* was a significant undertaking supported by many people along the way. I am deeply appreciative of the support I received from staff at Cygnus Applied Research, Inc. in data preparation and book production. Special thanks are due, in particular, to:

VP, Research and Client Services: Jeff Dubberley, B.A., M.A.
Associate Director of Research: Haihong Wang, PhD
Creative Director: Amanda Diletti-Goral
Senior Research Associate: Carolyn Veldstra, PhD (ABD)
Research Associate: Sarah Rietkoetter, BSc
Sales and Marketing Director: Theresa Horak

Their assistance in bringing *Donor-Centered Leadership* to life has been invaluable.

Out there in the world are three great men who are doing their bit to make the world a better and more interesting place. Jeffrey, Jonathan and Jason, I am so proud of you every day...and so very lucky.

CONTENTS

PART III – Holding Onto the Team You Build

PART I
Fundraising and Leadership

Chapter 1:
Behind the Revolving Door

Oh, that sick and sinking feeling.

Your most prized employee – the one who picks up everything so fast; the one who nails proposals in the first draft…and with perfect grammar, too; the one who makes donors want to give; the one who cheerfully adapts to your shifting priorities; the one you relied on to be there forever.

Now there she is, hovering in the doorway.

"Can I have a minute?"

"Sure, sit down."

She has a look of concern on her face but it's not a "something's-gone-wrong-with-the-campaign look." It's a look you've never seen before; it's a "let's get this over with" look.

And, even before the words are out of her mouth, you know. You know, and so you're unable to hear what she's saying. You're just catching the odd word here and there because you've redirected your senses to the emergency in which you now find yourself. You're trying to think logically while your whole being is moving at lightning speed through surprise, denial, anger and – oh, the irony – resignation.

You make an effort to come back to consciousness just as she reaches her main point.

"…So while I really appreciate how much I have learned here and, especially, the opportunity to work with you, I'm sorry to have to tell you…I'm leaving."

You know that now is the time to be gracious…and grateful. You should ask her about the new job. You should send her a signal that it's OK to be excited, that she's ready for and deserves a new challenge. You should say something that will become increasingly meaningful to her as she advances in her career. But the words don't come. You're doing what you have been hired and trained to do. You're in problem-solving mode.

Plan A is to get her to stay, but the tone of her voice and her body language say it's too late for that. So you move immediately to Plan B, and you try to list all the things that you'll need to do, in their proper order, to replace her. But you're not in the right frame of mind for lists, so you simplify. You focus on the critical path and how much time it will take to do all the things that you can't even think to put on that list yet.

You look across the desk at your excited, hesitant, hopeful employee who has done so much over the years that made you look so good, and you say,

"So, when's your last day, then?"

People Give to People

It's an old adage, and some might say a tired one, but it's still true. The quality of human interaction, customer service, donor relations – how one person treats and interacts with another – underpins all business success. And, when you're selling an intangible, an optional commodity, in fact one that will not even be consumed by the purchaser, the quality of people-to-people interaction in fundraising is the glue that binds donor to not-for-profit. In a field where building relationships is key, and where its practitioners acknowledge that doing so takes time, finding and holding onto good fundraisers is as integral to profit as finding and holding onto donors.

The length of time professional fundraisers stay with one not-for-profit, then, is a bellwether of the industry. And, on that front, there seems to be trouble. Nine out of ten Development Directors who manage fundraising staff feel that the rate of turnover in their organizations is a problem, and over half of CEOs have experienced the premature resignation or dismissal of their Chief Development Officer.

Supply and Demand

Adding to the problem is that there seem to be too few fundraising professionals for a growing not-for-profit sector. The strain of an under-resourced profession means that fundraisers are easily lured from one job to the next. As evidence of how serious this problem is, Directors of Development (or those occupying the top management positions in fundraising) say that they spend only three to six months in a new position before another not-for-profit or search firm asks them to consider a career opportunity. Fundraising program directors who manage specific areas of specialization such as direct marketing or planned giving are also in high demand. They report that it takes less than a year on the job before the courting begins.

The length of time fundraisers spend actively seeking new positions is another indicator of supply/demand imbalance. 62% of management-level fundraisers have never experienced any lag between jobs and this holds true for 68% who have no management responsibilities. Among those who have experienced any period of unemployment between positions, it was generally for less than a month; only 14% have sought work for longer than three months at least once in their careers.

Fundraisers also tend to move quickly, some say too quickly, up the seniority ladder and this, too, is a factor of supply and demand. Of the fundraisers in our study who started in non-management jobs, it took them only four years, on average, to rise to management-level positions.

The global recession that hit in 2007 and the sluggish economy that continues into the publication of this book, reinforced the connection between staff turnover and supply and demand. In the first few months of 2009, belt-tightening in Development Departments meant a freeze on hiring and even layoffs at some not-for-profits. 31% of fundraisers we studied who were planning to change jobs when surveyed in mid-2008 decided to stay put instead once the supply-demand factor shifted in favor of employers.

Entering and Leaving the Profession

Why people get into fundraising in the first place may offer another clue to the causes of rapid job change among Development professionals. Only 40% of survey respondents became fundraisers by choice, by responding to a job ad for instance or receiving advice from a career counselor. 44%, however, "settled" for a fundraising position due to lack of opportunity in other fields, or found that fundraising became part of their job when they thought they were hired to do something else.

Supply/demand imbalance is more than simply a dearth of people deliberately choosing fundraising as a career. Too many trained, experienced fundraisers are leaving the industry in favor of pursuing careers in other fields. Almost a third of Development professionals who were seriously considering a job change at the time we interviewed them were planning to get out of fundraising altogether.

Staff turnover in my multi-level not-for-profit has been the biggest impediment to our success. As a board member, I feel that the combination of staff turnover and poor management eats up half our time at board meetings. Settling these things down would free the board up to focus on raising money for a change.

Fundraising is a marathon, not a sprint. The longer you are at it, the broader and deeper relationships become. Plus you get to work with the most wonderful people in the world – donors and volunteers

The Big Pay-Off

In such a fast-paced world, where experts say that people will have ten to fourteen jobs before they are thirty-eight years old, is it realistic to think that there are constructive solutions to the problem of too-rapid staff turnover in fundraising? Yes, and the benefits of mitigating this problem are substantial. For example, adding twelve more months to the tenure of a non-management staff member, who had planned to leave after one year on the job, saves his not-for-profit almost 1.2 times his salary for a full year. More important, both employer and employee get to reap the return on their collective investment. The not-for-profit's time invested up front in training and mentoring now yields a more experienced staff member who, in year two, achieves results faster, solves problems more creatively (or avoids them altogether), and contributes as a fully functioning member of the team. The employee also benefits from living out a more satisfying career experience, rather than cycling through another apprenticeship period. And, when he does leave, he will be a much more valuable commodity to his next employer, while having the satisfaction of knowing he has served his current one well.

Extending job tenure along the spectrum of increasingly senior fundraising positions eventually leads to the biggest payoff of all – in planned giving. But, currently, this is where the gap is widest between what could be realized and what fundraisers are actually raising.

Among donors who have assigned a bequest in their wills, only 4% say they were influenced to do so by a representative of the recipient charity. While donors should be lauded for their initiative, fundraisers know that when they play an active role in negotiating major gifts (including planned gifts), more donors give and give more generously than if left to make these decisions on their own.

A fundraising bonanza is there for the taking. One out of three donors with a will, but no planned gift assigned, say they would definitely or very likely include a charitable bequest or give it serious consideration if asked by someone from a not-for-profit they respected.

Most not-for-profits are not negotiating planned gifts as part of their fundraising strategy. Among the minority who are, under-resourcing their planned gifts operation relative to potential is commonplace. Lack of appreciation for the net value of these gifts, and failing to understand how willing their donors are to offer them, contribute to the sector's failure to capitalize on this lucrative fundraising opportunity. However, premature staff turnover plays an important role, too.

Planned giving is a specialized field that demands maturity and experience. With the fundraising business starving for talent at every level, it is that much harder to staff planned giving adequately from among the industry's current practitioners. Addressing the supply/demand issue in professional fundraising as a whole will help, but it is not the only thing that needs to happen.

Resourcing fundraising more effectively also means being realistic about the inherent limitations of the business in developing the right kind of talent. Fundraising is comprised of two distinct fields – direct marketing and relationship fundraising – and someone who shines in the former may not be the best candidate for the latter. It will not be enough to enlarge the pool of fundraisers working volume-based programs and expect that this will take care of the problem. The highly profitable end of the business needs more fundraisers but a different breed of fundraiser as well.

The Essential Triumvirate

As vital as they are to growing sustainable revenue, professional fundraisers cannot do the job alone. Donors will not let them. In early 2009, when American donors were struggling under the weight of a severe economic downturn, the majority said they could still be influenced to give more money that year. At the top of a short list of things that could boost their philanthropy higher was "being asked to give by a leadership volunteer".

But, Board members are struggling with their own issues about fundraising, though job description rather than tenure is at the heart of the matter. 87% of volunteers who serve on Boards of Directors agree that they have specific responsibilities for raising money. They also acknowledge that being willing and able to fulfill these responsibilities affects the financial health of the not-for-profits they serve. At the same time, 68% say that there is significant room for improvement in how they and their fellow Board members contribute to fundraising. At the extreme end, 10% have noted serious conflict at the Board table over fundraising, resulting in premature resignations or unwillingness to serve a subsequent term. While this is unfortunate, it also points to a significant opportunity. Donors have strong views concerning the importance of leadership volunteers in fostering their desire to give and to do so at levels well beyond that which professional fundraisers can generate alone. If Board members can develop a better understanding of the role they should be playing, their confidence will rise and that will translate into action.

You can't call a friend once a year and ask for a favor if you plan on keeping that friend – you can't call a donor once a year and ask for a gift if you plan on keeping that person as a donor. Good development is all about relationships.

While leadership volunteers' lack of confidence about fundraising is crippling in its own right, it also contributes to staff turnover. As volunteers hesitate, staff move in to pick up the slack because "It's easier to do it ourselves than to depend on Board members to come through." And, volunteers often let them because "This really isn't our job anyway." This overloads paid staff and leaves them open to criticism for under-performance. Frustrated, but in high demand, they move on, pointing a finger at Board members as they head out the door. And the Board watches them leave with mixed emotions, remembering the days when volunteers used to raise all the money themselves...for free.

At the Heart of Fundraising Success

There is another crucial individual in every not-for-profit organization who has, perhaps, the biggest stake of all in fundraising success. How the Chief Executive Officer negotiates the relationship between fundraisers and Board members and, in fact, how she incorporates fundraising into the culture of her not-for-profit, determines whether her organization thrives financially or just survives.

CEOs do not have to be fundraisers themselves in order to have a huge influence on fundraising success, but a surprising number do have credentials. More than half of CEOs we surveyed said that fundraising knowledge and experience were critical to their landing the top job; only 18% said that fundraising skill was unimportant.

According to senior fundraisers, their CEOs hold the key to the whole Development team's success. Experienced or not, however, CEOs seem to be struggling when it comes to helping their Boards and professional staff maximize their performance. "Convincing or encouraging the Board to fulfill its responsibilities for raising money" was referenced by CEOs as the least enjoyable aspect of their own work in fundraising. "Finding qualified, professional fundraisers" was also high on their list of frustrations.

A Growing Demand and a Growing Opportunity

As the number of not-for-profits grows, the number that is raising money grows too, and, along with it, the demand for fundraisers. In 2000, 688,600 501(c)(3)s were registered with the IRS. Ten years later, that number had jumped to 979,901, a 42% increase . Even a recession did not stop the growth in charities, with IRS recording a 3% increase between April, 2008 and April 2009.[1]

---

[1] *The Nonprofit Almanac 2012*, National Center for Charitable Statistics, Urban Institute Press, October, 2012

In order to meet the growing demand for professional fundraisers, not-for-profit decision-makers need to focus on these priorities:

- address the issues that cause too many experienced professionals to abandon fundraising as a career and bring new thinking to the table that will inspire them to stay in one place long enough to make a measurable impact;

- redefine the fundraising job description for leadership volunteers, providing appropriate training and support to help them reclaim the high profile role that donors expect them to play;

- turn fundraising itself into a more desirable job for professionals and a less daunting task for volunteers and CEOs by bringing its methods in line with donors' needs and sensibilities.

Time is of the essence. The industry's most senior practitioners, who have enormous skill, who mentor younger fundraisers, and whose knowledge is the most valuable asset in the Development field, are on the verge of making this issue even more challenging. 20% plan to retire from the fundraising industry within the next four years; another 29% in five to ten.

The tenure of Development professionals can be extended; Board members can recapture their confidence and the extraordinary level of success they achieved before fundraising became professionalized; and CEOs can bring the whole team together. Is it worth the effort? Yes. One out of every two donors who made charitable gifts in 2011 said they could have given more , but that they held back, waiting for not-for-profits to get it right.

People move around a lot in this industry. Maintain good relationships with everyone you work with – you will likely meet up with them again.

This book is the culmination of five years of research with over 12,000 professional fundraisers, not-for-profit CEOs, leadership volunteers and donors. From their critical vantage points on the front lines of fundraising and philanthropy, they offered thoughtful observations and advice on how to build and sustain a high performance fundraising team.

Chapter 2:
One Thing Just Leads to Another

Fundraising Nirvana

I once met a not-for-profit organization that didn't need to raise money. I will never forget that meeting. It was in a coffee shop on a warm spring afternoon, somewhere in the southeastern United States. I had agreed to meet with the CEO of a small organization that worked in health and human services for the elderly. Earlier in the day, she had attended a workshop I had led and asked if I could give her some advice on how best to start a fundraising program. Over the course of our conversation, I learned that, almost one hundred years before, a grateful client had left a significant bequest to this small charity. The money had been invested well over the years, enhanced by several other unsolicited gifts contributed along the way. I asked the CEO how much money she thought they needed to raise in order to bridge the gap or expand services over the next few years.

"Well, none really," she replied. "We spend about eighty percent of the interest earned on our endowment each year, and roll the rest of it back into our long-term investment. When we want to expand services, we have the funds to do so."

"So, why do you want to raise money, then?" I asked.

"I feel as though we should." she said. "Everyone else is doing it."

Ah, fundraising nirvana. In my forty-year career, this is the only not-for-profit I've ever encountered that has reached this coveted state. But, in fact, this is the unspoken financial goal of every organization that raises money – to have an endowment and then build it to a level substantial enough to support annual operations indefinitely. Whether you get there the easy way, as this not-for-profit did by having a guardian angel with stunning foresight, or the hard way through decades or even hundreds of years of solid effort, the goal remains the same. Every not-for-profit is fundraising so that it can stop fundraising.

Fundraising Is a Business and It's All About Profit

The not-for-profit sector is exactly what its name suggests – a sector constituted to not make a profit. But inside hundreds of thousands of organizations that have been granted this status are bustling profit centers called Development or Fundraising Departments. They are charged with the opposite responsibility – to make as much profit as possible.

For-profit companies do not hesitate to invest in whatever resources are necessary to boost the sales of their products and develop new ones in order to maximize profit. Charities, on the other hand, allow their preoccupation with cost, bred in the not-for-profit side of their enterprise, to spill over into their business side in ways that inhibit fundraising success. While adopting a healthy profit-making mindset about revenue, one that expects fundraisers to secure as many generous gifts from donors as possible, they consider the expenditures that make this possible to be "unfortunate" and contrary to the spirit of how charitable organizations should operate. This serves only to prevent not-for-profits from maximizing net profit. Since only the net can be spent on programs and services, investing to increase net profit is a smart business and fundraising decision; doing otherwise allows old-fashioned thinking to trump reason.

While there is a generalized hesitation over spending money to make money, most charities do not have a grasp on how to allocate their budget resources to produce maximum results. They invest heavily, even to the point of irresponsibility, in high-risk fundraising events or short-term mass marketing activities. Through the latter, they bombard donors with relentless pleas for contributions, creating an environment of over-solicitation and mistrust among the very people they depend upon for revenue. These programs drive costs into the 40-70% range and give customers (donors) a good reason to be concerned about whether resources are being spent wisely. At the same time, decision-makers minimize or defer the introduction of more sophisticated fundraising methods that produce much higher revenue at much lower cost, but which also require more staff or staff with different skills. They argue, "We have to have the money now," missing the point that they can't have the money now because the requisite investment has not been made.

A small percentage of not-for-profits have figured it out and they have deservedly become the standard for fundraising success. Boards of charities not in that elite group point to those organizations' stunning achievements in fundraising, ostensibly as an incentive to their own fundraisers. At the same time, they ignore the reasons that set these organizations apart in the first place. The high performers are, most often, universities and colleges, but there is no secret about why they raise more money. They employ the largest contingent of fundraisers, investing in their training and supervision, and they run diversified Development operations, balancing high-cost mass marketing with low-cost major and planned gifts programs in order to effect a more reliable, and profitable, net return.

It's Not Just the Other Guy

While the ultimate responsibility for decisions that affect fundraising rests with the Board and CEO, fundraisers sometimes contribute to their own fate. They decry being treated differently from other non-fundraising staff. They want to be accepted as part of the team while insisting that no one else can do their job. Seeking inclusion rather than exclusion sets fundraisers up for the thing they hate the most, which is being told that their work requires no particular skill and that anyone can do it. The fundraising team is equivalent to the sales team in a for-profit company. Charged with unique performance objectives, fundraisers have to think and behave differently from their not-for-profit-oriented colleagues in order to be successful. They are up to their elbows in the very thing that non-fundraising staff (and, regrettably, sometimes their employers) abhor – making a profit. Of course they're different; thank goodness they're different; otherwise their colleagues wouldn't have a paycheck at the end of the week.

People who raise money are different as are their measures of success, yet organizations still tend to apply the same rules of employment and assessment methods to fundraisers as they do to other staff. Between 2008 and 2009 as the recession deepened, 53% of not-for-profits instituted a hiring freeze throughout their ranks, including in Development. Maybe they were concerned about a backlash if fundraisers were exempt from this edict. In addition, 24% laid off professional fundraisers, sending their Development operations into hunker-down mode to wait out the downturn. This is a short-sighted decision in an industry with a supply/demand imbalance in favor of professional fundraisers. It is also counter to the forward-thinking in which charities that raise money need to engage. A drop in the economy signals that it is time to buy, not sell. Just ask Warren Buffett what he does in a downturn, and America's second most generous philanthropist will tell you that this is when he invests.

A genuine love of people is the key to fundraising success. You can learn the rest of it from books and seminars, but being a good listener and being passionate as well as articulate about your cause are the essential things.

We are known inside the fundraising industry for our great working environment – team oriented and very collaborative. So, great fundraisers line up to work here.

Nirvana Is Achievable

It is not a fantasy, nor is it a matter of luck. All not-for-profits that raise money can reach the ultimate state of financial security described in the story at the beginning of this chapter, but most will not get there without professional fundraisers. Experts who are paid to raise money take on the time-consuming work that even the most dedicated volunteers cannot shoulder indefinitely. At one end of the business, professional fundraisers run systems that handle hundreds of thousands or even millions of donors at a time; at the other end, they negotiate complex gift arrangements with philanthropists who trust them with their private financial information and their even more private hopes and dreams.

Professional fundraisers stand behind campaign volunteers – encouraging, cajoling, inspiring and reassuring them towards mind-boggling goals. They ghost-write proposals that win seven-figure grants; they organize, run and clean up after fundraising events; they comfort family members at the funerals of donors they have grown to know and treasure. But perhaps the most important contribution that modern-day fundraising has offered the world is the chance for anyone to become a philanthropist, not just the privileged few. Where giving used to be limited to the business and social networks of members of Boards of Directors, today 66% of American households make recognized charitable contributions annually[1] as do 84% of Canadians over the age of 14.[2]

The Cost-Benefit of Professional Fundraisers

It is profitable to invest in the people who raise money and this applies to leadership volunteers and the CEO as well as to fundraisers. How these ultimate decision-makers are engaged in fundraising, and even how they set the tone about fundraising in their organizations, affect how much money will be raised. But, because CEOs have responsibilities other than fundraising and volunteers work for free, one automatically associates the fundraising budget with the cost of professional staff.

Professional fundraisers' value increases the longer they stay in the business. Many begin their fundraising careers in high-volume but relatively low-profit programs such as direct marketing and fundraising events. Over time, those with well developed people skills and the ability to steward relationships with donors and negotiate gifts migrate into the more profitable arena of major and planned gifts

---

[1] Center on Philanthropy Panel Study, School of Philanthropy, Indiana University-Purdue University, Indianapolis, 2007.

[2] Statistics Canada, Canada Survey of Giving, Volunteering and Participating, 2007.

and corporate sponsorships. Fundraisers who stay in the business long enough to get there, along with those who transfer in from progressive careers in other fields, are the industry's most coveted resource. They produce the highest revenue per donor and generate more than 80% of the profit.

What Motivated This Research?

Retaining fundraisers, then, whether maximizing their tenure within a single organization or ensuring that they stay in the Development field indefinitely, is a profit-making activity. So, I became increasingly interested whenever Development professionals responsible for hiring talked about a crippling rate of turnover in the industry. It seemed to be a problem at every level. They felt that the rate of staff turnover was high among young professionals in their first or second non-management job. This was not surprising to hear as it mirrors what is happening in the for-profit sector. But employers felt that staff turnover was problematic at the top of the fundraising pyramid as well. They cited difficulty finding, let alone holding onto, fundraisers with the requisite skill set and experience to populate major and planned gifts programs.

My head was full of questions. Was staff turnover in fundraising a real problem or just a perception? Was early career turnover behind a lack of good candidates for senior positions, or was this just a handy excuse to avoid investing in more sophisticated approaches to raising money? Was the direct marketing end of the fundraising business the right environment for developing candidates for high-level philanthropy? And, most important, could more profit be made by dealing differently with the issue of staff mobility in fundraising?

Research Objectives

With that in mind, I and my colleagues at Cygnus Applied Research shaped a series of research studies around these questions:

- What is the actual average rate of tenure among fundraising staff in various positions and at all levels of seniority? The answer could help employers measure their own organization's performance against objective benchmarks;
- How does the rate of job turnover, whatever it is, affect fundraising from the perspectives of fundraisers themselves, their employers, and donors? From donors, I was particularly interested in learning whether they notice fundraising staff turnover and, if so, whether it impacts their giving;

Staff turnover in fundraising is a big problem. It takes time to develop relationships and garner donors' trust. When a fundraiser leaves, it takes a good year or more to fill the gap.

If a donor senses high staff turnover, it leads him to question the business practices of the charity. He starts to pull away and that can be the beginning of the end.

What could inspire donors to give more generously than planned?

44% Ask less often
42% Specific information on what gifts are for
38% Measurable results of previous gifts
20% Asks that are less impersonal
19% Acknowledgments that make donors feel appreciated

- Can the rate of job turnover among professional fundraisers be mitigated if necessary and, if so, how?

The first research question is answered in the next chapter. The rest of the book is devoted to addressing the other two questions…plus one more. Cygnus conducts research annually with thousands of North American donors on issues that motivate or inhibit their philanthropy. Since 2000, the majority of donors participating in our studies have said they have more money to give but are holding back, waiting for certain things to improve. Even in a recession, donors seem to have room to grow their philanthropy. In early 2010 when donors were still feeling the full weight of the economic downturn, 72% of American donors and 66% of Canadians said they could be inspired to give more money this year, under certain circumstances.

Improving staff retention in fundraising will also improve the bottom line, but it is not the only thing that needs to be addressed if fundraising is to become substantially more profitable. Over the course of conducting several studies, the central issue of this research – the rate of staff turnover in fundraising – was exposed as a symptom of a bigger problem: the conflicting needs and expectations of fundraisers, their employers, their volunteer leaders, and donors. In fact, the fundraising system itself is identified in this book as an underlying cause of premature staff turnover.

How the Research Was Conducted

I first reached out to professional fundraisers in the United States and Canada. 1,143 volunteered to participate in a two-part online survey which investigated their employment history in Development, with particular emphasis on their career moves to date, the issues that motivated those moves, and respondents' long-term plans regarding their fundraising careers. Fundraisers who qualified to take part in the study categorized themselves in one of these four groups:

- **Development Directors** (or equivalent). At the time they participated in the research project, these senior professionals were the overall managers of the fundraising or advancement offices in their organizations or they headed foundations whose sole or main purpose was to raise money for specific not-for-profit organizations. Respondents in this category had the most senior responsibility for hiring and managing other fundraising staff.

- **Directors or Managers of specific fundraising programs**, such as direct mail or planned giving. Respondents in this category reported to the overall Director of Development or Advancement and were responsible for managing fundraising staff in their particular area of expertise.

- **Non-management staff** working in or supporting fundraising. These respondents worked in a particular program (such as direct mail) or area (such as donor relations) or had a diverse set of responsibilities in fundraising, but were not responsible for hiring or managing other fundraising staff.

- **Professionals working in one-person-fundraising shops.** A discrete category was established for respondents who were the only professional fundraiser in their organizations. Some had clerical or data entry assistants, but otherwise these sole practitioners carried out the full range of fundraising responsibilities by themselves.

Anyone who was employed in fundraising in a North American not-for-profit organization, whether full or part- time, was welcome to participate in our research studies. 82% of respondents were American fundraisers, 18% Canadian. 18% of all respondents were in their first position in fundraising at the time they completed the survey; 35% had been professional fundraisers for twenty years or more.

Participants were asked 219 questions and were given frequent opportunities to provide observations and advice. Due to the length of the surveys, which took several hours to complete, most questions allowed respondents to choose from a list of prescribed answers, but that list always included an "other" option to capture information and opinions that were not pre-supposed.

Just as the second research study was winding down, the economic recession was heating up. While its effects were devastating for donors and for not-for-profit organizations, the timing did present an opportunity to add to our growing body of knowledge. When surveyed in 2008, 39% of respondents said they were actively seeking a new position at that time. We were curious about whether the recession had mitigated that rate of turnover at all, or whether the specialized nature of fundraising and the profession's supply/demand inequity immunized fundraisers to a certain degree. We conducted a follow-up study in November, 2009, and discovered that the recession did indeed have an impact on professional fundraisers, though not perhaps to the degree that it affected other occupations. Only 27% had followed through and changed jobs once the recession took hold.

All Roads Lead to Leadership Volunteers

While our research uncovered a long list of factors that contribute to premature staff turnover in fundraising, we were intrigued by the number of issues we pursued that pointed back to leadership volunteers (members of Boards of Directors). While some Boards were singled out for praise by fundraisers in our study, far more were described as barriers to fundraising success. We felt that it was important to

The recession actually gave me the opportunity to pull the staff together to rethink and realign responsibilities for efficiency. The collaboration brought about a better understanding, acceptance, and feeling of ownership among the group.

give Board members the opportunity to speak about fundraising from their unique perspective.

We expanded our original research objectives to include leadership volunteers and, in 2010, conducted a study with 1,268 American and Canadian Board members. Among the issues we investigated was how volunteers defined their own, their CEOs' and their fundraisers' responsibilities in raising money.

We discovered that leadership volunteers and professional fundraisers definitely do not agree on "who is responsible for what" and concluded that neither defined their responsibilities in ways that actually maximize fundraising success. We also learned that while volunteers felt they should be participating in fundraising in a meaningful way, they had no idea what "meaningful" actually meant. Lacking proper orientation and largely untrained, leadership volunteers tended to operate within a safe agenda of peripheral fundraising activities. While this made them feel comfortable, it also denied their organizations the single most powerful asset that volunteers bring to fundraising – influence.

A second study in 2011, this time with 4,200 American and Canadian Board members, yielded even more information on what leadership volunteers need from their not-for-profit organizations to help them overcome their reluctance to raise money.

Wisdom from the Corner Office

Whether they are experienced fundraisers or have never raised a dime, CEOs influence how fundraising works more than anyone else in the organization. That was reinforced in our studies with both professional fundraisers and leadership volunteers, so we knew that surveying the top-paid staff person in not-for-profits would be crucial to answering the question, "What makes fundraising successful?" In mid-2010, 117 CEOs whose not-for-profits employ professional fundraisers completed our online survey. The study investigated respondents' level of satisfaction with their staff's, their Board's, and their own performance in fundraising. It also sought not-for-profit CEOs' views on issues that affected the tenure of Development staff, such as salary and fundraising strategy.

Among the three not-for-profit respondent groups – professional staff, leadership volunteers and CEOs – we found CEOs to have the most universal and pragmatic perspective. We also found them to be more willing to have their own preconceptions about fundraising challenged, if they were presented with a well-researched argument.

The Ultimate Arbiter

Research on fundraising conducted with those charged with the task of raising money is informative, but not fully reliable if the views of donors are not included. Confusion or guesswork about most issues concerning fundraising is usually cleared up when one turns to donors to seek their opinions. After all, it is their money – until they donate it – and so much goes into donors' decisions about whether to support a particular charity for the first time, or repeatedly. Donors are extraordinarily thoughtful about fundraising because philanthropy is so important to them and because they want their not-for-profits to be as successful as possible. Because my firm is grounded in research, it was second nature for us to turn to donors for their opinions on key issues that emerged from our earlier investigations with staff and volunteers.

In the spring of 2009 and again in 2010 and 2011, we conducted studies with thousands of donors in the United States and Canada. Among the many intriguing issues we explored were:

- Donors' experience with planned giving and their willingness to include a bequest to a charitable organization if asked by a trusted representative;

- Whether donors notice turnover among professional fundraisers and, if so, whether this impedes their giving;

- Whether donors could be influenced to stay loyal and give even more generously during a severe economic downturn;

- How donors' philosophy for giving and the ways in which they go about practicing their philanthropy, are changing.

On that last question we learned many important and often surprising things, but none with more potential to impact the future of fundraising than donors' evolution from reactive contributor to proactive donor. It used to be that donors had to cooperate with the dictates of the fundraising industry in order to be philanthropic. Fundraisers told them when and how to give and donors complied, sometimes enduring unappealing practices as they strove to make the world a better place. But, today, thanks to not-for-profits' own websites and third-party services that provide information on charities, donors have found a new independence that is changing the philanthropic landscape.

Five years of research answered some questions definitively, particularly those related to the causes of and remedies for rapid turnover among professional fundraisers. For employers experiencing this problem, the news is good. There are solutions that can extend tenure in both a particular job and a particular not-for-profit organization. But the research also uncovered something else. Fundraising itself – how it is designed and operated – contributes to the dissatisfaction that causes premature departure of staff, the reluctance to raise money among leadership volunteers, and minimally engaged CEOs.

Chapter 3:
Career Mobility Among Professional Fundraisers

They operate quietly, behind the scenes, but their influence is pervasive. They craft complex proposals that bring new ideas to life; coach leadership volunteers to land seven-figure campaign gifts; manage systems that bring in millions within days of a major disaster. And their talent and effort influence far more than just the raising of money. They shape public image and perception through the appeals they write and the programs they run, and they remind decision-makers about accountability for use of funds. But most important, they help people discover and rediscover the joy of philanthropy by introducing them to worthy causes and working steadily to turn those first tenuous gestures of support into lifelong relationships. They are fundraisers.

Improving Staff Retention Is a Profit-Making Activity

When one thinks of raising money, what springs immediately to mind are the programs that bring in the contributions and the donors who make the contributions. But money is also made – or lost – by how well or poorly the people who run those fundraising programs and develop those relationships with donors are managed. This applies to leadership volunteers with responsibility for fundraising as well as to professional staff.

One of the measures of how well a company or organization is managed is the average tenure of its staff. Satisfied staff are not simply people with a more positive outlook; they are people who are eager to come to work in the morning because they know they will be challenged to reach higher goals, encouraged to offer their ideas, respected by their bosses for the contributions they make, and surrounded by a group of co-workers with the same forward-looking attitude. A satisfied workforce reinforces all members of the team while sending the right signal to the industry as a whole. Especially in an insular industry like fundraising, word gets around quickly when Development operations are flying high – or failing – and good fundraisers beat a path to the door of top performers.

Cost as Investment or Just Expense

When a staff member remains loyal and excels at her job, the time it took and the cost incurred in hiring and training her is, in retrospect, a great investment. But the same time and cost applied to a new fundraiser who leaves prematurely and/or performs poorly will never be anything other than an unfortunate expense. There will always be staff turnover, of course, and there will sometimes be opportunities to grow the staff complement. What good managers strive for is to hire well initially and then maximize tenure in order to turn cost into investment as often as possible.

What It Costs to Replace a Professional Fundraiser

Even I was amazed when I worked it out. Putting a price on losing a high performing fundraiser requires taking into account expenses that are both above and below the line. What appears above the line is the cost of advertising a position, or the fee for hiring a recruitment firm, or the increased salary required to attract the best candidates. But, below-the-line costs are much more significant. They are, first and foremost, a factor of time – time from the departing employee diverted from raising money to winding down operations and preparing for his successor; time from the manager to handle hiring, orientation, and closer supervision of the new staff person; time from other members of the fundraising team to help their new colleague get up to speed.

Costs related to people make up the largest portion of the fundraising budget. This is just as it should be because those same people are the ones who bring in the money. But that also means that cost per dollar raised is affected every time an employee has to be replaced. The time it takes a manager to hire and orient a new fundraiser is time not devoted to his other work, including cultivating his own list of donors. It is rare in Development operations for managers to simply manage; they are almost always direct fundraisers, too, and the higher they climb the seniority ladder, the more crucial are their donors to the bottom line.

More time devoted to finding and training new staff is also time taken away from managing existing employees who are already trained and functioning productively. It is a common assumption that productive staff require less guidance and support from management, but this is not the case. Managers devote a disproportionate amount of their supervisory time to new staff, poor performers and disruptive employees, but these are not the people who are actually moving the Development operation forward. Time and budget applied to experienced, high performers is the best investment a manager will ever make in fundraising.

While every employment situation is different, the financial impact of premature staff turnover is quantifiable. Exposing the real cost of trained, productive staff lost too early is helpful to management in two ways. It can motivate employers to address the issues that lead to rapid staff turnover and it can help in salary negotiation. When an experienced, productive fundraiser asks her boss to match the salary offered by another not-for-profit that hopes to lure her away, her manager can only negotiate from a position of strength if he knows what it will cost to lose her.

Staff Turnover Affects Everyone

In a Development Department with multiple staff, the bottom line can be compromised in four different ways whenever time is shifted from raising money to dealing with staff turnover:

1. **The New Employee**: A fundraiser new on the job needs time to understand what he is selling (the organization and its programs and services). He needs training on the systems and procedures. If he works in major gifts, for example, he needs time to get to know his donors. If he is a copywriter in the direct marketing program, he needs more time initially to produce ready-to-publish scripts, appeal letters and communications than he will at a later stage. Naturally, the time he spends up front learning the job will eventually make him a better fundraiser. His productivity will improve as his knowledge and confidence grow, but in that early period of employment, allowances need to be made. This period of lesser productivity – or productivity gap – relates to a combination of costs associated with orientation, training and closer supervision plus monies not raised.

   How long does that initial period last? Our research determined that non-management employees require ten to twelve months to get to the point where they feel they are working as fully functioning members of the team, operating more or less independently and raising money at the expected level. Realistically, then, when setting fundraising goals for new non-management staff, employers need to have reduced expectations for performance for up to a year.

   Internally promoted staff are a different story, though, as are employees who graduate into positions through succession planning. These are the most cost-effective ways to effect job transition, and smart for so many other reasons.

When I compare the amount of money raised fundraiser-to-fundraiser over the course of a year, the staff who have stayed with us longer consistently raise much more money.

2. **The Person Responsible for Hiring**: A big part of the job of a supervisor or manager is to hire, orient, train and manage staff. How well she does those things ultimately defines her value to the organization. In fundraising, however, those with responsibility for hiring have other duties that either directly or indirectly affect the bottom line. This is especially true for Development Directors, whose unique influence with donors and leadership volunteers is critical to success in major gifts fundraising.

   It is true that, at the management level, a thirty-five hour work week seldom applies. So, one could argue that time spent hiring new staff and bringing them up to speed is simply the price one pays for the privilege of being in management. And, senior fundraisers might agree...to a point. We found that 50% of Development Directors work from five to twelve hours overtime each week. But, chronic overtime eventually takes its toll. Our research also noted that one in four managers left his last job due to unrealistic expectations related to time or the number of job responsibilities he had in addition to fundraising which made it impossible to reach revenue goals.

3. **Colleagues of the New Employee**: In high functioning organizations, it is not just the boss who supports employees and inspires them to reach ambitious goals. Team members support and inspire each other. Colleagues are the ones working on the ground and their wisdom from the trenches is invaluable. Sometimes colleagues contribute informally to helping new employees get up to speed; at other times, a member of the team may be officially charged with responsibility for new staff orientation. This latter option can have a positive effect on an experienced staff member who is seeking greater responsibility, while also providing the manager with another way of evaluating that person's future potential. But it can work the other way, too. Cohesiveness of the team is disturbed every time someone leaves prematurely, and there is always a possibility that the replacement may not gel with the group. Chronic staff turnover weighs heavily on the entire team, breeding a negative atmosphere inside the organization and increasing levels of stress. Practically speaking, the rest of the team's workload is increased when a position remains vacant for a time due to a sudden departure or dismissal, as well as during the initial employment period of the new hire. In the end, reduced productivity, regardless of the reason, means less revenue raised.

4. **Donors**: The higher one goes up the grid of fundraising programs, the more money a single staff member raises. Major and planned gifts officers raise money by cultivating relationships with donors so that, over time, they can steward generous contributions. Their growing knowledge of and sensi-

tivity to the needs of their donors also helps relationship managers identify the best time and way to make the ask.

For their part, donors are also aware of the importance of their relationships with major gifts staff. Many praised their gifts officers for the lengths they go to in order to make donors feel appreciated. For example, 60% of donors we surveyed said that relationship officers cut through red tape when necessary, providing them with information in a timely manner and making their giving experiences more rewarding.

On the flip side, major donors also expressed concern over the transition from one gifts officer to another, with 13% describing how the loss of a popular staff member affected their philanthropy in a negative way. Donors referenced making smaller gifts, taking longer to agree to making a gift, not making the gift at all, and, in some extreme cases, deciding not to include the charity in their wills. The majority of a not-for-profit's revenue comes from a relatively small number of donors who makes extraordinarily generous gifts. While 13% of that group is a statistical minority, it can represent a significant amount of lost revenue and a disproportionate impact on the bottom line.

The Financial Impact of Frequent Staff Turnover

If you struggle to reach higher goals, if new ideas seldom turn into action, if your Department feels like it is treading water, premature staff turnover may be the source of your frustration. The following three scenarios and accompanying calculations illustrate the impact of too-frequent staff turnover on the bottom line. Because fundraising goals, number of Development staff, and approaches to raising money differ from one not-for-profit to the next, these computations cannot be applied literally to any single fundraising operation. They serve to illustrate the crippling impact of frequent staff turnover and to underscore why it is worth addressing the problem.

Tenure and the Junior, Non-Management Fundraiser

Bill, age 24, is in his first professional job in fundraising. He works in the annual fund of a community-based social service agency as one of four staff reporting to the Manager of Direct Marketing. The direct marketing operation's annual goal is $1,000,000 and Bill's contribution to that goal is valued at $175,000. Bill's job includes drafting copy for solicitation appeals, updating data, dealing with donor inquiries or complaints over the phone, crafting thank-you letter copy and contributing to the organization's newsletter. Bill has been on the job for sixteen months and has just tendered his resignation.

I just started a job as a relationship specialist with donors. There have been five people in my position in the last five years – and it really shows. No engagement, low enthusiasm. Boy, do I have my work cut out for me!

As a donor, I get really tired of telling my story over and over again every time my gifts officer leaves. It's exhausting. Is this what they call "relationship fundraising?"

Donors watch and listen, perhaps more than not-for-profits realize. They worry that excessive staff turnover is a symptom of a more serious problem and wonder whether they are making the right choice in continuing their support.

What donors appreciate about Gifts Officers:

60% Questions/needs are addressed in timely manner
57% Feeling appreciated for gifts made
38% Being asked for gifts in a more personal way
37% Being better informed of how gifts are used
26% Being introduced to influential Not-for-profit reps

From this moment, until Bill's successor begins her second year on the job, unplanned costs will be incurred that are related to or caused by Bill's departure. Obvious end-of-employment payouts appear above the line, such as the cost of advertising the position, overtime paid to other staff if Bill's job is vacant for a period of time, and skills training in data management for the new hire. Another cost increase common in an industry where demand for talent outstrips supply relates to salary. Finding the right person to replace him may mean being willing to pay more than Bill was earning when he left. But these above-the-line costs are relatively minor when measured against the Departmental goal. What really adds up are the hidden costs in the form of time diverted from raising money.

The Productivity Gap Caused by Staff Turnover

It takes time to review and revise the job description in advance of posting the position. It takes more time to vet applications, conduct interviews, short-list preferred candidates, conduct second (and sometimes third) interviews, and negotiate the job with the top prospect. Once the new hire is on staff, still more time is required for job orientation, monitoring and assessing performance during the probationary period, and providing a more intense level of supervision during the first year. Why a year? If non-management respondents in our study said it takes ten to twelve months on the job before they are functioning independently and at full productivity, then fundraising is affected in two ways. Not only do employees in their first year require more support from supervisors and co-workers, but during this time they are not raising money at the level of their more experienced colleagues. This is understandable, of course, but the fundraising operation still takes a hit.

Table 1 illustrates the financial impact of Bill's departure after sixteen months on the job, taking the following assumptions and information into account:

- Work done by Bill and his three other co-workers is valued at $700,000 of the annual $1,000,000 goal, or $175,000 per employee. (The rest of the goal is attributable to the Direct Marketing Manager.) The new staff member replacing Bill will raise money at 80% of the rate of her longer tenured colleagues during her first year on the job. This is due to time required for orientation and training, and her somewhat slower pace while she learns. This is the productivity gap. It is the hidden cost of frequent staff turnover translated into money not raised. In this case, the productivity gap is $35,000.

- In his last two weeks of employment, Bill is less productive than before while he puts together an operations manual for his successor and attends to other matters.

- Due to short notice given by Bill, his position remains vacant for a month after he leaves.

Table 1: Cost to Replace a Non-Management Staff Member Who Leaves After 16 Months

Above-the-Line Costs	Value
Accrued vacation to departing employee (based on $42,500 salary)	545
Direct hiring costs: advertising the position	1,000
Salary increase to new hire @ 5%	2,125
Data System training for new staff	2,000
Productivity Gap – Money Not Raised due to Staff Turnover (% of $175,000 goal based on 240 work days/year)	
Wind-down period (5 days, based on salary of $42,500 – see note 1)	817
Bill's job vacant for 1 month (see note 2)	7,250
Productivity gap in Year 1 for new employee (20%)	35,000
Support from colleagues to help new staff member get up to speed (5 days – see note 2)	817
Total cost to replace a non-management employee	**$49,554**
Cost of staff turnover as a percentage of salary	**117%**
Cost of staff turnover as a percentage of annual goal	**28%**

Note 1: Bill's attention for these last five days on the job shifts from raising money to winding up his affairs. I have taken a conservative approach to this particular cost by only taking salary diversion into account. It could be argued that fundraised revenue would be compromised as well, but with three other colleagues on staff, it is reasonable to assume that they would pick up the slack.

Note 2: With an annual goal of $175,000, Bill would be raising approximately $14,500 per month, an amount jeopardized by his position remaining vacant for thirty days. I have cut that by 50% on the assumption that co-workers would pick up the slack to some degree and in the knowledge that direct marketing revenue does not flow in every month at the same level. Perhaps Bill was good enough to leave in the down period between campaigns!

The Impact of Short Tenures Over Time

The negative impact multiplies the longer short tenures are the norm. As Table 2 illustrates, it costs 300% more over four years to hire staff who stay for only sixteen months compared with the same size staff contingent whose members stay for three years. But the cost of staff replacement is just the beginning. Short stays among some staff affect the entire team. Frequent turnover jolts the working environment, necessitating overtime among other staff who now have to compensate. This

You never know what the past can teach you. I find that everything I have done in my varied career has culminated in the position I have now. Experience doesn't happen overnight.

eventually breeds dissatisfaction among loyal fundraisers which, in turn, affects their desire to stay, too.

Of course, the manager is very much affected by premature staff turnover. Hiring and training new staff is inherent in the Direct Marketing Manager's job description, so no management costs are implicated in Table 1 which concerns itself with replacing only one employee. However, with four members on the team and tenure averaging only sixteen months, in some years the manager will be required to replace four staff, not one. It is reasonable to assume that 10% of the manager's time would be devoted to hiring, orienting, training, supervising and evaluating a new staff member. Any additional hiring requirements start to impinge on his other responsibilities. The Productivity Gap now extends to the Manager as well.

Table 2: Impact of Shorter and Longer Tenures Extended Over Four Years

# of Staff Replaced and Cost of Staff Turnover @ $49,554/staff	Year 1	Year 2	Year 3	Year 4
16-month tenure				
- number of staff replaced	0	4	4	4
- total cost of staff replacement	0	$198,216	$198,216	$198,216
36-month tenure				
- number of staff replaced	0	0	4	0
- total cost of staff replacement	0	0	$198,216	0
Cumulative cost of staff replacement by end of 4th year				
- 16-month tenures	0	$198,216	$396,432	$594,648
- 36-month tenures	0	$0	$198,216	$198,216

Table 3 depicts what employers would rather experience, and the difference is dramatic. Costs related to hiring, training and supervising are incurred largely up front, of course, while the fundraising benefits of increased productivity accrue over the course of the extended tenure. The staff replacement cost for a single non-management employee who stays for three years is only 9% of revenue earned over the thirty-six month period of employment.

Table 3: The Cost/Benefit of a Non-Management Employee Who Stays for Three Years

Length of Stay	Direct and Indirect Costs
Year 1	49,554
Year 2	0
Year 3	0
TOTAL	$49,554
Revenue raised over 3 years	$525,000
Cost of hiring as a factor of revenue raised	9%

Investment/Return in Major Gifts Staffing

Michelle has nine years experience as a professional fundraiser. She started her career in fundraising events and donor relations and is currently in her first position in Major Gifts as a Major/Planned Gifts Officer for a mid-sized NGO. Michelle earns $85,000 a year and is responsible for raising $2 million annually in cash and expectancies. Michelle was hired five years ago and today is her last day on the job.

When she was hired, Michelle told her employer that she planned to stay in this job for five years to gain experience in planned giving, in particular. Six months ago, she and her boss had a planning meeting where Michelle reminded him that she would be leaving and recommended that the job of finding her replacement begin immediately. Michelle also suggested a sixty to ninety-day transition period during which she would introduce her successor to her donors and key prospects, forty-five of whom have been cultivated for a first-time or repeat major gift within the next eighteen months.

Michelle's boss was concerned about doubling major gifts salaries for a three-month period and, with Michelle's departure still half a year away, he was not in the right frame of mind to turn his attention to hiring her replacement. He was also secretly hoping that Michelle might change her mind and stay. After all, the economic climate was still sluggish and she might not have an easy time finding another job.

So, with other priorities occupying his time, the ad for an experienced Major/Planned Gifts Officer was not posted until six weeks prior to Michelle's departure. The first hiring attempt yielded four possible candidates. Two had accepted other offers by the time Michelle's boss contacted them for an interview; one more opted for a higher salary at the last minute; and the fourth candidate had a history of short job stays and was reluctant to provide a current reference. On Michelle's final day at work, the job ad was posted again.

It took two months to fill the position and the search only concluded successfully after Michelle's boss reluctantly agreed to a $110,000 salary for the new hire. The Board, alarmed at the cost, insisted that the employment agreement include a clause that made the new gift officer's employment beyond Year 1 contingent on raising $2 million in his first twelve months.

Paralleling the principle of the donor pyramid,[1] the value of a Development professional rises as she works higher up on the sophistication scale of fundraising programs. While they contribute approximately the same time to their organizations, Michelle raises almost twelve times the money through major gifts that Bill produces

---

How donors reacted after losing an effective Gifts Officer:

77% Had no impact on their giving
12% Made smaller gift
7% Took longer to make a gift
4% Stopped giving altogether

We can't build revenue from major donors because we can't seem to hold onto our gifts officer long enough to see progress. I'm at my wits' end.

---

[1] The donor pyramid organizes donors to a cause according to the value of their contributions. The pyramid shape reflects the fact that the majority of donors give modestly and that the number of donors decreases as gift values rise. At the top of the pyramid, a relatively small number of donors makes the most generous contributions and their collective value constitutes the majority of fundraised revenue.

Fundraisers' long-term career objective:

14% To become a CEO / GM
13% To turn a hobby into a career
13% To become a fundraising consultant
6% To become a teacher of Fundraising
5% To become a Development Director

in direct marketing. Impact of turnover is relative, too. New staff at the top end of the pyramid need less time than junior, inexperienced fundraisers to master their job duties, but they need much more time to build relationships with donors. At this sophisticated level of fundraising, costs must be viewed in the context of cause and effect. But that is not the perspective held by management or the Board in this particular illustration. Their unilateral focus on cost outlay was, in the end, very expensive for their not-for-profit. Here is the rest of the story.

> By the time Fred (Michelle's successor) started his new job, the position had been vacant for two and a half months. Fred was an experienced and capable gifts officer. After a one-week orientation, he began calling critical donors – those whom Michelle's excellent briefing notes suggested would be ready for an ask in the first quarter after her departure, a period of time that had already expired. Two of the five donors who took his call were not eager to see him. While Michelle had told them she would be leaving, they appeared to have redirected their attention to other giving options in her absence. Two others asked to delay a meeting to the following quarter. This was not an auspicious start.

> Fred turned to the Board for assistance in opening doors and re-engaging with past major donors but was told that Michelle had built these relationships herself. In one conversation with a leadership volunteer, Fred was reminded of the salary he had negotiated "and that he would now have to earn it".

> Fred worked diligently to cultivate donors and close major gifts, even winning over two Board members who helped him open doors with their contacts. Still, by the end of his first year on the job, he had raised only $900,000 towards a $2 million goal. He presented a report to his boss and to the Board on gifts in negotiation plus viable prospects that predicted the $2 million goal would be reached the following year. But the Board was not convinced, and Fred's contract was not renewed.

An additional outlay of $27,500, representing Fred's salary for a three-month transition period, would have all but guaranteed a different outcome. Lack of timely attention to rehiring plus reluctance to pay two salaries for a three-month period jeopardized $1.1 million in revenue. Put another way, had this not-for-profit been willing to invest in salary, it would have cost them only 2.5% of the additional monies that Fred would have raised.

Donor hesitation is real, so while the story of Michelle and Fred is just an illustration, failing to invest in staff transition has a real impact on the bottom line. Approximately 13% of major gifts donors we surveyed said they gave less, delayed decisions about giving or decided not to give at all after a trusted major gifts officer was replaced with someone new.

The Impact of Staff Turnover in Management Positions

Keith is the Director of Integrated Direct Marketing, responsible for online giving, direct mail, the internal call center and the social media presence of a national disease charity. Three managers and fifteen staff report either directly or indirectly to him. Keith earns $90,000 a year and has been in his job for two and a half years. During that time he and his team have increased revenue by 18%, even though the economy has been unstable for most of that period. Integrated Direct Marketing raised $7 million in the last fiscal year.

Keith reports to the VP, Development, who oversees a fundraising operation that grossed $16 million last year. $5 million of that goal was directly attributed to major gifts raised or influenced by the VP, CEO and Board; $7 million was raised by Keith's department, and $4 million came from all other fundraising activities.

Three months ago, a search firm approached Keith about a position similar to the one he currently holds. The job is at a national environmental organization which is led by a charismatic former VP of a Fortune 500 company. Initially, Keith dismissed the approach, but the search firm persisted and Keith gradually became more interested.

With a promise of a 40% increase in salary and a larger budget to explore new ideas (something that limited resources in his current job have prevented him from implementing), Keith eventually said yes. Earlier today, he tendered his resignation at the health charity.

Donors are thrown off their game by high staff turnover. Giving is extremely emotional and personal, and good fundraisers develop genuine relationships with their donors. It feels like abandonment when they leave.

In an industry experiencing more demand for proven, experienced talent than it can supply, this kind of scenario plays out daily. Readers will no doubt be divided in their views on this story. On the one hand, a 40% increase in salary is almost irresistible and why shouldn't Keith be rewarded for his expertise and success? On the other, whatever happened to loyalty and the commitment to the cause that Keith himself expressed so convincingly in interviews? There seemed to be no sign of dissatisfaction, yet suddenly here was his resignation.

Supply and demand is the issue on the surface, but the things that caused Keith to take another job after only two and a half years with the healthcare organization are compensation, innovation and leadership. These, and many other issues, are explored later in the book. For now, let's just look at the financial impact of replacing this high-functioning manager.

The more senior the position, the harder it is to precisely measure the cost of losing and replacing a key member of staff, especially one with management or directorial responsibilities. Two different managers, each fundamentally fulfilling his job

Donors appreciate it when they pick up the phone and can reach someone they know. If there is constant staff turnover, conversations keep having to start over again. This frustrates donors.

description, can produce vastly different results, and the resignation of one may be much more strongly felt than the departure of another. The quality of leadership and the synergy between manager and employees is intangible and hard to quantify. For example, there can be no precise answer to the question, "Of funds raised in a particular department or fundraising program, how much can be attributed to the manager?" It would require putting an accurate figure on the value of that person's management style, his propensity for innovation, and his sheer work ethic.

Because each situation is different, a single set of calculations cannot be applied in all instances of short tenures at the management level. The ones below are particular to the employment scenario about Keith. However, this information is still useful as a guide in determining the cost/benefit of fundraising managers in general.

In this particular example, the value of Keith's contribution to his department has been assessed at 25% of revenue earned, or $1,750,000 of the $7 million that the department raised last year. In measuring the impact of losing Keith, it is interesting to note that 99.8% of the cost associated with replacing him is hidden, related to time diverted from Keith, his staff and his boss – the Vice President of Development – which is then translated into money not raised. (If a search firm is used, then hidden costs are reduced to about 95%.) While I am all too aware that the eight-hour day is a relatively meaningless concept at the top, even Vice Presidents of Development reach their breaking point eventually. When too much time is spent replacing staff, it detracts from the more creative and productive time that the Chief Development Officer should be spending supporting the Board and CEO in securing major gifts and guiding and supporting the executive fundraising team. Equally important, short tenures in middle and upper management reflect badly on the boss. Hard to quantify as this is, the person at the top does more than anyone else to influence all employees' desire to stay – even in the face of other tempting job offers.

Who Knows Where the Time Goes...

From the moment he resigns until he actually leaves, Keith's job focus shifts and his productivity diminishes. That is a significant cost in itself, but the bigger impact relates to the ripple effect that his departure has on others. Short tenures magnify the problem by diverting time and jeopardizing revenue too often. Here is where the time goes:

Time from Keith, the Departing Director of Integrated Marketing

- lost productivity during Keith's final month on the job as attention is diverted from fundraising to winding up his affairs, compiling briefing notes for his replacement, and meeting with managers and colleagues on transition matters;

- a thirty-day vacancy of the position after Keith has left and before the new hire can start, due to the short two-week notice period stipulated in Keith's employment agreement. While the salary cost is saved for the month during which Keith's position is vacant, the transition costs are extended over that longer period of time, a much bigger problem in an industry where, literally, time is money.

Total: six weeks. Keith's department raises $7 million. His work is valued at 25% of that figure or $1,750,000 of the year's goal. Six weeks of that goal is equal to $218,750 in revenue jeopardized.

Time from the Boss

- if this is an internally managed hire, time from the boss is required for meetings with the departing manager, an exit interview (hopefully), preparing the position description, vetting applications, first, second and possibly third interviews, negotiations with the preferred candidate, possible renegotiations should the preferred candidate decline the offer of employment.[2] Whatever time this takes is time not invested in major gifts fundraising and department management that generates income (if a search firm is used, about half that time is saved);

- time to compensate for lost management during the month in which the position is vacant;

- time for orientation and support during the first three months of the new manager's employment (the higher one travels up the staff grid, the less time the new employee requires to get up to speed);

- time for a probationary period assessment.

Total: three weeks – The Vice President, Development, raises $5 million and is essential to the Board and CEO's success in fundraising as well. Three weeks diverted to dealing with replacing the short-tenured Director of Integrated Marketing means a potential of $312,000 in revenue not raised. If a search firm is used for the hire, about one week is saved, for a net loss in revenue of only $208,000.

Of course, one of the core job responsibilities of management-level staff is replacing employees or increasing the size of the team. So, reasonable time

Why candidates decline a job offer at the last minute:

35% Insufficient salary
34% Preferred a competitor's offer
6% Current employer matched salary offer
3% Benefits insufficient

---

[2] 36% of managers surveyed said that losing their preferred candidate to another organization in the final stage of negotiation was the most common reason why they had to start the hire over again.

spent in these critical functions is all part of a day's work. The problem arises when staff turnover is premature or where poor hires do not pass their probationary review. In those cases it is important to acknowledge that other progressive work in fundraising will be compromised and that this loss can be measured in real dollars that an organization fails to raise.

Time from Colleagues

- time to participate in the selection process;

- managers of other departments, such as major/planned gifts or fundraising events, play a role in helping the new manager adapt to the culture and learn how fundraising in one department integrates with the next. Other managers need to spend time getting to know their new colleague who is likely to have a different perspective on the job, one that affects those colleagues and the new manager's direct reports. How and how quickly the new team gels is important, but this process of adjustment takes time and, therefore, has a hidden cost.

Total: 3 colleagues, each losing one week over the transition through probationary period, for a total of three weeks. Colleagues collectively raise $4 million, and this loss of time jeopardizes fundraised revenue of approximately $83,300.

The New Hire's Probationary Period

- The new hire under-performs during the first six months at a rate of 20%. The Director of Integrated Marketing is responsible for $1,750,000 in a year, or $875,000 in six months. A 20% under-performance is valued at $175,000 in funds not raised.

Time from Direct Reports

- the three managers (Direct Mail, Online Giving, Call Center) who report to the Director of Integrated Marketing are most affected by the new hire as they contribute most of the orientation time. The time they spend reiterating what they already know and "managing up" can be significant. It is an essential investment, but time gone is time gone, no matter the reason.

- these managers raise $5,250,000 a year. Their on-the-job time and performance will be under pressure for six months, impacting their fundraising at, conservatively, 5% or $161,250.

Additional costs not related to time:

- internal hire: cost of advertising the position ($2,000) versus external hire @ 50% of the new hire's salary for the first year ($45,000). This calculation seems to imply that internal hires are more cost-effective but, in fact, the search firm cuts in half the Vice President of Development's time that would otherwise be devoted to hiring, saving 1.5 weeks or the equivalent of $156,000 in revenue for which the VP is responsible.

Table 4: Summary of What It Costs to Replace a Senior Fundraising Manager

Item	Internal Hire	Search Firm-Assisted Hire
Fees to search firm		45,000
Advertising the position	2,000	
Diverted time from staff translated into revenue not raised		
- the departing Manager of Integrated Marketing	218,750	218,750
- VP, Development	312,000	208,000
- other management colleagues	83,300	83,300
- under-performance of new hire during probationary period	175,000	175,000
- time diverted from direct reports' fundraising to orientation of new manager	161,250	161,250
Total cost to replace Keith, Integrated Direct Marketing Manager	**$952,300**	**$891,300**
Cost of staff turnover as a percentage of salary	**1058%**	**990%**
Cost of staff turnover as a percentage of Keith's goal	**54%**	**51%**
Cost of staff turnover as a percentage of Keith's department's overall goal	**14%**	**13%**

Turnover at the Top

How does one measure the value of a Chief Development Officer? In a Fundraising Department operating a variety of programs through multiple staff, the job of the most senior fundraiser is to inspire everyone else to give their all. Even if she doesn't have an independent file of major donors and a personal fundraising goal (which would be rare), the Chief Development Officer affects the fundraising performance of all Development staff, the CEO and the Board of Directors.

I made many attempts to calculate the financial impact on fundraising when a high-performing Chief Development Officer leaves an organization prematurely. But, while I could quantify the loss in less senior positions, I found it impossible to do so here. There are so many variables. Every scenario I hypothesized was particular to that situation and I knew readers would dismiss any example as too distant from their own experience. As well, I found research in the for-profit sector on the monetary value of top leadership to be equally vague, though many case studies exist on how brilliant CEOs have changed the culture of their organizations and led them to unparalleled profit.

I have seen a Development office completely fall apart when the Director resigned because no one else had developed relationships with any of the donors.

Restrictive reasons why fundraisers stay in their current jobs:

65% Shortage of other good jobs in the area
26% Contractual commitment to stay
14% Would have to forfeit retirement benefits
14% Difficulty finding jobs due to age

Perhaps, then, culture is the defining issue of top leadership; and the Chief Development Officer is responsible for the "fundraising culture". In the most positive examples, the culture inside a Development Department mirrors an equally positive culture organization-wide, inspired and reinforced by the CEO. But, other situations also commonly exist. An excellent Development chief can shield his team to some degree from an organization-wide culture that is less than positive.

According to Robert A. Cooke, CEO of Human Synergistics International,[3] positive cultures are ones in which leaders

- encourage and enable staff to approach work and interact with each other in ways that enhance their own growth and satisfaction;

- reinforce and inspire colleagues and staff to achieve goals through cooperation rather than competition (opposite to the territorial approach to fundraising often found in multi-level charities and even between fundraising departments);

- manage "prescriptively" by focusing on what is being done right, and guiding staff towards goals and outcomes rather than "restrictively" by focusing on mistakes, short-comings and constraining the actions of staff.

In studies of companies in which leaders created positive rather than negative cultures, Cooke found dramatic improvements in bottom line profit.

The greatest potential and the highest risk in fundraising are both embodied in the Chief Development Officer. Losing any high performing fundraiser too soon is regrettable; but losing the Chief Development Officer prematurely can be catastrophic.

A Picture of Job Tenure in Fundraising Today

While job tenure is not the only measure of the health of a profession, it is an important one. So, in a series of studies with professional fundraisers, job tenure was measured by several factors, some of which turned out to be significant, others less so. Gender fell into the latter category. Whether analyzed by fundraising position or by seniority, no meaningful difference was found between men and women regarding the length of time they tended to stay in fundraising positions.

Respondents whose most recent position was in management stayed longer on the job (4.4 years on average) than did non-management fundraisers (2.6 years).

---

[3] "Developing Constructive Leader Impact", Robert A. Cooke, PhD and Linda Sharkey, PhD, *Consulting Today*, 2006.

Fundraisers employed in one-person-shop operations – unique because they are both management and non-management simultaneously – stayed 3.7 years on average.

By far the most notable differences in tenure were found when respondents' length of stay in positions was analyzed by age (Table 5).

Table 5: Length of Stay in Last Three Positions by Age Group

Average Length of Stay	Respondents' Age			
	Under 30	**30-44**	**45-60**	**61+**
Most recent position	1.6 years	3.5 years	4.2 years	6.5 years
Second most recent position	1.8 years	3.0 years	4.0 years	5.8 years
Third most recent position	1.0 years	2.9 years	2.4 years	4.3 years

Among non-management professionals under thirty years of age who took part in our research studies, the average tenure in their most recent fundraising position was eighteen months. Taking their last three fundraising jobs into account, tenure per job averaged just sixteen months. These same fundraisers also said that it takes, on average, ten to twelve months in their new positions before feeling fully comfortable in their jobs and working at top productivity. While they undoubtedly produce good work as they are gaining experience and developing confidence, they also require closer supervision and more support from managers, as the scenarios earlier in this chapter described. So, if non-management fundraisers are changing jobs after sixteen months, they are giving their employers only four months of work at optimum output – not an attractive investment/return proposition.

Not surprising, tenure lengthens the older fundraisers become. More diverse job descriptions, higher pay, more responsibility and authority all play a role as do family commitments that lead fundraisers to seek greater stability. Sometimes, however, longer tenure is less a matter of choice and more one of circumstance. For instance, many respondents referred to being tied to a particular community because of their spouse's job, or living in an area where few progressive management positions were available to them.

Expectation versus Reality in Management and Non-Management Positions

Our research sought the views of Development managers with responsibility for hiring and/or supervising staff on what they considered to be an acceptable length

I joined this not-for-profit 28 years ago because of the job flexibility and benefits I was offered. But I'm still here today because of the confidence my VP has in me and the independence I enjoy.

What makes loyal fundraisers want to stay:

98% Career advancement opportunities
95% Positive workplace environment
84% Financial advantages

of stay for fundraisers in non-management positions. The latter were defined as fundraisers with no requirement for hiring or managing other staff. Managers' views were surprisingly consistent. Three years seems to be the standard for acceptable tenure for most non-management positions, especially those in which fundraisers interact directly with donors (major and planned gifts, corporate philanthropy and sponsorship, and donor relations). The exception was direct response or the annual fund. For workers who have little or no direct interaction with individual donors, most managers felt that between two and three years' tenure would be good value for money.

Actual length of stay for non-management fundraisers in their most recent positions was well within this desired timeframe. For instance, fundraisers working in direct response (direct mail, telemarketing or canvassing) stayed 2.8 years, and those working in donor relations 3.1 years. However, when those workers' tenure is analyzed by age, there is a notable difference between fundraisers under thirty, whose tenure is relatively short, and those over thirty, who tend to stay longer in these same positions.

Views differed, though not widely, on acceptable tenure for more senior positions in fundraising (Table 6). CEOs felt that five years of service from their Chief Development Officers was good value for money, and they are getting close to that at 4.8 years. Three years' tenure from annual fund or direct response program managers was considered acceptable, and that is actually being exceeded.

Table 6: What Employers Feel Is Appropriate Tenure in Fundraising Management Positions versus Respondents' Actual Tenure in their Most Recent Jobs

Fundraising Management Position	Appropriate Tenure for Managers of Fundraising Programs, According to their Employers	Actual Tenure of Management Level Respondents in their Most Recent Positions
Director of Development	5 years	4.8 years
Annual Fund/Direct Response Director or Manager	3 years	3.5 years
Donor Relations Director or Manager	5 years	3.7 years
Major/Planned Gifts/Capital Campaign Director or Manager	5 years	3.8 years

Five years was identified by employers as the job tenure benchmark for supervisors of practitioners in major and planned gifts programs, capital campaigns and donor relations (stewardship). These are the fundraising programs that employ professionals who deal directly with the most generous donors or those with the potential to give significantly more than they are currently contributing. Fundraisers who work in these programs generate most of their Development Departments' profit. Understandably, employers are looking for longer tenure in these highly sensitive and specialized positions, but here is where actual tenure (3.8 years) is falling short of expectation.

Job Tenure Among Sole Practitioners

10% of respondents in our studies classified themselves as "one-person-shop fundraisers". These multi-tasking practitioners are the entire Development operation embodied in one individual. One-person-shop fundraisers may or may not have clerical or data entry assistants (59% of our study participants did); but all responsibility for raising money on the staff side falls to these sole practitioners. One-person Development offices are more likely to be found in social or community service organizations than in any other kind of not-for-profit, though many health services, private schools, and arts organizations also tend to depend on a single professional to manage and execute their fundraising operations. While there are no meaningful differences between sole practitioners and other fundraisers in age, education or religious conviction, one-person-shop fundraisers are more likely to be female.

The average length of stay in their last position among one-person-shop fundraisers was 3.7 years while CEOs of not-for-profits that employ a single professional to do their fundraising felt that a tenure of five years or longer would be good value for money.

The Fundraisers Who Defy Tenure Statistics

While the average length of stay in their most recent positions for all respondents was four years, 14% had been in the same job for ten years or more at the time they were surveyed. Not surprising, these long-tenured fundraisers are statistically among the older participants in our research studies, and they are slightly more likely to be men. They are much more likely to work in higher education than in any other not-for-profit discipline and much less likely to be employed in the arts or social/community services. Fundraisers who have been in the same job for ten or more years are also considerably less likely to work in one-person Development shops.

Religious conviction is a notable characteristic of loyal American fundraisers, but not meaningful when we look at the characteristics of Canadian respondents with long tenures. 17% of Americans who have been in the same job for ten years or more identified themselves as "actively religious" versus only 5% who said they were "not at all religious". Among Canadians, though, 13% of long-tenured respondents were actively religious, whereas 15% were not at all religious. More than any other characteristic in the study, religious conviction is markedly different for Americans and Canadians.

59% of One-Person-Shop fundraisers have some amount of paid clerical and/or data entry assistance

Staying for 5 years in my first job has served me well. It showed my employers that I am stable, reliable and a good candidate for internal promotion.

I have been here for over 20 years and have loved every minute. I could go almost anywhere now, given my skills and experience, but I stay for the job satisfaction I enjoy. The accumulated benefits play a role, too.

I transitioned out of the corporate sector where I worked for 17 years so that I could make a difference. I wasn't sure what my contribution to the world was going to be, but it became clear to me when I became a fundraiser.

Loyal fundraisers also distinguish themselves from other study respondents by how they evolved into fundraising as a career. They were 25% more likely than their shorter-tenured colleagues to have come into the field from other occupations as opposed to spending their entire careers in Development. As well, they were more likely to have shifted into fundraising from other jobs inside the not-for-profit sector (50%) rather than coming from the for-profit sector (28%).

While more likely to be Development Directors, about 45% of respondents who have been in the same position for ten or more years manage or work in specific fundraising programs. Table 7 illustrates where loyal fundraisers are more and less likely to be found by job type.

Table 7: Programs in Which Loyal Fundraisers Are More Likely or Less Likely to Be Found

Fundraising Program	Likelihood of Employing Loyal Fundraisers [or] Likelihood of Engendering Longer Tenure	
	More Likely	Less Likely
Telemarketing/Call Center	X	
Canvassing		X
Special Events, Lotteries		X
Capital Campaigns	X	
Corporate Philanthropy/Corporate Sponsorship		X
Prospect Research	X	
Annual Fund		X
Data Management	X	

Prospect research and data analysis require unique skill sets, attracting practitioners who may not be on the typical career path in Development. These are also jobs that are not yet recognized as essential by the not-for-profit sector as a whole, even though they are. Specialists in data analysis or prospect research may find that there are fewer opportunities in their field, so they tend to stay longer in one position. Our research on tenure by position also found a greater tendency towards long-term loyalty among direct marketing fundraisers who work in call centers. Telemarketers and the companies and not-for-profits they work for are likely not surprised by this. I have heard so many accounts from owners of direct response firms about staff who, year after year, reconnect with the same donors on behalf of their clients. These callers have definitely built solid relationships, but they have done it entirely over the phone. That kind of job satisfaction, plus the effort that these companies make to retain good employees, contribute to their longer-than-average tenure.

Breakthrough goals, a compelling case, and the sheer intensity and profile of capital campaigns contribute to longer tenure among campaign staff. It is interesting to note, however, that incentives designed to keep staff on the job to the end of the campaign are not particularly effective. Only 29% of fundraisers who were offered bonuses if they stayed to the end of their capital campaign said that this was a factor that influenced their long tenure.

What is missing from Table 7 is just as interesting as what is included. Major and planned gifts programs are no more likely than other fundraising programs to generate longer tenure among practitioners. Since the essence of fundraising is relationship-building, this most sophisticated end of the Development field should be where the greatest job satisfaction is found. And, employers should be particularly motivated to influence the loyalty of their major and planned gifts officers as here is where length of stay has the biggest impact on the bottom line and where competition for talent is most intense.

Longer-than-average tenure seems to be a product of both job satisfaction and pragmatism. Among the qualitative reasons that respondents cited for remaining loyal, these were the most prevalent:

- Belief in the organization's mission or work – while this influences all fund-raisers, it has an even stronger pull for long-tenured practitioners;
- Strong connection with the organization's donors – long-tenured fundraisers were over 50% more likely to state this as something that influences their tenure.

On the practical side, these issues also have a positive influence on tenure:

- Holding one of the few coveted Development jobs in the area;
- Having access to an attractive benefits package (retirement benefits or family benefits, such as free tuition were especially noted);
- Having made a commitment to stay for a particular length of time;
- Assumed difficulty in finding another job due to age.

Greater Stability at the Top

Job tenure among Chief Executive Officers was not a deliberate focus of our research, but because we engaged CEOs in a study about managing fundraisers, we took the opportunity to ask about turnover in their own positions. 26% of Chief Executive Officers had been in their positions for ten years or longer at the time they joined our study. This is more than double that of Directors of Development where only 11% of survey respondents had held their positions for more than ten

My proudest accomplishment has been recruiting eight new business leaders for my agency's Board. This will have a lasting impact long after any donations that I secure are spent.

People feel amazing when they make a gift, and it's wonderful to be the someone who helps them feel that good.

Why senior fundraisers left their last position:

78% Career Advancement
30% Accomplished all I set out to do
39% Problems specific to previous position
39% Conflict with other members of organization
20% Family issues

years. High turnover among CEOs is relatively rare, but 17% of respondents we interviewed reported that four or more people had held their position in the last decade.

Tenure among leadership volunteers is, of itself, not a meaningful measure of either satisfaction or fundraising success at the Board level. By-laws meant to limit terms and ensure that Board membership is refreshed imply that the more common problem at the top is not high turnover but, rather, staying too long. However, it is still valuable to know whether Board members complete their terms and, if not, whether fundraising has anything to do with their early resignation. On that question, the news is good but the reason behind the positive statistic may tell another story. Only 10% of leadership volunteers we surveyed said they had ever left a Board position prior to their prescribed end of term for reasons connected to fundraising.

I found this surprising in light of both CEOs' and Development Directors' strong views as well as Board members' own assessment of their performance. CEOs said that their least enjoyable task was convincing their Boards to fulfill their fundraising responsibilities. Senior Development staff cited problems with the Board over fundraising as one of the top two reasons why they left their last position. For their part, Board members rated themselves a lackluster 4.4 on a scale of one to seven for the significance of their contributions to fundraising. Given those sentiments, I wondered why early resignation is not more prevalent among leadership volunteers. The answer seems to lie in performance expectations. Board members pointed out that there is considerable lack of clarity about their fundraising responsibilities at a leadership level and lack of accountability for meeting specific targets. In other words, there are no real expectations for fundraising performance placed on their shoulders and, therefore, no penalties for failing to meet them. I wondered whether professional fundraisers' and CEOs' inherent respect for leadership volunteers was manifesting itself in the wrong way. Were Board members being treated with kid gloves when they should be handed challenging fundraising goals and the resources required to meet them? Or, was the problem one of internal Board management? Were the Board and Development Chairs unable or unwilling to hold their fellow members' feet to the fire?

As it turns out, all of these things contribute to dissatisfaction at the top of many not-for-profits as it relates to raising money. Chapters 9, 10 and 11 provide more research data and recommendations to help leadership volunteers reach their own – and their donors' – fundraising expectations.

What Motivates Someone to Become a Fundraiser?

It was mid-morning on my first day as Director of Marketing and Public Relations at a local social service agency. I was sitting alone in my office trying to figure out how to create a voicemail message when Paul, Chair of the Fundraising Committee, appeared in the doorway.

"I only have a few minutes," he announced efficiently, "but I wanted to say 'hi' and see whether you have had a chance yet to review the Car Raffle and the Bowl-a-Thon files…and the notes I left on the upcoming Tribute Dinner. I'm particularly concerned about the Dinner as this will be our first attempt and we haven't yet nailed down the person we're going to honor. That means, of course, that the tickets aren't printed, though we do have a date – October 29th (it was now July 7th), and we've made the down payment to the hotel, which means we're committed. Anyway, do you have any questions?"

I hesitated a moment, then replied, "Paul, this sounds a lot like fundraising. You must have me mixed up with someone else. I'm the Director of Marketing and Public Relations."

"That may be so", Paul replied. "But you're also the fundraiser."

"I don't think so", I said, a measure of trepidation rising in my voice.

"Well, no one else is", he said emphatically, as if to end the debate right then and there.

I wasn't giving in that easily. I remembered I had the job ad in my briefcase. Pulling it out, I scanned it quickly and, much to my relief, found no mention of fundraising. I pushed it across the desk to Paul.

"See – Director of Marketing and Public Relations."

Paul gave the job ad a passing glance then paused for a minute. A strange look came over his face, akin to taking a swig from the milk carton whose contents had expired two weeks earlier. "Oh, yes…that… well…we were afraid that if we put the word 'Fundraiser' in the job title, no one would apply. But you're it."

Why someone might choose to work in fundraising in the first place can be important in knowing what will motivate them to stay in the field and, specifically, in a particular not-for-profit. It's the human resources equivalent of knowing why a donor gives at all and why he remains loyal to a particular organization when the choices are so numerous.

Only **38%** of fundraisers surveyed have ever considered Planned Giving as a career path.

Why respondents chose fundraising as a career:

33% Evolved out of other work
15% Responded to job ad
14% Inspired by volunteer activities
8% Recommendation of career counselor
6% Only job available / offered
5% Practical entry point into the non-profit sector

Today's professional fundraiser is more deliberately career-oriented than before, largely because raising money has become a professional career choice. Industry training and certification, demand in the not-for-profit sector for qualified practitioners, and the transfer of responsibility for fundraising from volunteers to paid staff, have all contributed to its evolution from activity to occupation.

All respondents were asked what motivated them to choose fundraising as a career. 40% entered the field deliberately by responding to a job ad, for instance, or by gravitating into professional fundraising through volunteering. However, a surprising 44% seem to have fallen into the work. Many in this latter group said they didn't choose fundraising but that fundraising chose them. Raising money was often referenced by more senior survey participants as an unofficial part of the job, one that only became apparent after they were hired.

In many respects, what motivates people to enter the Development field today is different from what influenced them twenty years ago. Table 8 illustrates.

Table 8: What Motivates Respondents to Become Fundraisers – Then and Now

Reason for Becoming a Fundraiser	Fundraisers with less than 5 years' experience	Fundraisers with more than twenty years' experience
Fundraising evolved out of other work/was an unofficial expectation of the job	26%	43%
My volunteer work inspired my interest in fundraising	9%	17%
Responded to a job posting	19%	12%
Fundraising was a practical entry point/enhanced my marketability for a career elsewhere in the not-for-profit sector	17%	7%
Fundraising was recommended to me by a career counselor or mentor	9%	8%
To enhance my marketability in the not-for-profit sector	8%	3%

While it is less likely today for someone to become a fundraiser accidentally or to step into fundraising professionally after raising money on a volunteer basis, there are a few things that have been consistently influential in drawing people into the field. For instance, it was just as likely twenty years ago as now for fundraising to be recommended as a career option by a mentor or career counselor. I was quite surprised to find this to be the case as fundraising was not viewed as a career twenty years ago in the same way it is today. This says less about the forward-thinking of career counselors two decades ago and more about the likely deficiency that exists today in marketing the profession strategically. The fundraising industry and its surrounding professional organizations could do more to sell Development to career advisors and career change specialists.

Where Do Fundraisers Come From?[4]

77% of professional fundraisers migrated into the industry from other professions, fairly evenly split between those who came from the not-for-profit sector and those who were previously employed in the for-profit sector.

It is interesting to note that among fundraisers with not-for-profit backgrounds, programs and services yielded more Development professionals than did administrative management or marketing/communications. The obvious advantage is that Development staff with experience in programs and services delivery are well versed in the issues for which their organizations are trying to raise money. Fundraisers with this kind of first-hand experience can be particularly compelling when describing the need or the opportunity to donors.

When fundraisers transitioned from the corporate sector they were most likely to come from marketing, advertising, communications and/or sales. These professionals are used to an environment that works to sales quotas and prospect pipelines – a decided advantage to a charitable sector still uncomfortable with bottom-line measures. However, a selling proposition to donors is far more complex than one to customers and the competition is considerably more intense. Convincing a donor to support the arts in the midst of an economic downturn, for example, is an art in itself.

Long-Term Career Intentions of Professional Fundraisers

While length of stay in a single fundraising position may be shorter than employers would like, the long-term picture is more positive. Among respondents confident about their long-term career intentions, almost three out of four intend to stay in fundraising indefinitely. This includes 20% who have their sights set on becoming a not-for-profit CEO, and feel (quite rightly) that fundraising experience will enhance their chances of securing the top job. For a profession in which more practitioners entered the field accidentally than intentionally, this is good news.

28% of all respondents were planning to leave the fundraising industry to pursue a different career path at the time they participated in the study. The two most prevalent reasons were "to pursue a personal passion" or to "enter or return to the for-profit sector".

---

[4] from the fundraising stork, of course.

Why respondents chose planned giving as a career:

47% Natural extension of major gifts work
11% Interest cultivated through conferences/trainings attended
5% Long-intended career goal
4% Compatible skills from working in private sector

My background is in marketing and I found it relatively easy to transfer those skills to fundraising. After all, it's about knowing your customer/ donor and communicating with them. However, I did take some general seminars when I first started to learn more about the specific fundraising programs we have here. This gave me a basic understanding of the fundamentals.

Table 9: Percentage of Respondents Planning to Retire or Leave Fundraising for Another Career Within the Next 10 Years by Current Occupation

Years to Retirement or Leaving Fundraising	Directors of Development	Fundraising Program Managers	Non-Management Fundraisers	One-Person-Shop Fundraisers
< 5 years	21%	18%	19%	19%
5–10 years	29%	25%	28%	34%
Total leaving within 10 years	50%	43%	47%	53%

Regardless of whether respondents intend to serve out their careers in fundraising or explore other opportunities before retiring, a fairly significant shift in personnel will be felt over the next decade. 50% of Directors of Development and 53% of fundraisers managing one-person-shops plan to leave the industry within the next ten years (Table 9). Age is definitely the main reason, especially for Directors of Development where 90% of those who plan to retire or leave fundraising are already over the age of 55 (Table 10). Table 10 also reveals some other interesting information about the intention to stay in fundraising or pursue other interests among practitioners between the ages of 35 and 55. The number planning to leave fundraising is higher among one-person-shop fundraisers than for other Development professionals. Other information provided by these respondents suggests that the pressure to raise money with insufficient staff resources, while earning lower salaries than colleagues working in larger Development operations, eventually exacts its price.

Table 10: Respondents Planning to Retire or Leave Fundraising for Another Career Within the Next 10 Years By Current Occupation and Age

Years to Retirement or Leaving Fundraising	Directors of Development			Fundraising Program Managers			Non-Management Fundraisers			One-Person-Shop Fundraisers		
	<35	35-55	>55	<35	35-55	>55	<35	35-55	>55	<35	35-55	>55
< 5 years	4%	13%	45%	18%	12%	36%	19%	15%	31%	17%	16%	32%
5-10 years	32%	23%	45%	16%	19%	45%	19%	24%	46%	17%	28%	47%
Total	36%	39%	90%	34%	31%	81%	38%	39%	77%	34%	44%	79%

Job Satisfaction and Immediate Intentions to Stay or Go

What distinguishes respondents who expect to stay in their current positions or with the same not-for-profit for an indefinite term (61% of all professional fundraisers studied) from others who are planning to leave? An interesting mix of both positive and negative factors is at play regardless of respondents' immediate career intentions.

Planning to Stay

Fundraisers with no intention to leave their current positions attribute their desire to stay to six key factors. By far the most popular is a strong belief in the importance of the organization and its mission (85%). This attribute far outstrips anything else as a factor that fundraisers say motivates them to stay, and, actually, I find that to be troubling. While it is heart-warming to have it affirmed, love of the cause is not something that can be tangibly improved or altered as a means of extending employees' tenure or fending off the competition. Employees don't evolve from loving to hating a cause over the course of their period of employment; they leave organizations for reasons that are connected with very tangible issues involving people and working conditions. So, if admiration for the cause is the thing that is holding someone in place, it will be insufficient when the competition comes knocking or when Development hits a rough patch. (I deal with this issue in more depth in Chapter 8 in a section called "Blinded by the Brand", in which our research revealed both employers' and employees' over-reliance on admiration for the cause as a tool in hiring, choosing jobs, and managing.)

68% of respondents said their intention to stay was connected to "being included as a respected participant in discussions and decision-making on issues affecting fundraising". I expected non-management fundraisers to say this was desirable and that it influenced their tenure. But four out of five Development Directors also identified this factor, even though these chief fundraisers should always be at the heart of decision-making on Development matters. Sadly, this is not always the case. In many not-for-profits, the fundraising goal, methodologies for raising money and the timeline for delivering results are determined in the CEO's office and at the Board table, then handed to the fundraisers as their marching orders. Not exclusive to, but particularly prevalent in, one-person-shop fundraising operations, this top-down approach sends entirely the wrong message. It says that fundraisers are not capable of contributing to the strategy for raising money while being on the hook for delivering results.

67% of all respondents said that being a member of an excellent team of co-workers was an important factor in their retention. Even 53% of one-person-shop fundraisers, who do not have fundraising colleagues, chose this option. They defined the "team" as broader than just Development professionals. Seasoned employers are definitely able to point to the times in their management careers when their team gelled and other times when it did not. An excellent team is a mark of excellent management, not a matter of luck. Some of the things that affect the quality of the team are determined during the hiring process. Others evolve over time through supervision, performance evaluation, recognition, and many other important and practical activities for which management is responsible.

Working for a boss I respect and admire influences 64% of respondents to stay in their current jobs. But, the attributes most valued in the boss differ depending upon who we surveyed. Directors of Development, in referring to their CEOs, felt that "asking for and valuing their employees' input" was the most important

72% of fundraisers surveyed said they plan to stay in the industry.

Another not-for-profit might be able to offer me ten times the salary. But if I got wind that the culture was bad, I wouldn't want it.

Why fundraisers plan to leave their current position:

74% Career / Financial advancement
70% Difficulties with position
60% Conflict/differences with other people in the organization
36% Achieved all that I could
34% Work-life conflict
32% Intention to leave the fundraising industry

characteristic of a great boss; Fundraising Program Managers appreciated their Directors of Development who "allowed staff to work independently".

A workplace culture in which management (the Board and CEO, in particular) exhibits a positive and supportive attitude towards professional fundraising was cited by 56% of respondents as a factor that influences tenure in a positive way. Professional fundraising has been a part of not-for-profit life for over half a century; but many charitable organizations still struggle with the idea of private sector support of third sector institutions. Unable to survive without it, but equally unwilling to embrace it, some not-for-profits keep fundraising and the people who do it at arm's length, hoping the money will appear without having to talk about it or without having to adjust internal practices in order to get it. Acceptance does not mean assimilation, however. Fundraisers' differences, especially their sales-oriented focus, make them good at what they do.

55% of respondents said that work conditions in which personal or family needs are accommodated have a positive impact on tenure. This is such a practical matter given the reality of life in the early twenty-first century and what it takes, both financially and in other ways, to raise a family today. Playing into this new dynamic is something which is not exclusive to not-for-profits but is definitely pronounced in the third sector. The majority of professional fundraisers are female, yet the salaries of women in Development in the United States are only 76% of those of their male counterparts (82% in Canada).[5] Paying women less than men to do the same job exposes not-for-profits as no better than the corporate sector, in spite of their focus on improving the human condition. From a business standpoint it is also short-sighted and costs not-for-profits in the long run. Women fundraisers work, on average, six hours of unpaid overtime per week on top of earning lower wages, and they shoulder the bulk of family care responsibilities.[6] Out of sheer necessity, therefore, women fundraisers with families are attracted to organizations that offer work conditions that ease the burden of their double careers. While resolving the issue of salary inequity is critical, smart employers will at least rethink their stance on telecommuting, job sharing, and leave for family situations. Most important, and this applies to men in fundraising as much as it does to women, performance evaluation for fundraisers should be focused on results in money raised; staff should not be penalized for the number of hours they didn't spend sitting in the office.

---

[5] *2012 Compensation and Benefits Study*, Association of Fundraising Professionals, U. S. and Canada, 2012. Available from http://www.afpnet.org/Audiences/ReportsResearchDetail.cfm?ItemNumber=11222
[6] According to the Bureau of Labor Statistics, their June, 2010 study revealed that 85% of women spend time doing household activities on an average day versus 67% of men, and that women who do household work spend an average of 2.6 hours versus 2.0 hours for men.

Sometimes, the intention to stay is more a factor of negative than positive circumstances. Nearly one out of three fundraisers not planning to change jobs said it was because there were few or no other equally appealing or well-paying positions in their geographical area. This observation was considerably more likely to be made by respondents working for universities or colleges (40%) than for any other type of not-for-profit.

Do Economic Swings Affect Fundraiser Retention?

The 2008/2009 economic downturn did impact fundraisers' mobility to some degree. 34% of respondents were intending to leave their jobs when we surveyed them in mid-2008, but that changed once the recession took hold. Cygnus conducted a follow-up study in the fall of 2009, seventeen months after our initial research. We found that 27% of respondents had actually changed jobs in a period of almost a year and a half, which suggested a slowdown in the rate of staff turnover in fundraising. When we interviewed employers (Directors of Development and Fundraising Program Managers), however, 59% felt that there had been no measurable improvement in staff retention in spite of the recession. The minority of employers, 31%, believed that fundraisers were tending to stay longer in their positions as a result of the economic slowdown.

24% of employers laid off one or more fundraising staff during the recession, in effect adding to the problem of high staff turnover in the industry.

Planning to Go

34% of respondents in our Study were planning to leave their jobs at the time they participated in the first research study in 2008. This figure does not include job change due to internal promotions but reflects only those respondents intending to leave one organization for another. At the time they joined the study, they were either in the process of negotiating a new position, had already secured a new job that they hadn't yet started, were actively job-hunting, or had simply made the decision to leave their current positions. While this group of respondents cited many reasons for intending to leave, it was interesting to note that almost one in three (31%) were planning to get out of fundraising altogether, though half of this group was hoping to remain working in the not-for-profit sector in some other capacity. Another 13% were on the verge of retirement. 17% of those planning to leave but not planning to retire were hoping to secure jobs within the not-for-profit sector but not in fundraising; 14% were intending to go into or return to the corporate sector or pursue a personal dream such as turning a hobby into a career.

I'm not all that happy with the position I have right now, but would moving somewhere else be any better in the end? Better the devil you know than the devil you don't.

Reasons why some fundraisers intend to leave the industry:

55% To work elsewhere in the not-for-profit sector
25% To work in the corporate sector
20% To follow a dream

69% of respondents said they had achieved all their career objectives in their previous positions.

By the time I decided to leave, staff dissatisfaction and turnover was so intense that I was questioning my own ability to do my job properly.

I'm jumping ship. It might be the "founder's syndrome" but I haven't been able to function at optimum productivity due to my not-for-profit's disorganization and lack of communication.

By a wide margin, the number one reason why respondents were seeking another job in fundraising was for better pay (48%). This is in spite of the fact that 70% of all fundraisers we surveyed felt they were already generously or adequately paid in their current positions. The supply/demand inequity in the industry means that fundraisers are often tempted with better offers and know that Development salaries are on the upswing. (During the recession, American fundraisers' salaries did decline by 2% between 2007 and 2008, but more than recovered by 2009, increasing over the previous year's level by 7%.)[7]

34% of respondents planning to leave were seeking a more senior position. 32% wanted to work in a larger not-for-profit with a bigger and/or diversified Development operation that offered more career advancement opportunities.

Not everyone's reason for leaving was positive or career-building in nature. 31% of fundraisers planning to leave were seeking another job in order to get away from an "old-school" approach to fundraising where they currently worked. This was most often described as an organizational culture in which key decisions about raising money were being made by people not willing to contribute to fundraising themselves or insufficiently knowledgeable about the length of time it takes to cultivate donors' support. An "old school culture" also referred to the tendency among organizational leaders to opt for short-term, minimally profitable fundraising ventures that were also very labor-intensive over longer-term but more lucrative strategies.

A fundamental disagreement between professional fundraisers and not-for-profit leaders (CEOs and Boards of Directors) about how money should be raised threaded its way through most of the research studies that support this book. Both fundraisers and their bosses had valid perspectives – to a point – the point at which fundraising beliefs and tactics intersect with donors' needs and sensibilities. Here, both "old-school" and professional views of how money should be raised were shaped on assumptions about what motivates donors to give and stay loyal, not all of which are correct.

The Unique Circumstances of One-Person-Shop Fundraisers

Meredith is the second full-time staff fundraiser for a community service agency. She has been with the organization for two and a half years, earns $39,000, and shares an administrative assistant with the Programs Coordinator. Her much-loved predecessor, with whom Meredith is often compared, held the job for fourteen years before retiring and developed most of the fundraising programs that raise money

---

[7] *2009 Compensation and Benefits Study*, Association of Fundraising Professionals, U. S. and Canada, 2009. Available from http://www.afpnet.org/Audiences/ReportsResearchDetail.cfm?ItemNumber=754

for this not-for-profit. Meredith is responsible for running the annual corporate and individual donor campaigns while the Board runs three fundraising events: a bowl-a-thon, a golf tournament and a combined auction/wine tasting fundraiser.

In the past year, a good deal of Meredith's time has been unofficially diverted to Board-managed fundraising events. She has spent many late nights in bowling alleys, filling in for volunteers who cancelled at the last minute; she has devoted the better part of six weeks to securing sponsors for the golf tournament, including many weekends visiting local retailers to ask for and pick up donations of items for the auction.

At the end of her first year on the job, Meredith was criticized by the CEO for spreading herself too thin. She asked for a full-time assistant to alleviate her time problems with fundraising events, but was told that there was no money in the budget. It was suggested that she learn to manage the Board more successfully as her predecessor had never had a problem with volunteers. At the end of her second year, Meredith's performance review noted a downturn in the corporate campaign even though the Board had produced a 20% increase in sponsorship value for their events. Meredith pointed out that she had secured many of the event sponsors, and several companies had "traded" their corporate gifts for the more attractive golf tournament sponsorships. She was reminded that it was very important to give Board members credit for success in fundraising events in order to maintain their enthusiasm, and that she should be more of a team player.

Four months ago Meredith resigned, giving one month's notice. The position has now been vacant for three months while the not-for-profit tries to find a suitable replacement. They have gone through the hiring process twice, the first time losing their preferred candidate at the last minute to another local not-for-profit offering a 50% higher salary plus a full-time assistant. They are in negotiation with their second-choice candidate and have offered a starting salary $10,000 higher than Meredith was earning when she left. In addition, they are willing to hire a contract fundraiser to work with the Board on fundraising events. The candidate is thinking about it, but has warned the agency that she is also considering other offers.

People are complex and situations that culminate in premature resignation or dismissal can seldom be traced back to a single issue or incident. This story unfolds in only four paragraphs, but it contains a long list of obvious and hidden problems that illustrate what went wrong. Even more troubling is that the not-for-profit is simply reacting rather than adopting a different approach that would stand a better chance of success.

These are the problems exacerbated by management:

- the salary is insufficient for the breadth and level of responsibilities, increasing the likelihood that only under-qualified candidates will be attracted to this position;

The key thing that one-person-shop fundraisers have been unable to accomplish:

43% Developing a fundraising plan
19% More/better donor cultivation
12% Better time management
12% Marketing
10% Convincing Board to participate in fundraising

Advantages of working in a one-person-shop, according to respondents:

37% Full control over planning
23% Sole ownership of successes
17% Autonomy
14% Variety of work

Disadvantages of working in a one-person-shop:

52% Too much work to be done by one person
31% Lack of collegial atmosphere
24% Lack of resources
12% Unrealistic expectations by Board/CEO

- salary levels and salary negotiations fail to take supply/demand into account as well as the basic logic of "you get what you pay for";

- deploying a "horse out of the barn" strategy to salary, agreeing to pay more only after the previous staff person has left for a better paying job, fails to account for the value of current staff and the cost of replacing them;

- a shared assistant means, inevitably, that the higher-priced fundraiser will spend too much time in administrative support, which is not a cost-effective use of a professional fundraiser's time and indicates a failure of management to make decisions on a cost/benefit basis;

- management's lack of respect towards their fundraiser is illustrated by a management style that measured Meredith's performance against some idealized former employee rather than against strategic fundraising goals;

- the not-for-profit is relying on an insufficiently diversified fundraising portfolio for success, one that is weighted in high-risk, time-intensive events that divert staff time from more lucrative and lower risk alternatives;

- in addition to lack of diversity in fundraising programs, there is an overall absence of strategy in decision-making on the part of Board, CEO and staff;

- the staff evaluation process is unprofessional. Criticisms are saved up for the annual review when it is too late to turn a negative situation around;

- a restrictive, rather than prescriptive, supervision style is in place, one which focuses on mistakes instead of accomplishments, denying staff a critical sense of accomplishment;

- a competitive, rather than collaborative, approach defines the Board/staff model for fundraising;

- the Board is shielded from responsibility for fundraising success simply because they are volunteers;

- a failure to budget staff support to the Board for their fundraising events jeopardizes the success of longer-term strategies that are managed by staff.

The problems are not all with management. Meredith contributed to her own poor situation and eventual resignation in these ways:

- failure to position to management the need for more staff within an investment/return proposition, condemning Meredith to running a chronically under-staffed fundraising operation and increasing the likelihood that she will not reach fundraising goals;

- lack of skill in managing up, especially regarding difficult matters such as ensuring the Board delivers on its own fundraising commitments;

- failure to prioritize her time in order to fulfill her own fundraising responsibilities;

- failure to use her CEO strategically to intervene with the Board when leadership volunteers were not meeting their own fundraising event goals;

- waiting until it was too late to point out problems to her boss that were preventing Meredith from meeting her fundraising goals.

Can Length of Stay Be Improved by Focusing on Length of Stay?

Replacing fundraising staff takes time, costs money, reduces efficiency, and puts fundraising performance at risk. So, no wonder Development managers are concerned about the tenure of their employees. But, while a span of time is the obvious way to define appropriate job tenure, is it the best way? So many factors other than length of stay determine whether an employee makes a worthwhile contribution to her organization before moving on. For example, Development Directors in our study felt that a planned gifts manager should stay in her position for five years. But, what if she stays for only three and a half years but, during that time, proves herself to be an exceptionally skillful manager? What if she has developed her staff to the point that they now close two gifts for every one they used to secure in the same period of time? While it's a shame to lose someone that capable, her organization definitely prospered from this manager's relatively short tenure and set a new standard for productivity in the future.

Because many factors need to be taken into account when assessing the value of someone's employment, I concluded that a more useful definition of satisfactory tenure is one that showcases accomplishment and satisfaction rather than simply time. The research data on tenure by position, age and other factors, plus the views and expectations of management, are all valuable to a degree; but, in the end, this definition trumps the numbers:

> *"A satisfactory tenure is a length of time at the end of which both employer and employee agree that their organization has been well served."*

This definition lessens the emphasis on time on the job and puts the focus instead on productivity. Productivity yields satisfaction and satisfaction is a hedge against premature departure. While not the only thing that will keep a good worker on the job longer, satisfaction with his current position is definitely something an employee takes into account when being courted by other not-for-profits.

The practical nature of fundraising is such that productivity is defined in the same way by both employers and employees – money raised. Fundraising is sales, though

I have only been in fundraising for 7 years, but in that time I have grown from the bottom to raising six and seven-figure major gifts. I think I am immensely better at my job because I have stayed in one organization.

How much longer respondents plan to work in fundraising before retiring?

19% Less than 5 years
28% 5-10 years
18% 11-15 years
13% 16-20 years
9% 21-25 years
7% More than 25 years

Fundraisers' greatest career accomplishment to date:

29% Amount of money raised
24% Role played in establishing strategic plans for organization's success
17% Successful stewardship of donors
15% Management of events or campaigns
14% Management of fundraising staff for success

Stay in a job long enough to understand what is expected of you and why you are being asked to do things a certain way. You might learn something!

Don't "hip-hop" around or your resume will look like Swiss cheese.

Short job stays are incompatible with how fundraising works. Donors give to people they trust and trust takes time to develop.

a rarified version in which the salesperson convinces the customer (donor) to pay for a product that someone else consumes. Our research definitely confirmed that salespeople are as driven to make the sale as are their managers. When we asked fundraisers in our study, "What has been your greatest accomplishment to date in your career?", the number one answer concerned the amount of money they had raised. The second most common response was cultivating relationships with donors that ultimately led to raising more money. This fundamental agreement between worker and boss means that half the battle is already won as soon as a professional fundraiser is hired. The other question, though, is "How must fundraising be designed and operated in order to create the best possible chance for success?" This is a challenging question to answer in an environment where key decisions are often made by those with the least knowledge about how fundraising works. The question is made even more difficult to answer because donors' needs and preferences are not static – they are changing with the times.

How Long Is Too Short?

While it makes sense to assess performance by measuring several factors in addition to length of stay, some tenures are just too short, period. An unacceptably short job stay is one in which the employee leaves before she is working relatively independently; that is, before she can be held responsible for the quality of her work and the decisions she makes. Because so much is invested in hiring, orientation, training and supervision, not-for-profits are short-changed when staff don't stay long enough to produce a profitable return.

Everyone we surveyed was asked how long they spent in their new jobs before reaching the point where they were working at full productivity. The more senior the position, the less time it takes, something that employers might not fully appreciate given the complexity of responsibilities at the top. Development Directors, for example, spend only six months in learning mode and those who are promoted internally spend even less. Non-management staff, however, need ten months before they are up to speed but their average tenure before leaving for another job is 2.5 years. When age is factored in, the problem is accentuated.

Of course, over an extended career, many professional fundraisers can point to a job they regret taking almost from the start, and the circumstances that led to their hasty departure. But it is fundraisers who exhibit a pattern of chronically short stays who offer no upside for their employers. Practitioners who have had, say, six jobs in six years, feel it demonstrates the breadth of their experience. In fact, it says something else entirely. It says that they have abandoned their positions just when they should have been assuming responsibility for the quality of their work and the decisions they make. These fundraisers are largely untested, and their short tenures are a warning to employers that they cost more than they are worth.

Why People Leave…and Why Their Bosses Think They Leave

There are two sides to every story. Development Directors planning to leave were more likely to blame deficiencies within the top management group for hastening their departure. They referenced lack of commitment to fundraising by Board members, failure to articulate how funds raised would be used (also referred to as insisting on raising all or as much money as possible "unrestricted"), and refusal to invest in fundraising, particularly staffing. On the other hand, CEOs who had experienced the premature departure of their chief fundraisers were most likely to attribute it to their fundraisers' own failure to reach assigned goals.

They are both a little bit right, and headed for trouble. Having not learned how to manage up, the Development Director is likely to find herself in a similar situation in her next job. Having not grasped what it actually takes to make profit in fundraising and to do so reliably year-on-year, the CEO and Board are likely to make decisions that set up their next Development Director for failure.

Premature Staff Turnover Is Not Inevitable

Among fundraisers we surveyed who left their last job for positive reasons, only 7% said they could have been persuaded to stay. This is not surprising given why they left. These Development professionals felt they had served their organizations well but had taken their careers as far as they could go within the limitations of the organizations or the size and scope of their fundraising operations. Some also left for reasons that they could not control such as family relocation. But, among respondents who left for negative reasons, 25% wanted to stay and would have done so if the situations that had prompted their departure were resolved. Poor pay, poor or no benefits, work expectations too broad for one person to handle, goals based on wishful thinking rather than evidence, management by fear, and the like, were reported as reasons why they left. Even a superbly managed not-for-profit that is highly successful in fundraising cannot keep all staff indefinitely. Nor would it want to, I suppose. But for managers and non-managers alike who are open to seeing things differently, opportunity awaits.

A strong resume includes length of stay plus impact and fundraisers can't have impact if they don't stay long enough in one not-for-profit. As an employer, I avoid applicants whose resumes reveal a pattern of job-hopping.

It's rare that there's just one thing wrong if someone isn't succeeding.

25% of respondents, in referring to their most recent job, said they could have been persuaded to stay.

28% of respondents have regretted at least one career move they have made. Among Directors of Development, **72%** have regretted one or more career moves.

The profitability of every business is compromised by poor hires, sub-standard productivity on the job, bad decision-making by management, and too-rapid staff turnover. But in not-for-profit sector fundraising, the scars are very visible. They show up on the ledger in black and white – or more accurately, black and red – as lower revenue and higher cost. But you don't have to accept the status quo. What it takes to build and sustain a high-performance fundraising team is within your grasp.

Chapter 4:
How the Fundraising Landscape is Changing

Money or Profit: It's Not the Same Thing

"Any fundraising activity can make money, but only certain ones make money profitably. Unfortunately, the fundraising system that is in place today is better at making money than profit."

I first made this comment about five years ago in the midst of a discussion with a client which had been going around in circles. It's not that I only figured this out recently; it's that it never occurred to me until then that I needed to say this out loud to a room full of fundraisers.

I had been advocating a restructuring of this client's Development operations, and I had the evidence to back up my argument. Donor attrition was crippling, gift values were stagnant and cost per dollar raised was unacceptably high. But this was a large national organization with a powerful brand, able to attract new donors easily. Their high volume/low gift value approach was all that they knew and it kept three hundred fundraising staff employed. My argument was falling on deaf ears.

Attempting to pull the debate around to the bottom line, I said, "Your CEO can only spend the profit that you make in fundraising. The way you are raising money now might produce a rise in gross revenue year-on-year, but it will not deliver more profit." The CEO was in the room and, up to this point, had been minimally engaged in the conversation. But he sat bolt upright when I said this as did several members of the Board who were also in attendance. Suddenly everyone was quiet, including the fundraising staff who, seconds before, had been strenuously advocating the status quo. I had hit a nerve.

Better or Just Different?

On the surface, fundraising appears to be considerably more sophisticated today than it was sixty years ago, but does it actually produce better results?

Anyone comparing gross revenue from fundraising then and now would conclude that the modern-day, professionalized approach to raising money is hands-down the better option. In 1971, giving totaled $130.22 billion (adjusted for inflation); in 2011 that figure had climbed to $298.42 billion, a 229%

increase. But the fair measure of growth compares philanthropy year-on-year against a consistent standard. In 1971, $130.22 billion represented 2.1% of America's gross domestic product (GDP); in 2011, $298.42 billion was 2.0%. True, 2011 was still a tough year for fundraising, which, at the time of publication of this book, has still not fully recovered from the recession that began in 2007. But, looking at all forty years between 1971 and 2011, philanthropy as a percentage of GDP was more often below than above the 2.1% benchmark.[1]

But what matters more is the amount of money that flows through fundraising into the operations of charitable organizations – i.e., net revenue raised. When the cost of fundraising is factored into the equation, the old-fashioned, low-volume-but-high-quality approach may actually have been the better performer. Today's most mature and diversified fundraising operations cost fifteen to twenty-five cents on the dollar while those that rely heavily on mass marketing and events can spend more than 50% of donors' contributions in raising money. Estimating a universal cost of fundraising at a conservative 15%, fundraising expenses were almost $45 billion in 2011. Today, salaries and fees which used to be contributed through volunteer labor make up the largest percentage of the fundraising budget. Considering the size of the professional fundraising industry today, has it grown philanthropy exponentially or substituted one way of raising money for another? And, given the vastly increased number of charitable organizations raising money, are today's fundraising tactics up to the challenge of resourcing the third sector?

Fundraising Then and Now: The Evolution of an Industry

There was a time when fundraising was almost entirely profit – back when volunteers raised all the money and fundraising had not yet become professionalized. Volunteers looked to others with an interest in their cause, and to colleagues and acquaintances for financial support. They knew their donors; they operated within the social codes of behavior of the times, instinctively using tactics that were comfortable to them and which they felt would be within the range of good taste. After all, whatever solicitations they made would be made back to them sooner or later. Fundraising was very personal then and while it engaged relatively few donors compared with today, it was highly profitable on a per-donor basis.

This was simply how fundraising was done for generations until, in the 1930s, new thinking about whether philanthropy could have universal appeal began to be explored. While it is impossible to pinpoint the moment that one approach to fundraising gave way to another, fundraising historian Scott M. Cutlip traced the

---

[1] Giving USA: The Annual Report on Philanthropy for the Year 2011 (2012). Chicago: Giving USA Foundation.

roots of volume-based fundraising to 1938 and the March of Dimes. President Franklin Delano Roosevelt had established a foundation to fight polio several years earlier, and each year on FDR's birthday "Birthday Balls" were held around the country to raise money. These balls were promoted by the media and Hollywood celebrities including Eddie Cantor who came up with the idea of asking the general public to get involved by contributing dimes and sending them directly to the President at the White House. Cantor called this campaign The March of Dimes. As Cutlip recounts in his book, "Desks and offices were stacked high with a flood of money-laden mail. The White House staff did little but open envelopes, sort mail, and count dimes for several days. All told, a total of 2,680,000 dimes ($268,000) were received in this first historic [mass fundraiser]."[2]

A decade later, direct mail marketing, which had existed in the for-profit sector in an organized fashion since the late 1800s, emerged as a fundraising strategy. The National Easter Seal Society was among the early adopters of direct mail, which they deployed as a means of broadening their base of donors.

The experiences of the March of Dimes and the Easter Seals represented a fundamental shift of emphasis away from a low-volume, low-cost, influence-based approach to raising money to a high-volume, mechanical one. This shift necessitated the professionalization of fundraising in order to maintain records on and solicit an ever-growing number of donors. Paid staff and the expenses inherent in mass marketing caused fundraising cost to rise, which, in turn, required not-for-profits to find more and more donors in order to keep these programs profitable. Redefining giving as a universal activity rather than the purview of the elite also served to reduce the per-donor value of gifts. More donors were required once again in order to compensate for more modest gift values.

Even with costs rising and gift values declining, though, fundraising in America remained buoyant. There was just so much potential. It was virgin territory back in the '40s, '50s and '60s, and average citizens were more than willing to give. As long as the number of charities engaged in volume-based appeals remained under control, fundraising potential seemed to be limitless.

But, the second half of the twentieth century saw explosive growth in not-for-profit organizations. The third sector in the United States quadrupled in the 1980s and doubled again in the 1990s and early 2000s. This growth is often cited as the impetus for an equally robust increase in the use of direct mail and other direct marketing techniques, but the reverse is actually more likely. It was the availability

As a board member and a donor, I don't really agree with the transition in fundraising from personal contact to email -- it's non-personal. I come out of sales where our motto was: "nose to nose, belly to belly, toe to toe brings in the sale."

---

[2] Fund Raising in the United States: Its Role in America's Philanthropy, Scott M. Cutlip, 1990, New Brunswick, New Jersey, Transaction Publishers (originally published in 1965 by Rutgers, the State University).

I tend to give more to not-for-profits that treat me as an individual and value my contributions. There are so many worthy causes and I can't give to them all. This is how I differentiate.

of mass marketing that made it possible for so many charitable organizations to emerge and build a financial base. Without direct marketing, many would have never survived beyond the startup phase.

A Philosophical Divide

The best thing about modern-day fundraising is that it gives all citizens – not just the well heeled and well connected – the opportunity to be philanthropic. The price paid, however, is less profit spread over substantially more charitable organizations and disagreement among decision-makers about how money should be raised. This lack of agreement is not surprising considering the system in place today is, in many ways, the philosophical opposite of how fundraising used to work. In the past, a fundraiser had a relationship with a prospect first, then the prospect became a donor. Now a stranger becomes a donor thanks to modern-day acquisition and then the solicitor has to figure out how to build a relationship with someone he doesn't know. This contemporary approach to fundraising can work, but it requires the people responsible for raising money – professional fundraisers, leadership volunteers and not-for-profit CEOs – to think differently and act cohesively.

Evidence from our research suggests that today there is a good deal of debate within this triumvirate about how fundraising should work and who is responsible for what. This disagreement is causing frustration, and this frustration is having repercussions. 40% of professional fundraisers said that conflicting opinions over how to raise money caused them to leave their last positions. They criticized Boards, in particular, for being unwilling to take modern-day practices into account or, worse, opting for short-term revenue activities over more lucrative, longer-term Development strategies. "We have to have the money now", was generally the reason.

How leadership volunteers define their own responsibilities in fundraising today says a lot about how unsure they are about the role they should be playing in a changing industry. 88% of Board members acknowledge they have responsibility for raising money, so at least there is agreement on that point. But, the job description that leadership volunteers assign themselves has them firmly entrenched in planning, supervising and showing up at events, when they should be using their unique influence to persuade donors to give. They used to do that job so well; now they are more likely to avoid it whenever possible.

For their part, Chief Executive Officers also commonly reference philosophical differences between themselves and their staff fundraisers about how money should be raised. The majority of CEOs we surveyed had experienced the premature resignation of their most senior Development staff member at least once. 42% said that disagreement over fundraising strategy caused or contributed to their fundraiser's early departure. Many Chief Executives also noted a lack of skill on the part of their Development staff in presenting a compelling argument that would have won decision-makers over and avoided such a drastic outcome.

Passionate debate over how to best configure a fundraising event or craft an appeal letter is one thing; disagreeing about how to realize the most profit from fundraising in a changing landscape is quite another. But, if CEOs, Board members and Development staff can get on the same page, their organizations will raise more money. That success will translate into job satisfaction, which, in turn, will cause fundraising staff and management to stay longer, and leadership volunteers to engage in more meaningful fundraising work.

How to Make the Most Profit

The good news is that all the fundraising strategies necessary for maximizing profit already exist; the bad news is that few not-for-profits are using them.

Most money given to charitable causes comes from individuals; people far outshine either corporations or foundations when their collective philanthropy is calculated. 81% of the $298+ billion raised in 2011 was contributed by individuals in outright gifts or bequests; 14% came from foundations and only 5% was donated by corporations.[3] In order to grow fundraising profit in a sustainable way, not-for-profits must put the majority of their talent and budget into raising money from individual donors. Corporate philanthropy, corporate sponsorship and grants from foundations are always important revenue sources, and they are especially so for not-for-profits in their earliest stage of financial growth. But this is short-term revenue, whereas individual donors can be persuaded to keep giving indefinitely as long as they get what they need.

Raising money from individuals includes two basic functions: volume-based appeals (direct marketing, participatory events and the like) where little if anything is known about the individuals who are being asked to give, and one-to-one appeals in which the objective is to get to know the donor well enough to secure increasingly generous contributions over time.

Imbalance is the fundamental problem today. There is too much reliance now on volume-based appeals in the mistaken belief that an organization can raise money

Every fundraiser and the not-for-profits they work for should remember that the money belongs to the donor. All they want in return is a sense that they got full value for their giving.

---

[3] Giving USA: The Annual Report on Philanthropy for the Year 2011 (2012). Chicago: Giving USA Foundation.

indefinitely – and profitably – through arms-length approaches alone. At the other end, there is too little investment in the growth of major and planned gifts programs – the sophisticated strategies that build gift value donor by donor and which raise money at a very attractive cost of about four to ten cents on the dollar. There are three primary reasons why major and planned gifts programs go underdeveloped in most not-for-profit organizations:

- lack of investment/return thinking and budgeting;
- fundamental reluctance among volunteers and even some paid professional fundraisers to interact personally with donors and ask them for money;
- failure to understand the difference between revenue and profit.

A cohesive, interdisciplinary approach to fundraising is one that prioritizes the movement of donors up and out of mass marketing and large-scale events into relationship fundraising.

Modern-Day Myths and Misunderstandings that Limit Fundraising Success

In the course of a century-long transition from very personal to very impersonal fundraising, some beliefs about how fundraising works have become so ingrained that they are now considered to be fundamental truths. Many are taught to students of fundraising as basic principles; others are assertively reinforced by senior practitioners and for-profit vendors of services to the fundraising industry. They serve to keep fundraising working one way when it should be adjusting to reflect changing donor behavior, and they limit profit.

Myth: The More Donors You Have, the More Money You Will Make

This is not true today, nor has it ever been true, and every capital campaign that fundraisers run disproves this assertion. A capital campaign is a time-limited, intense fundraising effort that raises an ambitious sum of money for a single purpose or a limited number of connected needs. The fundraising industry showcases one of its two greatest skills whenever it executes a capital campaign (the other being in planned giving). Capital campaigns are stunningly profitable; they reach for huge goals, spending only 5% to 15% of gross revenue to achieve dramatic results.

There are several reasons why capital campaigns raise so much money but a key strategy is that they avoid relying on volume of donors for their success. They would never reach goal if they did. Instead, they bring the best practices of prospect research, donor cultivation, gift negotiation and stewardship to the job of raising very generous gifts from as few donors as possible. Most campaigns raise 90% or more of their goal from fewer than 10% of donors, and they do not require a pool of hundreds of thousands of donors in order to define that core group of contributors. Capital campaigns often reach out to a larger group of potential donors towards the end to push the campaign over the top, but this final nod to volume is used more as a donor development strategy for the future than as an essential tool to reach the current goal. In fact, quietly raising a few more major gifts would be a much more efficient way to get to goal, and many campaigns do just that.

When not in capital campaign mode, not-for-profits seem to forget what makes these efforts so successful. They abandon what fundraisers know to be true, that "90% or more of money raised comes from 10% or fewer of the donors", and try instead to reach ambitious goals by appealing to a large volume of supporters through mass marketing. Direct marketing is designed to reach into a population of non-donors, to identify people with an interest in a particular cause, and to secure their initial support. It is good at that because that is the function for which it is designed. But acquisition is seldom profitable; as a matter of fact, James Greenfield, noted expert on fundraising cost-effectiveness, says that acquisition through direct mail can cost between $1.00 and $1.25 for every dollar raised.[4] Profit materializes through renewing the support of and securing larger gifts from as many of these donors as possible. Exactly as it works in the for-profit sector, the customer (donor) that a not-for-profit already has is more valuable than the one it might secure in the future.

Influencing existing donors to give again and give more generously than before requires an investment of time, ingenuity and money and here is where the mantra, "the more donors we have, the more money we will make", is exposed as untrue. Not-for-profits tend to accumulate more new donors than they can effectively steward within a limited budget. High donor attrition is the inevitable result. 65% of donors acquired through direct marketing never make a second gift; over 90% stop giving within five campaigns – most before they have contributed at a profitable level. The largest proportion of the fundraising budget is spent acquiring and reacquiring donors to make up for the premature exodus of those who come and go so quickly. This is an extraordinary waste of money and a poor use of professional talent.

This donor churn keeps a lot of fundraisers employed, however, and it floats a multi-billion dollar industry that solicits donors on behalf of not-for-profit clients. "The more donors you have, the more money you will make" is actually true for the

I don't want to receive 82 mailings after making one contribution. Add me to your mailing list but use email and other cost-effective communication methods rather than printing and mailing annual reports and newsletters. It's a waste of resources.

---

[4] Fund Raising: Evaluating and Managing the Fund Development Process, Greenfield, J.M., AFP/Wiley Fund Development Series, 2nd edition, 1999, John Wiley & Sons, Inc., New York, NY

Our fundraising goals are set by the board and they are wildly unrealistic. They are in the range of goals for hospitals ten times the size of ours. We have few donors and high patient turnover because we are a long-term care facility. I feel like a failure all the time.

vendors because they are paid for volume, not profit. Their contracts compensate them for the number of prospects they solicit and the number of campaigns they execute. The onus is on not-for-profits, however, to structure contracts differently so that they produce better results. Both vendors and internal direct marketing staff should be rewarded for retaining donors rather than replacing them and for flowing donors out of mass marketing into the hands of the relationship developers. The question should be, therefore, not "How many donors can we amass?" but "How few donors do we need from whom to build an increasingly profitable major and planned gifts program?"

Myth: "Losing Donors Is Not a Problem; There Will Always Be More Where They Came From"

A customer attrition rate over 90% would call for crisis intervention in any for-profit company but it has been going on for so long in not-for-profit fundraising that retaining only one donor in ten has become the accepted standard of practice. Direct marketing practitioners rely on donors' love of philanthropy and admiration for the work that charities do to keep them responding to appeals in large numbers. But the constant replacement of donors who have stopped giving with new supporters fails to take into account how fundraising revenue suffers as a result. 70% of donors say the first gift they make to a not-for-profit organization through a mass marketing appeal is, by their own standard, not generous within their means. They give modestly at first for one of two reasons: because they are following instructions, giving at one of the suggested gift levels in the appeal, or because they feel they should hold back until they see how the charity will respond. High levels of donor attrition, then, followed by robust donor acquisition, keeps average gift values artificially low. Sacrificing donors already in the system for new ones is simply not sound fundraising practice when the objective is making more profit.

Even if decision-makers continue to stubbornly drive volume at the expense of net revenue, it looks like donors are on their way to forcing the industry into a more balanced way of raising money. In their quarterly assessment of direct marketing performance, Target Analytics[5] evaluates six key measures that collectively chart the health of mass market fundraising. They are:

- Participation: the number of donors giving through volume-based appeals – regardless of how often or how much
- Revenue: total money contributed

---

[5] *Index of National Fundraising Performance*, a quarterly report by Target Analytics, a Blackbaud company, Charleston, SC.

- Revenue per donor: the average philanthropic value
- Acquisition: the percentage of non-donors solicited who gives for the first time
- Retention: the percentage of previously acquired donors who gives again
- Reactivation: the percentage of lapsed donors whose giving is renewed

As a donor during the recession, I worried that my financial situation might take a turn for the worse. On the other hand, I was very conscious that others were really suffering. I wanted to give more but I hesitated.

In an ideal fundraising world, all six measures would improve year-on-year and no doubt that is what happened before the marketplace became saturated with too many not-for-profits soliciting too often. Then, five of the six measures began to stall or head downward. But, revenue-per-donor continued to rise, masking the fact that participation, acquisition, retention, and reactivation were all on shaky ground. While this meant that a shrinking number of donors became increasingly responsible for direct marketing profit, charities could still make good money through volume-based appeals as long as nothing went horribly wrong.

But something did go horribly wrong when, between March 2007 and February 2009, the market crashed and the world was plunged into a deep recession. In a national research study that Cygnus conducted in February 2009, 63%[6] of respondents said they had been negatively affected by the economic turmoil, the majority quite seriously. Even so, donors were determined to remain philanthropic to the best of their ability. Some reduced the number of not-for-profit organizations they were supporting; others chose to keep giving to the same number of charities while reducing the value of their contributions across the board. With donor acquisition and lapsed donor recovery already in decline, the reduction in average gift value coupled with the rise in donor attrition hit the charitable sector very hard.

A sudden turn of events can catapult a growing trend into mainstream practice, and it is likely that the recession will have a long-lasting impact on the direct marketing landscape. Many donors have found that by contributing to fewer causes it is easier to manage their philanthropy. Others have abandoned traditional direct marketing because of its cost and especially because of over-solicitation. In an attempt to maximize the value of their gifts on the ground, donors are choosing to bypass traditional fundraising appeals in favor of going directly to a charity's website, doing their research and contributing online.

People are still giving; they're just doing it differently. As time goes by, it will be increasingly difficult for fundraisers to depend on volume-based programs for anything but the purpose for which they were designed – finding new supporters.

---

[6] *Philanthropy in a Turbulent Economy,* Penelope Burk, Cygnus Applied Research, Inc., Chicago, August 2009.

And even then, not-for-profits will need to reduce their expectations regarding the number of new donors they can acquire in a single campaign. In order to be profitable, a shift in focus and budget is required, one that emphasizes retaining donors who are already giving, rather than constantly having to replace them.

Misunderstanding: "Every Fundraising Program Must Make Money"

Direct marketing as it exists today consists of two basic functions: finding new donors (acquisition) and securing more and, hopefully, larger contributions from donors acquired previously (renewal). Not-for-profits accept that donor acquisition is seldom profitable, but they expect donor renewal to overcome this initial loss and turn a healthy net profit. But insisting on profitability in direct marketing actually forfeits a much more lucrative alternative. This is particularly so in direct mail.

A direct mail database houses a collection of donors who have been giving for different lengths of time and at different levels of generosity. It is not uncommon for 20 to 30% of direct mail donors to be contributing 70 to 80% of a program's revenue. Some donors give beyond the normal range because they have a special connection to the cause, because their capacity to give is greater, or simply because they have been giving for longer than other donors. Making larger-than-normal gifts is also a way in which donors signal their readiness for more personal stewardship which will lead to even more generous giving in the future.

The performance of the direct mail manager, like that of all other staff, is evaluated on several criteria, but this is fundraising, so reaching ever-increasing goals is a primary measure of his success. He cannot reach ambitious targets without a successful donor renewal program because that is where all his profit is made; and he cannot have a successful donor renewal program without holding onto the 20 to 30% of his donors who are contributing most of the revenue. Even though these donors are ready for the major gifts officer who could raise their gift values even higher, should the direct mail manager let them go, his revenue would plummet, he would receive a poor evaluation, and he might even lose his job.

Insisting that direct mail renewal be incrementally profitable ensures that major gifts fundraising, where much more profit can be realized, goes underdeveloped. The better objective for a direct mail renewal program would be to improve its donor retention rate while developing better informed and more satisfied donors who will be ready sooner to consider making major gifts. This requires investing in the things that cause donors to want to keep giving, such as meaningful information on what their gifts have achieved. It also means eliminating the things that cause donors to stop giving, like over-solicitation. In a diversified fundraising operation, most of the money is made in major and planned gifts from a relatively small percentage of donors. Instead of hoarding them in a program they have outgrown, the direct mail manager should be rewarded for guiding these donors up into the hands of the major gifts officer. When direct mail is not required to make profit independently, it can play a pivotal role in increasing profit where it really matters – at the top of the donor pyramid.

Misunderstanding: "Donors Give to Support Our Organization"

They do that only once it seems; after the initial contribution, a not-for-profit's reputation alone is insufficient to secure donors' ongoing loyalty. The proof is in the rate of donor attrition. 65% of donors who make a first gift to a particular charity never make a second and 90% or more stop giving within five campaigns.

Selling the brand (just the name of a well-known charity or the basic purpose of one that may not be so well known) is enough to attract a new donor. However, as soon as he writes that first check, or gives his credit card number over the phone or gives online, he evolves from interested outsider to inside investor. The value of the gift he has just made is not a factor. Every donor, no matter how much or how little he gives, feels like an investor whenever he contributes. An investor seeks return on investment; return on investment for a donor is information in the form of measurable results.

This is not well understood by fundraisers who feel that the approach that won the donor in the first place is the one that will work the next time. They continue to sell the brand when selling results is what is required in order to motivate donors' renewed support. Of course, charitable organizations *are* worthy, and that's what influences donors to open the envelope or take the call. But in an over-crowded fundraising marketplace, bottom-line results are a charity's most compelling asset. Donors are attempting to measure the effectiveness of the not-for-profits they are supporting in order to decide whether to give again and whether to give more. At the same time, they are evaluating their own performance as citizens and donors. They feel a momentary sense of satisfaction at the time they give, but they feel like real donors later when they learn that their giving actually accomplished something. That second wave of satisfaction readies donors for the next ask and increases the likelihood that both donor retention and average gift value – the two determinants of profit – will rise.

Since a measurable result on their previous gifts is the trigger to increased profit, it is logical to assume that donors must have their contributions assigned to something more specific than the welfare of the organization as a whole. Unassigned or

We are a very recognizable organization and come under scrutiny in a very public way which requires constant monitoring with the media, and developing trusting relationships with our local donors and media talent.

"unrestricted" gifts are not tied to anything measurable, leaving fundraisers with the frustrating task of attempting to sustain donors' interest and commitment to give by selling the brand over and over again. (See below, "We Need to Raise as Much Revenue as Possible Unrestricted".)

Misunderstanding: "You Don't Get If You Don't Ask"

In one interpretation, this statement is accurate because most donors, even when ready to make a gift, wait to be asked. However, this basic truth is often deliberately misrepresented to mean that constant asking is alright when it definitely is not. As a matter of fact, over-solicitation has become the number one reason why donors stop giving or why they make modest gifts when they could have given much more generously. Asking too often serves only to reduce profit.

"You don't get if you don't communicate" is the more accurate declaration. When a donor gives for the first time, the solicitation does most of the work. It brings the organization into focus and takes the prospect all the way along the spectrum from non-contributor to donor. After that, the solicitation never again singlehandedly accomplishes the job of renewing a donor's support. Making the decision to give again or not happens in between the asks; the solicitation is simply the donor's opportunity to declare the verdict.

Between the time a donor gives and is asked to give again, many things can influence the likelihood that she will say "yes" or "no" the next time. A thank-you letter received a month or more after the gift has been made, and which reads like every other thank-you letter she has ever been sent, deflates the donor's enthusiasm, causes her to question administrative efficiency, and makes her wonder whether anyone cares about what she has done. An original and personal thank-you note from a leadership volunteer, however, sent within days of receiving the gift, has the opposite effect. The donor is thrilled; she senses the administration is on the ball and has noticed her as an individual, and she is already thinking about how much more she will give next time.

Myth: "Donors Who Give Big Should Be Treated Better than Other Donors"

It is a fact that donors who give very generously *are* treated better than other donors – but should this be the case? Fundraising as we know it is designed on a reward/punishment model, and gift value determines whether donors will be heralded or just tolerated.

Donors who make contributions larger than the norm are singled out for praise in several ways: their gifts are acknowledged more promptly; the thank-you letters they receive are often more thoughtfully composed and signed by someone in a position of higher authority; their names appear in larger type near the top of the Honor Roll; they are assigned a gifts officer whose job it is to foster a closer relationship; and, for those who give very generously, they are offered the opportunity to designate their gifts to a program or project of their choice. Generous donors are rewarded.

Donors who give in the average range or, heaven forbid, very modestly, are told in no uncertain terms that they matter far less. Instead of a compelling thank-you letter, they get a pre-printed postcard produced in volume and pressed into service when the fundraiser gets around to it; their names appear at the bottom of the Honor Roll (if the value of their gift qualifies for placement on the list at all); they are assigned not to a gifts officer, but to an endless stream of hard-hitting appeals; and they definitely don't have a say in how their contributions will be used. Donors who give modestly are punished for having done so, even when they give within the range suggested in the direct marketing appeal literature.

The reward/punishment model is further frustrating for donors because the rules surrounding who qualifies for which treatment are seldom made public. There is a single or cumulative gift value that, when reached, triggers better treatment, but only the fundraiser knows what that figure is. The point at which a donor becomes an important donor is kept under wraps because publishing this information would contradict charities' public position – that all donors are important and that gifts of any value are welcome.

Categorizing donors based solely on gift value makes fundraising passive when it should be active and it leaves money on the table. Passive fundraising applies a single approach to all donors when asking for money, then treats donors differently after they give based on the value of the contributions they made. Active fundraising assumes there is greater potential in all donors, regardless of the value of gifts they are currently contributing. Active fundraising treats all donors like major donors in order to influence more of them to give more generously. Not surprising, donors respond more enthusiastically to an active fundraising approach; they step up their philanthropy and charities make more money.

The untapped potential of donors whose gift values are currently modest was brought to light in a recent Cygnus Donor Survey. Of the study's most generous donors (those giving $10,000 or more to charitable causes), 58% had made some of their gift transactions in response to direct mail appeals.[7] Their donations through the mail were not their largest gifts; in fact, direct mail contributions tended to

---

[7] *The Cygnus Donor Survey... Where Philanthropy Is Headed in 2011*, Penelope Burk, Cygnus Applied Research, Inc., Chicago, IL, April, 2011

I love getting personally signed thank you letters when I make larger gifts. I was very disappointed recently after making several $1000 gifts to a not-for-profit online. All I ever got in return was an online receipt.

My finances took a hit in the downturn. Now that things are recovering, I am giving more to the not-for-profits that treated me like a person and not like a bank account during the recession.

I never made a substantial gift to my college until someone connected with me personally. Sadly it took them almost 20 years to do that.

I'm certainly not going to knock on a charity's door and say, "Hey, I could give you $1,000," but I wouldn't hesitate to give at that level or even higher if I thought a not-for-profit had a compelling case and asked me to support it.

be among their most modest gifts. Many of these donors said they use direct marketing programs to quietly get to know charitable organizations that they have not supported before. But the fact that they could give much more, and are, in fact, doing so with other not-for-profits, is important information for Development professionals who design fundraising strategies and allocate resources. Almost every donor is capable of making more and larger gifts; good customer service (donor relations) is the key that unlocks their generosity. Fundraisers who wait for donors to make larger gifts first before treating them well have the process backwards and they pay a heavy price for that mistake.

Myth: "It Takes a Long Time to Cultivate a Donor from Modest to Generous Giving"

Well, it does within the fundraising system as we know it. But donors are actually willing to give far more generously much sooner if they get what they need earlier. Because direct marketers need to hold onto donors in order to make a profit, and because fundraising is passive when it should be active, donors remain locked into giving programs that do not reflect their real capacity or desire. We have tested donors' willingness to move quickly and dramatically up the giving ladder by offering them the kind of donor relations usually reserved for only the most generous contributors. It works. Among the 25-50% of test donors whose giving improves because of better stewardship, some 2-6% leap from entry-level contributions to major gifts in a single step. It seems that the tendency of donors to give just a little more each time they make a contribution is the result of fundraisers asking for just a little more instead of reaching for the stars.

Myth: "We Can't Spend Money to Raise Money Because Donors' Number One Concern Is Cost per Dollar Raised"

Cost per dollar raised is among donors' major concerns today, but that wasn't always the case. I first studied the degree to which donors are conscious of the cost of fundraising and how it impacts their giving decisions in 2000. Back then, it played no meaningful role in whether donors made a first-time gift to a particular cause or renewed their support. But the situation is different today. In research[8] conducted by my firm between 2009 and 2012, we found that the cost of fundraising as an issue that impacts giving had moved from inconsequential to significant. One in three donors now says that cost per dollar raised is an increasingly important factor in their decisions about which causes they will support and for how long.

---

[8] *Philanthropy in a Turbulent Economy* (2009) and *The Cygnus Donor Survey...Where Philanthropy Is Headed in 2010, 2011, and 2012* (3 studies), Penelope Burk, Cygnus Applied Research, Inc., Chicago, Il.

But, at the same time that donors scrutinize fundraising expense, they are also insisting on certain considerations from the charities they support, and those considerations cost money. For example, there is a price attached to the collection and dissemination of information; so, how do donors reconcile their concern over the cost of fundraising with their need for information on what their contributions are accomplishing? Fundraisers, CEOs and Boards have a point if they feel that donors are sending contradictory messages.

Throwing caution to the wind on fundraising expenditures is not the answer; nor is refusing to spend money on fundraising at all. The solution is investing in the things that matter to donors, while eliminating or reducing expenses related to the things that don't. What matters to donors means what causes them to remain loyal and make increasingly generous gifts. While this appears on the surface to be straightforward, there is much about fundraising that has become ingrained practice on the assumption that donors approve without actually testing those assumptions first.

One of the most vivid examples of the discrepancy between what influences donors and what fundraisers believe influences donors emerged in my research that led to the publication of *Donor-Centered Fundraising*. Fundraisers' long-standing conviction that donors want to be publicly recognized for their philanthropy was called into question when four out of five donors we studied said that public recognition influenced neither gift value nor retention. Considering the time and budget resources that Development offices apply to formal donor recognition, this was a shocking revelation. At the same time, donors lamented the sluggish issuing and poor quality of thank-you letters, and emphasized how the rare examples of great ones influenced them to give again and give more. While Development Directors were assigning up to 30% of their stewardship budgets to public recognition, they were spending almost nothing on lowly thank-you letters, not realizing that it was the latter that truly shaped donors' perceptions.

Not-for-profits cannot actually bring down the cost of fundraising by refusing to spend. This will work temporarily, but it cripples Development operations in the long run while being a major contributor to premature staff turnover. However, if fundraising spending is concentrated on strategies and products that influence donor retention and gift value, organizations will automatically become more profitable. Holding onto donors longer means that expensive donor acquisition can be reduced; increasing average gift values higher and sooner means that fewer costly solicitations are required. Cost per dollar raised declines automatically when not-for-profits fundraise more strategically.

The metrics for measuring fundraising success sometimes override a qualitative approach that would serve a not-for-profit better in the long run.

When the recession hit, we invested in wealth screening to augment our prospect pool when so many of our loyal donors simply couldn't give. It will take awhile to see the return on this investment, but it feels good to have made the decision and to have more potential donors to visit.

As a donor, my wallet opens up for projects that excite me. I'm more inclined to be generous for specific, rather than general, asks. When it comes to regular unrestricted giving, I'm consistent but I don't break the bank.

Misunderstanding:
"We Need to Raise as Much Money as Possible Unrestricted"

Insisting on unrestricted giving limits fundraising profit more than anything else while simultaneously exposing not-for-profits as having no strategic direction.

Unrestricted (or undesignated) gifts are contributions made by donors with no commitment from the recipient organizations about how the money will be used. Skillfully crafted online and mailed appeals and telemarketing scripts often cite Program X or Initiative Y as examples of how the money could be applied, but not-for-profits that solicit this way are careful not to pin themselves down. In insisting on unrestricted gifts, they demand blind trust from their donors regarding how the funds will be used and the level of progress that will be achieved.

For donors, unrestricted asks are the weakest solicitations, producing the poorest response rates and sub-par gift values. Holding back information on what a not-for-profit intends to do with the money they raise makes donors question whether fundraising is even necessary.

To illustrate unrestricted giving from the donor's point of view, let me take you back to my earlier description of capital campaigns, the single most profitable examples of cash-based fundraising. Imagine that your university or college decides to erect a new science building on campus and announces a $1 billion campaign to pay for it. They proceed to structure the campaign according to sound strategy (high level cabinet, experienced staff, healthy budget, communications and marketing support, prospect research, tight timeline, strategic progression of asks from highest to lowest value, etc.) There is only one thing they decide to leave out – telling donors what the $1 billion campaign is for. Do you think they will ever reach their goal? Of course not.

But reaching ambitious goals without a defined case for support is routinely expected of fundraisers as they raise money day-to-day in what is commonly called the annual fund. Because they are under pressure to bring in unrestricted gifts, fundraisers are relegated to selling the brand over and over again. Unable to see where their money is going or even why the organization needs it, donors respond by giving at levels far below their ability or by withholding their support altogether.

Why do Boards and CEOs insist on unrestricted giving when it compromises fundraising success so severely? Of the following positions that decision-makers commonly take, none is justifiable from a fundraising perspective. In every case, the opposite approach is advocated by donors in our research studies and verified through controlled testing. Since I cannot imagine that anyone in a position of authority would want to intentionally inhibit fundraising, other factors must be at play. These erroneous beliefs need to be brought into the open and recognized for what they really are:

- *Restricted giving puts donors in control of the agenda*

  In a restricted giving approach to fundraising, donors are offered information about how their gifts will be used before they make the commitment to give. Restricted giving does not mean that donors are given free rein to choose from all possible program options or, worse, allowed to apply their donations to initiatives entirely outside the organization's funding priorities. It is always within the not-for-profit's unilateral control to select the program or service that is their priority for funding.

  Some Boards and CEOs have experienced the occasional donor of means who promises a generous gift on condition that his personal, off-strategy idea is funded. It is frustrating and uncomfortable when this happens and a single experience can color decision-makers' views. The antidote to a donor who wants to co-opt the agenda are leaders who remain true to the mission, who recognize and use their own power of persuasion, and who are prepared to walk away from the money if the donor cannot be won over to their case.

- *We cannot fund overheads if donors' gifts are restricted*

  What are overheads? Is there actually any such thing? If you look at the expense allocations in any not-for-profit's audited statement (or the statement of a for-profit company for that matter), they all read pretty much the same: salaries, benefits, office supplies, travel, etc. Think about transposing your own statement to a blank sheet of paper. Would anyone who looks at it have any idea what kind of business you are in?

  Expenses are itemized this way because that keeps accounting and auditing practices uniform. But for fundraising and planning purposes, expenditures need to be expressed in a way that demonstrates what programs and services actually cost. This is cost-centered budgeting and it works like this:

  > Direct expenses plus apportioned salaries, benefits and any other staff-related expenses are attributed to each line of service, creating an accurate picture, program-by-program, of what it costs to operate. Any expenses still unattributed are assessed against this question: "Could this program or that service operate without incurring this expense?" Most of the time, an expense once labeled "administrative overhead" will now be recognized as essential to delivering services and fulfill-

There was a time when I didn't think twice about making a donation to a cause I believed in. That has now changed. As I'm watching my money more closely, I want to know exactly where it is going so I feel confident my donation is being used wisely.

*The days of "ask and ye shall receive"
and "dialing for dollars" are over.
The time has come for a much more
personal approach to fundraising.
Donors need to understand what
they are contributing to, why, and
what will be accomplished.*

ing the charitable mandate. If occasionally an expense item is found to have no bearing on the delivery of programs or services, it can be eliminated from the budget.

On the issue of whether and how to attribute the cost of fundraising, this is the one expense category that should be singled out for donors. You are justified in thinking that the cost of raising money should also be attributed across programs and services because, without fundraised revenue, programs could not be offered or offered at the same level. But when donors are considering who they will support and the level of gift they will make, the cost of fundraising plays a role in their decision. They want to know that they are giving to an organization that is not overspending on fundraising.

It is also important to keep in mind that most not-for-profits do not rely on private sector fundraising for 100% of their budget needs. Think about all sources of revenue that support your institution or charity – student fees, product sales, membership fees, etc. This revenue is all unrestricted and often comprises the majority of an organization's income. Only donors – individuals, foundations and corporations giving philanthropically – give with the expectation that their contributions will fund a specific and pre-determined initiative.

Cost-centered budgeting offers an added bonus to decision-makers. CEOs and Boards need information expressed in this way in order to understand the true cost of their programs and services, especially for planning purposes.

• *Gifts must be unrestricted to allow for maximum flexibility in programs and services*

This argument exposes the likelihood that the not-for-profit is operating without a strategic plan that maps the growth and evolution of programs and services over several years.

Many documents are called strategic plans when they are not, or are relied upon as planning tools when they are actually under-developed for that purpose. For instance, a vision statement that articulates the mission of the organization in general terms is not a strategic plan; neither is a guide that is short-term in duration covering, say, the current fiscal year only. 88% of CEOs we surveyed said there was a strategic plan in place in their not-for-profits, but 41% of them admitted their plan set only a general direction and did not include measurable objectives to be realized over more than one year.

A real strategic plan is one that defines measurable objectives to be reached in each program or service every year for a period of three years. Developed within these guidelines, a strategic plan becomes fundraisers' marching orders, dictating why money is needed and how it will be applied if donors give. It forms the basis of all solicitations and donor communications and is the single most important asset in raising money. Its multi-year duration takes into account the reality that measurable progress takes time and that not all fundable programs can produce stunning results in twelve months.

When decision-makers say they need maximum flexibility, it invariably means there is no strategic plan in place or, if there is one, it is not being followed. Maximum flexibility is not what a not-for-profit should be striving for; their objective should be maximum results. A multi-year strategic plan is the preeminent tool for the Board and CEO, enabling these top decision-makers to gauge progress, assign budget funds appropriately and evaluate their own effectiveness.

Other arguments in favor of unrestricted giving can also be traced back to the absence of a workable strategic plan. They include "Gifts must be unrestricted in case a new opportunity comes along that requires immediate funding." Leaders should definitely think big, but new ideas need time to be developed, researched, budgeted, tested, evaluated and blended into the overall programs strategy. When a real strategy is not in place, it is easy for decision-makers to jump from one thing to the next, leaving fundraisers and donors unsure of what they are selling and funding.

Working without a strategic plan or not adhering to the one in place is often a sign of leadership who do not feel they are accountable. This does not suggest confidence; rather, sidestepping accountability is more often an indicator of lack of confidence. Confident leaders expect to have their performance evaluated against measurable goals. Those unsure of their own ability tend to fear these same measures.

In some cases, a strategic plan is used to exert power or control. Rather than making it available to all staff as the unifying and inspiring document that it should be, a not-for-profit's plan is seen only by the CEO or circulated among a privileged few at the top. This is also an indicator of lack of confidence or ability to lead. Without a clear picture of where the organization is going, staff cannot innovate, challenge old thinking or, heaven forbid, outshine the boss. All they can do is what they are told.

My giving feels most productive when I can see specific results coming from my contributions, hence my preference for restricted donations. I do give unrestricted sometimes, but only small amounts.

Fundraising is a process. It requires time and a real commitment on the part of the not-for-profit and the Board to cultivate prospects and donors. We need to develop relationships, not just conduct financial transactions.

- *Restricted giving grants too much power to fundraisers*

  When donors are asked for money, they want to know why it is needed. If management cannot answer the question, fundraisers are placed in an impossible situation. Under pressure to raise more money but lacking the essential information that makes raising more money possible, they find themselves having to articulate the case on their own. It is unfair to blame fundraisers for usurping authority when lack of planning by management is the real culprit. If leaders expect donors to fund their not-for-profits, they need to anticipate the obvious question and take responsibility for articulating their case in measurable terms.

Fundraisers know that they could raise much more money if all gifts, regardless of value, were assigned to specific end purposes. Yet they quietly soldier on, doing the best they can under this severe handicap. I am intrigued by the fact that they are not in a state of collective rebellion. Are they afraid to rock the boat? Is the chief fundraiser too low on the seniority ladder to be influential with the CEO or the Board? Do they not know how to argue in favor of restricted giving?

On this important issue, fundraisers have two allies – their CEO and controlled testing. Proving that restricted-gift fundraising raises more than an unrestricted approach is easy. All that is required is to solicit a test group of donors with a targeted, measurable appeal while everyone else gets the "give to the annual fund" theme.[9] Then, take comfort in this important finding from our research. Only 19% of CEOs we surveyed were open to universal restricted giving; but four out of five would reconsider their position if presented with compelling evidence that restricted giving raises more money.

Misunderstanding: "We Have to Have the Money Now"

On my first day on the job in my first Executive Director position, I was informed matter-of-factly by the accountant that we were close to maxing out the line of credit, that we would be unable to meet the payroll sixty days hence, that the preliminary projection on our biggest fundraising event was down 30% from last year (assuming it didn't rain), and that there were two lawsuits pending for nonpayment of goods from suppliers related to an event that took place eight years previously. So, I do understand the CEO's or the Board's position when they say urgently to their fundraiser, "We have to have the money now."

[9] How to design and execute a controlled test in fundraising is fully explained in *Donor-Centered Fundraising*, Chapter 7, "Test Everything".

But when decision-makers insist on having the money now, they are choosing to expose their not-for-profits to a precarious funding situation that never ends. They might squeak through this month or this quarter, temporarily saved by a quick injection of cash. But, unless they lessen their dependency on high risk/low profit short-term fundraising, they will be back in the red before they know it.

If this is familiar, you can stop the cycle. The first thing to consider is that you should be reaching for more dependable profit, not more money, so deciding to, for example, immediately double your direct mail appeals to donors will produce a short-term increase in revenue but you will pay for that decision later.

One of the more interesting forensic investigations my firm has done in the past decade was for a national healthcare institution. We were hired to find out why their huge direct mail program had experienced a 40% increase in revenue in one year over the previous twelve-month period, and then, just as suddenly, a 65% drop in the following year. It was easy to see why revenue had shot up – the number of solicitations had doubled over the previous twelve months; but we could not account for the even more dramatic drop that followed – until we talked to donors. It turned out that, as solicitations began to increase, loyal donors thought they had forgotten to make their usually timed gifts, and quickly gave again, many with notes of apology. But, over the next year as the appeals kept coming thick and fast, donors went back to their bank and credit card records to find they had been duped. Their solution: stop giving. It turned out that the new direct mail manager had been put under tremendous pressure to bring in more money immediately. He did the only thing that a manager of direct mail has available to him – ask more often – and then found himself with a much bigger and longer term problem.

Once donors stop giving, it is difficult to get them back and expensive to try; most will never return. But even that pales in comparison to the lost future value of donors who were once loyal and now no longer contribute. Some might have evolved to the top of the giving spectrum over time, becoming major donors or leaving bequests in their wills. That is the real profit and the secure funding that can turn an unstable organization into a progressive, solidly funded not-for-profit. And that is what this organization forfeited by insisting on having the money now.

When facing an immediate financial problem, having the foresight to opt for more profit over more immediate revenue requires the CEO and Board to develop a bridging strategy that keeps the organization solvent in the short term. While it is their job to figure out how to buy time, they have every right to expect their fundraiser to step up with an evidence-based solution that will raise more money and produce longer-term stability. That solution is donor-centered fundraising.

Never compromise for the "quick gift". Be strategic, thoughtful and sensitive. More often than not, a "no" today turns into a "yes" tomorrow.

Donor-Centered Fundraising

In between today's high-volume approach to fundraising and yesterday's low-volume one sits a third option that is more profitable than either. This third option is right for a giving environment that is very different from that of even ten years ago and definitely a world away from fundraising in the mid 1900s. It is easy to understand; it focuses on the three things that make fundraising profitable; and it comes from donors themselves.

Donor-Centered Fundraising is donors' answer to this question:

> *"Once you have made a first gift to any not-for-profit, what would cause you to remain indefinitely loyal to that organization while giving at an increasingly generous level over time?"*

I have asked this question of more than 60,000 donors over several national studies since 1998 and the answer has always been the same. What donors want is a "donor-centered" approach to fundraising, which they describe concisely as:

- receiving prompt and meaningful acknowledgement whenever they make a gift;

- having their gifts assigned to a specific end purpose such as a program, project or initiative that is narrower in scope than the mission of the entire organization;

- receiving a report, in measurable terms, on what was accomplished with the gift (likely along with other donors' contributions) before being asked for another contribution.

Donors feel nothing when they receive poorly timed, stiff and impersonal acknowledgements for the gifts they make; but their hearts soar and their wallets open upon reading prompt, thoughtful and original thank-you notes that express the sincere gratitude of the writer. Donors are frustrated by solicitations that ask forcefully for money while providing no specifics on why it is needed; but they respond without hesitation, making it possible for not-for-profits to reach astounding goals, to campaigns that have clear and measurable objectives. Most of all, donors lament that reporting after the fact, if it happens at all, rarely includes accountability for how their contributions were spent and what was achieved; but, when this information is provided to donors, they are ready to give again almost immediately.

What a Donor-Centered Not-for-Profit Looks Like

Keeping in mind that profit is the objective, that profit is made by holding onto donors longer and securing more generous gifts sooner, and that donors themselves have defined donor-centered fundraising as the strategy that accomplishes this, this is what a donor-centered fundraising operation looks like:

Donor Acquisition

A mechanical approach to donor acquisition in which charities try to amass as many donors as possible gives way to a selective approach deployed to attract a limited number of new donors who are the best match for the organization. Increasing the volume of donors is no longer the focal point as not-for-profits realize that this is not what creates healthier profit. Because the focus has shifted to improving donor retention, donor acquisition can now be used strategically. Reallocating some of the donor acquisition budget into donor retention improves gross revenue without increasing fundraising cost, something that is attractive to both donors and not-for-profit leaders. However, when donor acquisition is called for, it is designed with far more care and precision and is fully resourced in order to achieve the best possible result.

Investment/Return

Donor-centered fundraisers are careful to use direct marketing for the purpose for which it was designed – to acquire new donors. They know they cannot rely on it to generate profit indefinitely and so begin taking a proactive approach through donor relations as soon as new donors come on board. Fundraisers in a donor-centered operation also recognize that most donors could be persuaded to give more if they were given what they need. They invest early in the three things that donors say influence loyalty and generosity in order to generate higher profit later. Donors reward that kind of respectful and proactive approach to fundraising by responding sooner with more generous gifts and by staying loyal longer.

Donors Are Accountable Too

When donors receive a donor-centered approach and still some stop giving anyway, fundraisers know they can let those donors go. Fully confident that they have offered everything necessary to sustain donor loyalty, fundraisers make the wise decision to shift precious resources to the donors who are still responding rather than waste money soliciting non-responsive supporters for years. Donor-centered fundraisers let go gracefully in the knowledge that they are holding onto far more donors than before, while understanding that theirs cannot be the charity of choice for everyone.

Real recognition is not something you do at certain intervals in your relationship with donors, nor is it a momentary thing. It is pervasive. Recognition is between the lines in the letters you write, in the tone of your voice, in the welcoming handshakes of your Board members. Recognition is inseparable from the people who give it.

On one level, Donor-Centered Fundraising is simply the obvious and the right thing to do; on another level, it is the guarantee of a future with your donors and the vital ingredient to raising much more money.

I made a token gift in memoriam to a not-for-profit I'd never supported before. I would have supported them again if I had been treated better. I never got a thank you note but was relentlessly solicited. If I had been thanked properly (or at all), I would have continued to give, and made increasingly larger contributions.

Moving Up

Most donors say they could be even more generous than they are now, so it is not surprising that an approach that is advocated by the people who give has the power to unleash their philanthropy at a whole new level. Fundraisers who deploy a donor-centered approach ready their donors more quickly for major and planned gifts and are prepared to respond when donors signal their interest early. Small, slow increases in gift value are understood to be a product of how typical fundraising operates rather than a reflection of donors' ability to give. So, in a donor-centered environment, fundraisers steward donors from an entry-level gift to a major gift as early as the second ask. This early attention is worth the effort because every donor who leaps from introductory-level giving to major gifts makes a substantial impact on the bottom line.

Respecting Time

Donor-centered fundraisers understand that the relationship between not-for-profit and donor is a partnership, not a dictatorship. While charities' need for money may be urgent, donors require time to consider requests and time to fulfill obligations to other organizations before prioritizing someone new. Donor-centered fundraisers do not settle for the small gift that can be won immediately because they know they will be giving up the larger gift that requires contemplation and stewardship.

It's Not Just the Thought that Counts

I've often asked a room full of fundraisers, "How do you build a relationship with a donor?" After some understandable hesitation due to the scope of the question, I have then suggested they tell me what they might do with or for a donor that did not involve asking for a gift. Out pours a long list of both typical and not-so-typical ideas, from publishing donors' names in the annual report, to holding a donor recognition event, to sending birthday and holiday cards. I usually have to cut this discussion off at some point because the list becomes so long. I've never heard a fundraiser suggest an idea that donors would label inappropriate or offensive. Fundraisers are both sensitive and conservative and would be mortified if they did something that caused donors to be angry or embarrassed. Then I would ask a second question: "It is unlikely that you will have either the time or the resources to do everything, so which ones are the most important?" Because they are all gestures of appreciation in one form or another, opinions differ about what should stay and what should go.

On the many occasions when I have asked a similar question of donors, like "What would you consider to be a valuable or meaningful way for a not-for-profit you admire to build a relationship with you?", their response often begins with, "I know that fundraisers' hearts are in the right place and that they mean well, but…." And then they mention the token gift that they would have rather not received or the named recognition that they didn't really want.

In donor-centered fundraising, just because something might be termed a thoughtful gesture, that doesn't mean it should occupy a spot on fundraisers' to-do list. With tight budgets and limited time, fundraisers need to spend their resources on strategies that produce results. The research behind donor-centered fundraising was conducted for the very purpose of discovering what, among all the possible things that fundraisers could do, truly influences donors. It turns out that once they have been thanked in an original and personal way and, later, provided with a report in measurable terms on what has been accomplished with their previous gift, donors consider fundraisers to have fulfilled their end of the bargain. A relationship now exists because each partner has met the other's expectations.

Giving donors other stuff in addition to measurable results is considered thoughtful but unnecessary; but attempting to satisfy donors with something other than measurable results is counter-productive. It serves only to focus their attention on the cost of whatever was provided and the time that was diverted from more important activities. It causes donors to wonder about the cost of fundraising and whether a healthy percentage of their contribution will be allocated to the charitable work they thought they were supporting. And, it makes them wonder whether fundraisers have their priorities straight.

Adapting to a Changing World

A donor-centered Development operation adjusts how it raises money to reflect donors' changing tastes and behavior. Donor-centered fundraisers are objective about the fundraising programs they manage or work in, knowing that evolving preferences can make certain programs more or less popular over time. They don't take it personally if theirs is a fundraising program that is falling out of favor with donors. They keep their eye on the real prize, which is the rising average gift value among all donors across all giving strategies, along with improvement in average tenure. At the same time, they respect emerging trends, testing donors' receptiveness to new communications strategies and solicitation techniques. They know that their donors live in the real world, that the real world is changing all the time and that fundraising must adapt along with it or risk being left behind.

The Ten Most Important Tenets of Donor-Centered Fundraising

1. Higher profit is the objective of all fundraising, and that can only be achieved by holding onto existing donors and inspiring them to make increasingly

Meaningful information on their gifts at work is the key to donors' repeat and increased giving. Communication is the process by which information is delivered. Fundraising under-performance, therefore, is actually a failure to communicate.

If we wait for donors to make major gifts before we make a special effort to acknowledge their support, most of them will never get there. It's direct contact and its inherent gesture of respect that reinforces donors' giving and influences them to give again. In essence, the "thank you" is the ask. It's as simple as that.

generous gifts. Attempting to increase profit substantially by increasing the volume of donors not only does not work, it actually reduces profit as a disproportionate amount of the fundraising budget must be diverted into managing the volume instead of making more money.

2. Selling a not-for-profit's "brand" or mission only works once – when donors are first acquired. Thereafter, only measurable results on what happened with their last gifts will compel donors to continue to give indefinitely and at increasingly generous levels.

3. In a donor-centered fundraising operation, all donors, regardless of current or accumulative gift value, are thanked promptly and personally whenever they make a gift.

4. All donors, regardless of the value of their most recent gift, are provided with measurable results achieved with their last donation before being asked to give again. Information on how gifts are being used is never withheld from donors who give below a certain threshold.

5. Donor-centered fundraisers assign every gift, regardless of its value, to a program or project narrower in scope than the charity's mission as a whole. They never reserve designated or restricted giving for donors who make the largest gifts but recognize that all donors have a right to know what they are funding.

6. Donor-centered fundraisers never over-solicit. They respect their donors' definition of over-solicitation which is "being asked to give again before learning what was accomplished with the last gift".

7. Donor-centered fundraisers do not acquire more donors at any one time than can be properly served with personal acknowledgement and well-timed, meaningful communication. Budget resources available for stewardship dictate the maximum number of donors that a Development Office can support.

8. The majority of donors, at the time they are acquired, are actually capable of giving much more generously than their initial gift suggests. Donor-centered fundraisers showcase high quality gift acknowledgement and stewardship to these donors right from the start in order to inspire them to give much more generously as early as the second ask.

9. Public recognition is less effective at influencing loyalty and generosity than is meaningful information on what donors' gifts are accomplishing. Donor-centered Development Departments understand this and, therefore, assign more financial and human resources to gathering and disseminating information to donors than to recognizing them publicly. Donors consider

private acknowledgement in the form of thank-you letters, personal phone calls or private meetings to be superior forms of recognition and more powerful in influencing their future giving.

10. Leadership volunteers (Board members) and other honored personnel such as Deans, Artistic Directors and CEOs, have innate fundraising power due to the positions they hold and the stature they have gained in the community. In most fundraising situations they are more influential in securing generous gifts and in influencing donor loyalty than are other not-for-profit personnel, including professional fundraisers. In a donor-centered Development operation, these highly influential leaders are actively engaged in fundraising.

Fundraising in the 21st Century: Leaders Required

Adopting a donor-centered way of doing business takes the heat off fundraisers for the things they cannot control, but replaces that unfair pressure with an expectation of ambitious revenue growth through an approach that is endorsed by donors. There is much more money out there and donors want to give it; but fundraisers and not-for-profit leaders need to cast aside stereotypical thinking and negative fundraising practices in order to claim their share of the philanthropic pie.

The fundraising myths and misunderstandings described in this chapter are the key barriers to change, but another is simply the idea of change itself. An entire industry of change management specialists exists to help private sector companies overcome their inertia so that they can grasp profitable opportunities that are right in front of them. It is no different in the not-for-profit sector, except that neither the ready resources nor the culture exists inside charitable organizations to make it easy for them to reach out for this assistance. There is also a lot of pressure exerted by some vested interest insiders and external suppliers to keep fundraising working exactly as it does now, even though an alternative approach would raise much more money.

While variety is fine, there is still a right way and a wrong way to do things in Development. There is a body of knowledge out there; there should be no excuse today for not-for-profits that keep reinventing the wheel.

Connected by a common understanding of what makes money and what holds fundraising back, Boards, CEOs and Professional Fundraisers will discover that problems that used to be pervasive can be solved for good, and that issues that seem so complicated now have clear and straightforward solutions. When fundraising is shaped to deliver what donors need instead of what decision-makers think they need, more profit is the unavoidable result.

PART II
Building Your Best Fundraising Team

Chapter 5:
Planning to Hire

Retired from hockey since 1999, Wayne Gretzky, Canadian sports icon, is still the National Hockey League's all-time scoring leader. When asked how it was that he always seemed to be in just the right spot on the ice to score a goal, he explained that he skates to where the puck is going to be, not to where it is.

Hire for the Future

When hiring for any position, these are the two questions you are trying to answer:

- Can the candidate do the job in question?

- Can the candidate be instrumental in moving the entire Development operation to where it is going to be, or will he likely work within the boundaries of where fundraising already is?

Focusing solely or largely on the position you are trying to fill when hiring narrows the discussion, limiting the candidate's contributions during interviews and depriving you, the employer, of a more sophisticated means of assessing her suitability for the job and for your organization.

That makes the latter question the more important consideration when hiring, regardless of the seniority of the position being filled. It deserves the majority of your time and attention because gaining insight into the creativity, flexibility, capability and simply more senior potential of a candidate helps answer the other question about his likelihood of staying for an acceptable period of time. In Gretzky fashion, if you hire for where you want your employee to be in five years, and not just for the immediate task, you score goals (or reach the goal, to be more accurate). After two or three years as a member of your team, someone hired in a non-management capacity might be managing people on a project or permanent basis; a writer might be an editor; a major gifts officer might be heading the department. Look for those skills and hire with your future in mind.

To Hire for the Future, You Have to Know Where You Are Going

Achieving long-term Development objectives requires having a multi-year fundraising strategy against which candidates can be assessed. If this makes you shudder at the prospect of spending weeks or months developing a sophisticated plan before you can hire, you can rest easy. Here is where the donor-centered alternative described in the previous chapter offers a pragmatic multi-year picture that is easy to construct and which can be used as a vetting tool with candidates for any position.

Table 11 depicts a typical approach to fundraising planning by forecasting revenue in the fundraising programs that the not-for-profit deploys. This is revealing on several fronts:

- each fundraising program is expected to make more money each year.

- each fundraising program is expected to make money independent of each other program.

- the plan is focused on revenue alone rather than on revenue and donors.

- the plan fails to take giving trends and changes in donor behavior into account.

Table 11:

A Typical Plan for Revenue Over Five Campaigns Expressed by Fundraising Program

Fundraising Program	Campaign				
	1	2	3	4	5
Catalogue sales	70,000	78,000	85,000	100,000	125,000
Direct mail	60,000	75,000	80,000	90,000	100,000
Online giving	45,000	65,000	90,000	125,000	150,000
Walk-a-thon	30,000	35,000	40,000	45,000	50,000
Major gifts	250,000	300,000	350,000	400,000	500,000
Planned gifts	150,000	175,000	200,000	300,000	400,000
Total	605,000	728,000	845,000	1,060,000	1,325,000

Expressing fundraising planning in this manner creates a counter-productive mindset among fundraising staff. For a Development operation to make as much money as possible, it needs to transition donors through entry-level giving programs into major gifts. Movement is the objective, not growing revenue in programs that do not have the ability to maximize donors' philanthropy.

Illustrating a fundraising plan differently will set the stage for raising more money. Table 12 is a forecast from acquisition through five renewal campaigns where donors are initially acquired through a direct marketing approach. Over five campaigns some donors move up to more generous giving and become classified as major gift donors. Others remain giving at a level typical of direct marketing programs, although the average value of their gifts triples between acquisition and the fifth campaign. Equally important, donor retention is featured in this forecast. The number of donors remaining active from one campaign to the next reflects industry standards for retention/attrition in mass marketing programs.

Table 12: A Typical Fundraising Plan Expressed in Terms of Donor Acquisition, Retention and Gift Value Growth

Campaign	Volume of Donors/Net Retention	Average Gift Value in Direct Marketing	Revenue from Direct Marketing	%/# Donors Transitioning into Major Gifts	Average Major Gift Value	Revenue from Major Gift Donors
Acquisition	2000 / n/a	$50	$100,000	0%/0	n/a	$0
Renewal 1	700 / 35%	$65	45,240	0.5% / 4	$1,000	4,000
Renewal 2	400 / 20%	$85	33,660	1.0% / 4	$1,250	5,000
Renewal 3	300 / 15%	$100	29,400	2.0% / 6	$1,500	9,000
Renewal 4	200 / 10%	$125	24,125	3.5% / 7	$1,750	12,250
Renewal 5	180 / 9%	$150	25,800	4.5% / 8	$2,000	16,000
Total by program			258,225			46,250
Total revenue	$304,475					

Expressing fundraising objectives by donors rather than by fundraising programs demonstrates where opportunities lie should budget and talent be redistributed. For example, the movement of only 29 donors into major gifts yields revenue equaling 18% of all funds raised over six direct marketing campaigns (including acquisition). This kind of forecasting makes it easy for the Development Director to know how much more money could be raised by increasing staff in major gifts, for example, or by enhancing donor communication so that more donors are drawn upwards from the direct marketing operation.

The Donor-Centered Alternative

Table 13 is also focused on acquisition, retention, gift value and donor movement, but with a difference. This table represents the Donor-Centered Fundraising Plan where changes in donor behavior and preferences have been taken into account. Fierce competition for new donors along with donors' own inclination to support fewer causes means that acquisition numbers are declining in the United States and Canada. And, while a new not-for-profit with a compelling mandate may acquire donors at a better rate initially, sooner or later it joins the ranks of 1.4 million other not-for-profits competing for donors and funds. At that point, this organization's planning needs to reflect the realities of fundraising in the twenty-first century. Fewer donors may be available to them now but there is significant untapped opportunity when it comes to donor retention and improving gift value.

Table 13: A Donor-Centered Fundraising (DCF) Alternative to Typical Fundraising Plans

Campaign	Volume of Donors		Net Retention		Average Gift Value		%/Volume of Donors to Major Gifts Officers		Total Revenue in Direct Marketing		Revenue from Major Gift Donors	
	Typical	DCF	Typical	DCF	Typical	DCF	Typical	DCF	Typical	DCF	Typical	DCF
Acquisition	2000	1000	n/a	n/a	$50	$50	0% / 0	1.0% / 10	100,000	$50,000	n/a	10,000
1st year	700	450	35%	45%	$65	$80	0.5% / 4	3.0% / 14	45,240	34,880	4,000	17,500
2nd year	400	350	20%	35%	$85	$110	1.0% / 4	4.5% / 16	33,660	36,740	5,000	24,000
3rd year	300	300	15%	30%	$100	$150	2.0% / 6	6.0% / 18	29,400	42,300	9,000	31,500
4th year	200	250	10%	25%	$125	$200	3.5% / 7	8.0% / 20	24,125	46,000	12,250	40,000
5th year	180	200	9%	20%	$150	$260	4.5% / 8	10.0% / 20	25,800	46,800	16,000	45,000
Total							29 MG Donors	95 MG Donors	258,225	256,720	46,250	168,000
Total Revenue – Typical Fundraising Plan with 2000 Donors									$304,475			
Total Revenue – Donor-Centered Fundraising Plan with 1000 Donors									$424,720 (+ 39.5%)			

Table 13 begins with 1000, rather than 2000, donors who are acquired through a more selective process that targets best prospects. New donors give initially at the same $50 level, but their average gift value rises sooner and higher because they are giving in a donor-centered environment. Encouraged and rewarded by their Director of Development for donor movement, direct marketing staff put their creative energy into transitioning donors into the hands of relationship officers where more money per donor can be raised. For their part, stewardship managers and relationship officers collaborate with direct marketers to communicate effectively with donors as soon as they are acquired. They know that improved donor retention will mean a larger pool of better cultivated prospects for major gifts officers. The last two columns in Table 13 illustrate the most important achievement of a donor-centered approach. More donors become major gift donors and their contributions are more generous, on average, than those of donors in a more typical fundraising approach.

In the donor-centered model, there is no longer an expectation that heavy volume will drive fundraising success. Rather, the Donor-Centered Fundraising Plan relies on brilliant and compelling cases for support and excellent donor-centered stewardship to inspire more donors to stay loyal, give more generously and, equally important, evolve into the hands of the major gifts officers sooner. With only half the number of donors acquired initially, the donor-centered strategy in Table 13 makes almost 40% more money in the same period as the more traditional approach.

Revenue Trumping Cost

Table 13 illustrates how a Donor-Centered Fundraising Plan raises more money (i.e., improves gross revenue). But this superior approach also reduces fundraising cost by shifting emphasis from high-cost/low-revenue to low-cost/high-revenue strategies.

Between the two options available for improving cost per dollar raised, cutting cost is an inferior option to increasing revenue. The former stifles innovation and compromises stewardship which is essential for creating upward movement among donors. The latter invests strategically in order to influence donors to give more generously. In any not-for-profit in which cost of fundraising is prohibitively high, a donor-centered approach will gradually eliminate this problem through improved donor retention and higher average gift values. Cost-cutting is acceptable in a donor-centered Development budget, but it happens in areas that tend to escape the axe in typical fundraising. A donor-centered plan moderates the cost of acquisition and related data input and administrative expense by reducing the volume of prospects and dealing with fewer donors overall. It also looks critically at solicitation volume, often reducing the number of appeals per year in order to prevent excessive donor attrition due to over-solicitation.

A shift in thinking concerning cost is signaled on several fronts when a donor-centered approach to fundraising planning is adopted. The message communicated to staff and especially to the CEO and Board of Directors is that cost per dollar raised is significantly reduced when the upward movement of more donors is achieved. In a fundraising operation that has been relying on volume to make money, this is the only way that the cost of fundraising can be brought in line with donors' and leaders' expectations. Refusing to hire more staff, or withholding information from donors post-gift in order to limit cost, serves only to increase donor attrition and stifle growth in average gift values. But increasing average gift value among more retained donors reduces cost automatically.

Collaboration, Not Competition

Though fundraisers want their supporters to give more generously, typical Development Departments are structured to hold donors in place, not to raise their sights and inspire higher-level giving. This is a problem which exposes how pervasive the lack of understanding is about what inspires donors to give more generously and how profit can be maximized. Donor-centered planning reminds everyone of the real objective, and rewards staff for innovations that speed up donors' transition to major and planned gifts.

My biggest frustration revolves not around raising money but attributing it. There is tension among staff in one program and the next over who gets credit for gifts.

In a donor-centered environment, fundraisers must cooperate with each other in order to be successful. Much to the chagrin of people who give, fundraising is often structured on a competitive model instead of one that paves a smooth road to the major/planned gifts officer. The central advancement office competes with its school- or faculty-based fundraising operations; national headquarters competes with its local affiliates; and, even in a single Development office, one program competes with the next for donors and money. This is the unfortunate hallmark of fundraising today. While employers may think that furthering a sense of competition among their fundraisers motivates everyone to raise more money, it actually impedes fundraising growth. Coming at them from all sides serves only to make donors feel that the not-for-profit they are supporting is disorganized, that it over-solicits and that it spends too much money on fundraising infrastructure. This, of course, affects their willingness to keep giving.

As the primary directive for all members of the Development team (not just management), the Donor-Centered Fundraising Plan clearly articulates the ultimate goal as well as where and by when significant change and improvement are expected. By focusing on donors and their sustained loyalty rather than solely on fundraising programs, the Donor-Centered Plan re-orients staff to what really matters. With retention and upward movement of donors the goal, staff no longer need to hoard donors in entry-level programs just to keep those programs looking healthy. Rather, they are rewarded for the opposite behavior because that is what is more lucrative.

Donor-centered planning resolves a major revenue-limiting problem – the siloed configuration of Development Departments. Looking at planning from the perspective of donor movement, managers of direct marketing and other entry-level programs can see the inherent limitations in the programs they run, as well as their advantages. Encouraged and rewarded by their Director of Development for retaining donors and moving them higher, they put their creative energy into transitioning donors into the hands of relationship officers where more money per donor can be raised. In a donor-centered Development operation, everyone collaborates and, as a result, everyone wins.

Donor-Centered Planning and Its Impact on Staff Retention

Reliable fundraising planning starts with number of donors, percentage retained and moved up, and average gift value, and ends with revenue. So, not-for-profits that begin their fundraising planning process by saying, "We expect our Development Department to raise $X" and plug that figure into the budget, are working backwards and setting themselves up for premature staff turnover. Just like salespeople in the for-profit sector, not-for-profit sector fundraisers are only satisfied when they make the sale (i.e., close the gift) and reach the goal. If they fall short they will be disappointed with their own performance, but human nature means they will also be looking externally to deflect some of the responsibility. Failing to reach a strategically researched and achievable goal is cause for employers to question staff capability and the quality of supervision. Failing to reach an arbitrary goal is reason for a fundraiser to look for another job.

Planning Accomplishes Half the Job of Hiring

The simplicity and brevity of Table 13 belies the wealth of information it contains about fundraising. It also reveals much about the people who manage Development and the direction in which they are taking their organization. Your own version of this chart will speak volumes to your current staff as well as to job applicants (or at least to the ones you would want to hire). Here are the key messages that this concise table transmits to anyone perceptive enough to read between the lines:

- this not-for-profit's fundraising operation is focused on increasing profit in the Development operation as a whole, not necessarily in every fundraising program;

- they know that it is donor retention, not exponential growth in the number of donors that creates more profit;

- they have built their plan in the knowledge that most of the profit in fundraising is raised in major and planned gifts operations. They understand that the job of other fundraising programs is to hold onto as many donors as possible and move them as soon as possible into the hands of the gifts officers;

- they have taken donor trends and industry research into account in their planning process. The five-campaign forecast assumes that donor acquisition at historical levels will likely be unachievable in the future;

- they have analyzed their own donor retention/attrition statistics and changes in gift value and they have used real data to forecast future revenue goals;

- their objectives are ambitious, yet achievable. There are no unrealistic figures plugged into the plan;

- management staff at this not-for-profit are looking long term for the level of achievement they are predicting. They know that the ambitious growth forecast in the Plan cannot be realized in one year. (This also says to candidates that the organization is looking for fundraisers who can think in terms of what can be accomplished over a strategic length of time, not in one year which is the norm);

Lack of success is not due to a shortage of plans; it's due to plans being disassociated from the people who have to carry them out. If your staff aren't developing the plan with you, you'll never get the best out of your team.

- in this organization, all fundraising programs and the staff who manage and work in them are connected and working collaboratively, not competitively;

- fundraising data and planning information is not developed and held in confidence by management. On the contrary, it is shared among all staff in order to encourage creative thinking and inspire everyone to work together to reach ambitious goals.

Your Donor-Centered Plan clearly expresses the goals you intend to meet, and by when and how you will achieve them. It also tells you what skills you should be looking for in candidates and even whether you need to hire at all. With this plan at the ready you are way ahead because the hardest part of hiring has already been done. All that remains is to bring your best game to the art of finding the right person.

Chapter 6:

How to Attract Top Fundraising Talent

Survey Question: What is the most nagging issue you have encountered in your career up to this point?

Respondent: It is staffing. It is easy to find people who have a passion for our mission but very difficult to find people with both passion and fundraising experience. When we do, they are seldom willing to work for the salary we can offer.

Then there's the workload. The pace is frantic here and even the most seasoned fundraisers say they were unprepared for that when they joined our team.

I just filled one fundraising position last week that has been vacant for some time. Yesterday I learned that my other direct report is leaving. It's enormously frustrating.

The reasons that fundraisers leave their jobs prematurely are varied and numerous, but some find their origins in the hiring process. At the very moment when employer and candidate are showcasing the best of themselves to each other and when the stakes are so high for both, it is unsettling to think that things may already be starting to go wrong.

For employers, it takes precious time and costs money to hire; for employees, changing jobs is one of the ten most stressful life experiences a person can have. So, everyone's primary objective should be to commit fully to the hiring or job-seeking process in order to maximize productivity and satisfaction and minimize the possibility of premature resignation or dismissal.

Besides bolstering your chances for longer tenure, hiring well has delicious secondary benefits that affect your entire Development operation. A good hire is a candidate for promotion to increasingly more responsible positions. Equally important, a good hire sets a new standard of performance for all future employees who take on that position and for the rest of the fundraising team.

Of course, hiring well in order to raise more money applies just as much to selecting the CEO and electing members of the Board as it does to hiring Development staff. The skills required may be different, but the

I'm feeling that trends in job mobility make it inevitable that people will move on. But I find that tenure can be extended for awhile by offering fresh challenges and growth opportunities periodically.

What CEOs say makes it hard to hire good fundraisers:

59%   Salary not competitive
15%   Weak leadership
9%   Staff too small for volume of work
6%   Poor reputation of organization

impact of poor hires at the top is catastrophic while great hires propel fundraising to an extraordinary new level. Chapter 9 is devoted to hiring strategically at the top in order to improve management and decision-making on all fronts, including fundraising.

Do You Really Need to Hire?

Your Donor-Centered Plan based on numbers of donors and their evolution into higher giving offers the opportunity to think differently about the staffing complement you need. When the focus is on fundraising programs and a vacancy arises within one of those programs, the natural reaction is to fill it. But now you might ask yourself, "Do we really need to rehire this particular position or are time and talent required elsewhere along the donor spectrum?" It may be that you can shift human resources from one area of fundraising to another, though it is good to be realistic about whether the talent required for direct marketing is compatible with the requirements of major/planned gifts officers. It is also possible that you do not need to hire at all at this time. A shift in emphasis away from heavy donor acquisition to donor retention, for example, could mean that you already have the right staff complement and skills for your needs.

However, not needing to hire any more staff is definitely not the same as not being permitted to. The common cry, "We can't hire any more staff", is the same as saying, "We don't want any more money." When each staff member is familiar with the whole plan and is both capable of and motivated to play his role in reaching the goal, the more staff you have, the more money you will make. Having a skeleton fundraising staff is nothing to be proud of. It means you are missing big opportunities for revenue growth.

Positive versus Negative Reasons for Hiring

There are two great reasons to hire – to expand the size of your Development operation in order to capitalize on opportunity or to replace someone who has been promoted internally. In both situations, your objective should be to hire the least senior position, providing more employees than just the one who is targeted for promotion with the opportunity to take on new responsibilities.

The unfortunate reason for hiring is to replace someone who is leaving your organization prematurely. Hiring well will likely not eliminate this problem entirely but it will definitely reduce the instances of short job stays. In the long run, hiring well will save you time and money while lessening the risk inherent in introducing a new member to the team.

How to Find Great Fundraising Staff

If you have ever been responsible for hiring or supervising staff, you will understand the sinking feeling upon learning that a productive employee is leaving. It is usually too late to turn things around at this point, and this only adds to the frustration. Head down, teeth gritted, you march along that well trodden path again, setting aside your own work and stealing from the time you should be giving to other staff, with the added worry that the next hiring effort may not achieve a better result.

All hiring carries an element of risk. You hope that the new fundraiser will be a good fit, full of innovation and an extraordinarily hard worker. You hope she will breathe new energy into the entire Development team, floating all ships higher as the saying goes. But it doesn't always work out that way. Sometimes things go terribly wrong. Sometimes the new hire doesn't pass her probation; sometimes he turns out to be great at selling himself but not so good at selling your cause to donors. Sometimes, you have to start all over again.

Your Best Hire Already Works for You

When faced with the need to hire, promoting from within is by far the best option. It is not just a little more preferable than hiring from the outside; it is substantially superior in several important ways, all of which minimize risk while saving money. I am not referring to lateral moves here, but to promotions which offer staff more senior roles and greater responsibility.

There are practical benefits to promoting from within, then replacing the less senior position vacated due to the promotion:

- the more senior the job, the harder it is to find a qualified candidate who is also a great fit;
- it often takes longer to fill a more senior position than a junior one;
- the higher you go on the seniority ladder, the greater the possibility that your preferred candidate will be considering several job offers simultaneously. Consequently, you might lose out to the competition at the last minute.

It is more costly and riskier to hire senior employees through an external search than it is to promote internally. But, reducing cost and risk is just the beginning. Promoting from within means no gap of time during which the more senior position goes unfilled. An internally promoted candidate needs no orientation to the organization, and may need very little orientation to the job itself, especially if she moves up through succession planning, (See Chapter 13). Promoting internally

An internal candidate's knowledge of the organization, its politics and people translate into getting up to speed immediately. There is a lot of credibility in hiring internally and it sends a great message to the rest of the Department.

31% of respondents were promoted internally into the position they now hold

Do CEOs favor internal promotion over hiring externally?

52% Both viewed as equally important

33% Preference for internal promotion

7% Preference for internal promotion, with external hiring for augmenting staff complement

through succession planning, in particular, eliminates second-guessing among other staff and ensures a smooth transition from one supervisor or manager to the next. This eases stress and the temptation for other staff to look elsewhere in order to avoid the unknown.

Perhaps most important, when an employee is promoted internally it sends a message to the entire department or organization that management believes in its people and rewards them for their effort and their loyalty. 37% of professional fundraisers said they left their last place of employment because they were unable to secure a more senior position where they were.

Three predominant reasons cause employers to look elsewhere when hiring instead of committing to a promote-from-within policy:

1. **Absence of qualified candidates on staff.** Of course, the requisite qualifications and experience are critical when filling any position; but conducting an external search because there are no qualified candidates on staff speaks to failure of management, not inadequacy among staff. Commitment to internal promotions places the onus on managers to prepare employees for more senior roles, but also to hire staff in the first place who demonstrate the ability to produce beyond their initial job description.

2. **House-cleaning.** Employers hire externally instead of internally in an attempt to overcome a negative culture which has built up over time. As long as the root of the problem rests with the person or persons who have left, this can be productive, but house-cleaning is no guarantee that the problem will not re-emerge. The best antidote to a dysfunctional Development workplace is a Donor-Centered Fundraising Strategy – a plan for raising money that refocuses everyone's attention on reaching ambitious, yet achievable goals, coupled with management training. A Development operation in distress may very well need a superman from the outside to reverse a negative culture, but it should only need him once. After that, management training and results-based planning will make a promote-from-within policy both possible and preferable.

3. **The lure of the unknown.** "We believe in promoting from within but we just want to see who else is out there." This is a common sentiment among decision-makers but it is interpreted by employees as paying lip service to promoting internally. Only 7% of CEOs we surveyed were fully committed to internal promotions as an operating policy. 33% said they had a "decided preference" for promoting from within and 52% saw internal and external hiring as equally desirable. Perhaps Table 14 would change their minds.

Table 14: Cost and Risk Implications of Replacing a Successful Director of Development: Internal Promotion versus External Hire

Activity	Internal Promotion	External Search
Direct and indirect cost of hiring	$0	$30,000 to $75,000
Time position is vacant between old staff leaving and new replacement starting	0 days	Up to 90 days
Time required for orientation to the organization and the new job	0 days	Up to 90 days
Lower productivity during initial period on the job	Up to 60 days	Up to 180 days
Other staff leave due to uncertainty or to follow the departing Director	Likelihood minimized	The risk exists
New Director takes department in a different and, ultimately, less successful direction	Unlikely	Possible

The buy-in is already there with staff promoted internally. They still need lots of training and support as they move up, however.

My greatest achievement has been staying with the same not-for-profit for 11 years. I have grown from a part-time data entry clerk to the Director of Individual Giving responsible for $3 million in contributed revenue.

Managers who do not favor internal promotions over external hires deny themselves the big reward. They incur all the risk and expense of hiring, orienting and training staff, then opt for risk and expense all over again by re-hiring externally instead of cashing in on their initial investment by promoting internally.

It takes time to evolve to the point where you can promote from within unconditionally, but you can start moving in that direction now by taking these steps:

1. When filling positions at the bottom of the seniority ladder, do so with a "hire for the future" attitude, one that assesses candidates for both their ability to handle the immediate job and their potential to assume more senior responsibilities. Being over-qualified, for example, should not be the reason that eliminates an otherwise exciting candidate; it should be the deciding factor in choosing this candidate over someone else who fits neatly into the job today but whose ability to meet your future needs is unknown.

2. Adopt a policy of succession planning now – not just for the Vice President or Director of Development position but for any and all jobs that include responsibility for managing others.

3. Assess current staff on a continuing basis for their readiness to take on more senior roles.

4. Invest in the training necessary to ready staff for promotion.

5. Reorganize or redefine jobs in order to provide more and better opportunities for promotion.

Among **29%** of respondents whose full time job included responsibilities other than fundraising, these duties were referenced most often:

73% Marketing
69% Organization management
38% Volunteer training
32% Programs Delivery
27% Administration
22% Finance

Is Your Fundraising Department Structured to Facilitate Internal Promotions?

Both seasoned Development managers and the fundraising industry's youngest practitioners identified a structural weakness in certain Development Departments that limits potential for internal promotions. Many respondents described their staffing configuration as one of extremes, with a few highly experienced practitioners on the executive team but many fundraisers on the front lines reporting to that small management group. Both directors and non-management fundraisers said there were too few positions in between. This configuration denies young fundraisers, in particular, the opportunity to take on more senior responsibilities within a progressive, yet protected learning environment. Because it is not realistic to shoot for the executive office at their age, young fundraisers quickly deduce that they will have to leave if they want to build their careers.

At the same time, fundraisers in the most senior positions say they are overloaded. Among Directors and Managers planning to leave their current positions, 34% referenced responsibilities so comprehensive that it was impossible to fulfill job expectations. If managers need to be relieved of some of their duties and non-management personnel are eager to assume more, this sounds like an opportunity just waiting to happen. Here are two practical solutions:

1. Identify short-term projects that accomplish a fundraising objective while developing the staff member's skills in areas such as strategic planning, balancing multiple responsibilities, testing new concepts, creative problem-solving or managing staff.

2. Divide one job into two or three increasingly senior roles with titles that reflect their higher level responsibilities.

A truly productive organizational culture lies somewhere between the old approach with multiple layers of middle management and a flattened reporting grid that is more popular today. The former made businesses (and not-for-profits) too cost-heavy on the administrative side; the latter ignores the need for gaining incremental experience in managing people.

Expanding opportunities for career growth automatically increases the need for supervision. Management-level fundraisers who are already over-burdened with responsibilities may resist. But short-term investment in more or different supervision pays off in long-term profit. Besides keeping good staff longer, promoting internally, and proving commitment to internal promotions by doing it, draws top fundraisers to your organization, and deepens a sense of loyalty among all staff.

Internal Promotion Is a Delicate Dance

While promoting from within is the best hiring option, it is tricky to establish a culture that truly supports this policy. Supply/demand imbalance in fundraising is the reason.

Even when the Chief Development Officer or CEO endorses the policy, an opportunity for internal promotion can be quietly thwarted by an applicant's existing manager. The future boss's gain is the current one's loss as the cost and time involved in filling the vacancy is simply passed from one department to another. In an attempt to stave off what they see as internal staff poaching, managers have made it known that they do not want their staff to pursue internal job opportunities. Some fundraisers we surveyed said they were told they would be letting their boss and colleagues down if they applied for a job in another program or department. Others said the working relationship and atmosphere changed for the worse after their boss learned they had put their name forward. Still others, after failing to win the promotion, found out that their current boss had hinted broadly that they were not yet ready for more senior responsibilities.

Respondents who had had a poor experience in pursuing internal promotions emphasized the importance of confidentiality. There are many reasons why someone will withhold the fact that he is applying for a job in a different not-for-profit until he has a conditional offer of employment. Internal applicants are less in control of the flow of information and must rely on Human Resources and/or the potential new boss to be very discreet. At some point the new employer will turn to the applicant's current manager for the key reference, but up to that point, internal staff should be accorded the same discretion and confidentiality as any other external candidate.

Adjusting the Culture Regarding Internal Promotions

Managers can adopt a competitive attitude in which they try to dissuade their staff from pursuing internal promotions, or they can champion a deliberately collaborative approach. The latter involves supervising and mentoring staff in order to prepare them for jobs with increasing responsibility inside their own organizations. For this to work, top management must endorse the collective goal (financial and otherwise) over the secondary goals of any individual department or fundraising program. Additionally, there must be a benefit to managers who invest so much time and money in making their staff desirable prospects for higher-level positions.

20% of respondents who have been offered an internal promotion have turned it down.

Organizational and attitudinal problems contributing to why fundraisers left their last position:

34% Unrealistic timeframe for meeting fundraising goals
33% Lack of direction on how funds would be used
32% "We have to have the money now"
27% Insufficient fundraising budget
24% Additional responsibilities beyond fundraising
24% Resistance to innovation
14% Resistance to adopting better fundraising strategies

Why some respondents have turned down a promotion:

27% Desire to achieve a goal in current job
26% Family/personal reasons
18% More senior position seemed less interesting
16% Lateral rather than upward move
15% Prospective manager less capable than current boss

These are some ways in which managers can be credited for actively developing staff to take on more senior positions:

- reference managers' skill, effort and collaborative attitude in formal and informal performance reviews;

- thank managers publicly – in staff, committee and Board meetings – for contributing to staff retention by training and mentoring their staff well;

- allocate time and budget in their schedules to hire, train and supervise. Overloading good managers with these responsibilities on top of other job expectations extends their work day, leads to exhaustion and eventually drains the enthusiasm of even the most positive managers. Modifying other responsibilities keeps them sharp while acknowledging how much you value this work;

- offer a "train-the-trainer" status to managers who are especially capable in staff retention and mentorship. Invest in their capacity to teach other colleagues and/or have them design an internal management training program;

- pay managers better who retain staff longer and who do an excellent job of preparing their reports for internal promotions.

In the end, the best way to retain staff is to be the best manager in your not-for-profit. 27% of staff who have turned down at least one internal promotion said they were more committed to staying in their current position in order to achieve goals that they were working towards; 15% said they stayed where they were because the other manager was a less capable or less appealing boss.

The Best Time to Hire Is When You're Not Hiring

Fundraisers who have worked in the industry for a while will likely recall the direct mail industry term, "white mail". It refers to a gift that comes through the mail but cannot be traced back to a particular solicitation. The reply envelope has not been used; there is no pledge card accompanying the check that would otherwise identify a particular appeal; and the donation may have been received outside the active fundraising timeframe. While few in number, white-mail donors often distinguish themselves with higher-than-average gifts and longer loyalty. And, of course, they are acquired free of charge. White-mail donors are especially important because of the trouble they go to in order to give. They also signal a potential giving future that is well beyond the value of the initial unsolicited gift.

There is a parallel to white-mail donors when it comes to hiring. They are candidates who do not wait for a job to be posted before making their interest in your organization known. I have hired many staff who reached out to me before

I reached out to them, and I have never regretted it. Proactive and decisive, these candidates do their homework, zeroing in on your not-for-profit as a desirable employer because they feel the fit is right.

You can capitalize on this important resource. First, always make time to see candidates who are proactive in this way. "We'll keep your resume on file" is the same as saying "Thanks, but no thanks" to someone who has gone to the trouble of singling you out. Of course you are busy, but this is an opportunity that you should grab whether or not you have a position to fill right now. Connecting with someone who could be a great addition to your team helps you broaden your thinking about the skills and perspectives you need to boost fundraising performance. On the practical side, because fundraising is an industry experiencing a supply/demand imbalance, it is wise to welcome unsolicited inquiries.

Broadcasting your staffing needs only when you are actively seeking an employee is equivalent to speaking to donors only when you want their money. The second thing you can do to attract future fundraisers is to have a steady conversation going on with them about what it's like to work in your shop. You can build a low-cost bridge between your not-for-profit and professional fundraisers by using your website judiciously. Every time it leads to a good hire, you save all the time and cost of a formal search. A Career Landing Page (see later in this chapter) is an excellent first step.

Showcase Yourself

Great bosses attract great employees. Build your public profile by, for example, speaking at conferences, authoring a blog on leadership, doing media interviews. Have a video on your website in which you talk about what it is like to work in your not-for-profit. How you reference your organization and the people who work for you will say a great deal about you as a manager or leader and it will cause good candidates to seek you out. According to our research, "appealing qualities of the boss" is the second most influential reason why fundraisers choose one job over another.

Hold Exploratory Interviews with Unsolicited Candidates

When there is no specific job opening to focus your thinking, it is easy for meetings with unsolicited candidates to drift or to be too general to be useful. It may also be some time before you return to this person's file when a job does open up. So, it helps to develop a candidate profile to be sure you record information that will jog your memory later and which you can also use immediately as an initial vetting

People-related reasons why fundraisers stay loyal:

83% Inclusive environment that allows staff to participate in strategic decision-making
75% Positive relationship with co-workers
68% Positive relationship with boss
60% Positive attitude of management towards fundraising
22% Same cultural background as donors or co-workers

tool. Because the candidate has approached you, you can assume that he is coming to the meeting with specific and insightful questions. What he is looking for and the conversation that ensues should help you assess his suitability as much as he is assessing yours. There is only one opportunity for a first impression, so your comments on deportment and the initial conversation leading up to the purpose of the meeting are particularly important.

Table 15: Sample Candidate Profile for Interviews with Unsolicited Candidates

Category / Item	Information/Comments
Candidate name/contact info	Jean Tomlinson.
Interview date	Friday, March 12, 11:00 a.m.
Meeting with - Name/title - Department	Ben deSilva, Director of Development.
Attire/deportment	Professionally attired; slightly conservative; compatible with fundraising sensibilities.
In the first minute	Great smile; firm handshake. She noticed the kayak paddle standing in the corner; asked about the sport and my favorite routes.
Current/most recent position and employer	GH Financial; account exec serving customers with $1 million + portfolios
Seniority in current/recent position	8 years; no experience managing other staff.
Why candidate sought us out	Has participated in our ½ marathon for the last 3 years, raising over $10,000 in pledges. Sits on Employee Giving Committee at GH Financial where our sponsorship proposals have been considered. Seeking to transfer skills with high net worth customers into compatible role in NFP sector.
Questions from the candidate - has done homework on our NFP - originality or informed nature of questions	She asked whether we knew the philanthropic potential of our donors and whether that potential was being maximized currently – a good question from someone who wants to transition into major gifts fundraising. Was I open to non-traditional candidates for fundraising positions? Would she have to get specific fundraising industry training before I would consider her seriously? She did not ask about how our Board participates in fundraising – don't think she made the connection, given that she does not have professional experience inside a NFP.
How candidate responded to information shared about our organization - active listening - strategic context	6/7 for using what I told her as a jumping off point for another question. Active listener and learner. She asked for my assessment of how developed our Planned Giving Program is relative to current potential and where I expected the value of this fundraising program to be five years from now. I strongly suggested she acquire formal training in planned giving to round out her natural abilities from working in a compatible field
Post-meeting follow up by candidate - sent "thanks for time" email or letter - had other questions evidently sparked by the conversation	Yes – there was a thanks email in my inbox before 5 the same day. No additional questions.

Category / Item	Information/Comments

Active follow up by candidate
  - date
  - date
  - date
	[Interview on March 12, 2011]
	- March 16/11: received hand-written thank-you note.
	- April 30/11: follow-up email expressing continued interest (see attached).
	- June 10/11: email noting our job posting for Dir of Major Gifts, expressing continuing interest should this new hire result in department expansion.

Internal follow up
  - date
 	
  - date
	- June 10/11: I forwarded candidate's June 10th email to Assistant to Dir Major Gifts to be flagged in file for attention when Director is hired
	- Aug 2/11: followed up with new Dir Major Gifts re candidate; asked that she be interviewed as someone who could bring for-profit customer perspective to Major/Planned Gifts Team; advised Dir Major Gifts to inquire whether Jean has pursued training in planned giving

Strategic Selection: How to Raid the Competition with Class

I cringe when I hear the more common name for strategic selection – predatory hiring. This term accurately describes the double-barreled objective of a company when it steals a staff member from another corporation. It is simultaneously enhancing its own ability to make money while crippling its competitor.

Thanks to the limitless potential of philanthropy, not-for-profits do not have to overtly or covertly attempt to stifle other charities' fundraising efforts. However, while intentions are noble, charities use each other as training ground for their own future staff all the time. It is very common for mid-level and senior Development managers to be courted aggressively by other not-for-profits. As a matter of fact, Directors of Development spend only three to six months in a new job on average before they are approached about another one, usually through a search firm.

Strategic selection works both ways, so your first objective should be to make it as difficult as possible for other not-for-profits to lure away your staff. That is accomplished by offering an irresistible work environment and a challenging, progressive career. Your best staff will still be courted by others, but, when they are, they will be weighing the known benefits of staying with you against the unknown risk of leaving.

Using Professional Search Firms

Most managers we surveyed agree that search firms are valuable for approaching candidates who are working in other not-for-profits, something many employers felt was too awkward for them to do directly. Search firms are an advantage in several other ways as well, as long as they have a good track record in the professional fundraising field. Development Directors and CEOs we interviewed said that lack of knowledge about the fundraising industry was the most common criticism when an experience with a search firm was less than satisfactory.

Advantages of search firms
according to employers:

80% Advisory role / expert
perspective
67% Eliminates time-consuming
work
67% Broadens the search pool
inside known fundraising
industry
67% Reaches beyond fundraising
industry for candidates

Advantages of search firms from
candidates' point of view:

26% Extensive knowledge of
hiring organization
14% Facilitation of negotiation/
hiring process
11% Source of job leads even
when not actively searching
10% Extensive connection to the
labor market

Two out of three CEOs reported that search firms eliminate the time-consuming legwork involved in sourcing appropriate candidates. These same CEOs may not be valuing that legwork in monetary terms, however, as the cost of their services was cited as the primary disadvantage of using search firms. CEOs also noted that search firms often find more and better applicants than not-for-profits can attract on their own. As well, 80% of CEOs said they value the advisor role that search firms bring to the hiring process. It is not uncommon for search firms to help their clients define their operational strategy or their case for fundraising before they reach out to potential candidates. Search firms are their clients' advocates; they work diligently to make them look as attractive as possible to qualified fundraisers, a decided asset when dealing with an industry in high demand.

Using Your Staff as Informal Search Consultants

A team that gels is an invaluable asset. You can feel it when a group of skilled and motivated individuals comes together, and so can they. Your staff may not be able to fully articulate why their team zings, but they know that it does and they have a sixth sense about who would add value to the group. So, engage your staff in identifying future candidates.

Fundraisers connect with each other through professional membership associations and other networking groups. Encourage your staff to attend educational conferences and informal luncheons where they can build professional networks. To some degree, this extends to online professional support groups, as well, though both you and your staff may balk at the time it takes to wade through the daily barrage of postings.

The key thing is to send the message that active participation in professional membership associations is a boon to you – the boss – as well as to your employees. Paying for or contributing to your staff's annual membership dues further advantages you as a desirable employer while leveraging your influence. Fundraisers always have a million reasons why they are too busy to attend their own association's events but when you pay the fee you can insist that they get out of the office. Changing one's environment renews creativity and peer networking is a cost-effective form of professional consultation. Charge your staff with two responsibilities – bringing back educational information for the benefit of the rest of the team and sourcing their future colleagues.

Advertising for Candidates

Advertising for fundraisers is last on the list of options for hiring because it is the least effective way to find great staff when compared with promotion, encouraging unsolicited inquiries, and strategic selection. If you find yourself facing the prospect of advertising a position, you have likely missed a better hiring option. Have you passed over someone inside your department who is ready or near ready for a new challenge? Have you talked to your staff about the skills and experience you are seeking and whether they know someone who fits the profile? Have you remembered to review resumes already on file from unsolicited applicants? And, is this an opportunity for reorganizing rather than re-hiring? All these options are less time-consuming, less expensive and more proactive. When you have to advertise, you are limited to the collection of resumes you receive. Sure, you are not forced to hire from these applicants, but that only reinforces the argument that advertising can be time-consuming, expensive and risky.

That said, if you have decided to advertise a position, there are ways to do it better in order to improve your chances of attracting the best candidates.

1. **Approach the task with the right attitude.** Do not assume that you will be choosing from among many eager applicants for your coveted job opportunity. Instead, take the position that you are the one in competition for talent – because you are. This mindset helps you craft job ads and conduct interviews in ways that showcase your competitive advantages.

2. **Emphasize your attractive selling features to fundraisers** – the things you do better than other organizations. Fundraisers who are happily settled in their current jobs and who are not thinking about a change still peruse the ads. You cannot interest these "non-candidates" with a description of your mission statement; but you might be able to pique someone's curiosity when you say that you have won a national "Employer of the Year" award for the last three years in a row.

3. **Do not rely on your name and mission to be your primary selling feature** because it is everyone else's primary selling feature too and, therefore, no one's unique advantage.

4. **Do not allow your ad to read like a contract.** It is meant to inspire the desire to apply, not to remind applicants of the endless list of tasks that the winner will have to carry out.

5. **Consider the medium.** Ads for fundraising positions are increasingly posted online through membership associations. In that format, they all look very

Why **10%** of candidates were critical of search firms:

15% Limited knowledge of the position or field
9% Created distance between candidate and employer
8% Provided inaccurate information about position
6% Too focused on commission to be made

Disadvantages of search firms according to employers:

94% Cost of service
47% Does not guarantee candidate will stay
40% Does not guarantee candidate's quality or suitability
7% Difficult to find search firms that specialize in fundraising

There is a big difference between great and mediocre search firms. A good search firm communicates really well and clearly understands their client's expectations. They invest time and talent up front in getting to know the client's culture and unmet needs and they can articulate what makes a client unique. They also stay on deadline.

Where are the fundraisers with the combination of people and analytical skills? The two seem to be mutually exclusive.

I have trouble finding staff with flexible talents. My grants-writers don't have the inclination to get out there and meet with donors. They stay at their desks and focus on application deadlines.

similar due in part to the job posting template to which customers are expected to adhere. Resist anything that forces you to conform to everyone else's advertisement style. This is not a level playing field – yours is the better organization and the superior job, and you are paying good money to make your ad stand out from the pack, not blend in with it.

6. Take human nature into account. First impressions are formed as you read the opening paragraph of the candidate's cover letter; his first impression of you is formed as he reads the first three lines of your job ad. In typical electronic ads, what is visible first is the name of the organization, the title of the position and the title to whom the position reports. Within the rest of the visible space before scrolling is generally something about the history of the organization. This is a poor substitute for what could be in this crucial space to make good candidates sit up and take notice. Drop the organizational history and the reporting criteria and answer this question instead: "If you were limited to one sentence only, what would you say to a very desirable candidate in order to sway her decision in your favor?" Just as in any other electronic communication, you have to come straight at the reader with the best you have to offer, then back up into your supplementary information once you have her attention.

7. Weed out inappropriate candidates from the start. If you are seeking an experienced Director of Development with a track record of taking other not-for-profits' fundraising to impressive new heights, then do not shy away from saying so in your advertisement. Firmly state your bottom-line requirements in order to minimize the time-wasting nuisance of having to peruse too many applications from unsuitable candidates.

8. Use your job ad to send candidates to your website. The diligent ones will go there anyway, but there is a distinct advantage to a two-tiered approach to advertising a position. With your website as the main event, your ad can be shorter and, depending upon the medium, less expensive. Brevity plus focus makes your ad even more attractive – emphasize your advantages that will make desirable candidates pay attention. Imagine a candidate who, impressed by your concise and compelling electronic job ad, clicks through to a short video of your Development team in which your staff is enthusing about reaching a fundraising goal early and the pivotal role their boss played in this achievement.

Let Your Advertising Do Half the Work of Hiring

Your job ad can conform to someone else's requirements or it can accomplish what you are paying for. Below is an example of the type of ad typically seen by fundraisers; following that, the same position expressed in quite a different way. The difference in tone and style causes your job to be noticed; the difference in content causes you to be noticed.

Major/Planned Giving Assistant

Posted date: Aug 29, 2013
Closing date: Sep 14, 2013

Department: Strategic Partnerships & Development
Reporting to: National Director, Development
Location: Washington, DC

About The Global Environmental Association

GEA, a global environment charity, is one of the world's largest and most respected independent conservation organizations. GEA is active in over 100 countries with almost 5 million supporters.

GEA's mission is to stop the degradation of the earth's natural environment and to build a future in which humans live in harmony with nature by conserving the world's biological diversity, ensuring that the use of renewable natural resources is sustainable, and promoting the reduction of pollution and wasteful consumption.

In North America, GEA has a history of outstanding accomplishments. Currently we are focusing on preventing climate change as well as investing in long-term conservation efforts in key sensitive wilderness habitats. This is an exciting period for GEA.

What appears above is all that can be seen in the email without scrolling. There is no information about the position in the key viewing area, other than the job title. I have spared you the agony of reading three more pages of information, none of which showcases GEA as a place where fundraisers would want to work or the job as a stimulating challenge. Ads like this are typical. They may yield applicants who are qualified on paper but they do nothing to further the selection process. Great ads, however, cause potential candidates to vet themselves – well qualified, high performers find the opportunity irresistible and submit their resumes; marginal players weed themselves out before you ever know they considered your job opportunity. This reduces the employer's workload, speeds up the review process, and increases the not-for-profit's chances of making a great hire.

I left a job with a wonderful, flexible, supportive organization, one that gave me autonomy and authority and have landed in a job where I am either ignored, made to feel unimportant or micromanaged. I thought I had done my due diligence, but not enough I guess.

Here is the same job ad rewritten to achieve a better result. Considering the examples above and below, which version would make you wish you could work for this organization?

Research Partner for Over-Achievers

Behind every high performance major gifts team is one person who makes their stunning success possible. *Could it be you?*

The Global Environment Association (GEA) works under the radar, bringing major players together locally, nationally and internationally to tackle some of the world's most serious environmental problems. While we have received three awards for innovation in the last decade, we are most proud of the amazing team we have assembled that made those awards possible. Our fundraising staff is a critical part of our team. This highly motivated group has tripled philanthropic revenue in only seven years, but now they need a superb research specialist/analyst and overall task-master to help them take Development to the next level.

If you love the idea of being the power behind the throne, [click through] to discover what it's like to work at GEA. Once there, you will learn more about how this new position, combined with your exemplary skills and varied work experience, can add huge value to our team. We're eager to welcome the right person on board, so please apply no later than [date]. Our fundraising brain trust works out of Washington, DC, where the city buzzes, where you'll find the best espresso anywhere, and where the fruit trees bloom in March (not May)!

What Your Candidates Need to Know

Think about your own job for a minute. Its key responsibilities can be summed up in a single paragraph, but if you were to itemize all the things you actually do, the list would go on for pages. A common mistake made by people who craft job ads is that they use the list of duties that would be appended to an employment agreement as their advertisement. But, these are two different things. Most electronic job ads are unnecessarily long, perhaps because it costs the same to post one paragraph as it does to post three pages. But opting for the everything-and-the-kitchen-sink version is counter to your objective. Dry and unimaginative, these lengthy substitutes for enticing advertisements do more to turn good candidates off than on.

Your Website Is a Powerful Hiring Tool

Use your job ad to whet their appetites; then offer potential candidates an even more exciting experience on your website.

Clicking through to your "Career Landing Page", prospective employees will be presented with concrete information about the available position and equally important information about your not-for-profit's work environment. After all, the chosen candidate will be spending the better part of his waking hours in this job, so this is your opportunity to bring your hidden assets out into the open.

The Career Page carries the prospective employee through learning more about the job to completing an application form designed to make your hiring work as efficient and successful as possible. A common template makes scanning applications a breeze while allowing for apples-to-apples comparisons of candidates. Information on the job itself is comprehensive enough for a potential applicant to know whether he is qualified, but still concise enough to be enticing. (The longer the job ad, the more the candidate will feel that the workload is impossible, something that is a deterrent, not an enticement.)

Your Career Page is not only valuable when a position is available. It sends a powerful message to those proactive potential employees I referenced earlier in this chapter – the ones who don't wait for a position to be posted before approaching you about future employment opportunities. Through this creative resource, you will build a file of excellent candidates faster, meaning that your need to advertise will lessen over time. Your Career Page will also serve as an internal resource for your staff, reminding current employees that they are your number one resource for future talent. And, your Career Page is a boon to your search firm if you use one, speeding up their orientation to your not-for-profit and giving them an inside view of your working environment and management style.

Information about the job is just a small part of what an effective Career Page offers. It describes the work setting (physical) and work environment (atmospheric) through narrative and photos. It shows off your office space if you happen to have a particularly attractive, unusual or even funky setting. It references working conditions that make you stand out, such as how you advocate flex-time work schedules, that you have an onsite daycare, or that staff love your organization's roving food cart that dispenses health-conscious meals. It says things about current staff that would not be common knowledge such as awards they have won both professionally and personally. It showcases you, the employer, in ways that make

When interviewing candidates, make sure they understand that their performance will be measured using quantifiable metrics. That tends to scare away those who would only succeed if measured by "softer" criteria.

people want to work in your organization, such as how you engineered an atypical work schedule so that a staff member could qualify for the national sailing team. It includes quotes from employees about what it is like to work for your organization (and for you), action-oriented photos showing staff at retreats, doing community service, celebrating reaching your fundraising goal, and the like.

Here is a sample Career Landing Page on our company's website; http://www.donorcenteredleadership.com/career

Featuring the organization and position referenced about, this sample career landing page might spark your own creative ideas about how to use your most important communications vehicle – your website – as an ally in the hiring process. The unique nature of your not-for-profit, coupled with your ingenuity and particular perspective, will make your Career Page an important asset in the highly competitive pursuit of top fundraising talent.

Our sample page includes:

- a short video from the CEO, talking about his staff, what they have accomplished lately and how he enjoys working with them;

- a group photo of the Development Team with whom the new hire will be working. In the case of my imaginary organization, the photo includes a 360^0-view of the office space which happens to be charming, having been restored from an abandoned warehouse;

- a photo and short bio of the person to whom the new hire will report;

- information and photos about the on-site daycare, a particularly attractive employment benefit that has been the difference between winning and losing the not-for-profit's preferred candidate on more than one occasion;

- a photo and caption of GEA's baseball team competing in a recent tournament;

- a quick story about "Working Lunch Wednesdays", a fabulous idea introduced by a staff member where, once a week, departments take turns catering a themed lunch for the rest of the staff;

- more information about the job, including a brief narrative called, "A Day in the Life of Our Research Partner". This is a new position, difficult to describe by simply articulating the job responsibilities. This narrative brings the job alive;

- an entry portal to the application template and the technicalities of applying for the job.

Your own Career Page will bring your office environment alive so that candidates can see what makes you tick. But creating your Career Page also offers an opportunity to further staff retention. This is an excellent project to assign to your younger staff who are completely at home in the medium, who may be more recent hires themselves with fresh memories of the experience, and who are definitely eager to take on more responsibility. This concrete project will test their ability to collaborate, to expand their creative abilities, to think from the outsider's point of view, to work within a budget, and to meet deadlines.

The Prospect Pool Is Bigger than You Think

As I arrived at a conference venue in Colorado Springs, a vibrant, young woman immediately caught my attention. She was coming towards me with hand outstretched and a huge smile on her face. "Welcome, Ms. Burk", she said. "Let me help you get settled, then I want to introduce you to some people who are really looking forward to meeting you." She then escorted me over to the Conference Chair and her colleagues. Once assured that I was engaged in conversation, my young greeter quietly slipped away to continue her work.

I watched her manage the room as it filled with delegates. That beautiful smile and warm handshake were there for everyone. She addressed delegates by name as they arrived and had something upbeat to say to every person she welcomed. She was everywhere, making sure the details of the day were attended to but without drawing attention to herself.

The annual Philanthropy Day celebrations were held over lunch and they included presentation of the "Young Fundraiser of the Year" award. Introducing the winner was this person's boss, who leapt energetically to the stage and grinned his way through his prepared speech. He talked about how quickly his young staff member had grasped her responsibilities, how she always volunteered for new assignments, and how both donors and fellow staff were captivated by her delightful personality.

When she was called up to the stage, I was not at all surprised to see that the winner was the same vibrant young women who had helped me earlier. Addressing her boss, she said: "I have no idea why you hired me. I was fresh out of college and all I knew was that I wanted to work in the not-for-profit sector and that fundraising might be exciting. In the job interview, I became quite worried, though, because everyone in the room was talking about "Development" and I didn't know what that word meant. So I just kept smiling and telling them that I was willing to do anything, and I guess it worked because here I am." Everyone laughed.

I thought about this young, award-winning fundraiser's boss who had had the good sense to look beyond his employee's inexperience and lack of technical knowledge, and hire her instead for the qualities she possessed that could never be taught in a classroom.

I find that few people actually "plan" to become a fundraiser. It seems to happen to certain people who have the right set of skills and personal characteristics. Therefore, I'm always looking for people with these traits.

Whenever there is a supply/demand imbalance in favor of the supplier, prices rise. In the fundraising industry, too few qualified, experienced practitioners for too many jobs means Development professionals are in an advantageous position when negotiating starting salary or raises. This puts smaller-budget not-for-profits at a disadvantage when competing for talent against universities, national charities and big-brand institutions. This imbalance produces secondary consequences. The availability of jobs, and the urgent need among charitable organizations to fill them, allows credentialed fundraisers with very little experience to move up the seniority ladder quickly – sometimes too quickly. High expectations are placed on their too-junior shoulders long before they are ready to manage staff or have earned the credibility needed to be persuasive with the Board and CEO. Under pressure to deliver before they have learned how to do it, they move on prematurely, often blaming top management for not seeing things their way or the Board for not pulling their weight.

Do You Have to Know Fundraising to Be a Fundraiser?

Opening up the job market to workers with compatible skills will help appease the demand for professional fundraisers and it will add value to the industry.

The technical side of fundraising involves knowing how the methodologies for raising money work. Dispensing technical knowledge is the core activity of fundraising courses, degree programs and conferences; assessing practitioners' grasp of technical knowledge is the function of elementary-level accreditation programs. Both training and accreditation are a boon to a fast-growing industry that is transitioning from job to career status. But, while technical knowledge can get fundraisers into junior positions, relationship-building and fundraising management require other skills and plenty of work/life experience. When not-for-profits fill mid-level and senior positions, and when they have to compete aggressively for those key staff, they should be getting Development professionals who can make strategic decisions based on reliable data, who have a keen sense of customer service, and who can manage people – in both directions.

These skills are not tied to fundraising; they are developed in ambitious, career-oriented workers in every industry, and they are highly transferable. It takes very little time to learn the technicalities of fundraising but it takes a lifetime of practice to become expert at everything else that makes fundraising successful. And, because raising money is all about persuasion, compatibility and other very human qualities that are simply not present in everyone, there is a certain kind of individual – trained in fundraising or not – who will do well at the top of this field.

Great fundraisers possess that je ne sais quoi – that special something that cannot be taught in a classroom and which defies assessment through examination. The young fundraiser from Colorado Springs has it and the person who hired her knows it, though he might have been hard-pressed to explain exactly why at the time he offered her the job. Often summed up in words like talent, personality, intuition, creativity, insight and persuasiveness, these qualities manifest themselves in ways that achieve extraordinary results. They make the difference between a thank-you letter that acknowledges a gift and one that makes the reader's heart soar; they take a donor from conversation to decision without her ever feeling she has been sold; they bring someone's gift to life through words as vivid and compelling as a photograph. And, when these traits are present in managers, their staff stay loyal longer and produce better results sooner. Excellent fundraising managers influence up as well as down, instilling confidence in members of the Board and fostering a determination to succeed.

Good Fundraisers Come from Everywhere

77% of professional fundraisers we surveyed did not begin their careers in fundraising. 40% moved into Development from other disciplines inside the not-for-profit sector, and 37% came from outside the third sector entirely. Not surprising, fundraisers transitioning from the for-profit sector were most likely to have come out of marketing/communications or sales. Not so, however, for respondents who moved into fundraising from elsewhere in the not-for-profit sector. 22% became Development professionals after working in programs and services. This was especially true for one-person-shop fundraisers, where 28% transitioned into fundraising from careers in programs and services. Management, marketing and administrative support were also common jumping off points for respondents who became fundraisers after working in other third-sector jobs.

On the one hand, fundraisers with not-for-profit backgrounds in programs and services offer their employers an interesting opportunity. They are viscerally connected to the mission, able to communicate a vivid picture to donors of what they are funding. But, it takes more than passion and knowledge about the case to raise money. Creative writing, marketing, negotiating, closing and staff management skills are also essential to fundraising success. On the other hand, fundraisers with for-profit backgrounds may come into their new jobs highly experienced in negotiating and closing, and comfortable with meeting time-limited sales targets. This is a boon to charities trying to improve net fundraising results. But these fundraisers may not fully appreciate how different it is to sell a quality of life argument to someone who will receive no tangible benefit from the organization's services, let alone close the sale in an industry swamped with equally

I learned early on to get involved in the bigger Development picture through CASE, ADRP, etc. Opening my mind beyond my own organization has actually served to keep me in this job much longer than I would have otherwise stayed.

What respondents did in the for-profit sector before transitioning into fundraising:

22% Marketing/communications
21% Sales
14% Business management
9% Administration
9% Finance

worthy competitors. Working within a very limited budget, maneuvering through several layers of decision-making, and having no one available to assist with support work are all hallmarks of life in the not-for-profit sector. This may represent a major adjustment for new employees coming out of business.

In a turbulent economy, fundraising is somewhat of an oasis. It is a growing profession with increasing opportunities, an anomaly in a world of shrinking job options. A career in fundraising is attractive to highly skilled and experienced "outsiders" seeking a new path in a changing world. And, as it has done for some time, fundraising lures people in their mid or late careers who are looking for a more meaningful work experience. But, with its emphasis on growing credentials and credibility in the field, fundraising as a profession runs the risk of becoming too insular. When jobs are posted only to people already inside the industry, when conference sessions are led only by fundraising experts, when courses are designed to teach how fundraising already works but not how it could work, Development misses a big opportunity to…well…develop. Acknowledging the importance of inside knowledge while welcoming outside expertise would give not-for-profits and their Development operations a decided advantage.

Does someone have to know fundraising to be a fundraiser, then? Yes, in the end, but perhaps not necessarily in the beginning. The technicalities of fundraising can be learned quite quickly either on the job, or on the job in combination with targeted training and education. Employers should hire for the harder or impossible-to-teach skills, something that will instantly expand the prospect pool. The fundraising industry cannot produce enough practitioners on its own through traditional channels; atypical hires are a must in a growing industry and a hedge against a profession that would otherwise define itself too narrowly.

That said, the fundraising industry is no place for people who think they don't have to learn how fundraising works and that their corporate or other career experience makes them an instant and unconditional asset. An "I'm here to show you the light" attitude is unwelcome in the not-for-profit sector, and justifiably so. Working in fundraising is simultaneously demanding and humbling and not a good fit for candidates who think their very existence is a gift.

How to Diversify Your Staff Complement

Both language and location matter when seeking staff from inside or outside the established Development industry. Where you advertise is important. Increasingly, ads for professional fundraisers are posted through a service offered by Development membership associations. But only established fundraisers see these advertisements, and even then, only fundraisers who are members of those associations receive your job postings. Advertising in the career section of daily newspapers will expose your job to a wider audience; but even more targeted advertising in trade publications or on the websites of professional associations may get you directly in front of the people with the skills you want.

If you are seeking a donor relations specialist, advertising inside the communications industry will alert writers, journalists and communications experts to your position. You can approach your search broadly or narrowly inside this industry because there are many associations that represent specializations within the profession. Posting your job ad with the Association of Health Care Journalists, for example, will yield highly experienced candidates in both communications and healthcare, who are likely to have career backgrounds that complement but don't replicate your core professional fundraising group. Your primary advantage remains your own website. Your organization's brand and the good work you do will beckon potential employees to your site. Once there, your Career Page will inspire great people to apply for posted jobs or contact you to express their interest in working for your not-for-profit organization.

The language you use on your website or in external job postings can attract good outside candidates with transferable skills while still being appealing to experienced professional fundraisers. These brief excerpts send two quite different messages though they are marketing the same position:

Planned Gifts Associate – Minimum Qualifications
This position is suitable for a senior Development practitioner with at least ten years' diversified experience in Advancement. Proven knowledge of complex gift arrangements and associated tax laws is essential.

Relationship Specialist for Prominent Philanthropists
This position offers a vibrant and rewarding career to either a seasoned fundraiser with ten or more years of progressive experience (including a track record in major and planned gifts) or a corporate sector sales and relationship associate with a solid background in managing high net worth clients.

Words of Wisdom from Those Who Have Gone Before You

Respondents who have transitioned into fundraising from other careers offered advice through our research study to others who are thinking of doing the same thing. From a management perspective, what they suggested is noteworthy for both Development Directors and CEOs who want to shorten the orientation period and help their new staff produce early results.

I was a lawyer before becoming a not-for-profit manager. I had no idea how much time I would spend dealing with people-management issues and staff turnover. It's very draining.

Advice from fundraisers who
transitioned from other fields:

23% Take fundraising courses/
training
19% Articulate transferable skills
15% Volunteer

*In making a career transition
from the financial planning field,
my single best advantage was
the mentorship offered to me by
a seasoned veteran inside the
fundraising industry.*

Learn How the Industry Works

23% of fundraisers who came into Development from other careers said that taking fundraising courses made their transition much easier while reaffirming fundraising as a career choice. Transitioning fundraisers also said that specialized training in a particular branch of Development, such as planned giving, was decidedly advantageous. It was interesting to note that even short-term training or exposure to fundraising was considered helpful. A two or three-day industry conference, for example, provides an overview of the profession and introduces novices to the lingo of the industry.

People wanting to transition into fundraising from other professions are often proactive about approaching potential employers in off-hiring times in order to leverage their transferable skills. (See "unsolicited candidates" referenced earlier in this chapter.) Unsolicited candidates are a great resource but those who also have no direct fundraising experience are at a disadvantage when competing for positions that have already been posted. Employers perusing resumes may stop reading when they realize that certain candidates have not worked in not-for-profit organizations or that their non-profit experience is not in fundraising. If they get to the first interview stage, candidates in transition may have a tough time getting shortlisted. Here is where fundraising training is a decided advantage. Candidates with compatible skills who pursue fundraising education before seeking Development jobs send several positive messages to potential employers: they are serious, they are willing to put time and money into improving their marketability, and they respect the fact that fundraising is a profession requiring knowledge and training.

Employers can also use formal fundraising education as a tool in assessing the potential of unsolicited candidates who are transitioning out of the corporate sector. Chances are that a suitable position will not be available at the moment the information meeting is held. As an employer, if you suggest that training is warranted, it will be valuable information should the candidate follow or not follow your advice.

Respondents who successfully transitioned from other fields also advised anyone wanting to do the same to join one or more professional fundraising associations. As much, if not more, is learned through informal networking, a hallmark of professional associations. At the same time, membership affords a degree of "inside status", even if the transitioning member has yet to secure a job in the industry. Respondents further suggested that volunteering on the Executive or an event committee signals a serious commitment, something important when trying to making connections and build a profile inside the profession.

Use Fundraising Language When Defining Your Skills

19% of respondents said that it is important for employees hoping to transition into fundraising to identify their transferable skills in ways that resonate with potential employers. This means defining their knowledge and skills by using language common to the fundraising business. For instance, experience in customer service translates into experience in donor relations or stewardship. Having a solid track record in up-selling existing clients or customers can be compared with cultivating donors from annual fund contributions to major gifts. And, improving the rate of repeat sales with existing customers sounds very much like improving performance in donor retention.

The following sample resume highlights the career experience of John Smith who, at first glance, might be eliminated as a candidate for a senior fundraising position. But, on closer inspection, his credentials are highly compatible with those of a major gifts officer or manager of a major/planned gifts department. Note also how Mr. Smith's knowledge of not-for-profits is woven into his resume.

My colleagues who are not in fundraising think that our profession is nothing but fun – having lunch with donors and going to parties all the time. They should try it for a week.

John Smith
Curriculum Vitae

Private Banking Associate	Greenbay Bank, Greenbay, CA state-wide bank specializing in serving individual clients; managing a roster of 75 private banking clients with portfolios of $1 million to $1.5 billion; investment increase averaged 6.7%/year; also manages GBG Philanthropic Fund of $132M *See Appendix i*	2007 to present
Private Banking Associate Int'l Office, Hong Kong	Greenbay Bank, Greenbay, CA responsible for 140 private banking clients with portfolios under $1 million investment increase averaged 17.5%/year *See Appendix ii*	2002 to 2007
VP, Product Marketing	Arc Pharmaceuticals, San Francisco, CA Fortune 500 Pharmaceutical company head of marketing, managing staff of 300 in four countries, annual budget of $40 million; also managed $5 million Arc Sponsorship budget featuring Johns Hopkins, American Cancer Society, Hospice Assn of America *See Appendix iii*	1995 to 2002
Dir, Client Services	TWD Agency International, New York, NY boutique ad agency serving int'l clients managed 10 account executives and $75 million annual budget; grew clients by 100% during tenure; negotiated pro bono services for 10 not-for-profits including Habitat for Humanity whose 30-second PSA won Gold at Nat'l American Media Assn Award '94 *See Appendix iv*	1990 to 1995
Senior Associate	TWD Agency Int'l, New York, NY responsible for creative for American Red Cross, Save the Children and Doctors without Borders files in addition to several international corporate clients - $14 million annual budget *See Appendix v*	1992 to 1995

The actual skill set is more important than number of years of experience. There are a lot of slackers out there.

Get Volunteer Experience

15% of professionals who transitioned into fundraising from other fields said that volunteer experience was a decided asset. Serving on Boards of Directors was considered valuable, especially when it included active engagement in fundraising, particularly in gift negotiation. There can sometimes be a catch, however. I have known many leadership volunteers who were very successful at fundraising, thanks largely to the influence their volunteer positions afforded them. After transitioning into paid staff roles, the same people sometimes found their donor/friends to be less receptive and raising money from them a lot harder. This is not surprising. While the connection remains, the extraordinary influence of volunteer status is no longer there to make the ask irresistibly compelling to donors.

Not-for-Profits Need Expertise, Not Rescue

Transitioning employees add extraordinary value to Development when they bring their skills and fresh perspective to fundraising, adapting their knowledge to their new environment as they go. Less effective are corporate sector recruits who think that not-for-profits should operate more like businesses. Even though fundraising is the profit center inside the not-for-profit entity, the sensibilities and decision-making processes inherent in third-sector organizations do not lend themselves to corporate-style operations.

When transitioning staff (and some leadership volunteers) say their not-for-profit or their Development Office should operate more like a business, they are wasting energy on something that is neither possible nor desirable. What it would take for a charitable organization to be businesslike is exactly what it takes for a profit-making company to be businesslike – large staff contingents, big budgets and a customer base (donors in this case) who are unconcerned with how much money is spent getting the product to market (i.e., raising money).

Not-for-profits can learn many things from people who transition from the corporate sector. But the reverse is equally true. The right attitude, along with an endless capacity for hard work under trying circumstances, will be transitioning employees' best advantage.

An Alternative Approach to Requesting Applications

In the mid-eighties, I was preparing to return to the real workforce after having had three children. During the ten years in which I was called a housewife, I did contract assignments in between changing diapers, doing my stint at co-op daycare, keeping the house in livable order, chauffeuring, entertaining, and a million other things. Any reader who has had a similar experience knows exactly what this is like; anyone who hasn't has never really had their stamina or their ability to multi-task put to the test. I decided to rejoin the workforce just to get some rest.

Worried, however, that the business world might have passed me by while I was distracted by motherhood (it hadn't, by the way), I thought I should brush up on my job application skills. I went to the public library and checked out the only book not already out on loan. I cannot remember its name and it is long since out of print. I do remember, though, that it was shorter than a hundred pages in length with a picture of the author on the front cover, staring directly into the camera. He was wearing a dark blue business suit, white shirt, and a tie that was definitely not making a statement of any kind. (This may have had something to do with why the book was still on the library shelf.)

Its uninspiring book jacket notwithstanding, this short how-to contained extraordinarily valuable information, and I have come to appreciate its wisdom more and more the longer I am in business. It turned out that the author had previously been employed in human resources for the Federal Government where he reviewed about two hundred applications a day. The advice he offered in his book came from the perspective of someone devoting less than one minute to a single application before recommending it for the "A List" or the bin. I used all of his advice, especially what he recommended regarding formatting one's resume to make it stand out from the crowd. Soon after I read this book, I submitted my resume to a local not-for-profit that had advertised a position. I got the job and learned later that the way in which my resume had been crafted (following Mr. Blue Suit's advice) drew the attention of the Executive Director and got me short-listed. My own persuasiveness, buoyed by the prospect of escaping a 24/7 career in domestic science, did the rest.

Resumes that Rock

Mr. Blue Suit's resume template is a boon to job applicants but it is also a sanity-saving tool for employers. Especially now, in an age where most applications are submitted electronically, employers can – and should – insist that applicants use a template that they stipulate. This significantly reduces the time employers must spend perusing resumes initially, while enabling an apples-to-apples comparison of candidates' qualifications and suitability.

I highly recommend the template that Mr. Blue Suit suggested (which I used to list the career experience and qualifications of John Smith on Page 119). Mr. Blue Suit advocated a one-page summary containing limited yet specific information. The summary is laid out in three columns, with the most critical information for employers in the left-hand column (taking natural eye movement and reading left to right into account). The three columns contain:

If you transition into fundraising from other professions, keep an open mind and listen to experienced people in the biz. It's your responsibility to connect the dots from your former profession to fundraising.

- Left-hand column – job title
- Middle column – name of organization with one-line description if necessary, followed by the applicant's key accomplishments while in the job
- Right-hand column – period of employment

As an electronic file that links from your Career Page, your application template will serve you even better if you limit the number of characters available for each entry. This is especially important for the middle column where applicants will be tempted to say too much. [See our example at www.donorcenteredleadership. com/career/apcover, which prompts applicants to describe their jobs in terms of accomplishments or outcomes delivered, as opposed to simply offering a list of their responsibilities.]

Our Career Summary Page lays out resume information so that employers can answer the following questions in less than one minute:

- *Has the candidate worked in progressively responsible Development positions over his/her career in fundraising?*
- *Is the candidate's level of experience sufficient for the posted position?*
- *For what type(s) of not-for-profits has the candidate worked?*
- *What are the one or two most significant and measurable fundraising accomplishments that the candidate has achieved in each position?*
- *Has the candidate been promoted internally at least once?*
- *How long has the candidate worked with each organization referenced in the resume?*
- *Are there any red flags such as successive short stays, gaps of time that are not accounted for, lack of visible progress up the seniority ladder or leapfrogging into senior-level positions without the requisite experience or training that would warrant such a move?*

Behind this summary, applicants can include as much information as they like in the form of appendices. Employers who read the summary and feel the candidate is not suitable for the job will not have to read further. Employers who like what they see on the summary page, however, will find the appendices irresistible.

The following are two examples of one-page resume summaries that demonstrate just how much is revealed about a job applicant in a single page and how easy it is to compare and prioritize candidates when you opt for a common application template. The job under consideration is Associate Director of Development for a mid-sized state college with a staff of sixty in the advancement office. Following each resume are the reviewer's notes. Reviewing and note-taking took less than two minutes for each.

Resume Example 1

Director of Development	**Goldenview Community Center** a multi-purpose center serving 15,000 seniors fundraising revenue growth from $1M to $4.5M annually; endowment built from $6M to $20M; managing staff of 12. *See Appendix i*	2005 to present
Director, Major and Planned Gifts	**Goldenview Memorial Hospital Foundation** regional hospital serving seven counties in Indiana and a population base of 4.5 million established strategic planned giving program; increased annual revenue through major gifts from $2.5M to $5.5M; managed 6 staff.	2001 to 2005
Campaign Coordinator	**Easton Performing Arts Center, Easton, MI** 350-seat repertory theatre, opened 2005 hired after $25M campaign stalled; raised $6M in 9 months. *See Appendix iii*	2003 to 2004
Gifts Officer	**Easton State College, Easton, MI** renowned for environmental education and entrepreneurship member of 7-member major/planned gifts team; personally responsible for raising $2M annually (achieved); citation for drafting College's first campus-wide Stewardship Plan. *See Appendix iv*	2001 to 2004
Events Manager	**Easton Big Brothers/Big Sisters** local chapter of renowned national social service agency turned around declining revenue from three long-term, volunteer-led events improving revenue from $300,000 to $1.2M in two years *See Appendix v*	1999 to 2001

Over eleven years, this candidate has engineered a strategically progressive career, rising from a manager of fundraising events to his first job as a Director of Development. In all but one position, he has stayed in his job for as long as or longer than the average industry tenure. His front-line fundraising experience spans events, major gifts, capital campaigns and planned giving, so he is well versed in most aspects of fundraising, the exception possibly being direct marketing. The applicant has lived in two states and has worked for not-for-profits in the fields

If you transition into fundraising from other professions, keep an open mind and listen to experienced people in the biz. It's your responsibility to connect the dots from your former profession to fundraising.

of social services, higher education, the arts, healthcare and recreation. He was internally promoted once.

The candidate has increased fundraising revenue by what appears to be a healthy margin in each position he has held. He has had progressive supervisory/management experience since 2001.

Note: It appears that the candidate joined the Easton Performing Arts Centre team towards the end of their campaign which would account for the tenure of only one year. Check this out.
Note: Check out his knowledge of direct marketing due to the size and scope of the direct mail and online giving programs that fall under this position.

Recommendation: an "A" list candidate; review full resume and consider for next step.

Resume Example 2

Interim Manager	Women for Equal Opportunity, Austin, TX	2011 to 2012
	advocacy agency supporting pay equity and other issues filling in during Exec Dir's maternity leave; overseeing staff of 15, including Development Dept. of 4. See Appendix i	
Stewardship Co-Ord	World Food Program, Boston, MA	2010 to 2011
	NGO redirecting surplus food and supplies to third world created first stewardship program, managing staff of 6. See Appendix ii	
President	JYC Consulting, Albany, NY	2010
	full service fundraising and communications firm serving upstate New York provided individualized services for a variety of not-for-profits. See Appendix iii	
Fundraising Manager	Albany Arts Council, Albany, NY	2008-2009
	overseeing body for municipally-owned arts facilities co-ordinated special events for facilities sponsors; investigated private fundraising potential. See Appendix iv	
Writer/Editor	Open Door, Kansas City, MO	2008
	public information office for Kansas City Municipality copywriting and general marketing for City-funded not-for-profits. See Appendix v	

Special Events	Easter Seals, Midwest Regional Office, Kansas City	2007 to 2008
	responsible for copywriting, editing, design coordination, and marketing for events where Easter Seals is the designated beneficiary; 30 events/year. See Appendix vi	
Writer/Editor	About Town, Kansas City	2006 to 2007
	contributed and edited stories to magazine aimed at tourists and business travelers. See Appendix vii	

I thought I was hired for the skills I could bring to my new position. But I soon understood that my new boss expected me to relearn everything "their way". No matter how experienced you are, be ready to eat humble pie when you start a new job.

This candidate has held seven positions in seven years. Positions seem to be relatively unrelated, not progressing in an increasingly senior capacity in fundraising. Four of the seven positions are not in fundraising, though they are in the related fields of communication, administration and consulting. The consulting position appears to be a self-employment period between jobs, due to its short duration and lack of specifics regarding clients and work achievements. The longest tenure in any one position seems to be two years, though 2007 to 2008, for example, could represent a period as short as a few months. The most recent management position is an interim role, covering a maternity leave, in which the candidate may have been acting in more of a caretaking capacity than leading the organization forward in new ways.

This candidate has lived in five cities in seven years. Key accomplishments in fundraising positions make no reference to the amount of money raised.

Recommendation: under-qualified as a candidate for this position; "C" List

The Cover Letter

I disagree with Mr. Blue Suit's advice on cover letters, but only because the times have changed. He advised that, because the resume itself was fully informative, the letter that accompanies it needed to say only:

Dear sir or madam:

Enclosed please find my resume in response to your advertisement for the position of Director of Annual Giving.

I look forward to hearing from you in due course.

Sincerely,

As the book was written in the early seventies, Mr. Blue Suit's youngest readers would have graduated from high school in the sixties. People of that generation, or older, could write – they did not graduate if they couldn't – and their diplomas or degrees confirmed that they had acquired an acceptable level of skill. That is not the case today, sadly, which is why the letter now forms an integral part of any application. The resume gives employers a clue, but the style of this concise summary speaks more to the applicant's ability to write marketing copy than prose. The accompanying cover letter provides employers with a first impression of the candidate's style when interacting with donors, his grasp of language, and his ability to be discreetly persuasive.

An excellent letter…

- contains no spelling or grammatical errors. If it does, you should throw the application out without reading further. When so much is at stake for the candidate and, yet, she still sends you sloppy correspondence, it is an unintentional warning that, if hired, her work will be executed to an even lower standard.

- is addressed personally to the individual to whom resumes are to be sent. No "Dear sir" or "To whom it may concern". If you did not provide this information in the job ad or on your website, but an applicant goes to the trouble of finding out the name and title of the person who should receive his resume, consider this a point in his favor.

- speaks directly to and about the job in question. This reassures those who review the application that a templated letter was not used. Preformatted letters are problematic because their content is non-specific, leaving the impression that the applicant may be mass marketing herself to every job advertised rather than approaching job-hunting strategically. Templated cover letters also raise the possibility that they have been crafted by a third party in order to mask the applicant's poor writing skills.

- answers any specific questions that you have asked candidates to address. This shows employers that the applicant is paying close attention. Addressing a specific request in the letter also requires the writer to craft original correspondence.

- avoids claims that cannot be substantiated. In a surprisingly common example, an applicant will declare himself the best candidate for the job. He is attempting to communicate confidence, of course, but the message received is something else entirely. Only the employer is in a position to make that assessment.

Apart from these must-haves, the qualities that make a cover letter stand out are as individual as the applicants themselves. I have often lingered over correspondence that demonstrated the author's effort to learn about my company and its work. Because my firm is rooted in research, I look for that combination of initiative, evidence-based thinking and curiosity that characterizes all Cygnus employees. Two or three brief paragraphs of original composition say a lot about the writer. Some of that information appears on the page; most of the insight that the reader gains can be found between the lines.

The A-B-C Method for Short-Listing Candidates

Vetting applications the traditional way can be time-consuming and leave those responsible for short-listing fraught with doubt. The three-column resume template will significantly reduce the time required to review submissions and my A/B/C process for categorizing applications will streamline the job of short-listing.

As a first step, consider only the information provided on the one-page, three-column template. (Anyone who did not submit her application on your required template should be placed in the "C" group without further consideration. She is not good at following instructions.)

Review each application for adherence to the criteria that this template prioritizes. The sample template described earlier was designed to reveal:

- whether applicants' careers to date have progressed along a path that, on paper, qualifies them as candidates for the job on offer;
- whether there were unexplained employment gaps;
- whether candidates stayed in previous positions long enough to make an impact or had chronically short job stays;
- whether the organizations for which applicants worked made them attractive as candidates;
- whether candidates demonstrated measurable achievements in the jobs they held at a level that made them worth interviewing.

The one-page template represents your hiring bottom line, so you may need to adjust it to include something else that is essential to your organization or the position in question; but Mr. Blue Suit's example answers key questions concisely, allowing employers to move efficiently to the short-listing process.

There is a lot of crossover between fundraising and other professions. The ability to build relationships with people, organizational management, communication -- they're skills common to all business, not just fundraising, and they are skills that can be learned. The key thing is having the right temperament.

I think the turnover rate of fundraising staff is related to loss of passion. When Development professionals stop focusing on the mission of the charity they work for and start focusing on the numbers, it's the beginning of the end.

B Stands for But...

The A/B/C process for short-listing applicants works, but only if you let it. "A" candidates meet your bottom line requirements and that, in turn, makes you want to investigate more. You will now be eager to read the letter accompanying his resume and at least scan the appendices which give you more information about the candidate's career history. Just because the letter sits on top of the resume, by the way, does not mean you have to read it first. It is backup to the more critical employment history information, though it does reveal a great deal about the person behind the stats. If you are still intrigued or excited by this candidate, she now belongs in the A pile.

"C" candidates do not meet your basic requirements for qualification or they raise red flags for other reasons. Mr. Blue Suit's template makes it impossible to conceal problems unless the candidate has not told the truth. But if that is the case, certain interview questions and diligent reference-checking will help you separate genuine from contrived information. Red flags such as rapid job turnover or lack of specific achievements are easy to spot. Resist the temptation to read further. No matter how appealing the accompanying letter, for instance, this applicant is not qualified for the job. Into the "C" file she goes. When all applications have been reviewed and filed, take the C file, send everyone in it a "thanks but no thanks" acknowledgement, then shred the file.

The "B" file is where most applications will accumulate. Not quite fully qualified – but not a disaster either – B candidates have deficiencies but not to the extent that you are willing to give up on them. *There is a grammatical mistake in the cover letter* **BUT** *everyone confuses "its" with "it's"[1] these days. He only stayed fifteen months on average in his last two jobs,* **BUT** *he might have had a good reason.*

The thicker the B file becomes as you vet and categorize applicants, the likelier it is that these factors are present:

- there is hardly anyone, or there is no one, in the A file;
- the job has been vacant for some time and everyone is feeling the strain of handling more responsibilities;
- this is your second kick at the can. Your preferred candidate from the last hiring attempt took another position at the last minute.

The "B" file is the "But..." file, and it reveals your reluctance to trust the process, a reluctance which understandably stems from the pressure you are under to get this

---

[1] That one drives me crazy!

hire done. **BUT**, as many wise Development Directors pointed out in our research, you will regret it if you hire someone whose resume, interview or reference left you wondering. A seemingly minor deficiency will turn into a major problem on the job. I concur with the managers we surveyed. Whenever I have had to let someone go, or when the employee sees the writing on the wall and leaves first, I have returned to the personnel file. After reviewing the job application and my notes from interviews and referees, I see clearly what I had refused to see before.

The "B" File Exception – Over-Qualified Applicants

When all other criteria are positive, being over-qualified alone is not a reason to downgrade an applicant to the "B" File. Managed strategically, over-qualified staff can be a boon to your fundraising operation, but you must include discreet questions in interviews to know whether you have an asset or a liability under consideration (see Chapter 8, Interviewing Over-Qualified Candidates).

How to Handle the "B" File

On the day you finish categorizing all applicants, do not be tempted to re-visit the B File. Instead, leave it till tomorrow. Go home, take your significant other out for dinner, go to a show, have a really good glass of wine – whatever reminds you that you are no longer on the clock. Then, get a good night's sleep. Go to work the next morning rested, energized and confident. Take the "B" file, send everyone in it a "thanks- but-no-thanks" acknowledgement, and then shred it.

The A-Team

The "A" file contains your candidates. If you have only one candidate in the A file, remember that you will be hiring only one person for the job. If you have no one in the A file, then ask yourself these questions:

- Did I overlook an excellent internal candidate who is ready or near ready for a promotion?
- Have I developed a Career Landing Page to attract unsolicited candidates?
- Did I remember to review my file of unsolicited candidates?
- Have I asked my staff to identify someone in their circle of influence who would make a good member of the team?
- Should I be calling someone whose work I admire and asking her to have lunch?
- Was my job ad original and enticing or did it read like everyone else's ad-vertisement?

During interviews, be sure to talk about bottom-line expectations and how the new employee will be evaluated against them. I would rather have a "B" product and an "A" fundraiser than the other way around.

You may be facing a good deal of work and even a cultural shift in thinking in order to re-position your not-for-profit as a coveted destination for fundraisers. Do not be discouraged. The time you invest in hiring the right staff and managing them well pays off in a team that wants to succeed, that is confident in its ability to reach and exceed goals, and whose members stay loyal longer. In other words, hiring and managing well *is* fundraising.

Chapter 7:
Salary and Benefits in the Real World

A friend of mine has carved out a progressive – and impressive – career in fundraising and marketing over the last thirty years. She has held increasingly senior positions in prominent healthcare institutions, arts organizations and, now, in higher education. She is very accomplished and equally at ease both managing staff and being on the front lines developing relationships with major gift donors. She is particularly astute when it comes to recognizing opportunities for creative sponsorships thanks to her early career in corporate marketing.

Now in her mid-fifties, my friend has often mused about the final chapter of her fundraising career. Not that she isn't happy where she is; but if that perfect job in an amazing not-for-profit were to come along...that would be the icing on the cake.

Well, it did. A renowned children's hospital was seeking a Senior Director to lead their biggest ever capital campaign. The hospital Board had just approved an international pediatric oncology center devoted to finding cures for some of the most virulent childhood cancers. Their requirements for Campaign Director were a perfect match for her background. Moreover, my friend had survived childhood leukemia herself; her connection to the cause was visceral.

I have never seen her so excited. Not surprising, she breezed through the preliminary interviews and was placed among the finalists. But she was much more subdued after the next interview. My friend was offered the position but learned she would have to accept a 15% cut in pay and a benefits package far less attractive than the one she already enjoys. She would also be commuting a much greater distance to the office, adding ninety minutes to her work day.

I suggested she speak to an accountant – perhaps the lower salary would put her in a better tax bracket and maybe there was room to maneuver with her future employer on benefits and work schedule. After all, a top campaign job like this makes severe demands on a fundraiser for meetings in off-hours with donors and volunteers.

Several discussions later, negotiations appeared to be at an impasse. While my friend sought the middle ground by suggesting a compromise salary she could live with, there was no movement by the other side. "We can't do it; it's out of our control", the Director replied. "Pay scales are set across the whole hospital by job category, and your job has been categorized as a C-9. This is all we can offer." Her potential employer then added, "Why don't you take a little more time to think about it. We would really love to have you join our team."

She did think about it. For a week my friend re-ran the numbers and developed a list of pros and cons about staying where she was versus taking on this new challenge. In the end, she decided to accept the reduction in pay and benefits in order to follow her dream. She arranged another meeting with her prospective employer to give her the good news.

Her soon-to-be boss was almost jubilant until my friend brought up the subject of a flexible work schedule. "While I'm prepared to accept a reduced salary and benefits package", she said, "I'm also looking at a costly and time-consuming commute; so I assume you don't have a problem with me working from home when I'm writing proposals, for instance, or adjusting my hours to take evening and weekend meetings into account." "Actually, I do", said the Director. "I expect all my staff to be in the office between the hours of nine and five. I feel it's important for the team to work together and, besides, if I need to meet with you, I don't want to have to chase all over town to find you."

My friend told me later that this was the moment when everything changed. "I felt a shiver run up my spine", she said, "when I realized that I had just been given a preview of the Director's management style. Suddenly I knew that this was not the place for me."

Give and Take in a Changing Work Environment

"Level playing field" is a hackneyed phrase but an entirely appropriate description of the hiring process. After the new staff member is hired, he will never again enjoy outright equality, but, while negotiations continue, both employer and candidate have very strong cards to play. They are like two worthy opponents, with each other their ultimate prize.

Knowing what your advantages are – and are not – will guide you in being resolute about the things that you can control and flexible about those you cannot. As the employer, you have every right to expect your fundraising team to reach the net revenue goals laid out in your plan. If you have developed a strategy based on real evidence, one that takes donor trends into account, ambitious results can be achieved and you should not settle for anything less. You can also be resolute about certain other things. How those goals are reached is vital; fundraising must be conducted in ways that are compatible with the sensitivities of your not-for-profit and ethical. You must be confident that overall goals will be reached, meaning that regular interim reporting from fundraisers is a must. And, you have the right to expect your team to interact with each other and with you in a businesslike and respectful way; productivity grants no one the right to act like a jerk in the office, souring the work environment for everyone else.

But even though you are the employer, there are things over which you do not have unilateral control. Being resolute about them when you should be flexible leads to hiring the wrong person or the right person under the wrong terms. Candidates who feel they have been outwitted on issues where they could have taken a firmer stand start looking for another job at the first sign of dissatisfaction. In the end, employers always end up paying the price in premature resignation and/or under-performance.

You need time before you hire to think through the issues that will make or break your negotiation. Salary is number one because, more than anything else, winning your preferred candidate depends on getting this right. Benefits and related working conditions are sometimes just as much of a deal maker or breaker as salary. They are a significant negotiating advantage that few not-for-profit employers fully appreciate.

You Get What You Pay For

Once the hiring process begins, it takes on a life of its own. Sure, the employer wants to get the job filled as quickly as possible and get back to her other work; but candidates are also on a critical path and the good ones may be considering several opportunities simultaneously. Being taken off guard in the midst of a negotiation by something that you have not carefully considered in advance can cause negotiations to stall and leading candidates to opt for the competition.

Readers may be thinking, "Well, of course employers are in control of salary. We tell candidates what we are willing to pay and if they won't work for that, they can go elsewhere." You are right, but the critical objective is to hire the person who can get the job done and that job is meeting your fundraising goal. If you lose your preferred candidate over salary and have to settle for another applicant about whose skills or fit you are less confident, you are putting your most important goal at risk.

At this time in the evolution of fundraising as a profession, practitioners wield more power than employers on the issue of compensation. In the research that informs this book, not-for-profit CEOs, Directors of Development and other professional fundraisers provided conclusive evidence about the relationship between salary and fundraising success. This is what each group had to say:

Chief Executive Officers

1. When asked, "What is the number one issue that has caused your preferred candidate for the top fundraising position to decline your job offer," 58% cited the salary they were willing to pay.

2. Only 21% of CEOs feel they offer competitive salaries in order to attract the best candidates for key fundraising jobs.

We pay less than our competitors and, as a result, are perpetually two or three people short of our staffing needs. Being lean sure presents some challenges.

Management's view about salary scales for fundraisers:

65% Fundraisers are adequately paid
8% Fundraisers are generously paid
28% Fundraisers are underpaid

3. 25% of CEOs feel that their chief fundraiser is currently underpaid, but, among this group, 70% still expect top performance from these individuals, irrespective of compensation.

4. Among CEOs who have experienced this, 44% said that salary is the number one reason for premature resignation of their chief fundraiser.

Directors or VPs of Development

1. 35% of Directors/VPs of Development reported "not being able to offer a competitive salary" as the number one cause of unsuccessful hiring attempts.

2. On a scale of 1 to 7, with 1 being "not at all important" and 7 being "essential", top Development Directors rated "offering competitive salary" at 5.7 when hiring management-level fundraisers and 5.4 for mid-level Development personnel.

3. When a valued employee makes it known he is leaving to take a position elsewhere for better pay, only 5% of chief Development Officers say they offer to match that salary if the employee will agree to stay; an additional 54% said they might do so under certain circumstances; and 41% would not do so under any circumstances. (Among those who would definitely or possibly offer to increase the staff member's salary, the majority did not know what their outer limit was for negotiation. 19% of respondents were willing to offer up to 10% more and 16% said they would consider matching any salary level in order to keep a particularly valuable staff member.)

Development Professionals

1. 35% of survey respondents who are the most senior fundraisers in their organizations said that the salary they were offered or which they negotiated influenced them to accept their current position more than anything else.

2. 37% of all professional fundraisers surveyed said they left their last job for a higher salary elsewhere.

3. On a scale of 1 to 7, with 1 being "not at all important" and 7 being "essential", chief Development Officers rated the role that competitive salaries play in their desire to stay in their current jobs at 5.2; middle management fundraisers gave the connection between salary levels and retention a 5.3 rating. Respondents who were the sole Development professionals in their organizations (one-person-shop fundraisers) rated salary at 4.9 on the 7-point scale.

4. Among Development Directors planning to stay indefinitely in their current positions at the time they participated in our study, 32% said that the salary they are paid strongly influences their loyalty.

5. Among respondents who were planning to leave their positions when we surveyed them, 40% of Development Directors, 54% of mid-level fundraising managers, 52% of non-management personnel and 51% of one-person-shop fundraisers were leaving for higher pay elsewhere. Regardless of the category of respondent, "leaving for higher salary elsewhere" was the number one response by a wide margin. This is in spite of the fact that 70% of all fundraisers surveyed felt that they were already either generously or adequately paid in their current positions.

58% of fundraisers surveyed feel they are adequately paid; **12%** feel their salary is generous, and **30%** feel they are underpaid.

All this evidence points to an inescapable conclusion: salary is the number one reason why fundraisers leave for another position or why your preferred candidate opts at the last minute for someone else's job offer. So, inflexibility on salary is tantamount to eliminating yourself, not the candidate, from the competition. As long as supply/demand inequity in the fundraising industry favors job applicants, this will remain the case. What should be unacceptable to employers is not getting exemplary results after compensating generously.

Obstructions and Opportunities

The strategies in Chapters 6 and 8 will help you identify excellent fundraisers quickly, weed out under-performers before they appear on your payroll, and hire in the most cost-effective manner possible. This practical approach to developing your staff team also includes being realistic about employment trends over which you have little or no control and recognizing opportunity when it presents itself. Salary is that most frustrating barrier to successful negotiations; employment benefits represent an opportunity that is waiting to be recognized.

So, what do you have to pay to land your preferred candidate? There is published information in the Development field that you can use as a guide in estimating fundraising salaries. (The Association of Fundraising Professionals and Charity Village are popular sources of information on salaries.) But, once again, supply/demand inequity may require you to be more flexible. 37% of CEOs we surveyed said that fundraising salaries offered in their organizations are not competitive and that they frequently lose good candidates as a result. Another 43% agreed that the compensation they offered was not a hiring advantage but that they were still usually successful at winning the candidate of their choice. CEOs who said this should be credited for their persuasiveness and for managing a not-for-profit with a great

I was excited to come here because of my not-for-profit's fabulous mission. But, to be honest, the 20 days vacation and the 12% flat retirement contribution after one year were pretty influential, too.

Financial incentives offered to **21%** of respondents:

79% Bonus for reaching a specified goal

8% Bonus to leverage tenure through to the end of a specified timeframe

13% Other bonuses such as allowances, educational assistance, etc.

reputation. But, the reality is that the number one reason why senior fundraisers leave a position prematurely is for better pay elsewhere and this premature loss is far more expensive than paying competitively from the start.

The more senior the position, the more you should expect to compete for talent on the issue of salary. But, rather than focusing on the salary range you have paid before or even what the industry standard might be, it is actually more constructive to consult your own Donor-Centered Fundraising Plan. You may find, for instance, that a single direct marketing officer raises, say, $250,000 a year but a major gifts officer raises eight times that amount. Is your pay scale for major gifts officers substantially higher than that of direct marketing staff? How hard is it to find someone with the skill and experience that a major gifts officer must have in order to close six and seven-figure donations? Be open to paying well for profitable results.

Financial Incentives

Financial incentives over and above salary are not all that common in Development. This may be, in part, because certain incentives such as commission-based compensation are frowned upon by the AFP, which has published an extensive opinion paper on the subject.[1] But, 21% of respondents said that some kind of financial incentive is part of their compensation package, the most usual being a bonus in the form of a percentage salary increase or set dollar amount for reaching or exceeding a goal (79%). 8% of fundraisers who receive financial incentives referenced bonuses designed to leverage their tenure through to the end of a campaign.

Financial incentives do not seem to be particularly effective and perhaps that is why they are less common in fundraising than they are in corporate sector sales. What they are paid is important to fundraisers at the time they are actively seeking and negotiating a new job, or when they are being courted by another organization. However, once salary has been agreed upon, compensation does not continue to be a primary measure of satisfaction on the job.

It was interesting to find that financial incentives meant to influence staff to stay to the end of a capital campaign were particularly ineffective. Though the number of respondents with this experience was small, 72% who were offered this kind of bonus said that it was not a factor in their eventual decision to stay or go. It is common practice to lay off campaign staff after the goal is reached, with the job of pledge collection and ongoing donor communication falling to a much smaller

---

[1] *Professional Compensation...A Position Paper*, Association of Fundraising Professionals, Ethics Committee, Arlington, VA, 2001

team. Campaign fundraisers know they are likely going to lose their job and also when that will happen; they also realize that several or even many fundraisers with similar credentials might enter the job market at the same time if everyone stays to the end of the campaign. Most fundraisers said that choosing to leave was an easy decision when weighing the security of a new full-time position against the temporary enjoyment of an end-of-campaign bonus.

The Subtle Negotiating Advantage of Creative Employment Benefits

I was captivated while being escorted on a tour of the national headquarters of a leading not-for-profit in disaster relief. The building was a combination of ancient and modern architecture, at once bearing witness to the organization's illustrious history while sending an equally powerful message of its modernity. Everywhere, glass met granite and quiet contemplation met bustling technology. It was a marvel.

My colleague who was kind enough to show me around saved the high point of our tour to the end. Its impact was not lost on me. In sharp contrast to the stone-carved frieze that surrounded it like a picture frame, a huge window forced everyone who passed by to pay close attention. Behind it were rows of computer screens, electronic maps and layers of sophisticated equipment. Noticing where my attention was riveted, my tour guide/colleague said, "It's either the storm or the calm before the next one behind that window. We know whether something monumental is unfolding somewhere in the world by what we can see through the glass." She continued: "A siren sounds at the first indication of a disaster, and people pour out of their offices into this command center. They are here for days or even weeks at a time."

I imagined the command center in full swing and blurted out, "There must be a whole system of services that moves swiftly into place to keep staff focused on the job and able to work those long hours. It must be amazing to see it all come alive." "What do you mean?" she asked.

"…Like caterers, dry cleaners, child care – whatever staff need so they don't worry about what's going on or not going on at home while they are here around the clock."

"Oh, good grief," she replied. "We don't have that sort of thing. We're a charity."

Benefits are a Hiring Advantage

The benefits you offer to employees can be a significant advantage, both in securing the candidate you want and in influencing the retention and productivity of the staff you already have.

Experience has taught me to ask this question in interviews: "Does this position include retirement and continuing education benefits and is there flexibility in scheduling work hours?"

Atypical benefits that could inspire staff to stay longer in their current position:

52% Option to work from home
51% Flexible hours
42% Additional vacation time
32% Communication tools
28% Comp/Lieu time

Standard benefits available to
respondents:

98% Paid vacation
95% Paid sick leave
93% Medical insurance
92% Retirement plan
84% Dental insurance
82% Life insurance
72% Disability benefits

*In my job, the benefits make up for
low salary. I get free full healthcare
benefits which are extended to my
family.*

Only **18%** of respondents said
that professional leaves or
sabbaticals are possible in their
organizations.

Topping an unimaginative list of benefits referenced by respondents in our studies was paid vacation time, though American fundraisers were more likely to make this reference than Canadians.[2] Paid sick leave, basic medical insurance and retirement plans were part of a benefits package for over 90% of respondents, though retirement plans did not necessarily include a co-payment by the employer.

Beyond this basic list, few benefits that would be defined as creative or atypical were available to fundraisers who participated in our study. Only 4% of respondents worked a flexible schedule – defined as a work day not confined to a standard 9 to 5 schedule. Only 2% of fundraisers we surveyed enjoyed professional development opportunities paid for by their employers. 3% received a parking allowance and 2% had a company-paid cell phone. Looking at fundraising managers and directors only, the benefits picture is still not much better. 63% received no benefits at all. Only 10% worked in organizations where flex time existed; 8% could access some paid professional development; 5% had a cell phone provided by their employers and 4% had some or all of their professional membership dues paid by the organizations for which they worked.

Time Is Everything

Benefits that are meaningful to employees are those that make it easier for them to maneuver through life -- not life as it was in 1970 but life as it is today. 63% of professional fundraisers we surveyed have responsibility, whether alone or jointly, for financially supporting children or other family members. As I referenced in Chapter 3, the majority of fundraisers are women and women tend to shoulder the lion's share of domestic responsibilities while being paid 76% of the salaries of their male counterparts.[3] At the same time, 93% of our survey respondents said they work unpaid overtime averaging 7.8 hours per week. In other words, fundraisers work six days a week while being paid for five. Time is their number one concern.

In the larger context, anyone attempting to sustain a middle-class existence today, whether working in the not-for-profit or the for-profit sector, is fighting an uphill battle. In 1970, it took 41.5 hours of work per month to maintain middle-class housing (rent or mortgage); by 2000, the labor requirement had risen to 62.4 hours per month.[4] The cost of housing forces more people to live further away from work in order to keep their families in suitable accommodation. That lengthens

---

[2] Anything required by law was less likely to be labelled a benefit by respondents. In Canada, employers must provide a minimum of two weeks of paid vacation to fulltime workers. In the United States, there is no minimum paid vacation required by law.

[3] *2012 Compensation and Benefits Study*, Association of Fundraising Professionals, U.S. and Canada, 2012

[4] From 'Gauging the Pain of the Middle Class', Robert H. Frank, New York Times, April 3, 2011.

commuting time, which, in turn, robs time at home. Workers today return to the office on Monday morning to de-stress from their whirlwind weekend into which they have tried to cram all their domestic and family responsibilities. There is just no time to get everything done.

Not surprising, then, when we asked respondents to identify employment benefits that would be meaningful to them, their opinions were informed by the world in which they live; desirable benefits related to time were at the top of their list. According to fundraisers, these benefits would affect their retention in a positive way and/or influence their decision when considering a new position:

- 52%   the option to work from home as necessary;
- 51%   flexible hours while on the job;
- 42%   vacation time in addition to that provided by law or by practice in the organization;
- 32%   a company-paid cell phone;
- 28%   comp time (lieu time in Canada) for overtime worked.

One could argue that even the cell phone is a benefit prompted by the desire to make the best possible use of time. For those who commute long distances to work, who attend off-hour meetings, donor visits and events or who travel out of town on behalf of their employer, a business cell phone allows fundraisers to use time efficiently while maintaining contact with their families.

Other benefits popular with respondents were:

- 24%   portable computer;
- 23%   professional development;
- 22%   reimbursement of professional membership dues;
- 20%   sabbaticals.

Employee Benefits Work for Employers, Too

Jason Fried, co-founder and President of 37signals, and a popular Ted Talk speaker, has been asking this question of workers for more than ten years: "Where do you go when you really need to get something done?" What they don't answer is, "the office". Employees are much more likely to say they accomplish important work in a room at home, somewhere in the community like at the library or in a coffee shop, or while mobile on a train or plane. And time is a factor, too. Important things tend to get done very early in the morning or late at night or on the weekends – in other

I consider myself to be flexible as an employer. If a staff member needs time off, that's okay as long as the work gets done.

I value flexibility over everything else, especially the ability to leave – guilt free – if an emergency arises with one of my children.

words, outside regular business hours. Fried points out that businesses (and not-for-profits, too) spend a lot of money on offices and they expect their staff to be there, yet that is not where employees tend to get their work done.[5]

Of course, in-office time should be structured to improve this situation, but when two or more people are in the same workplace, interruptions are bound to happen. So, employers who insist that their staff be in the office from nine to five (plus overtime) are settling for sub-standard work outcomes. Flexible work hours and working outside the office should be encouraged by employers as a means of elevating productivity, (see Chapter 12, "Time and Productivity").

There are other arguments for providing benefits identified by respondents in our study that are equally attractive to employers. Like the cell phone, a portable computer means efficiency wherever the employee happens to be working. If employers expect a staff team that is consistently innovative and motivated, professional development is a must. Not-for-profits that choose not to subsidize the cost of professional training, or compromise the education budget whenever the economy weakens, are contributing to the problem.

Reimbursing professional membership dues allows employers to support their fundraising staff in a way that is greatly appreciated but which costs very little. Encouraging membership in at least one professional association by subsidizing dues also makes free or inexpensive training available to staff while hooking them into networking forums that add to their knowledge on a less formal level.

I was pleased to see sabbaticals on the list of fundraisers' most valued benefits. Considered a foreign concept outside academia, sabbaticals – along with professional exchanges – renew the creativity and drive of your most senior fundraisers. The Development profession includes a relatively small number of very experienced and talented leaders. There is little available for them through traditional learning forums, which must cater to more junior practitioners in order to serve a broad cross-section of members and practitioners. But top Development professionals need to be inspired, too, and they need opportunities to recharge.

Lifelong Learning – A Two-Way Benefit

CEOs we surveyed agree that employment benefits are influential in helping secure preferred candidates and extend employee tenure. 71% of CEOs said that subsidizing professional development for their fundraising chiefs is their number

---

[5] *Jason Fried: Why Work Doesn't Happen at Work*, TED, Ted Talks, November, 2010, http://www.ted.com

one advantage among the benefits they offer. This is a very encouraging statistic but I wonder whether these not-for-profit leaders really understood how powerful a tool they had on their hands when they were responding to our survey. In one of the studies we conducted towards the end of the 2007-09 recession, we found that only 19% of managers surveyed said their professional development budgets had remained intact over the period of economic decline; 32% said training subsidies had been eliminated altogether and 40% saw a significant reduction in their budgets. Among those whose allocations for professional development had been eliminated entirely during the recession, only one in three said that budgets were partially or fully restored once fundraising showed dependable improvement.

Professional development is an essential management tool, not an expendable perk because training is as beneficial to management as it is to the staff who experience it. When management reduces or eliminates professional development subsidies or allows their budget to go unspent, they are kicking themselves in the shins.

Professional development achieves the following:

- Preparing staff for more senior responsibilities, especially as they relate to managing other people;

- taking staff out of their day-to-day setting, giving them the opportunity to see their organization, their fundraising operation and their own specific responsibilities more objectively;

- expanding a not-for-profit's sphere of influence through professional networking and, simply, through meeting new people;

- adding to the overall repository of knowledge inside a not-for-profit and, in particular, its Development Office;

- re-energizing staff, contributing to higher productivity and longer tenure;

- solving or alleviating certain management problems by addressing them in a different way.

To illustrate this last point, I had an executive assistant many years ago with exemplary customer relations skills, a meticulous approach to work and a manner that made her an all-around delight to have on staff. But she had a weakness when it came to appreciating her own strengths and weaknesses. She felt she should be on a career path towards management and approached me several times about a promotion. I hesitated, however, because I had not seen signs in her performance that made me think she would be effective in managing other staff. On the other hand, I had to admit that her current job might be preventing her from showcasing a latent talent in that direction. So I assigned her a few projects that would allow me to observe her in this capacity.

Benefits that CEOs feel are most helpful in attracting good candidates:

71% Professional development
67% Generous vacation time
55% Flexible work hours
52% Retirement benefits
49% Medical benefits
42% Work-from-home option

I am a life-long learner and believe that cross-pollination of fundraising ideas is very healthy for professional growth. Without outside training, development staff become jaded and lack creativity.

In my early career, I didn't have sufficient know-how to be choosy about jobs. But now, my life is different. My husband has a comfortable income so I am drawn to jobs that perhaps don't pay so well but have opportunities for professional advancement.

She did not perform well. Over time I tried to discourage her ambitions towards management, emphasizing how well she produced when working on her own. She was undeterred, however, and growing increasingly dissatisfied with the job that she did so well.

Our professional development program included a budget allocation for each member of the staff, and 30% could be spent at the staff member's sole discretion. The only stipulation I placed on that 30% was that staff had to prepare and present a summary of what they learned to the rest of the group upon their return to the office. One day, my executive assistant informed me that she would be taking a two-day course for managers, led by a prominent university in our city. I looked at the course prospectus and felt it was an ambitious choice, but she seemed very determined, so I wished her the best.

She returned from the course with an entirely different demeanor. At the staff meeting a few days later she summarized what the course had featured – a case study approach to some very complex staff management scenarios. Then she said, "I spent two days immersed in the issues that preoccupy people in management positions. By the end of the first day I knew that a manager is not just a person whose hard work has been rewarded with a better title, a bigger salary and a larger office. By the end of the second day, I knew that I was nowhere near ready to assume a management role…and I'm beginning to wonder if that's what I even want. I guess I have some thinking to do."

My EA learned something in two days that she would likely have never accepted from me. This experience, difficult as it was, became a catalyst to a self-assessment in which she appreciated, perhaps for the first time, the unique talent she had and the extraordinary value she brought to the company. What she did may not have been wrapped in a management title, but it was no less essential to our success.

What Needs to Be Learned

Giving staff control over part of their professional development allocation is a smart strategy. This is especially so in fundraising where there is no such thing as useless knowledge. If a fundraiser uses her personal training budget to learn how to make stained glass, you can bet that she will soon open a door with a donor because of this new-found knowledge. She is also very likely to develop prospects she would have never reached had she not connected into a whole new social circle. Professional development that is focused on mastering the technicalities of fundraising is worthwhile, but it cannot do the job of developing a well-rounded senior practitioner.

There is an aspect of professional development that must be orchestrated by the most senior Development staff and which should command the lion's share of any professional development budget. It is management and leadership training. Most staff see themselves on a career trajectory towards management. They may imagine management to be the mastery of systems, policies and programs, but it is not. Management can only be practiced, not perfected, because it is almost entirely about guiding, training and assessing the performance of people. Those who commit to managing other people well take on a career-long commitment to learning and improving their technique.

It is disheartening then, that over 50% of managers we surveyed said they had no training whatsoever in the management of people prior to becoming a boss for the first time. Only 19% worked in an organization where management training was recognized as a valuable asset and where employees with leadership potential were guided through a progressive management training program.

Training at the Top

When it comes to the fundraising industry's most senior practitioners, training may not be the best word to describe the professional development needs of this invaluable collective human resource. But that does not mean that fundraisers with twenty or thirty years of experience in management do not need – or want – good training experiences. The problem is the scarcity of programs or forums geared to their level of seniority and the specialized nature of their work. 30% of all Directors of Development we surveyed said they were unable to find any suitable training opportunities.

Tailor-Made Benefits

There are no rules about what can and cannot be offered to fundraisers as employee benefits; there is only commonplace practice which has served merely to narrow people's thinking. Excellent benefits are practical while reflecting who you are, what you do and how you do it. Your organization or your fundraising operation might function very differently from the norm, and this may impact your expectations of fundraisers at certain times. As the earlier story illustrated, large-scale relief agencies receive a huge influx of gifts when a disaster strikes and for the period that follows, in which the disaster and need for funds is experiencing intense media attention. If fundraisers need to work round the clock at these times, employers have a wonderful opportunity to look after their people well. Managers of fundraising operations that are dramatically cyclical, demanding extraordinary hours at certain times, could poll staff about the problems that were created in their

---

Management training received by fundraisers before managing staff for the first time:

50% None
19% Internal training
17% External courses

Positive impact of training programs on staff retention:

41% Skills development
23% Shows staff they are valued
22% Networking / benchmarking opportunities
17% Staff appreciate employer who provides training
14% Creates enthusiasm among staff

There are so many good fundraising jobs that I can afford to have strict rules about the jobs I apply for. My #1 – I won't commute more than 30 minutes.

personal lives during the last such intense work period. From that information, a basket of relevant benefits could be developed that staff can access during the next such demanding period. Watch what that does for employee morale and how it plays a positive role in staff retention.

Neither your organization nor the demands placed on your fundraising staff need to be extraordinary, though, to warrant made-to-measure benefits. Ask staff to describe a typical Saturday and you will be treated to a litany of tasks that makes any workday to-do list pale by comparison. How can innovative benefits reduce that Saturday whirlwind so your staff can truly enjoy their time away from the office?

A frustrating and stress-inducing conflict between work and home obligations involves appointments for professional services. When the furnace dies, the plumbing heaves or the washer repairman says he'll be there "sometime between 8 and 6", your employee is distracted and it costs you in lost productivity. Consider assembling a team of bonded professionals available to provide services to your employees. They pick up the key at the office and get the job done while staff are focusing their time where it belongs – on the job. You may be able to negotiate a good deal on professional rates if your staff contingent is large enough. Benefits like this cost your not-for-profit nothing while sending a strong, positive message about how much you care.

To jumpstart your creative thinking, here are some atypical benefits available to staff in several corporations and associations. What matters is what you and your staff would find appealing, but something on this list might resonate or spark a better idea:

- *McGraw Wentworth*, a provider of group benefits, offers on-site pickup and return of clothes that need laundering;
- *Cooper Pest Solutions'* service technicians and salespeople can use company vehicles for commuting to and from work;
- *Dealer.com*, which helps auto dealers with their online marketing, serves locally grown organic treats in its on-site café. Employees can have their subsidized meals delivered to their desks if they are on deadline;
- *Akraya*, an IT staffing company, sends professional cleaners to employees' homes every two weeks;
- *Patagonia*, the outdoor-apparel maker, grants employees two weeks of fully paid leave to work for the green nonprofit of their choice. (How about not-for-profits considering the reverse, where fundraisers spend two weeks

of every year in the sales or marketing departments of corporations they admire?)

- *Buttoned Up Inc.*, an organizational company based in Ann Arbor, Michigan, offers its small staff (seven employees) flexible work schedules designed to cater to each employee's family/life circumstances. Among other things, options include working from home one day a week or working longer hours over two or three days instead of the traditional five-day, nine-to-five schedule;

- *Creative Business Resources*, a Phoenix-based HR outsourcing firm, instituted an employee volunteer program that offers participating staff additional paid time off to do volunteer work on their own time, up to a certain limit;

- *iAnywhere Solutions*, a wireless and mobile software provider in Waterloo, Ontario, permits employees to work from home and covers the cost of their internet connections. Reasons for working from home vary from needing a day without distraction to taking care of children due to school closure, illness and the like;

- *Beloit Memorial Hospital* in Wisconsin offers a "recuperation station" where employees can bring their sick children to be looked after at no cost during business hours;

- *Scottrade*, an online trading and investing firm, will consider opening an office for an employee who wants to relocate to an area where a branch does not currently exist. The company has already done this for more than twenty employees;

- *ePrize* is a Detroit-based company sourcing interactive prizes for its clients' promotions and loyalty programs. With offices situated near the Detroit Zoo, ePrize provides employees with Zoo memberships and guest passes. Appreciated by ePrize staff, the gesture also helped the Detroit Zoo keep attendance viable during the height of the recession, reminding donors and sponsors that the community still needed its Zoo;

- *Arrow Strategies*, a recruiting firm in Michigan, offers employees a free concierge service. The concierge does everything from picking up items at the store to letting out the dog. They also have an on-site dentist for routine procedures so employees don't have to schedule most dental visits on their own time;

- *Google*, no explanation required, offers….onsite bicycle repairs, onsite haircuts (hopefully, not from the same person), masseurs, a de-stress room where employees sit in massage chairs while gazing into huge aquariums, personal trainers, nutritionists…and the list goes on.

I would love to think that it's our case or my management style that attracts good fundraisers. But I think it's our benefits package which is outstanding. Oh, well, whatever brings them to my door!

Allow staff to "own" their positions and encourage them to think out-of-the-box. It's not a luxury; it's a necessity.

The main priority for me is having a flexible work schedule. With a husband who works all hours, I am the primary caregiver to our children.

From the Ground Up

Encourage everyone to take part in creating your benefits program, and be sure to include the views of staff who are single or have no children. These employees work a disproportionate amount of overtime because they cannot fall back on the ultimate excuse, "I have to pick up my kids from daycare by 5:30." The carefree, fun-filled life of the single employee is a myth if he is always in the office.

Developing your tailor-made benefits program is a great project that you can assign to a staff member seeking new responsibilities or an employee targeted for management training. Among other things, the skills required to execute a project of this nature include:

- gathering input from staff with diverse life experiences and needs;
- researching how other companies or not-for-profits have used creative benefits to solve problems;
- analyzing how investing in tailor-made benefits will enhance productivity and results;
- budgeting the program;
- creating an internal marketing strategy for the benefits program that achieves the organization's goal of furthering its image among employees.

Once developed, your benefits program should not remain static; rather, it should expand and adjust to reflect changing times and staff priorities. Most benefits will not cost employers anything other than the time required to consider them and make them accessible. But having a policy that welcomes innovative solutions to work/life challenges, and then bringing that policy alive, showcases your organization's creativity and, especially, how much you care for your staff. Your benefits program makes you look good while reminding staff why they love working for your organization. This, in turn, impacts the tenure of existing staff while also being a hiring advantage. Giving visitors to your Career Landing Page a taste of your unusual and creative employment benefits will lead to more good fundraisers applying for posted positions. And, if it comes down to this, an enticing benefits program offers your preferred candidate yet another reason to choose your excellent career opportunity over your competitor's job.

Put a Price on Your Deficiencies

Ask yourself this question: "Are there issues that appear and reappear which cause staff to leave or which contribute to losing our preferred candidate to someone else at the last minute?" If the answer is "yes", then dealing with them is more sensible than hoping the next candidate will see it your way. Exit interviews with departing employees (referenced in Chapter 13) are a boon and, if questions are standardized, will reveal common issues over time that you can work to change or eliminate. And take the time to hold meaningful discussions with candidates who decline your job offer. At the moment you are reeling from the realization that you are back at square one, it is hard to be objective. But, this is exactly when you need to find the professional distance required to hold this conversation.

Most important, if you put your losses in financial terms, you will be more motivated to take action. The calculations in Chapter 3 will remind you what it costs to hire a fundraiser or to lose one prematurely. This should put you in the right frame of mind to solve the problem.

> If you hire for results and not for time spent sitting in the office, both you and your employee will be winners. If your employee is able to reach your ambitious goals while working a flexible schedule, both in time and location, then brilliant you for hiring such a top performer and advocating a work environment that maximizes productivity. She is happy; she intends to stay; you are getting exemplary results – nirvana.

It makes me crazy that we spend more money on keeping our copy machine working than we do on keeping our staff happy.

Chapter 8:

How to Select the Best Candidate

I had applied for a fundraising position with an advocacy group for women. After an initial interview with a hiring committee consisting of two staff members and the Chair of Fundraising, I was short-listed as one of the finalists. At my second interview with the CEO and Board, I had the distinct impression that I was the favored candidate. I could tell from the body language that I was answering questions to the Board's satisfaction. Members were smiling and sitting forward in their chairs, fully engaged in the conversation – always a good sign.

As the meeting progressed, questions investigating my fundraising knowledge and management style gave way to inquiries of a more philosophical nature. What was my view concerning pay equity? What contributes to the glass ceiling for women in the workplace? And then, "Are you a feminist?"

I paused. "It depends on your definition", I replied, and waited for someone to clarify. Instead of receiving an explanation, I felt the room get a couple of degrees colder. "Either you're a feminist or you're not", said the Executive Director, with just the barest hint of irritation in her voice. "And, if you're applying for a key position in an organization that advocates for women, you should know."

"I'm even more eager to hear your definition, then", I replied. A few of the board members around the table shot glances at each other. The Executive Director stared at me as if to say, "I supported your candidacy and now you are letting me down." The Chair started tapping the tip of her pencil on the board table. I could feel the job slipping away. "If you're not going to answer, then I guess that concludes the interview", said the Executive Director.

I left feeling awkward and a little embarrassed, but also thankful for the accidental insight into how this organization makes decisions and how it deals with staff members who ask questions.

The most rewarding thing about doing research with senior Development professionals is the treasure trove of wisdom that weaves its way through every study we conduct. In our research on staff turnover, the advice from management-level respondents regarding interviewing candidates was particularly valuable. I have included it here, along with some of my own experiences and observations from those on the other side of the table – the candidates themselves.

Revisiting Candidates' Applications

Before conducting interviews, it is wise to verify the facts stated in your "A list" candidates' resumes. It may save valuable time later and, possibly, avert a disaster. This does not mean confirming the accuracy of claims of success in previous positions; both the interview(s) and reference-checking will accomplish that. Facts that should be verified in advance include academic institutions attended, degrees attained, certifications earned, and scholarships, grants or awards won. Eliminate, without hesitation, anyone found to have falsified any of these credentials. It speaks volumes about the ethical and practical issues you are bound to face if you proceed with the hire.

High levels of involvement with professional associations can sometimes be a warning sign, especially if this is combined with frequent position changes. Over-involvement is the issue here, not contributing to the work of an association per se. Volunteering for the AFP, AHP or any other professional fundraising association is a very good thing but, unless you deduct that time from your fundraiser's salary, you are paying for that volunteer work. Ask directly about the number of business hours per month that are consumed by this activity, and then check this out specifically with references.

Be careful about hiring on the basis of family, alumni or Board connections. While it may mean valuable networking possibilities, it can also place you in a compromised position as the employer.

You may also wish to revisit the short check-list in Chapter 6 to make sure you have correctly categorized the candidates who are now on your A list and about to be interviewed.

Is Your Candidate Interesting?

Adopting a donor-centered approach means advocating internal promotions as your primary hiring policy. So, even when you are filling a junior position, you should be assessing candidates for their future potential. This means exploring whether they have certain skills and life experiences that make them attractive prospects for more senior roles, especially those that build relationships with donors. This is where the most lucrative fundraising happens, making major/planned gifts officers a uniquely valuable resource.

In order to build successful relationships, Development professionals must attract donors' attention – in writing, over the phone and especially in person. To do that, fundraisers must be interesting enough for donors to want to interact with them. What makes fundraisers interesting are the same things that make anyone interesting – their hobbies, the people they know, the places they've been and the things they have learned. Of course, they must also be active, engaged listeners, but a stimulating conversation is one in which the donor *and* the fundraiser are fully participating, sharing with and learning from each other.

The only subject that fundraisers do not tend to talk about with donors is fundraising, particularly its technicalities, yet job interviews tend to be focused on just that. So altering how you conduct in-person interviews will help you gain valuable insights about the other side of your candidate – the personal, qualitative side which, in the end, will be what matters most when a significant ask is in the making. Here are some suggestions:

> *Setting:* Consider where you hold interviews. A general purpose, windowless office or boardroom with bare walls is a barren and unforgiving space. There is nothing for your candidate to notice and remark upon. But a room that looks inviting and lived in replicates a fundraiser/donor setting to some degree, and gives you a chance to assess the candidate's observation skills and ability to converse off-the-cuff. Hold interviews in offices that are alive – art on the walls, pictures on the desk, interesting furnishings and perhaps a view.

> *Mannerism:* Greet the candidate as you would a donor. If the interviewer or interview panel is sitting behind a desk or table as the candidate enters, it feels more like an inquisition than an interview. Stand up and come out from behind the desk; shake hands; engage in small talk. "Small talk" is a misnomer; this critical banter sets the tone in any meeting or interview and communicates volumes to each person in the room. Small talk has big implications.

> *Information Sharing Before Interviewing:* Consider a two-part interview. Job interviews are already such anxiety-ridden experiences for candidates that I prefer to set a climate that lessens rather than magnifies their nervousness. My objective in an interview is not to test my candidate's ability to withstand stress; checking references will give me all the information I need on that front. Over time I have come to prefer a two-pronged approach to interviewing that establishes as comfortable an atmosphere as possible. I meet with the candidate initially to talk about our company's goals, how we conduct research with donors, the history behind the concept of "Donor-Centered Fundraising" for which I and my firm have become well known, etc. Before long, the candidate forgets

Fundraising is such a people-focused and relationship-focused profession that it lends itself well to those with transferable skills. Public relations, marketing, writing and editing, financial and legal knowledge, volunteering – all are skills that make someone a preferred candidate for a good job in Development.

Be open-minded when considering candidates. Don't look for the same things one candidate to the next.

he is in an interview and becomes fully engaged in the conversation. He asks questions, makes observations, draws conclusions and shows me a critical side of himself that would not otherwise be revealed so soon. Now, in a relaxed atmosphere where his attention is refocused on the work our firm is trying to achieve, I get a better picture of what inspires his enthusiasm, how he processes information, and what he would be like on the job. Assuming I am feeling positive about the candidate, I then shift the interview to questions that explore his credentials and experience, which he can now contextualize within a deeper understanding of our company. (Sometimes I defer this discussion to a second meeting, giving him time to think about what he has learned and use it to position his skills accordingly.) I find that exceptional candidates shine and less capable ones are exposed through this approach. Candidates who do not ask questions or engage in the conversation, or who have trouble holding a conversation with someone in a position of authority, are not suitable for my business – or for yours, I would expect.

Here is a valuable question to ask of candidates after they have had a chance to learn more about your organization and the job: "*What do you think it will take for you to be successful in this position?*" This important, big-picture question demands that candidates examine their own abilities and experience in the context of your not-for-profit and what you are trying to achieve. If you respond to the answer with the question, "*Tell me about a previous position/situation where you displayed those qualities*", you will have learned much about your candidate before getting down to specific interview questions that explore credentials and experience. This may be as far as you need to go with some candidates; with others, these two questions will be the start of a fascinating search experience.

Focus on the Person: Explore candidates' personal interests and non-fundraising accomplishments before you get into the fundraising questions, rather than bringing them up as an afterthought at the end of a tough interview. This could include their academic and extra-curricular areas of study, where they have travelled, their hobbies and special interests. What they say and how they engage in this conversation can be very telling. For instance, working out or being into fitness is not much of a conversation starter; but, being a long-distance runner who has competed in the Boston Marathon – well, that's fascinating.

First Impressions

Not only a first, but a lasting impression is created within the first thirty seconds. How you feel as you greet the candidate and for those first few moments afterwards is important, so make sure you document your impression before moving onto the prepared interview questions. How did the candidate contribute to establishing a positive tone? What did she notice and comment on? Other valuable first impressions are formed by the receptionist and/or your EA who first see the candidate or talk to her on the phone, so be sure to include their views as part of your assessment.

Experienced interviewers point out that candidates are motivated to show you their best when applying for jobs and this includes dress, demeanor, level of engagement and preparation, among other things. If you are hesitant about any of these things, which are fundamentally important in an industry that depends on building relationships, remember – this is the best it is going to be.

Has the Candidate Prepared for the Interview?

A candidate who seems to have made little effort to check you out before you check him out is not a serious contender for an important Development position. Prospect research is essential in fundraising, including when the prospect is the potential employer. How a candidate responds to questions you ask and what he asks you in return will tell you whether he has done his homework. Questions like these get to the heart of the matter:

- *How do you differentiate our case from that of other not-for-profits working in animal welfare?*

- *How do you assess our social media presence at this time, and where do you see opportunities for improvement?*

- *What caught your attention about our website?*

How to Phrase Interview Questions

Many management-level fundraisers suggested that interviewers should avoid using theoretical or conditional language when asking questions. For example, do not ask a candidate, "How would you begin a conversation with a donor in her home if this is the first time you have met?" Instead, say, "Think about the most recent time you met a donor for the first time where the meeting took place in her home. How did you begin the conversation?" Positioning the question in the past tense gives you so much more information. You will know, for a fact, whether the candidate has

Fundraising is very difficult, so good candidates wear their successes like a diplomatic sash. If a candidate plays down his accomplishments, it isn't humility.

Take a wider view. Don't make hiring decisions based on just what they did in their last job or two. Look at the whole person for their fit within your existing team. Often, specific skills that may be deficient can be taught. Fit is an intangible that is either there or not there.

had this experience. If he has, you will gain insight into his skill in this important aspect of donor cultivation.

There is no doubt that successful fundraising requires the efforts of professional staff, leadership volunteers, the CEO and sometimes other staff. But, when conducting interviews, it is important to determine the degree to which your candidate has contributed to the success she is referencing. Several management-level fundraisers who took part in our research recommended asking a question like this: "*Who made the ask for the most generous gift secured in the last year where you work now (worked previously)? Was it you and, if not, how did you support the solicitor who asked for the gift?*"

What to Listen For

Take note of candidates who tend to use the word "we" rather than "I" when responding to questions, especially those concerning meeting performance targets. Sometimes candidates deflect attention from their own under-performance or secondary role by claiming the success of the group.

Beware of candidates who over-promise, suggesting an ability to raise unrealistic sums of money quickly. You did not get to where you are by living and working in a vacuum. There is no magic bullet out there that you have not discovered; nor is there a new fundraising revelation that you missed hearing about. Do not fall for an over-the-top pitch. On the other hand, take seriously candidates who are thoughtful about fundraising goals and timeframes and who ask questions about the criteria used to set those targets. Give credit to candidates who are upfront enough to ask other probing questions such as, "What role do the CEO and Board play in fundraising?" "Is there a time-limited strategic plan with measurable benchmarks for growth?" "What is your organization's position concerning restricted versus unrestricted gifts?" And, of course, be prepared to answer them.

Blaming others for the candidate's own under-performance is a red flag, especially if the candidate is referring to a job in which she managed other staff. Under-performance by reports is actually a failure of management; failure to set achievable goals; failure to supervise effectively; failure to take responsibility. In the case of a candidate who was not previously in a management role but is casting blame elsewhere for his performance shortcomings, this is what you can expect will go on behind your back if you hire this individual. On the other hand, take seriously candidates who take responsibility; who can admit failure but are also able to tell you what they did to overcome it. People who have never experienced failure are either too green for your challenging fundraising environment or they are deceiving themselves.

Weeding Out Chronic Under-Performers

Grant, who has a fifteen-year history in a variety of non-management fundraising positions with nine not-for-profits, was hired by an arts organization to raise money from subscribers and members. Though slow to find his footing in his new position, at the end of his third month on the job he was performing well enough to pass his probation and be placed on permanent staff. But, by the end of Year 1 he had reached only 60% of his goal. During this period, he was absent from work for personal reasons twice as often as other staff. As well, two of his colleagues quietly made it known to the Manager that they had been compensating for Grant's absences and lack of focus on the job by picking up the slack. Grant was dismissed at the end of his first year. In order to get him out the door quickly and with as little fuss as possible, he was paid double the required severance.

Management-level respondents in our studies were encouraged to tell us about the problems they experience when hiring and how our research might serve them most effectively. The issue they referenced most often was identifying and weeding out chronic under-performers during the hiring process. These troublesome candidates are particularly adept at selling themselves but far less capable once on the job. While chronic under-performers are definitely the minority among Development professionals, they can wreak havoc inside a not-for-profit and monopolize managers' time and attention.

We turned to Development Directors and Managers for examples of questions they use in interviews to address this difficult problem. Happily, we got more than we asked for. It turned out that the same interview questions serve both to expose chronic under-performers *and* showcase fundraisers who excel. The hard-earned wisdom of senior practitioners is evident in how they articulated their key interview questions. What they ask, and how they ask it, compels candidates to be specific and prevents them from claiming their department's or their colleagues' accomplishments as their own personal achievements.

Effective interview questions get the job done, regardless of who is being interviewed. The only requirement of employers is that they resist allowing secondary issues, such as their urgent need to accomplish the hire, to prevent them from hearing what is actually being said.

Regrettably, I've known many people in fundraising who were hired because they were really friendly and the Board and CEO were swayed by their upbeat demeanor. Cut through the veneer and demand accountability.

Interview Questions Recommended by Survey Respondents

Candidates' Breadth and Depth of Experience

Please share an example of a campaign that you personally conducted, from inception through feasibility study through completion. This question will reveal information about the candidate's strategic abilities, staff management skills, tenacity and orientation towards the goal.

Describe the approach you used in your last position to turn annual fund donors into major donors. Questions like this one definitely separate the linear from the big-picture thinkers in fundraising. This particular example speaks to the core challenge of fundraising: stewarding donors' generosity to a level that even they may not have contemplated, and doing so amidst fierce competition from other not-for-profits. How the question is articulated forces the candidate to stick to the facts and not veer off into a theoretical response.

What is the largest gift amount that you have ever personally requested from a donor? This clarifies whether your candidate's experience is within the range expected of fundraisers in your not-for-profit.

How many gifts did you secure last year from individual donors in the following gift ranges: over $10,000; over $25,000; over $100,000; over $1 million. Not only does this very specific question tell you more about the candidate's ability to secure gifts of extraordinary value, but it reveals whether she can keep several balls in the air simultaneously.

Similar to the previous question, but focused on another area of fundraising: *How many grant applications did you write that were successfully funded last year?* Phrased this way, the question focuses on the candidate's output in quantifiable terms. Similar questions can be articulated for securing gifts from corporations or negotiating corporate sponsorships, though the latter are business relationships whose success requires a sound knowledge of marketing.

Meeting Fundraising Goals: Attitude and Achievements

In the last year in your current/last position, what was/were your fundraising goals? Please describe your performance against those goals. What were your end results? Non-monetary goals are legitimate, but monetary ones must be included, as this is fundraising.

In your current/last position, what is/was your goal for the number of contacts to be made with donors in a typical month? How often did you meet or exceed that goal? It is not necessarily true that the more contacts a fundraiser makes in a month, the more money he will raise. So how your candidate responds to this question will give you insight into how she prioritizes her work in order to maximize results.

Have you worked within a metrics-based, bottom-line performance shop before and, if so, how did you respond to having your performance evaluated in this way? All employees, regardless of their positions, should work to specific bottom-line goals, but in fundraising the numbers (dollars) are easy to measure. Some fundraisers are motivated to get up in the morning by these very tangible targets; others have difficulty coping in this bottom-line environment.

How, specifically, has fundraised revenue increased under your direction? This is a pretty basic question, but you might be surprised at how many employers do not think to ask it.

Describe a situation in which you delivered beyond expectation in your current/most recent job. This could mean beyond the employer's or the candidate's expectation, and either interpretation will produce interesting information.

What techniques have you deployed successfully to secure visits with reluctant prospects and donors? Once they have their donors' attention, fundraisers are very good at selling their case and stewarding donors along the ask spectrum towards "yes". But, getting in the door is the toughest part of the job so be sure to cover this issue when you interview candidates who are responsible for closing major gifts and corporate sponsorships.

Think about the largest gift you personally secured in the last two years. Please walk us through the steps you went through from identifying the prospect to closing the gift. The answer to this question reveals the candidate's understanding of donor psychology, his skill in crafting a proposal that inspires the donor to give, and his ability to manage the complexity of relationship fundraising. It will also reassure employers about the depth of knowledge and range of experience of the candidate.

Assuming the candidate does not freely offer this in his answer to the previous question, this is an important supplementary question: *what were the barriers or difficulties you had to overcome to bring that ask to a successful conclusion?* Fundraisers who close gifts at or above the targeted level with each of their prospects and do so effortlessly are extraordinary. I have never met one, however. Your candidate's

Look for indicators of strength and commitment, such as external volunteer experience and/or college courses. Make sure that your candidate is not just looking to make more money.

answer to this question will demonstrate his resilience in the face of adversity and his ability to learn from mistakes.

What has been your proudest fundraising achievement in the last five years of your career? If the answer does not reference a goal reached, a gift secured, or a donor relationship saved or moved to the next level, probe for this specifically. Positive sentiments about working with an excellent staff team are laudable, but great fundraisers' pride of accomplishment comes from bringing in the money.

Overcoming Failure and Disappointment

Describe your least successful campaign or ask for which you were responsible. What have you learned from that disappointment and how have you put what you learned into action? Your candidate's response will allow you to assess her maturity (no one does it right all the time), her ability to analyze and solve problems and, especially, how she learns from mistakes and changes her approach to minimize the possibility of repeating them. Defensiveness and/or blaming co-workers or volunteers are warning signals.

What problems did you encounter in meeting your fundraising goal in your last position, and what steps did you implement to make sure it was attained? This is an excellent way to phrase a question that explores the candidate's ability to solve problems and recover from setbacks. It is particularly useful if he claimed that he has never had a failure in response to the previous question.

Why the Candidate Is Applying for Your Job

What is it that caught your attention about this job and inspired you to apply? While your candidate's letter that accompanied his resume may have satisfied you on this question, it doesn't hurt to ask it outright. The answer will tell you whether this is someone who is applying for every fundraising job that is posted or whether he is making strategic choices based on honest self-awareness. This is also one of those questions that should be a delight to answer and perhaps a momentary relief amidst other more demanding queries.

Why did you leave your last job?/Why do you want to leave your current job? You should feel reassured if your candidate is seeking a new job because she accomplished all that she could where she is now (or in the position she most recently held). But, be sure to explore why she feels there are no other meaningful opportunities for career development where she currently works. You should be trying to hire staff who will be assets well beyond the job currently available, especially if you adopt a policy that prioritizes internal promotion.

Any reasons for leaving her last job other than lack of opportunity to build her career should be fully explored with your candidate. While there may be a lot of truth in statements like, "I left because the Board consistently failed to fulfill their responsibilities in fundraising", you should focus on the role your candidate played in the Board's failure to produce. Ask her to assess her own skills and results in managing up, and then, if she becomes one of the finalists, be sure to explore this same issue with her referees.

Motivation and Innovation

What re-energizes you and keeps you moving forward when things are not going well at the office? Does the candidate have a life and/or interests outside work from which he can draw inspiration and which motivate him to keep going? However he answers this question will be revealing about your candidate's coping skills and how he solves problems.

What is your favorite part of the job? This question gives the candidate a break from more grueling interview questions while allowing you to find out what makes her heart soar. But, if her answer is not integral to closing a gift or reaching a goal, be cautious.

What can you bring to the job that is new? There is a world of wisdom from experience in the fundraising industry concerning what works and what should be avoided. But, there is still room for innovation, especially in donor communication and in moving donors more quickly into major and planned gifts. By exploring your candidate's innovative side you are letting her know that you welcome – and expect – new ideas. This says a lot about how you manage staff and the atmosphere of free-thinking that you are fostering in your Development operation.

Describe a situation in which you offered a time-saving idea to the team. "Not having enough time" is fundraisers' number one complaint, so it is very impressive when a candidate can identify time-saving strategies.

The real value in a candidate's responses to the previous two questions is in how he answers this one: *tell us about a situation in which you challenged conventional practice in order to accomplish something important.* Good ideas are only useful if adopted, so explore with the candidate how he stewarded his idea from conception to implementation.

Career decisions for me come down to the person I work for. Is my potential new boss ethical? Is he a kind and decent person? I check this out behind the scenes and never move if there is any doubt.

Critical Questions for Management-Level Candidates

Most of the above questions apply equally to management-level fundraisers and those on the front lines. However, additional questions for candidates applying for supervisory positions are necessary to satisfy employers on issues concerned with strategic direction and the management of people.

On Strategic Thinking and Direction

Describe how you would spend your first ninety days on the job if you were offered the position. New managers enjoy a honeymoon period during the first few months. During this period, they are given leeway for their lack of familiarity with the organization and their views carry additional weight (much like those of a consultant). This is an opportunity not to be squandered, so how candidates applying for management-level positions answer this question will be very revealing.

Describe how you created your most recent fundraising plan and the process it and you underwent to have it approved. This question is suitable for candidates for manager of a specific fundraising program or department or for the Director of Development. How candidates answer it tells you whether they deploy a top-down or a collaborative style when managing staff. Probe for the role that reports played in developing the fundraising plan and how the candidate encouraged and stewarded their input. This question also opens the door to an exploration of whether the candidate sees fundraising programs and the people who run them as independent silos or as part of a genuinely integrated system designed to move donors seamlessly up the generosity ladder. The latter approach is more successful but it puts greater demands on managers, especially Development Directors, to supervise more creatively in order to change long-held views about how money should be raised.

On the Management of Staff

Describe a recent management experience in which you mentored a member of your fundraising team, guiding him or her from under-performance to success. Questions like this one speak to the candidate's character as well as to her talent for managing for optimum results.

The previous question invites this interesting follow-up query: *What was it about this staff member that made you feel your investment of time and effort would be worthwhile?*

What is the most difficult staff management issue you have faced in the last five years of your career? Please include in your answer why you chose this particular example and how you worked through the problem.

A practical and revealing follow up to the previous question is: *Looking back on this situation now, what would you have done differently?* If the answer is "nothing", be cautious. Top managers are always questioning their abilities and decisions concerning staff management, not because they are overly critical of themselves but because looking for ways to improve their performance in the future is all part of the job. More than anything else in business, when it comes to the management of people, one can strive for perfection but never fully attain it.

Describe a recent experience in which you orchestrated the resolution of a conflict. What was the nature of the conflict, who was involved and what was the outcome? [supplementary] *If you had the same issue to deal with again, would you handle it differently and why?* This supplementary question gets to the heart of the matter in management – not that managers are managers because they do everything right, but that good managers are successful because they analyze their own performance and willingly learn from their mistakes.

Describe how you handled a significant issue around workload management with someone who reported directly to you. Fundraising success is related to time invested, so making sure staff use their time productively should be a constant preoccupation of fundraising managers.

Regarding your own workload, describe how you handled managing your own portfolio plus your reports' multiple projects. What do you feel you managed well?; what do you feel you did not manage as well as you would have liked; and what did you learn?

On Interacting with Leadership Volunteers and the CEO

Describe a recent fundraising situation in which the Board and you/your staff team had significantly different views. What was the outcome and how would you analyze the role you played in "managing up". How an organization handles the big issues in fundraising such as restricted versus unrestricted gifts, or short-term revenue versus long-term profit determine whether it will prosper or merely survive. While the Board and CEO make the final decision on policy matters, professional fundraisers are instrumental in bringing reliable data and a sound argument to their employers. What they present and how they do it says a lot about their ability and how they are respected by decision-makers. (By the way, if the candidate does not understand what it means to "manage up", she has probably not had to deal directly with leadership volunteers or the CEO.)

I took training in analyzing different work styles. It helped me adapt my own style to meet the needs of a diverse staff who learn in different ways. I am a much better manager today as a result.

I've learned the hard way to always ask in interviews about the involvement of the CEO and the Board in fundraising.

Tell me about a situation in which you worked effectively with a volunteer fundraising group to achieve a goal that you felt would be difficult to attain. Motivating Board members to use their influence while co-operating with the agreed approach to an ask requires particular skill and maturity. The very best fundraisers are able to inspire their volunteers to deliver when needed and in a way that works best for the whole team.

Fundraising Metrics

Several research study respondents suggested that candidates who are applying for positions that include budget-setting responsibilities should be asked questions such as these: *when forecasting fundraising revenue, what do you take into consideration? Or, what metrics were used to measure success in your most recent position?*

I agree that these are important questions, but they are much more useful as a means of rating candidates if they are connected directly to your Donor-Centered Fundraising Plan.

Interviewing Short-Listed Candidates in the Context of Donor-Centered Fundraising

Chapter 5 described how a Donor-Centered Fundraising Plan focuses budget and talent on retaining donors longer and increasing average gift values sooner. This is becoming increasingly important as more donors concentrate their support among fewer charities and demand measurable results as the prerequisite of their longer loyalty and greater generosity.

A Development operation that is donor-centered works from revenue forecasts that are based on the analysis of the department's own donors and their giving patterns. And it relies on staff to bring their creative ideas to the table in order to capture and sustain the attention of the giving public. So, it is wise to investigate candidates' ability to interpret data and conceive innovative solutions during the interview process. Any fundraiser can learn to think and work in a donor-centered way, but candidates who already display that kind of approach to decision-making are an advantage from their first day on the job.

The best way to handle an interview focused on donor-centered fundraising is to separate it from other issues that are important to cover. Ideally, a first interview with "A list" candidates identifies a shorter list of finalists by exploring qualifications, experience and compatibility. Even if only one candidate remains at this point, a second donor-centered interview is still important because it answers the employer's single most crucial question: "How will this candidate help move our entire Development operation forward towards the goal?"

Give your finalists your one- or two-page Donor-Centered Plan and some time to think about its implications before the next interview. If you are reticent about revealing proprietary financial and other information, then create a table like this one, brought forward from Chapter 5, which illustrates the issues that you have prioritized, but substitutes artificial numbers.

Table 13: A Donor-Centered Alternative to a Typical Fundraising Plan (from Chapter 5)

Campaign	Volume of Donors		Net Retention		Average Gift Value		%/Volume of Donors to Major Gifts Officers		Total Revenue in Direct Marketing		Revenue from Major Gift Donors	
	Typical	DCF	Typical	DCF	Typical	DCF	Typical	DCF	Typical	DCF	Typical	DCF
Acq.	2000	1000	n/a	n/a	$50	$50	0% / 0	1.0% / 10	100,000	$50,000	n/a	10,000
1st year	700	450	35%	45%	$65	$80	0.5% / 4	3.0% / 14	45,240	34,880	4,000	17,500
2nd year	400	350	20%	35%	$85	$110	1.0% / 4	4.5% / 16	33,660	36,740	5,000	24,000
3rd year	300	300	15%	30%	$100	$150	2.0% / 6	6.0% / 18	29,400	42,300	9,000	31,500
4th year	200	250	10%	25%	$125	$200	3.5% / 7	8.0% / 20	24,125	46,000	12,250	40,000
5th year	180	200	9%	20%	$150	$260	4.5% / 8	10.0% / 20	25,800	46,800	16,000	45,000
Total							29 MG Donors	95 MG Donors	258,225	256,720	46,250	168,000
Total Revenue – Typical Fundraising Plan with 2000 Donors									$304,475			
Total Revenue – Donor-Centered Fundraising Plan with 1000 Donors									$424,720 (+ 39.5%)			

Here are some sample interview questions for three different positions in this donor-centered not-for-profit. Note that they are all about thinking and working differently in order to achieve ambitious goals. They explore applicants' ability to break free of the restraints of a typical siloed approach to raising money. Candidates who have engineered innovative solutions in other jobs or even those who have had their creative ideas rebuffed, will shine in donor-centered interviews.

1. Manager of Direct Marketing

   a. *If you only had to acquire half the new donors this year compared with the number acquired last year, but had the same budget to work with, how would your approach to donor acquisition change? What would you be able to do that you have only wished you could accomplish up to now?*

b. *With direct mail, online giving and our internal call center at your disposal, how would you configure these fundraising programs to improve donor retention rates, especially in donors' first two years where attrition is most severe?*

c. *Post-gift, what have you found to be the most effective strategy to retain donors?*

d. *What characteristics or behaviors have you found to be accurate signals of donors' readiness for the major gifts officer?*

e. *What would you do with a donor who exhibits these characteristics?*

f. *If you had a budget to test something in your field, what is the question you would be most eager to answer?*

g. *What is your big-picture philosophy regarding the role of direct marketing in the fundraising continuum?*

2. Director of Donor Relations

   a. *Focusing on donors currently giving through our direct marketing programs, what would be your strategy to improve five-year net retention from 9% to 20%?*

   b. *What in your experience tells you that your proposed strategy will work?*

   c. *Our plan is to double the number of donors who transition out of introductory level fundraising into major gifts in each year for the next five years. What role would your donor relations strategy play in this transition?*

   d. *What would you not do that might be considered common practice in donor relations, and why do you feel this is ineffective?*

   e. *Our plan projects a 75% increase in average gift value among donors retained in direct marketing programs by Year 5. How would your approach to donor relations inspire donors to give more generously while they are still making contributions through a program that is less personal than major gifts?*

   f. *Once a donor is in the hands of one of our major gifts officers, what is the value-added you would bring to the top of the donor pyramid as Director of Donor Relations?*

   g. *How would you work with our Board of Directors to maximize the impact of donor relations in order to achieve the goals expressed in this plan?*

3. Major/Planned Gifts Officer

    a. How soon after acquisition is a donor ready for the major/planned gifts officer, and what evidence from your experience supports this opinion?

    b. If you had access to the entire database of donors and free rein to take any donors you wish into your portfolio, which ones would you choose and why?

    c. What do you see as the opportunities within our flagship fundraising event to move more participants into the major gifts arena? Describe your ideal role in this event that would cause more event-based donors to become major donors sooner.

    d. How would you use our Board and our CEO to meet the major/planned gifts objectives of this plan?

    e. After negotiating a first major gift from one of your donors, how do you know when this donor is ready to entertain a request for a second significant contribution? How would you handle this relationship when under pressure to bring in more money by the end of the fiscal year?

    f. Imagine a meeting of the major/planned gifts team. What would you discuss and decide that would help meet the objectives of this plan? Who else would you want to have in such a meeting, if anyone?

These questions may have caused you to catch your breath, so you can only imagine how a candidate, already under the stress of applying for a job would react if they were thrown at him. Big questions require big thinking and thinking takes time. The objective here is not to trip someone up in an interview. You are trying to answer that second big question by exploring where the candidate is situated along a scale, with one end being "locked into the fundraising system as we know it" and the other end being "highly innovative, thriving in an atmosphere of change". The sample questions above and, more important, the ones you develop that reflect your own ambitious planning, require both your and your candidate's contemplation.

Discussing References with Candidates

Interviews commonly work their way through questions related to skills and experience and then top candidates are asked to provide references. But, there are some very useful questions concerning references that you should pursue directly with your candidates.

Tell us how you made a difference at [name of organization listed as a reference,] and is it alright if we ask them to confirm this information? This question suggests to candidates that they should be objective about their own accomplishments. It

When I accepted my current position, I thought my employer was seeking an innovator and a change agent. But soon after I started, it became apparent that they actually would prefer to maintain the status quo.

warns those who tend to magnify their achievements that you will verify the facts with previous employers.

Similarly, you should ask this question: *What would your previous employer/ supervisor say are your particular strengths and weaknesses?* Then be sure to ask the same question of the referee.

In fundraising, donors can be important secondary references for any position involving relationship management or fundraising leadership. This question was suggested by several managers we surveyed: *Can you provide me with the name and contact information of a donor with whom you have negotiated a major gift within the past year?*

Involving Other Staff in Candidate Selection

Several respondents recommended having at least two other people in your organization interview "A list" candidates independently, then meet to compare impressions. Others suggested having finalists meet with a staff group. Doing this does not compel you to hire the candidate they prefer but it certainly gives you a great second opinion. Your staff team has inside knowledge that you, as the employer, do not have because they work and see things from a perspective you cannot experience. They, like you, have the best interests of the organization at heart and are motivated to find the most qualified and capable person to add to the team, so let them play that role as constructively as possible. (Your staff's most important inside knowledge, by the way, is what it is like to work for you and the type of employee who thrives under your leadership. You cannot be objective about this no matter how hard you try.)

Interviewing Over-Qualified Candidates

The last time the economy faltered, many Development Directors were faced with the prospect of reducing staff. Among them was someone who heads the Fundraising Office of a prominent healthcare institution. Not wanting to lose her highly skilled fundraisers and, along with them, the investment she had made in their training and supervision, the Development Director offered an alternative to those targeted for layoff. Four major gifts officers and prospect research associates could stay on full time if they agreed to spend part of their day doing basic donor data support. So, these highly experienced fundraisers went to work part-time in data input in order to save their jobs.

It wasn't long before one of them asked for a meeting with the Development Director. "I'm seeing something interesting", she said. "There is a large group of donors who gives modestly but regularly. They are not being stewarded because each gift averages less than twenty dollars. But they give from five to ten times a year. I think someone should be talking with them as they seem to be signaling interest in a closer relationship."

She was right. The group of donors making small but frequent gifts was targeted for special stewardship. Many became major donors; many more joined the recurring gifts program. Revenue from these donors soared thanks to an employee who brought all her skill and experience plus her fresh perspective to a job for which she was substantially overqualified.

It's a reflection of the times. In the five years leading up to publishing this book, unemployment in the United States doubled. In such a tough environment, job-seekers just want to work, and they are grateful for a chance to get back into the ranks of the employed, even if it means being over-qualified for the positions available to them.

While the demand for fundraisers is on the rise overall, the Development field has experienced periods where it was more difficult for practitioners to find suitable employment. The most recent 2007-2009 recession is an example where one in four not-for-profits we surveyed said they laid off fundraising staff. So, whether it is economically driven, a result of the evolving popularity of fundraising methods, or a factor of demographics like age, there will always be over-qualified candidates in the job market. On that last point, 36% of non-management fundraisers we surveyed were over the age of 50. Many had enjoyed successful, progressive careers that included management positions with significant responsibility. But they wanted to live out the last years of their employment working directly with donors, often in major and planned gifts. They are technically over-qualified, I suppose, but only if the assessment criteria define qualification in terms of management seniority.

As an employer, you may be somewhat reticent about hiring an over-qualified candidate. You are right to ask yourself, "Will he handle the job differently from his predecessor whose approach was compatible with my management style?" "Will she become bored and want more responsibility?; "Will he challenge the status quo?"

But hiring over-qualified fundraisers also means hiring people who bypass the learning curve, are able to make an early contribution beyond the job description, and bring experienced perspectives to the complex world of fundraising. Whether these new staff members perform in these very desirable ways, though, is as much a product of how they are managed as how they motivate themselves.

Doing well in fundraising is largely a product of interpersonal skills, writing ability and organization. Any intelligent, mature person can learn the ropes.

Instead of dismissing over-qualified candidates over fears about what might go wrong, why not interview them and find out whether they could add a unique dimension to your fundraising operation. Table 16 illustrates how similar questions, posed from different perspectives, yield very different results.

Table 16 – How to Ask Questions of Over-Qualified Candidates

Questions Phrased in a Critical Manner that Reveal the Employer's Reticence	Better Questions that Explore Positive Potential
I see you are over-qualified for this job. Why did you apply?	Since you appear to be over-qualified for the position, what was it about the job or our not-for-profit that inspired you to apply?
I see you have worked in fundraising for more than twenty years, including holding management positions. Why would you be applying for this less senior job?	At this point in your career, what are you seeking personally or professionally that this job on the front lines of fundraising might offer you?
You would be reporting to someone with considerably less experience than you have. Are you OK with that?	Talk about the challenges of reporting to someone whose fundraising and management experience might be less senior than yours. What working style and relationship would optimize the experience for both of you?
We encourage our staff to be team players here. How will you fit in as someone more senior (read "older") than the rest of the group?	There are challenges inherent in reporting to someone from a younger generation. Please talk about how you would establish and sustain an excellent working relationship in this situation.

Is Hiring from Outside the Profession More Trouble than It's Worth?

Inside knowledge of fundraising can be helpful and it can be limiting at the same time. Focus on what you are trying to achieve with this hire, and ask yourself whether knowing the details of how fundraising works is really the key skill you need. What can be learned on the job? What skills are you attempting to hire that would be difficult to teach or that you don't want to have to pay for while someone learns them?

Fundraising is not rocket science and its technical aspects can be learned on the job, especially if employers use apprenticeship for orientation (see Chapter 10) and specialized fundraising training for continuing education. When face-to-face with a donor, your fundraiser will not be talking about fundraising. He will be telling the story of your case and learning as much as he can about the person on the other side of the coffee table. When sitting in front of her blank computer screen, your fundraiser won't be thinking about the technicalities of mass marketing acquisition. She will be putting herself in the shoes of the people you serve and drawing upon her skills as a writer to illustrate how your donor's philanthropy is making the world a better place.

Even if transition time is longer or orientation has to be designed differently, you will benefit from filling some fundraising positions with staff from atypical career paths. Diversifying your talent base in Development is important in order to avoid shaping a department with a cloistered perspective about how fundraising should be operated. It is a credit to the profession that aspiring Development professionals can take specialized fundraising courses and become certified before or soon after entering the field. But that also means that students learn the established views about how money should be raised and are rewarded with top marks for accepting the status quo. That would be fine if the established views about fundraising and, in particular, about what motivates donors were all correct. But they aren't. Some beliefs and practices are out of synch with donors' changing attitudes about philanthropy; others are simply not adjusting fast enough to keep up with modern-day communication and technology.

The antidote to a fundraising operation that thinks too narrowly or conforms too readily is a staff complement with diverse backgrounds. Fundraisers with backgrounds acquired inside the Development field are important in preventing expensive mistakes or wasting scarce resources by reinventing the wheel. In turn, staff who come into fundraising from other fields ask, "Why do we do things this way?" or "How do you know donors actually prefer this?" or "Have you tried this approach which produced better results where I used to work?"

Fundraising is a service and a means to a bigger end; it is not the end in itself. It should adjust and shift and reinvent itself as necessary in order to capitalize on opportunity in a world that is adjusting and shifting all the time.

Hiring the Chief Development Officer

Hiring the right Development Director is easier if you prepare to hire by considering the other two members of the management team – the CEO and the Board of Directors. They are extraordinarily important in furthering donors' desire to give more generously and they are the ultimate decision-makers concerning how fundraising is resourced and executed. Every senior fundraiser hire should be planned with your CEO and Board of Directors in mind.

If you are a CEO not knowledgeable about fundraising, make it your goal to learn the business. Be a visible, enthusiastic champion of both fundraising and the people who do it.

Consider Your Staff Leader First

While it would be wonderful if all CEOs loved to raise money, couldn't wait to meet with donors, and drew people like a magnet whenever they walked into a room, it doesn't always work out that way. Fundraising definitely improves when CEOs are willing participants, but that doesn't mean that every Chief Executive is comfortable in this arena.

The degree to which your CEO is an asset for fundraising may depend upon when she was hired. Fundraising experience and skill are more likely to be required than optional for today's chief executives. Our research found that 52% of Chief Executive Officers said fundraising know-how was critical to their winning the job. An additional 26% said that it was important and helped position them as the preferred candidate. But, many not-for-profits have long-serving CEOs, hired at a time when ability to raise money from the private sector was not so crucial. They may not be shining stars in fundraising but superb leaders in many other ways. No matter where your CEO sits along the fundraising continuum, it is advantageous to hire a Chief Development Officer whose skills complement, not duplicate, those of your CEO.

Whether and how the CEO influences the Board of Directors on fundraising matters is a primary consideration. 55% of Chief Executive Officers we surveyed said that convincing Board members to fulfill their responsibilities in fundraising was the least enjoyable part of their job as it relates to raising money. This is definitely a problem. Development professionals, no matter how skilled or how senior, should be able to turn to their CEOs for leadership on critical fundraising matters. This would include sensitive issues like achieving 100% giving among Board members, influencing volunteers to engage in major gifts asks, and preventing their Boards from diverting too much professional Development staff time into high-risk/low-return fundraising events.

It can be frustrating for fundraisers when their Chief Executive Officer performs poorly in situations involving donors. For example, perhaps your CEO is uncomfortable in group settings or at events, reluctant to approach people he doesn't know, or poor at starting or sustaining a conversation. He attends the event because he has to, but hovers in the shadows. When he does interact it is with his staff, rather than with donors, because talking with staff is safe and familiar. While this is unfortunate, it is unlikely that you will be able to re-engineer these personality traits. The more practical approach is to ask this question: "Under what circumstances does our CEO come out of his shell?" Perhaps he stumbles in group settings but excels in one-on-one conversations, becoming animated and truly engaging when he talks about the work his not-for-profit is doing. So, when hiring the head of Development, you should be looking for someone with the ability to compensate for the boss's shortcomings and with the right professional attitude — one that supports her boss in situations he finds difficult.

Seeing the CEO's assets and shortcomings objectively makes it easy to shape interview questions that will help you find a compatible match. For example,

- *Describe how you would support your CEO at an event for donors, knowing that he performs very well in one-on-one situations but less well when interacting with a group.*

- *In this situation, how would you introduce the CEO to a donor, and how might you contribute to the conversation initially to bring these two people into comfortable communication with each other?*

- *What would you be sure to learn or do beforehand to help your CEO contribute meaningfully to donor cultivation at the event?*

In organizations where fundraising is progressively successful, the Chief Executive Officer and the Development Director are a formidable team. They play off each other's strengths in order to negotiate extraordinary gifts from donors and help Board members play their role as successfully as possible. They also compensate for each other's weaknesses in the knowledge that no single person can possess every fundraising advantage. The CEO and the Development Chief accomplish much more as a cohesive duo than they ever could separately.

Consider the Board When Hiring the Chief Development Officer

There is room for improvement in the working relationship between Development professionals and Boards of Directors, and it starts with each having a better appreciation of their own and the other's assets and limitations in fundraising.

84% of leadership volunteers acknowledge they have direct responsibility for raising money even though their organizations employ professional fundraisers. In spite of this positive finding, Boards are not confident about what their responsibilities actually are, in part because their not-for-profits employ professionals to raise money. For their part, fundraising staff feel they have to be responsible for everything, or the money will simply not get raised. This lack of clarity makes it easy to draw erroneous conclusions and point fingers when fundraising gets tough.

The relationship between Boards and fundraising success is explored more thoroughly in Chapter 9. For now, how you answer these two straightforward

Paid fundraising staff are great, but the CEO must be an active partner in raising money.

Board members tend to over-simplify fundraising. They believe it's no big deal until they become directly involved in the asking process. At that point, they're often out of their depth.

Boards perform better once they understand that fundraising is not asking for money; it's offering people the opportunity to make a positive difference in the lives of others.

questions about your Board gives you practical insight into the kind of Development Director you need:

- *Do all our Board members make charitable contributions to our organization on a regular basis and at a level that is generous within each member's means?*

- *Do all Board members willingly participate in raising money for our not-for-profit?*

Not-for-profits that can confidently answer "yes" to both questions should be seeking a Development Director whose focus will be largely on expanding the professional side of fundraising in order to move your not-for-profit to a higher level of performance. The positive culture has already been established that makes this possible; bottom-line productivity is now the objective. Your Donor-Centered Fundraising Plan described in Chapter 5 is the roadmap you need to maximize results.

On the other hand, organizations answering "no" to one or both of these questions need a chief fundraiser who can help the Board (both directly and indirectly through the CEO) transition from its current mindset about fundraising to one that makes it possible for them to raise money more successfully. Effecting this transition is critical because once all Board members give and contribute meaningfully to fundraising, their not-for-profit never again has to accept a lesser standard of performance.

Experienced fundraisers who apply for management-level Development positions almost always ask questions about the Board, particularly the two questions above. Where the Board goes, there goes their own potential for success and their job satisfaction. 51% of chief fundraisers said that, when all Board members give, it makes them much more eager to work for that not-for-profit and causes them to stay in the job longer. Conversely, 34% said that when they do not have a 100% giving Board, their work is harder and less satisfying and it contributes to their premature resignation.

Not-for-profits should be prepared to answer questions about their Boards related to fundraising willingness and capability. Employers can and should be proactive on this issue by opening up the conversation themselves. Framed in a way that is not critical of the Board but merely factual about how it contributes to fundraising currently, questions such as these can tell you whether the candidate in question is right for you at this time:

- *While 70% of our Board members make philanthropic gifts to our organization, 30% do not, and these are most often members who have been on the Board for a long time. How will you approach this situation to help us achieve 100% Board member giving?*

- *What steps will you undertake to assist our Board in becoming measurably more successful at asking donors for gifts? How will you gauge progress towards the ultimate goal?*

- *How will you give direction to the Board on fundraising matters in ways that respect their role as the organization's ultimate decision-making body? How do you know your approach will work?*

In my opinion, smaller fundraising operations lacking clear opportunities for advancement have a much tougher job retaining staff.

When my firm conducts fundraising research studies for clients, they often want to know how their performance compares with that of other organizations in the same field. It is easy to speak in relative terms about long-term donor retention, average gift values, the percentage of donors moving from modest to significant giving and the like. But the real measure of success for any not-for-profit that raises money is its people; and, among the staff, top management has the greatest influence of all. The CEO and Chief Development Officer working as a cohesive team can make good things happen. But, when the Board steps up as well, there is no limit to a not-for-profit's fundraising potential. Every hour invested in helping the Board become fundraising leaders in their community is time very well spent. Hiring someone with the ability to orchestrate that transition should be every not-for-profit's goal.

The Special Nature of One-Person-Shop Fundraisers

Our study included a contingent of fundraisers running one-person Development operations. Sole practitioners tend to be generalists, rather than specialists, due to the all-encompassing nature of their job descriptions. For almost half of our one-person-shop respondents, this was the literal definition of their job – they were the entire Development Department embodied in a single individual. 59% had some clerical or data entry assistance, though rarely was that support full time. One-person Development Departments are most likely to be found in social service agencies, but many arts organizations and secondary schools also employ sole practitioners.

Our research found that one-person-shop fundraisers derive their job satisfaction from being in control of the entire fundraising operation. They "own their success" as many respondents pointed out. Both autonomy and variety matter to these fundraisers. They are motivated by the myriad responsibilities they have and, along with them, the silent competition they hold with themselves to see whether they can handle it all. They value flexibility in their work schedules even more than do other fundraisers we surveyed. This includes working from home, working flexible hours, and working for a not-for-profit that accommodates family matters.

There are special considerations to take into account when hiring one-person-shop fundraisers. Employers should seek applicants who are exceptionally good at managing their time and who understand investment/return as it relates to their job descriptions. On that latter point, a sole practitioner is pulled in many directions. She (four out of five are women) needs to know whether half a day spent crafting a grant proposal or the same amount of time spent supporting the Golf Tournament Committee produces a better return on investment for the organization.

Not-for-Profits in Transition

Whether they realize it or not, charities with one paid fundraiser on staff are in the midst of organizational change, and that includes change in how funds are raised. They are no longer enjoying the benefits of being the "new kid on the block" with founding Board members who are willing to do whatever it takes to bring in the money. On the other hand, they are also not yet diversified in how they fundraise, nor do they have the budget (and usually the experience) required to consistently make wise investments in their fundraising future.

Not-for-profits at this stage sometimes hire a junior fundraiser who compensates for lack of experience with limitless energy. The priority for organizations that hire this way is to alleviate the workload without relinquishing the more hands-on approach to decision-making that the CEO and, especially, the Board are used to. This can work well as long as the fundraiser is clear about where her authority begins and ends. Another option for not-for-profits in transition is to seek a fundraiser who has managed a larger shop with diversified programming, including major and planned gifts. His fundraising experience at the more profitable end of the spectrum will help guide a small shop down a better path; his management experience will position him well to help the Board and CEO make forward-thinking decisions. A more experienced, sometimes older, fundraiser is more likely to have the credibility with decision-makers that will be necessary to help them engage in more sophisticated ways.

Whichever direction is chosen, interview questions should take into account the unique circumstances of one-person-shop fundraisers. Here are some examples:

- *What is a balanced approach to fundraising, in your view?*

- *Our cost per dollar raised is currently 60%, due largely to a fundraising portfolio weighted in events. What would you do in your first year on the job to move us in a less risky and more profitable direction?*

- *Describe your number one strength in working with board members to help them add value to fundraising?*

- *What is your most prominent weakness when it comes to the Board and fundraising?* [follow up] *How will you overcome that weakness if you are hired?*

- *How do you help a board move to a more sophisticated approach without dampening the enthusiasm of those who organize our fundraising events?*

- *What kind of physical work configuration regarding hours and location of work would you consider to be ideal?*

- *How do you know when you need more staff in fundraising or when you simply need to manage your time differently?* [follow up] *Describe your time-management strategy.*

- *Describe what you need from your CEO in order to be successful in fundraising*

A not-for-profit with only one fundraiser on staff still needs a Donor-Centered Fundraising Plan. Give your finalists your version of Table 13 (Chapter 5) and some time to study it, then ask this question:

- *How would you prioritize your work in order to accomplish this Plan's goals?*

Checking References

A prominent university and the cancer world reeled when, in 2010, the lead investigator of a research team was suspended. He had become renowned for stunning success in individualizing treatment based on cancer patients' own biomarkers. But, it had come to light that his resume referenced a Rhodes scholarship that he had never been awarded. Peer reviews later uncovered obvious errors and mislabeling that easily discredited his research.

The investigator left the University, but soon resurfaced at a cancer treatment center in another state. It had been further reported that he had hired an online reputation management firm to position him in a more favorable light. The firm worked diligently to ensure that the researcher's falsified resume, faulty research and the retractions from renowned medical journals that had previously published his papers no longer constituted the majority of top online search results.

I always assume two things about the people who work for me – competence and good will. I maintain those assumptions until proved otherwise, which seldom happens.

Ten Things About Reference-Checking from Those Who Learned the Hard Way

Once again, management-level fundraisers in our study came through with invaluable advice about checking references. Their wise counsel includes, in some cases, how to phrase questions to referees to be sure you get the information you need.

1. Always clarify the referee's working relationship with a candidate and how long they worked together, regardless of what appears on the candidate's resume.

2. Find out if the referee is related to or a friend of the candidate. This definitely colors the reference and you will need to balance information from this individual with at least one other referee in a strictly professional capacity.

3. Checking the official references that candidates provide is important, but you should also make informal inquiries through your own network. Colleagues, leadership volunteers and your own staff can be great resources or they can lead you to people who are. It's a big industry but a small world in fundraising – everyone knows everyone.

4. Be realistic about the questions that referees can and cannot answer. For instance, chemistry is essential – no referee can tell you how your preferred candidate will gel with your staff team. Review your list of reference questions before picking up the phone and ask yourself, "Can a referee really enlighten me on this issue?"

5. Listen for unsolicited, positive praise. If your referee steps in and takes over the conversation, waxing eloquent about the candidate, this is a big green flag. But, be sure to follow up with this query: *"Why, then, are you letting this person slip through your fingers?"*

6. Avoid asking questions that can be answered with a "yes" or "no". Rather, phrase them in ways that encourage referees to answer in a more descriptive fashion. For example, *"Did the candidate meet her fundraising goal last year?"* invites a one-word answer. But, the same question positioned this way will reveal what you want to know: *"Talk about the candidate's performance in light of increasingly challenging fundraising goals. Where would you say she met or exceeded performance expectations and where did you feel she needed extra support?"*

7. Whatever you ask of referees should be phrased in the same way you asked the question of candidates. A nuance shift can leave you no longer comparing apples with apples.

8. Phrase questions that explore difficult issues in a constructive way. This will put your referee at ease, keeping him focused on the information you are seeking and not whether he should downplay or avoid talking about something that might prevent the candidate from being hired. For example, instead of asking, *"What are the candidate's weaknesses?"*, consider this alternative: *"Everyone has weaknesses in some area. Can you give me advice on this candidate's shortcomings and how we should support her in order to ensure success?"*

9. Do not mentally hire your preferred candidate before checking references or you will be reluctant to hear what is actually being said.

10. When asking questions of referees, listen both to what they are saying and how they are saying it. If their answers are evasive, if they hesitate too long before replying, they may be trying to send you a message. Here is a portion of a reference I once gave. It's a classic case of failing to "hear between the lines":

> Prospective Employer: *"Can you talk about the kind of supervision that best suits this candidate?"*
> Referee: [Pause] *"I would have to say that he needs close supervision."*
> Employer: *"Can you elaborate?"*
> Referee: [Even longer pause] *"He needs specific, time-limited goals. It is challenging for him to stay focused on one thing."*
> Employer: [Having mentally hired the candidate already] *"It sounds like he is very creative with lots of ideas. That was evident during interviews which is one of the things that put him on the list of finalists."*
> Referee: *"Creative…that is one interpretation, of course."*
> Employer: *"Would you hire this candidate again?"*
> Referee: [after another lengthy pause] *"No, I think this was not the best fit for him."*
> Employer: *"What about hiring him for another job in your organization that would be more compatible with his talents?"*
> Referee: *"It would be unlikely."*

The candidate in question was hired…and then fired four months later. I remember that about a year after that phone call I ran into the Development manager who had conducted the interview. She said, "It was a blow when someone who had seemed so good during interviews turned out to be such a disappointment on the job. I was unnerved and particularly critical of the role that I had played in hiring him in the first place. So, before I sought his replacement, I went back through the hiring process to try to pinpoint

Many employer references are unwilling to say anything negative about a former staff member because they are afraid of being sued. Try to pick up on inflections and other clues that signal reluctance. You will need other reference sources in that case.

Check out candidates with "unofficial" referees. We tell candidates that we will do this as a last step after checking the official references.

where things went wrong. When I reread the notes I took from our phone call, I was stunned. You were trying to warn me but I was not willing to hear that message. I now listen differently during interviews with candidates but, especially, in conversations with referees."

You might be surprised why someone who had obviously not performed well at my firm would use me as a reference. I certainly was, but it is possible that employers from other places he worked would have been even less generous with their opinions. I also did not know that my name was on this individual's reference list or that he had applied for this job. So I was unprepared for the call when it came and unable to think about the job and him in ways that might have allowed me to offer a more nuanced review of his performance.

Of course, this story invites the question, "Why did I hire him in the first place?" I, too, failed to do my due diligence. I made two fundamental mistakes – he was a friend and I had no first-hand knowledge of his performance at work. I made assumptions that I should not have made based on a non-professional relationship. And then I failed to check references at all, which meant I carried the friendship connection right into the business environment. Ah, well, I was greener then. Live and learn.

Twenty Clincher Questions for Referees

1. *Would you hire this person again…into the same job?* It is the last part of this question that is most important.

2. *Did the candidate meet your specific targets and expectations?* While respondents advised not to phrase questions that evoke a "yes" or "no" answer, on the issue of reaching the goal you simply need to know whether your candidate came through. If the answer is "no", you can then ask the referee about degree of responsibility. For instance, Were there any obstacles to reaching the goal that were out of the candidate's control? An obvious one is that the goal was a figure pulled out of the air and not based on known donor data.

3. *Can you verify, on or off the record, the accuracy of information in the candidate's resume, specifically [reaching fundraising goals, educational qualifications, awards, etc.]*

4. *Can you tell me how the candidate made a tangible difference in your fundraising results?* This could go either way, of course but it is an important question that asks the referee to define what it is about the candidate that differentiated her performance from that of other colleagues.

5. *Compared with other fundraisers who have worked for you in a similar capacity, where would you place this candidate for overall performance – the best you've had, in the top third, middle third, lowest third?* Ranking the candidate against others who have done the same job allows for a highly objective assessment.

Go to colleagues, board members, peers, etc. to get beyond the typical HR restrictions such as, "All I can confirm is his/her dates of employment".

6. *Could you have achieved the same level of success in your fundraising operation without this person?* A variation on the theme expressed in the previous two questions, but a good way to articulate it nonetheless.

7. *Was the candidate promoted internally and, if so, how many times?* A positive answer to this question is a big green flag; regardless, you should ask a follow-up question that takes the "Peter Principle"[1] into account. Was he just as successful in his current/most recent position in your organization as he was in more junior jobs where his performance warranted promotion?

8. *If you were doing a performance evaluation of this candidate today, what would you share with me regarding issues that need attention going forward?*

9. *Can you share how this candidate handles poor results?* This important question can lead to a supplementary one on the candidate's working relationship with peers and/or her management style in the face of performance falling short of expectation. It can also take the conversation down another path. Fundraising is a business fraught with disappointment and how Development professionals handle the highs and lows of raising money is very important. Does she stew over a fundraising failure or pick herself back up and move on?

10. Assuming the referee is giving a glowing account or a very positive one, *Why did you not attempt to retain this individual on staff?* It's an obvious question but one that you might not think to ask when the referee is effusive with praise. This question brings the conversation back down to earth.

11. *The pace of work here is intense. Can you describe how the candidate functions while under pressure?* To avoid the referee simply responding, "very well" or something equally uninformative, ask him to describe a specific fundraising situation that was highly charged and how the candidate maneuvered through the challenge.

12. *What is the best style of supervision for this individual?*

---

[1] An observation formulated by Dr. Laurence J. Peter and Raymond Hull, asserting that employees tend to be promoted on merit until they are promoted into a position that is beyond their competency. Now no longer qualifying for another promotion, they tend to be left in place rather than demoted, forcing subordinates to "manage up" in order to limit the damage and get work done. *The Peter Principle: Why Things Always Go Wrong.* Laurence J. Peter and Raymond Hull, William Morrow/HarperCollins Publishers, New York, NY, originally published in 1969.

13. *How would you advise we manage the candidate for best results if we hire him?*

14. *Did this candidate seek opportunities to go beyond her prescribed duties while working for your organization?* This speaks to innovation, capitalizing on opportunity, and having pride in one's own work.

15. *If I hire this candidate, what challenges do you think I might be facing six months from now?* This is an interesting question because it asks the referee to think back and assess the candidate he originally hired against the staff member who is now fully oriented to the job and functioning more-or-less independently.

16. *What was this person's most significant contribution to your not-for-profit?* Something should stand out and, no matter how the referee responds to this question, the information will be important. For example, this response – She was an inspiration to her colleagues, always willing to help them succeed and consistently creating a positive, "can-do" environment in the office – speaks to the candidate's leadership potential, giving you another reason to hire her before someone else wins this prize.

17. *What are the characteristics of the candidate that enhanced or inhibited the department's or group's performance?* You will be particularly glad you asked this question if the referee identifies negative traits that interfered with the team's ability to perform.

18. *What about attendance?* While the objective should be meeting the goal rather than being at one's desk by 9:00 a.m., there are times when attendance matters. For instance, does the candidate tend to arrive late to internal meetings? That behavior says, "I am more important than the rest of you." You may wish to explore this further if the referee has any concerns on this issue.

19. *Does the candidate communicate proactively or do you always have to take the lead?* Deference is considerate – to a point; taken too far, it can stifle progress. Not being proactive, especially when communicating up, is problematic in fundraising. You need your staff to give you early warning when goals are in jeopardy and to have enough confidence to offer better alternatives to your ideas from time to time. If everyone waits for you to take the lead all the time, you might as well be a staff of one.

20. *What feedback have you had from donors about the candidate?* If the candidate was responsible for building relationships with donors and was particularly skillful at doing so, the referee should be able to answer this question. No feedback does not mean that the relationships established were negative,

but it could mean that they were not particularly memorable or interesting. (See "Is Your Candidate Interesting?" earlier in this chapter.)

"I Don't Want My Boss to Know": A Reference Dilemma

At any moment in time, one in three fundraisers is looking for another job, so employers should not be surprised when the one-in-three applies to a member of their own staff. Nonetheless, it's frustrating and disheartening when good people leave and not all bosses react in a positive manner when they hear the news. For that reason – and others – some job candidates are reluctant to provide their bosses as references. You have every right, however, to know why a candidate is unwilling.

If you are so inclined, you could accept an "interim" reference, but a friend or colleague should not qualify in that role. The referee should be someone who is clearly senior to the candidate such as a Board member, a client of the applicant if he currently works in a consulting firm or his boss from his last position. However, if this candidate eventually becomes your first choice for the job, you should then insist on speaking with his current employer. While there may be nothing to worry about, have your radar up as you listen to what the employer/referee has to say. Things are not always as they appear on the surface.

Always, Always, Always Check References

On the day that a tyrannical staff member finally left a prominent healthcare institution, her employees and colleagues quietly got together at a local restaurant to "celebrate". Over the course of four years, this individual's angry outbursts and demeaning management style had been responsible for the premature resignation of nine members of the Development team. The conversation around the table underscored the relief that everyone was feeling over this individual's departure. Finally, having made enemies out of just about everyone on staff, she had seen the writing on the wall.

Someone offered up a toast: "Here's to her never being able to do this to another fundraiser ever again."

"Not so fast", said a member of the group who had been sitting quietly at one end of the table. "She has landed a job with even more management responsibility than before – just twenty miles away at XYZ Healthcare Institute."

"How is this possible?" someone eventually asked, breaking the stunned silence. Everyone knew that their VP, who was the obvious referee, had been carefully considering how she would handle questions about her former employee's management style. But, in the end it wasn't necessary. The call never came.

I should have listened to my colleagues who warned me about going to this organization. I have regretted that move from my first day on the job.

It seems obvious that you should always check references, but it is actually quite easy for a potential employer to get swept up in the good vibes and instant connection created when an interview goes really well. Combined with wanting to fill the position as quickly as possible, it is easy to become over-confident about one's own ability to judge character. Remember, this is fundraising, so you should expect candidates to be excellent at selling themselves. Remain objective and do your reference checking in the cold light of day.

Interviewing Works Both Ways

By the time you have reviewed her application, made informal inquiries among your colleagues about her achievements and work ethic, conducted two or more increasingly in-depth interviews, and checked her references, you will have learned a lot about your candidate and invested a great deal of time and effort in the hiring process. But has she done the same? What if, before submitting her application, she checked you out as thoroughly as you investigated her? Maybe she had lunch with a member of your Board; maybe she talked to one of your major donors about how you steward relationships; perhaps she emailed a former employee to find out why he left and to ask for an assessment of your management style. While big and getting bigger all the time, the fundraising industry is still a fairly closed shop. It is easy to find out whether your not-for-profit is bleeding professional fundraisers and why; whether you are a respectful and collaborative manager or a tyrant; and whether your Board rolls up its sleeves or runs from the room when raising money is on the agenda.

While it might be a little unnerving to think that your candidate has put you and your not-for-profit under a microscope, if she has and has still applied for the job, then you must have passed the first test. Excellent candidates will come to interviews prepared to investigate their red flags and you should not be caught off guard when they do. Their probing questions are not meant to point a finger at your organization's fundraising deficiencies; rather, candidates want to know if you are flexible about working differently in order to produce better results.

Early in my career, I took a fundraising job with a not-for-profit that was seriously in debt. Angry creditors were knocking at the door and the organization was relying on weather-dependent, high-cost fundraising events for almost all its revenue. What persuaded me to take the job anyway was everyone's forthrightness. No one tried to withhold information or downplay the problem. On the other hand, they weren't wringing their hands in despair, either. They just wanted to develop a better approach to raising money and they were looking for someone who would work hard and provide reliable advice. I delivered for them and this challenging experience opened up a progressive career in Development for me. We both won.

Here are some of the questions that good candidates will (or should) ask and the issues behind the questions that they are exploring:

Do you have a strategic plan in place?

It takes time to earn donors' trust and cultivate them towards major gifts. If the CEO changes priorities often rather than working steadily towards accomplishing stated goals, it compromises fundraising success. A Development professional's credibility is on the line with donors when he is negotiating gifts. If his not-for-profit changes direction in mid-stream, it is both difficult and embarrassing for a gifts officer to explain why yesterday's priority is no longer an important funding objective. This leaves him having to start all over with donors – at least with the ones who are still willing to hear a new pitch.

What is your position on the designation of gifts to specific programs and services?

This question is tied to the previous one concerning the strategic plan. Fundraisers know that focusing donors on a single or a short list of linked objectives raises far more money than selling the brand or a shopping list of initiatives. All fundraisers want to raise as much money as possible for the organizations that employ them, and designated (restricted) giving is the way to do it (see Chapter 4).

Is Development represented on the executive team that makes key planning decisions?

Not-for-profits that answer "no" to this question reveal their lack of sophistication about the role that fundraising plays in branding and marketing. All fundraising appeals and related communications have the capacity to enhance or compromise the brand. Your charity's chief fundraiser needs to be part of the central decision-making group so that Development reflects the appropriate tone and content from the start. Yes, you can send endless drafts back to the drawing board, but why waste that kind of time and money? Empower your Development head to produce compelling, winning communications from the start by insisting that she take responsibility at the highest level with the rest of your executive team.

If you ran an automobile company and expected your customers to design your product, you would end up with a pathetic alternative to transportation that never left the driveway. On the other hand, if you never took your customers' views into account, you'd be – well – nuts. There's a parallel in fundraising. Not-for-profits should never let a single donor or group of donors entice them off their strategy with

Three things I learned during the job interview enticed me into the position I now hold. 1) The not-for-profit has been around for 121 years; 2) they have a long-standing and well-established fundraising program; 3) they have an endowment which means they are forward-thinking.

the promise of funding. But not taking donors' opinions into account is equally short-sighted. Donors are embedded in your community, they have a valuable and unique perspective, and they want you to succeed. Your core strategy is shaped by the team at the top and your Chief Development Officer brings donors' views to the table – if she's there, that is.

What is your CEO's attitude towards fundraising?

A good fundraiser is able to work with any CEO, whether he is or is not an experienced fundraiser himself. The only impossible working relationship pertains to a CEO who sees fundraising as a necessary evil. He refuses to play a useful role himself, lessening the potential for success, then blaming the fundraiser for below-par results. His negative attitude towards fundraising cannot help but be transmitted to other non-fundraising staff, leaving Development personnel isolated. It is not uncommon for fundraisers who work in this type of atmosphere to be addressed in derogatory terms like "money-grabbers" and, when they complain, be told they have no sense of humor. This "them-and-us" attitude is more common than one might think. 36% of fundraisers in our study left their last job, at least in part, to get away from a negative view that employers and/or colleagues held about fundraising. Good work cannot get done in this kind of atmosphere, so fundraisers tend not to stay long in organizations that want more money but are unwilling to adjust their thinking in order to make raising more money possible.

How does your Board engage in fundraising?

There are Boards whose willingness to give and uncanny ability to raise money take fundraisers' breath away. And there are Boards that struggle with everything to do with fundraising. 35% of Development professionals we surveyed said they left their last job, at least in part, because their Boards failed to contribute meaningfully to fundraising. In many cases, the Board's lack of engagement was compounded by poor decision-making, making it that much harder for staff to reach ambitious goals.

Leadership volunteers influence donors more than anyone else, so professional fundraisers need this rare and most valuable asset on their side. When candidates ask in interviews about the Board, they may be dreaming about a group of powerful influencers that never has to be asked twice to bring home the bacon; but they will be delighted if they are applying to a not-for-profit whose Board shows up and tries their best (see *Hiring the Board* in Chapter 9).

What is your position on investment/return in fundraising?

Good fundraisers need to know that decision-makers will invest in fundraising when investment is warranted and, equally important, that they understand the role that time plays in building profit. It is not investment when revenue must be found to offset a cost incurred in the same fiscal year. That is cash-flow insecurity. Investing means shouldering cost for a period of time beyond the present year's fundraising budget. It means drawing from a reserve, for example, or making budget adjustments in some other area to provide Development with the resources it needs.

When a candidate asks this question, he is assessing your willingness to move up the ladder of fundraising sophistication. Will you invest in the introduction or expansion of planned giving, for example, or will you miss golden opportunities to grow profit simply based on a reluctance to spend money to make money? (Of course, you can – and should – be ready with your own questions. *On what basis would your candidate argue for such investment? Describe how, in your last job, you prepared and presented a request to decision-makers for new investment in fundraising. Did you win or lose the argument and why?)*

What style of working relationship works best for you (or the person to whom I will report)?

Your candidate may have already had work experiences where she thrived or suffered under managers who used one supervisory approach or another. So, she will be motivated to avoid repeating bad experiences. This question allays her fears while sending a positive message to potential employers – that the candidate is willing to adapt her style of interaction to suit the boss – something an employer managing a diverse team will welcome.

What are the possibilities for internal promotion?

As long as it does not appear to be more important to the candidate than other questions concerning the immediate position being filled, this is an excellent and important query. A smart employer will see this question for what it is – the mark of a candidate who is confident and ambitious – characteristics that are valuable assets in a professional fundraiser. A candidate who looks beyond the immediate position to the future is also expressing a desire to broaden his career experience by *staying*, not going.

When applying for jobs, I take into account how "donor-centered" the organization is. Are they using best practices and do they have a strategy, or does direction change with the changing whims of the CEO?

What convinced me to take this job was that the people here are just so ambitious. They aren't mired in old practices and outdated traditions; they are very focused on moving forward.

Factors that influence fundraisers' career choices:

68% Brand / Mission of organization
18% Appealing qualities of the boss
13% Clear strategy for growing programs
2% Clear strategy for fundraising

Blinded by the Brand

When considering a new position, are fundraisers as thorough in their search as the questions above imply? To the detriment of both candidates and employers, they are not. In our study, we asked professional fundraisers to identify the key factor that convinced them to accept the positions they now hold. By a wide margin, respondents identified the mission or brand of the not-for-profit organization. We asked these same respondents why they had left their last positions. Those who did so for negative reasons referenced pivotal issues such as difficulty with the boss, a desire to get away from an "old-school" approach to fundraising, and lack of a clear strategy for fundraising growth. No one said they left because they didn't like what the organization stood for.

I wondered if fundraisers become more strategic about job-seeking and selection as they gain more experience, with mission taking a back seat to more measurable concerns. After all, the mission is still the mission, whether the Development operation is excelling or dysfunctional. So, in a follow-up study, we asked senior Development Directors to look back on the fundraising positions they had held and tell us which of the following three factors most strongly influenced their most recent career decision:

- brand, mission or reputation of the not-for-profit;
- evidence that the not-for-profit had a clear and realistic strategy for fundraising growth;
- appealing qualities of the person to whom the respondent would be reporting.

71% said that the mission of the organization is what caused them to take the job; only 14% referenced the not-for-profit's strategy for fundraising growth; and only 15% said that the appealing qualities of the boss won them over.

Mission is important, of course. When success relies so heavily on ability to persuade, the job is much easier if the fundraiser is passionate about the organization he is selling. But, frankly, I've never known a not-for-profit that I couldn't get passionate about. That's the thing about third sector organizations – they exist to save lives or make lives worth saving – what's not to love? But if love of mission overrides more practical concerns when job-seeking, then candidates may end up reliving their last poor experience. More important, the new employer may unwittingly hire someone with a hidden problem.

The Brand Blinds Employers, Too

What if a candidate reveals during interviews that she left her last position because the Board refused to fulfill its fundraising responsibilities, but then fails to ask in an interview about the role that your Board plays in raising money? This could be a sign that she is putting too much faith in your enticing mission at the expense of seeing your not-for-profit objectively. And you may be tempted to do the same. In our survey with Chief Executive Officers, we asked respondents for their organization's greatest advantage when it comes to hiring good fundraisers. By far the most frequent response was the mission or brand of the not-for-profit (52%). An additional 27% of respondents referenced the high profile status of their organization, something that is closely associated with the brand. Only one in four CEOs identified an exceptional work environment for staff and a mere 10% said the salary and/or benefits they offer are a major hiring advantage. It appears that over-reliance on the brand as a deal-closer is a problem not limited to job-seekers.

When You Are the Candidate

If you are in the market now for a new position or considering a move in the future, then this information will help you see your job search from the perspective of your potential employer. In answering the sample questions that appear earlier in this chapter, you will see what strengths you have that you can showcase in your resume and during interviews. You will also realize how you might be a weaker candidate in some areas that are important to employers. Here is where you should concentrate your efforts before applying for a coveted position.

Do You Really Want to Go?

While starting a new job is exciting, the risk that you may be moving from frying pan to fire is always there. Will your boss turn out to be a tyrant? Will you uncover negative fundraising practices that have contributed to high donor attrition? Compared with other fields where supply and demand are more evenly balanced, it is easier to find a job in the fundraising industry, especially for experienced practitioners. That makes it tempting to abandon an otherwise good position when you run into difficulty. But, if you consider your longer term career aspirations – and if those aspirations include senior management or top leadership – you will only be a serious contender if you have held steady through the tough challenges, learning to solve problems and overcome obstacles.

I should have done my homework. I was dazzled by the famous brand of this long-standing not-for-profit. Once inside, however, I discovered that they were seriously dysfunctional.

There are three justifiable reasons to go, but, even if you happen to be in one of these situations, you should still ask yourself, "Could I have done more or approached the problem in another way in order to bring about a different outcome?" The situations are:

- within the context of both you and your employer agreeing that you have excelled at the job you have now and would be in line for a promotion, you have asked and been told that there are no more senior positions into which you could move within a reasonable period of time;

- you are unable to get the career-building experience you need in the organization where you currently work. This might include, for example, gaining first-hand experience in planned giving but working in a not-for-profit that is not engaged in this form of fundraising (short-sighted as that is);

- there is a fundamental disagreement about how funds should be raised where you work now and you know this is leaving money on the table. You have already taken all reasonable steps to help decision-makers see things differently, including presenting evidence through research and testing that another approach is more profitable. However, they are unwilling to move forward.

You do not have to wait for your boss to come to the realization that you should be promoted, that your great idea should be adopted, or that superiors should take your advice more often. You can be proactive without having to leave. But, the old adage that you cannot change other people's perspectives or behavior directly is absolutely true. You must learn to think like decision-makers think, asking yourself before you present your argument, "If I were my boss, what would I need to know, why would I want to know it, and how would I want the information presented to me in order to make the best possible decision for my not-for-profit?" Remember, while your ideas and concerns are valid, the people to whom you report are dealing with equally serious issues on a larger scale. But never forget you are a fundraiser. No one knows better than you how to win over a reluctant prospect with an irresistible proposal.

How Do You Define Success?

If you are seeking a new position, or trying to determine whether you should stay where you are, answer these two questions:

- How do I define success in this job – i.e., the state of having accomplished all that I set out to achieve?

- What are the benchmarks that tell me I am progressing in the right direction and that I will ultimately succeed?

Having a goal without thinking through how that goal will be accomplished makes you passive about your own career when you should be active and it leaves success to chance – both yours as a professional fundraiser and that of the organization for which you work. Answering these questions forces you to look well beyond the enticing mission of your not-for-profit to determine whether this job is a good fit for you at this time.

How to Get the Job You Want

If you want to land your dream job, do not wait for it to be advertised – go after it. The advice I gave to employers in Chapter 6 on how to find the best candidates applies equally to fundraisers who are seeking positions. The best ways to win a great job involve:

- positioning yourself for an internal promotion. Take on projects and extra assignments eagerly. They enhance your qualifications immediately while showcasing your skills and willingness to work to your boss. What are the characteristics that you would be expected to exhibit in the more senior position that you have your eye on? Demonstrate those characteristics now in the job you currently hold. Employees who get their own job done, while contributing positively to the success of the group, showcase their management potential and signal their readiness for more senior responsibilities.

- going after the job you want. Waiting for a job to be posted is not strategic. Instead, target several not-for-profits that work in a field that inspires you and approach them when they are not hiring. Employers would much rather hire someone who pursues them – it saves them the time and cost of conducting a formal search and it showcases your enthusiasm and proactive approach. It is also much more enjoyable and less stressful to actively pursue a future job than to apply for an already-posted position. Because there is less at stake, you will be more relaxed in interviews, more engaged and less worried about making a mistake. Similarly, the potential employer will be looking at you in a wider field of vision – not just assessing your skills and experience against the narrow framework of a job that he is trying to fill as quickly as possible.

- meeting with a decision-maker in a not-for-profit you admire to discuss the possibility of working there in the future. Doing this when you are unemployed shows initiative; but reaching out in this way when you already hold down a good job is even more impressive.

- building a network of colleagues you admire. Tell them you would welcome the opportunity to be part of their team if a suitable opportunity comes along. Meanwhile, if their manager is on the ball, he will be mobilizing his own staff to look out for good people like you.

31% of respondents have had the experience of negotiating with two or more potential employers simultaneously.

- getting involved – but not overly involved – in your professional organization. The executive team and Board of the association are influential industry insiders who are constantly dealing with staffing issues in their own shops.

- continuing your professional education, even if your employer cannot or is unwilling to cover the cost. Do not limit yourself to educational opportunities within the fundraising industry. There are excellent resources in the for-profit world and, in many cases, content is largely transferrable to Development.

- making yourself increasingly interesting to donors. Pursue hobbies, go places, learn new things. Maximize your personal time in ways that make you happy and add value to your life. This will open doors to more donors while making you eager to get up each morning and go to work. Well rested and inspired by life, you will get more done in fewer hours and your attitude will be brighter. That will be noticed by your boss, which, in turn, will position you well for other opportunities. By insisting to yourself that you stop working and have some fun, your work – as well as your life – will improve.

Applying for Advertised Positions

Going after internal promotions and positioning yourself for jobs before they become available are the superior job-seeking strategies. But, every once in awhile, you may come across an advertised position that is very enticing. When applying for a posted job, this will improve your chances for getting short-listed:

- Craft a winning resume on Mr. Blue Suit's model described in Chapter 6. Most important, define each position you held by the goals you reached or exceeded, the ideas you innovated and the other non-financial achievements you realized.

- Create a letter that someone will be eager to read and which expresses your enthusiasm for the not-for-profit to which you are applying. A well constructed resume showcases your skills and accomplishments but it cannot answer the question, "Why do you want to work here?" The tone and content of your narrative should make it apparent that you are not simply responding to every posted job ad that comes along but applying for this position in particular, after careful consideration of both the opportunity and the not-for-profit. Communicate how this job offers you an exciting challenge at this point in your career.

"I Can't Believe I Did Something That Stupid!"

Avoid these common mistakes that get job applicants short-listed....for the waste basket:

- Linking your resume to your Facebook account. I click the link every time, by the way. The information I find is always very revealing and it never enhances the applicant's chances of getting hired by my firm. What you do in your off-hours is your business, but if I learn from your Facebook page that you won first prize in the beer-drinking contest each weekend last month, don't be surprised if I don't hire you. I don't want you and your deteriorating brain cells on my team on Monday morning. If you are applying for a job – or happily employed for that matter – take advantage of all possible privacy controls on your Facebook or other social media account.

- *I am pleased to submit my application for the position of Development Coordinator at Global Enviromental Foundation.* Always re-read your cover letter (more than once if you are sending an email) because a single spelling mistake can eliminate you from the competition. Your potential employer assumes that you are putting your best foot forward when you apply for a job. If you make sloppy mistakes in such crucial correspondence, she will be reluctant to put you through to the interview stage.

- *I am pleased to submit my application for the position of Development Coordinator at Global Environmental Foundation.* OK, that's better....except for one minor detail. This particular application is going to the Greenwood Humane Society. Cut-and-paste applications are risky. You are better off writing an original letter to accompany each job application. Starting from scratch lessens the chance of making expensive mistakes and gives you the opportunity to say why you are applying for this particular job.

- implying, or saying outright, that you are the best candidate for the position. Even if your qualifications are a perfect match for the job ad's stated requirements, only the employer can determine whether or not you are the best candidate. Claiming that you are will make you appear conceited, not confident.

How to Handle Over-Qualification if You Are the Candidate

If you are over-qualified but still eager to win the job, you should approach the interview realistically. Your first objective should be to set the interviewer or interview panel at ease, persuading those on the other side of the table that you are willing to roll up your sleeves and get the job done. Keep bringing the interview back to the concrete deliverables associated with the job and how you are the candidate who can reach or exceed the goal, on time and with minimal supervision.

I took a gamble by resigning in the expectation that my not-for-profit would beg me to stay and offer me more money and more senior responsibilities. It didn't happen. I wish I had the chance to do it over again; I would be much smarter today.

I was actively courted for a new job and left another job I loved to take it. Within three weeks, I knew I had made a mistake. I don't know what to do.

Being a team player will be on your potential employer's mind. Bring the issue up yourself if it is not referenced by the interviewer. Think of a recent situation in your career where you worked effectively with a diverse group of staff or where, as a manager, you inspired your staff to be successful. Acknowledge that your experience does not give you privileges over other colleagues but that it does give you insight into how to help them reach their potential as you strive to reach your own.

Why Did You Leave Your Last Job?

You must expect to be questioned about why you left your last position (or are intending to leave your current one) so ask yourself the question first. If you are leaving for any reason with a negative connotation, it is important to be introspective about how you contributed to the outcome. What role did you play in allowing the relationship between you and your boss to deteriorate? What did you fail to do or to do well enough that caused your team to fall short of the goal? Why did your enthusiasm for the job or the organization wane? No experienced employer will accept an assessment that the fault lies fully with your previous boss. Laying blame elsewhere will be interpreted as a reluctance to take responsibility.

Take time to think about the supervisory or management style under which you thrive and the kind of work culture that enhances or inhibits your ability to perform. You can wow any potential employer with a beautifully phrased response to a challenging question, but that is not the point. If you are leaving a less than satisfactory work experience, now is the time to think through how you will handle things differently when a version of the same problem arises again – because it will.

You should also think about the qualities you are seeking in an employer – who and what you need to help you get to a better place. Are you the kind of employee who bottles everything up inside because you are reluctant to express your views when you have the chance? Is fear of failure so intense that your first reaction to under-performance is to look for a scapegoat? Are you poor at motivating yourself to reach ever-increasing fundraising goals? On the other hand, do donors find you engaging and persuasive? Do your written communications make delighted readers catch their breath? Do your colleagues praise your loyalty and trustworthiness?

Look for a boss who will help you capitalize on your strengths while working with you to overcome your weaknesses. Employers will appreciate you on many levels if you tell them how you are trying to make yourself a better fundraiser.

After engaging in honest self-assessment about why you are leaving your current job, after thoroughly investigating your potential new employer, and after presenting your skills and career hopes as well as you possibly can, that little voice inside your head may still be whispering, "Be careful." Take your time and be sure before you accept the job. Your integrity and your future are on the line.

The same applies when the shoe is on the other foot. After screening applicants carefully, after interviewing short-listed candidates to the best of your ability, and after checking references diligently, you may still have doubts about your finalist. Even if you cannot precisely articulate why you are unsure, do not proceed with the hire. You will regret it every time.

Chapter 9:
Hiring the People Who Lead

John Campbell was the best boss I've ever had. I try to remember his leadership as I manage a department of six young professionals, because I was a young fundraiser and mother when John was my boss. John was collaborative, hard working, focused on relationships. He never took sole credit for our department's successes (which were substantial). He said thank you meaningfully and often. He used to say he was smart enough to hire great people and get out of their way so they could succeed. I try to remember that advice every time I'm hiring someone. He made sure the President of the hospital was aware of the work I did as an Assistant Director. He allowed me to shine in front of Board members. He assigned me responsibilities based on my ability – not my title – including multi-million-dollar proposals. I was allowed to grow under John's leadership and this was a key reason why I stayed for many years.

John died ten years ago at the age of 42 and there are so many times I wish I could thank him for his leadership and for the influence he had on my life.

Every Job Is Connected to Every Other Job

It takes the combined efforts of professional fundraisers, Chief Executive Officers and leadership volunteers to maximize fundraising success. According to donors, each of these three key players brings something unique to the job of raising money.

Volunteers have the one thing that paid staff can never possess – influence. A quick thank-you call from a volunteer can turn a first-time donor into a permanent supporter. A word of praise from a member of the Board can inspire a corporation to sponsor an event for years. A personal request from a leadership volunteer can land a gift that puts a fundraising drive over the top. The charitable sector is well aware of the power that leadership volunteers bring to fundraising. No not-for-profit would ever dream of embarking on an ambitious capital campaign without first assembling a team of committed volunteers to lead the effort.

Donors see volunteering as the highest form of community service and volunteering in positions of responsibility, as represented by Board members, even more laudable. Donors will go to extraordinary lengths with their philanthropy at the encouragement of leadership volunteers.

Chief Executive Officers have a different and no less critical role to play in fundraising. While Board members have influence, CEOs have authority. Donors look to CEOs as the gatekeepers of the not-for-profit organizations that they support. CEOs own the strategy and are responsible for getting results. When donors consider funding new or existing programs, they look to CEOs for assurance that their money will be wisely spent.

Professional fundraisers have neither influence nor authority bestowed upon them, but they are still extraordinarily important to fundraising success. The people who are paid to raise money hold the most complex jobs in fundraising. They earn donors' trust by cultivating meaningful relationships, playing the dual roles of facilitators and advisors. Donors see paid fundraising staff as the guardians of their philanthropy, entrusting them with personal and financial information that they would never divulge to Board members or CEOs. In order to be as effective as possible, professional fundraisers must also be internal facilitators and advisors. This particularly delicate aspect of their jobs requires them to manage up so that their CEOs and Board members bring their respective authority and influence to bear at the right time and in the right way.

A Matter of Role Confusion

Board members, CEOs and professional fundraisers were all surveyed on their views concerning fundraising responsibilities. Each group was offered the identical list of fundraising job functions and asked to identify who was responsible for what. (Note that respondents were asked to say who *is* actually responsible, not who *should be*.) The most interesting finding was the extent to which the three groups disagreed.

Chief Executive Officers' responses were the most realistic, reflecting the broadest insight. CEOs seemed to have a good grasp of who is best suited to execute tasks related to raising money. Board members and professional fundraisers seriously missed the mark, but not in the same way. Board members stood out for resisting responsibility in areas where they should be using their discreet influence with donors. Professional fundraisers took the opposite stance, claiming every aspect of fundraising as their job. No doubt unintentionally, they revealed a weakness regarding their own ability to help Board members and CEOs play their fundraising roles effectively. They also tended to be unrealistic about the kind of task and the volume of work they could accomplish on their own as professional fundraisers.

Table 17: Disparate Views on Fundraising Responsibility Among Board Members, CEOs & Professional Staff

Fundraising Activity	Board Members			CEO			Professional Fundraisers		
	Board	CEO	FR Staff	Board	CEO	FR Staff	Board	CEO	FR Staff
Offering names/information on prospects	X			X					X
In-person "asks"			X	X					X
Thank-you letters to donors			X		X				X
Thank-you calls to donors			X	X					X
Attending events to meet and socialize with donors	X			X					X
Conceiving/planning fundraising events			X			X			X
Executing fundraising events			X			X			X
Determining the case for fundraising			X	X					X
Evaluating fundraisers' performance	X			X					X
Developing the fundraising strategic plan	X		X	X					X

Responsibility or Suitability?

Board members assume too little responsibility and professional staff assume too much, and both do so out of uncertainty. Board members worry about having the time available to raise money and/or that they will be unsuccessful when they try. Paid fundraisers worry that if they don't do it themselves the work will not get done, regardless of who could actually have the best chance of success. So they claim responsibility for everything in a futile attempt to prevent things from falling through the cracks. While CEOs are more realistic, they tend to let their Board members off the hook concerning tasks that leadership volunteers most certainly should be shouldering.

Perhaps the problem is responsibility itself. It is entirely understandable that busy leadership volunteers are reluctant to take on responsibilities additional to those they already have – especially ones that require skill and confidence and which must be executed outside Board meetings. But if they understood how influential they are and how much they are admired by donors, they might look at fundraising differently. And, if CEOs saw their Board members as a fundraising asset that no one else can replicate, they might put more effort into encouraging their volunteers to play a productive role. They would certainly have a better shot at success. Board members are more likely to be persuaded into action by their CEOs than by paid fundraising staff.

The issue, then, is not responsibility but suitability. Positioned as "who has the know-how or the influence" rather than "who is responsible", it is easier to line up fundraising tasks behind the person (or the title) with the best likelihood for success. Table 18 references the same job functions itemized in table 17, but assigns duties by best chance of success and by taking donors' opinions into account. Note that, in almost every case, two and sometimes all three parties are required to collaborate in

I know that a board is critical to fundraising success. I also know that you're only as good as the volunteer who has been serving the longest. In our case, this is someone who will not contribute. I need to get this person off my Board.

Most Board members feel that they can give staff a name and the donor will respond to our call. Board members do not see the need to get involved.

order to produce the best result. Regarding conceiving, planning and executing events, a Fundraising Committee of the Board would logically be charged with those responsibilities, but the Board, in their overseeing role with all Committees, would remain responsible for ensuring the event's success.

Table 18: Who Has the Best Chance of Success with Donors?

Fundraising Activity	Board	CEO	Fundraising Staff
Offering names/information on prospects	X	X	X
In-person "asks"	X	X	X
Thank-you letters to donors	X	X	X
Thank-you calls to donors	X	X	X
Attending events to meet and socialize with donors	X	X	
Conceiving/planning fundraising events	X		X
Executing fundraising events	X		
Determining the case for fundraising	X	X	
Evaluating fundraisers' performance		X	
Developing the fundraising strategic plan		X	X

Shared responsibility does not mean that two or more parties are equally responsible for a single task – something that leads to everyone waiting for someone else to make the first move or to take on the toughest part of the job. In an environment where responsibility is shared but talent is recognized, two or three parties have distinct, yet symbiotic roles to play in most fundraising activities. These examples illustrate.

Offering names/information on prospects. Board and Committee volunteers are well positioned to offer prospects from their networks, and so are CEOs, especially those who have a high profile in the community. But, while they could bring those names forward, they often hesitate and this is understandable. Just because they are known to the volunteer doesn't mean they are actually good prospects for fundraising. Meanwhile, their Development chief is managing a donor database that is overflowing with names, all of whom at one time or another chose to support their not-for-profit. It is very productive to bring some of those names forward to Board members and the CEO and ask them to identify leadership connections that could move these donors up the giving ladder or re-engage those who have lapsed.

In-person asks. Yes, the influence and authority of Board members and the CEO give a not-for-profit a much better chance of success. But that is actually not the case when it comes to the most lucrative fundraising program of all. Negotiating planned gifts (largely but not solely bequests) requires the solicitor to have specialized expertise and often involves the disclosure of donors' personal financial information. In this most profitable fundraising program of all, influence is no longer the asset it usually is; skill and impartiality are required and professional fundraisers have both.

Thank-you letters. Professional staff should definitely be drafting thank-you letters but Board members should be signing them. "Signed by a leadership volunteer" was one of the twenty characteristics that donors said make thank-you letters stand out and which influence their future giving.[1]

Thank-you calls to donors. My extensive research on the subject confirms that calls made by Board members and CEOs which thank donors for gifts just received extend loyalty and increase future gift values (i.e., make more profit). But charities running large campaigns often gain more new or renewing donors than Board members can acknowledge promptly and personally. While no one can match the influence of a leadership volunteer, donors still appreciate receiving a thank-you call from a professional fundraiser. Furthermore, Development staff deserve to enjoy the number one perk in fundraising, which is talking to donors when they are not asking for money. It turns a bad day into a good one and inspires fundraisers to keep reaching for the goal. Staff – and volunteers – should do this every day.

Governance versus Management

Table 17 exposed Board members' role confusion on key fundraising issues related to governance (where the Board belongs) and management (where it does not). Board members felt that professional fundraisers were responsible for determining the selling case to donors. This is definitely not the job of staff. It is the responsibility of the Board itself, in consultation with the CEO, to articulate the strategy for programs and services growth, in measurable terms and within a specific timeframe. After this is done, fundraisers can be counted upon to wordsmith the case, making it as attractive as possible to donors. Boards that assign the job of defining the case to fundraisers are, in effect, allowing staff to decide how their not-for-profits will carry out their missions while relinquishing their most important task and exciting privilege as governors of the organization.

Boards we surveyed also felt they should be evaluating the performance of fundraising staff, when that is actually not their job. Doing so crosses the line into staff management, which is the sole purview of the Chief Executive Officer. The only staff member whose performance the Board evaluates is the CEO herself. The

Our CEO should be more supportive of fundraising and fundraising staff to the Board rather than letting them push their personal agendas off on staff.

---

[1] *Donor-Centered Fundraising,* Penelope Burk, Cygnus Applied Research, Inc., Chicaho, IL, 2003.

Viable candidates are those who can think and reason broadly, keep confidences and steward donors and prospects.

What makes a highly effective fundraiser? Someone who can work closely and influentially with the Chair of the Board, convincing this top volunteer to engage in fundraising without him realizing that he is being managed.

same applies to planning. It is the job of the Board and CEO to establish the overall strategy, but plans for carrying out that strategy, including the fundraising plan, should be developed by the CEO and his staff.

Understanding Who Does What Best Is the First Step to a Good Hire

Hiring the people who lead is easier when responsibilities are converted into talent needs, and tasks into opportunities for success. This is not just a mental exercise to make fundraising appear less daunting. It is a practical approach to raising money that prioritizes the advantages of influence and authority that Boards and CEOs bring to the table. Apprehension subsides and confidence rises when leadership volunteers and top executives understand how much they are admired by donors and how willing donors are to reach for the stars when approached by the right people in the right way.

What Separates Great Fundraising Chief Executives from Other Not-for-Profit CEOs

When hiring a new CEO, the Board is seeking that special someone who can excel at a variety of tasks, only some of which relate to raising money. But when a Chief Executive Officer has characteristics and credentials that are fundraising assets, Development soars to new heights. The CEO is not just an additional source of paid fundraising manpower. Fundraising staff, leadership volunteers and donors all agree that the CEO plays a different and highly critical role in Development. Her knowledge of how fundraising works – his skill at managing staff – the role she chooses to play with donors – whether and how he exerts influence on the Board – all shape the tone and direction that fundraising takes. The CEO can unilaterally make or break the entire Development operation.

The research studies that contributed to this book were constant reminders of the pivotal role that CEOs play in fundraising. Satisfied Directors of Development with lengthy tenures gave considerable credit to their bosses for creating a workplace culture that motivated fundraisers to stay longer in their jobs and work more productively. 83% credited their CEOs for ensuring that the Director of Fundraising is an active and respected member of the senior decision-making team. 60% referenced the positive and supportive attitude their CEOs have towards fundraising which motivates their desire to stay. The importance of this latter attribute cannot be overstated. The Chief Executive Officer exerts more influence on staff and leadership volunteers than does anyone else in the organization. A signal from her that fundraising is a positive force and a priority sets the right tone with all staff and with leadership volunteers whose commitment to fundraise actively is vital.

The Fundraising Advantages of Great CEOs

Chief Executive Officers participating in our study and who had substantial management experience identified these leadership advantages they bring to fundraising:

- **they prefer a collaborative approach to fundraising management.** Progressive CEOs eschew a top-down management style for a truly collaborative working relationship with their Chief Development Officers. The order of seniority remains intact, but collaborative CEOs understand that seasoned Development managers bring a unique skill set to their not-for-profits. On most issues, they operate as partners rather than as bosses and employees. Charities often look with admiration and envy to top universities whose fundraising prowess and campaign goals are legendary. Collaboration is the hallmark of these successful institutions, with the chief fundraiser holding Vice Presidential status and working as a close colleague of the President.

- **they see fundraising leadership as one of their core jobs.** Great CEOs do not shy away from fundraising. They are fully engaged in the knowledge that their commitment breeds success which, in turn, means higher quality programs and services delivered to more people. Their engagement is not just philosophical; it translates on the ground into meaningful time spent with fundraising staff, active engagement in donor cultivation and asks, persuasive interaction with the Board and active involvement in the community.

- **they set clear expectations and demand accountability.** Ambitious and focused CEOs are as demanding of their fundraising staff as they are of themselves. They earn their staff's respect and achieve better results because they set clear expectations for Development based on fair and measurable performance criteria.

- **they credit and recognize fundraising staff for their achievements.** The best Chief Executives put all the necessary elements in place for fundraisers to succeed, then give the credit to their staff when good things happen. Top-flight CEOs never miss an opportunity to offer praise – privately to fundraisers themselves and publicly to other staff and, especially, to the Board. Exemplary CEOs do not take personal credit for achievements in fundraising, even when they deserve to do so. They know that when they

My CEO truly enjoys fundraising because he sees what it accomplishes in changing lives. He is a great story-teller.

I may be different from a lot of CEOs. I truly enjoy fundraising and I love working with my Development team. I understand fundraising on both a philosophical and an economic level.

Characteristics of great bosses, according to fundraisers:

40% Strategic / goal-oriented
40% Supportive of fundraising staff
34% Supportive of fundraising as a core activity
28% Understands his / her role and plays it effectively
25% Skilled in "making asks"

acknowledge their staff's achievements, they are using their power in the most positive and productive way possible.

What Development Directors Look for in a Great Fundraising Boss

Directors of Development identified these key behaviors, management tactics and leadership skills of CEOs that make them the bosses that fundraisers want to work for:

- **they are goal-oriented.** Fundraisers are salespeople, driven to reach specific, ambitious targets and they look to their CEOs to set or ratify them. Setting fundraising goals is both a science and an art; goals must be ambitious enough to inspire fundraisers to work at peak performance but still achievable in order to prevent a sense of failure from permeating the Development office. Finding that sweet spot requires tempering desire with objective evidence. CEOs with an understanding of fundraising data and donor history have an advantage. Those who also know enough about fundraising to question less productive but ingrained practices while recognizing innovative ideas are better equipped to set ambitious yet reachable goals. Even CEOs who are highly experienced fundraisers themselves do a better job of goal-setting when they establish targets collaboratively with their Development chiefs. Setting unrealistic goals or setting goals unilaterally creates a "them and us" relationship between leadership and those charged with raising the money. In this top-down culture, management by pressure, criticism and fear often trumps the more progressive alternative.

- **they adopt a strategic approach to fulfilling the mission.** Great CEOs always know what they are trying to accomplish this year – and three years out – and they have a measurable, evidence-based plan as their roadmap. This plan is also their fundraisers' selling case to donors and the single most important tool in raising money. The strategic plan rouses donors' imagination and inspires them to commit gifts within a set timeline.

  Given its importance, it is troubling that only 59% of CEOs surveyed said their organizations have such a plan in place. Without a strategy that articulates specific measurable goals to be reached in each program or service, fundraisers are relegated to selling the brand over and over again (see Chapter 4).

- **they are respectful and supportive of fundraisers' professional judgment.** CEOs who are characterized this way resist the "old-school" approach to raising money in which high-risk, high-cost fundraising ventures are valued as much as or more than sophisticated, relationship-based strategies. CEOs who respect their fundraisers' judgment do not believe that "anyone can raise money". They know that fundraising is a profession requiring specialized knowledge and progressive experience. They trust their fundraising staff's judgment and seek their advice on the best ways to raise funds sustainably.

- **they are aware of the importance of the role they play as CEOs in making fundraising successful.** Effective CEOs do not divest all responsibility for fundraising to professional staff; rather they remain responsible for the overall success of fundraising just as they do with any other aspect of the not-for-profit. They also use their unique influence as CEOs to increase the chances of success.

- **they are supportive of fundraising when dealing with the Board.** Great CEOs establish a positive culture throughout the organization but especially at the Board table, instilling confidence in leadership volunteers as they strive to reach ambitious fundraising targets. CEOs who bring a positive attitude about fundraising to the Board are able to engage more members in the work of raising money while making it easier for staff to hold volunteers accountable for results.

- **they are skilled at interacting with donors and asking them for gifts.** It is the job of Development professionals to ensure that donors are asked for gifts that are generous within their own means and that no donor or potential donor falls through the cracks. Fundraisers draw on many resources to accomplish this, including their two most valuable assets – their Board members and their Chief Executive Officer. The individual and collective influence of top leadership can inspire donors to take their philanthropy to extraordinary heights. When a CEO is both an impressive representative of the organization and effective at stewarding donors and asking for gifts, professional fundraisers know they have the best possible advantage for fundraising success.

Characteristics of CEOs that Disadvantage Fundraising

Development Directors and one-person-shop fundraisers who were planning to leave their jobs were asked to identify the characteristics or behaviors of their CEOs that inhibited efforts to raise money. These issues were noted most often:

- **lack of direction from the top concerning how funds raised would be used.** 45% of fundraisers who were planning to leave expressed frustration about this issue. Without clear direction from leadership that answers donors' number one question, "Why do you need my money?", fundraisers must settle for fewer donors and less-than-generous gifts.

The best CEO I ever had influenced people to do a lot of things – donors to give, volunteers to give time, and staff to perform at the very highest level.

Though top management is supportive of fundraising in general, there is little real understanding about the difference between good and bad fundraising. We sometimes divert a lot of precious time and resources into risky ventures with low return.

Characteristics of poor bosses on fundraising matters, according to respondents:

20% Unrealistic timeframe for raising money
19% Does not assess performance objectively
16% No objectives–based strategies in place
12% Insufficient fundraising budget
12% Reluctant to make asks

- **unrealistic expectations concerning the timeline for reaching fundraising targets.** Opinions about the length of time it should take to reach a fundraising goal (or to close a single ask) divide professional fundraisers and their bosses more than any other issue. 24% of Directors of Development and 26% of one-person-shop fundraisers identified unrealistically short timelines for raising money as a main reason behind their intentions to leave their current jobs. But 49% of CEOs who were also surveyed on the issue said that failing to reach the fundraising goal on time was due to substandard performance by their Development staff. CEOs were much less likely to question the efficacy of the goals and timelines that had been set.

The timeline issue is symptomatic of a bigger problem. It definitely takes longer to raise money if fundraisers have to work without the benefit of the influence that their Board members and the CEO bring to the job. Influence secures an appointment without weeks' worth of cold calling; influence allows solicitors to move more quickly to the ask; influence ups the chances of getting "yes" instead of "no"; and influence makes bigger asks possible. CEOs and Boards estimate the time required to reach goals based on what it would take if they were raising the money; then they assign the job to their paid fundraisers who can never have that kind of influence precisely because they are paid to raise money. Timelines need to be adjusted if the CEO is divesting responsibility for raising money to paid fundraisers. But, if the CEO remains ready to use her influence whenever it is called upon, and ensures that the Board does the same, ambitious targets can be met sooner.

Timelines are also unrealistic if they fail to take into account donors, their current commitments and the way they make giving decisions. On this issue, capital campaigns prove themselves superior, once again. In a pre-campaign feasibility or market study, research explores whether potential donors warm to the case and whether they will give if the campaign proceeds. But these studies also explore donors' other philanthropic commitments that could prevent them from giving if the campaign were to launch in the near future. Donors' personal timelines are carefully considered by the consultants who conduct these feasibility studies so that they can advise their clients on both the campaign's viability and the length of time it will take to reach the goal.

In day-to-day fundraising, however, this strategic and common-sense approach to setting goals and timelines goes out the window. Goals are set based on need for the money (the more serious the need, the shorter the fundraising timeline) instead of on evidence that the not-for-profit has enough cultivated donors and a strong enough case to make reaching the target by a particular deadline possible.

- **failing to assess staff's performance objectively and/or regularly.** Regular feedback and support from their bosses keeps fundraisers driving towards the goal; and meaningful supervision and guidance helps them avoid disasters. Development staff need timely performance reviews because they are always working to specific targets and deadlines. CEOs who are less knowledge-able about fundraising or less skilled as leaders may keep their fundraisers at arm's length, leaving them to achieve objectives and solve problems on their own. In fact, CEOs do not need to be experts at raising money themselves in order to manage fundraisers effectively, but they also cannot distance them-selves from this management role and still be effective Chief Executives.

Assessing fundraisers' performance in a timely fashion simply requires put-ting formal and informal reviews on a schedule and sticking to it. This is a challenge for busy CEOs, but, if they knew how it affected the bottom line, they would prioritize rather than avoid this job. Staff who receive regular, objective feedback raise more money. Success heightens satisfaction which, in turn, lengthens their tenure. Performance reviews facilitate a simultane-ous increase in revenue and decrease in cost, (see Chapter 11).

Regularity of performance reviews is important; what is evaluated during reviews is equally vital. On this issue, there appears to be much confusion among CEOs and even among Directors of Development about what con-stitute meaningful evaluation criteria. Chapter 11 also reveals the typical measures that employers rely on and the different measures that are actually more useful when evaluating the performance of professional fundraisers.

- **setting Development budgets that are insufficient to support fundrais-ing growth.** Most CEOs and Board members surveyed agreed that invest-ment in fundraising was important or, at least, inevitable in order to real-ize a greater future return. However, opinions differed significantly on the length of time that decision-makers should invest in new fundraising strate-gies before expecting to recover the outlay. 31% of CEOs said they would invest in fundraising only if return on investment could be realized in the same fiscal year, something that is actually a cash flow, not an investment, decision. 39% felt they would be willing to invest for 18 months, a period of time that is generally insufficient to achieve sustainable growth in rela-tionship-based (major gifts) fundraising where profit is highest. Only 30% of CEOs would invest in a new fundraising initiative for two years before expecting to recover their initial investment. This is actually the minimum period of time that Development needs in order to produce any degree of sustainable return.

The thing I can't deal with is a boss who doesn't keep her fundraisers informed. It makes us look stupid in front of donors and it leaves donors suspicious that our own organization doesn't trust us with important information.

- **being reluctant or outright unwilling to ask donors for gifts.** This was noted far more often by one-person-shop fundraisers (27%) than by Directors of fundraising operations with multiple staff (12%). When all responsibility for raising money falls on the shoulders of a single individual, it is critical that the CEO and the Board act as a high level resource for fundraising.

- **having a negative or unsupportive attitude towards fundraising.** This was noted by 53% of Development staff who were planning to leave their jobs. Most said their CEOs were keen to have the money that Development staff raise but reluctant to make either procedural or attitudinal changes that would establish a more favorable climate for fundraising. Not surprising, these CEOs do not play a meaningful role in fundraising themselves. In some extreme cases, resentment that their not-for-profits are compelled to raise money in order to survive permeates the working atmosphere.

How to Hire a CEO Who Makes Fundraising Soar

If a beloved CEO is leaving, you will be praying for another to come along who is just like her. If you are finally unloading a tyrant, you will be hoping to avoid anyone who reminds you of that individual. By all means study those positive and negative traits so that you are better equipped to conduct a good hire. But resist basing your assessment of candidates on the individual who went before. A better way to hire is to focus on practical and measurable qualifications and experience and ask questions that showcase these attributes. This will allow you to rate candidates objectively against one another, which, in turn, will reveal the best possible staff leader for your organization at this time.

There are certain big-picture attributes in high performing CEOs that are a boon to fundraising. At the same time, these qualities also benefit their not-for-profits in many other ways. CEOs who develop a profile in the community and who are well spoken and confident in media interviews, for example, attract high performing staff in all disciplines, not just in fundraising. They act as magnets to community members who are seeking rewarding experiences as leadership volunteers. They also make under-achievers think twice about applying for jobs in their not-for-profits. Great CEOs exert positive influence in every direction.

Hiring the Person Who Will Hold the Board's Feet to the Fire

It is a particularly delicate situation when interviews with CEO candidates turn to fundraising. Whether the hire is conducted internally or involves a search firm, Board members will be interviewing candidates at some stage. They will be keen to know how candidates would manage a team of professional fundraisers (or the sole practitioner in a small shop) in order to increase productivity. But will they really want to explore how candidates would manage the Board in order to improve fundraising productivity among volunteers? It takes objectivity and humility for a Board to acknowledge its own deficiencies. It also takes maturity to ask CEO candidates how they would help the Board do a better job, especially in fundraising which may not be high on leadership volunteers' list of favorite activities.

While search firms add considerable value to the hiring process overall, the role they play as intermediaries between clients and candidates is a particular boon to fundraising. Firms with a track record in providing counsel to not-for-profits on management and/or fundraising are particularly adept at assessing the Board's fundraising strengths and weaknesses and seeking CEO candidates who are a good match. Boards that prefer to handle this key hire without help of counsel will benefit from examining where they perform well or need to improve in raising money. The section, "Fundraising Expectations Should Align with Board Members' Talents", found later in this chapter, and Table 28 in Chapter 12, will help Boards conduct that self-assessment before interviewing CEO candidates.

Phrasing Interview Questions Advantageously

When we asked CEOs to identify their fundraising advantages, many referred to their management style. Energetic, open-door, fair, motivational, supportive and, especially, not prone to micro-managing, were most often cited as traits that helped them secure and retain good fundraisers. Being credible, having passion for the cause, being flexible, having high expectations and other laudable qualities were also referenced.

When hiring a new CEO, interviewers should expect to hear these descriptions but they are not very useful when considering the merits of one candidate over another. It is important to dig deeper to determine whether candidates have what it takes to lead. Characteristics like being credible or flexible or fair are the conclusions you draw by assessing other things that are more tangible. No one would apply for a job by referring to herself as lacking credibility, being inflexible or acting unfairly. So, when considering how to phrase questions effectively, interviewers should ask themselves:

- *Am I relying on something that is impossible to assess about this candidate's qualifications for the job?*
- *Does the question I am asking truly illuminate how the candidate will make decisions, manage staff, etc?*

The best advice I could give a CEO is this: If fundraising is not your strength, admit it and be willing to learn. Let your fundraiser know that she reports to you but you are listening to her and letting her take the lead when her expertise warrants it.

The left-hand column of Table 19 includes some common generalizations that candidates make when asked to talk about themselves in relation to fundraising or managing fundraising staff. On the right are examples of interview questions that will elicit much more valuable information. These questions focus on specific actions taken or results achieved, from which interviewers will be able to conclude whether candidates possess the admirable traits they espouse.

Table 19: Translating Characteristics into Questions that Facilitate Measurable Assessment of CEO Candidates

How Candidates Define Their Management Skills by Characteristic	Questions that Define Management Skill by Action
I care about donors	How many calls a month did you make to donors (in person or by phone) in your last job? Describe your most successful relationship with a donor and how you built it over time.
I believe in professional development	In the most recent recession, what was the fate of the professional development budget in your organization – was it reduced, eliminated altogether, maintained, or increased – why? How do you assess the kind of professional development that your chief fundraiser requires?
I am strategic	What information and data do you expect your chief fundraiser to give you so that you can determine whether or not fundraising is headed in the right direction? Describe a situation in your recent career in which you intervened early to prevent a potentially negative outcome in fundraising? What were the signals that caused you to step in? How did you turn the situation around?
I am a good mentor/coach	What is the difference between being a boss and being a mentor? What are the three most important attributes of a mentor or coach? Pick one and describe how you used it in your current job to cultivate a skill or inspire achievement in your Development Director.
I am passionate about the organization/ mission	So are we…or some such response. Then move on to the next question (see Chapter 8, Blinded by the Brand).
I have high expectations of my fundraising team	How were fundraising goals established in the organization you last worked for? (Probe for information that demonstrates that goals were based on actual past performance, not on need or conjecture.) Describe how you managed your chief fundraiser in a situation where he/she failed to reach a pre-established fundraising goal.
I am not a micro-manager	What do you need to know from your chief fundraiser in order to set or approve the fundraising goal? How do you assure accountability by your fundraising team for reaching the goal? At what intervals do you expect to be updated on progress towards the goal? Why is this schedule most appropriate for managing fundraising? Describe a recent situation in which you had to intervene because an interim target was not going to be met. Explain what you did to get fundraising back on track.

Interviewing CEO Candidates about Fundraising

Professional fundraisers, leadership volunteers and the CEO have different, yet connected, roles to play in making fundraising successful. And the CEO's job is definitely the trickiest. She must manage up and down simultaneously, motivating both Board and staff to succeed. The CEO must also be directly engaged in key major asks and relationship-building. Donors look to the Chief Executive Officer as the person who really knows whether and how their gifts will help accomplish measurable progress.

The description in Chapter 8 about how to create an optimum environment for interviewing fundraisers applies equally to interviewing candidates for the position of Chief Executive Officer. Holding interviews in rooms that are "lived in", coming out from behind the desk, engaging in informal conversation first – these things and more set the stage for a productive interview while answering your most important question, "Is this someone we would enjoy working with?" Candidates' answers to specific interview questions will paint the rest of the picture.

Qualities that are a boon to fundraising will reveal themselves in those first few minutes. Look for:

- a sense of presence or charisma – if it is there, you will feel it as the candidate enters the room.

- a manner that puts people at ease while making them feel important. People with this quality are genuinely interested in other people. If you are in conversation with someone who exhibits this characteristic, you are the only person in the room.

- a positive outlook. While anyone applying for an important job will be making every effort to adopt a positive demeanor, genuinely positive individuals have a "can do" attitude towards work and life, including the tough stuff like tackling major challenges and effecting change. They exude confidence – not over-confidence, but a calm appreciation of their own ability, earned over years of learning the hard way: through living.

Getting Down to Business

The following sample questions acknowledge the singular role that a CEO plays in fundraising while also focusing on the bottom line. They are examples only; the actual questions a not-for-profit asks would relate to its particular Development portfolio and priorities and, especially, what it hopes to change or improve in order to increase fundraising profit. The interview panel must also be sufficiently well informed about fundraising in order to understand whether candidates are offering valuable insights. The Chief Development Officer should be a member of the interview team.

- **Candidates' Knowledge of Fundraising:** When CEOs we surveyed were asked to identify their single best advantage in attracting and sustaining the loyalty of good fundraisers, what they said and didn't say were equally revealing. The asset they referenced most often was their own knowledge of fundraising.

Some CEOs used to be professional fundraisers themselves, something that is becoming increasingly commonplace. However, even more CEOs have never been fundraisers, yet they understand the complexity and demands of the job and are very successful at hiring and retaining good Development staff.

Knowing what fundraising is and knowing how to increase fundraising profit are two different things, however. As the interview shifts to the subject of raising money, the first objective is to find out how much the candidate knows about the business. A candidate who understands, for example, that the objective of all fundraising is to move donors up to a state of "giving generously within their own means" has a more sophisticated understanding than one who focuses on increasing revenue in a lower level fundraising program. These sample interview questions illustrate:

Describe your philosophy regarding the role that fundraising plays in the not-for-profit where you currently work (worked recently). Candidates' answers to this question reveal their attitude towards fundraising, the single most important determinant of whether fundraising will thrive or experience a setback under their leadership. Candidates with an aversion to fundraising or who think they can dissociate themselves from Development hurt their not-for-profits' efforts to raise more money.

Please walk us through fundraising as it is structured in your current organization. Be sure to describe how one fundraising program impacts the next. This is simply a more restrained way of saying, "Tell us what you know about raising money so we can evaluate your level of sophistication on this subject."

What changing donor trends are you seeing that influence how you manage fundraising staff? CEO candidates who actually realize that changes are going on, such as donors choosing to support fewer causes or making giving decisions more independently rather than passively responding to appeals, display an insight well above the norm. They are also incredibly valuable leaders because they make budget decisions, interact with the Board and manage staff in ways that take this information into account.

What is stewardship, in your view, and how do you measure its value on fundraising's bottom line? If you find a CEO candidate with an enlightened view on this subject, he is definitely a fundraising industry leader. There is a big difference between impactful and superficial stewardship. The former focuses staff time on crafting personal and inspired acknowledgements and communications that provide measurable information in order to grow productive relationships with donors. The latter occupies staff time with perusing token gift catalogues and manufacturing gift levels and benefits on the mistaken assumption that this influences giving.

How would you advise your Development team in building a robust donor base under the age of 40? CEO candidates who acknowledge that there are vast differences from one generation to the next are an asset for fundraising certainly, but also for not-for-profit branding, marketing and definitely staff management.

What is your position on investing in fundraising? How long are you willing to invest before that outlay is fully recovered? As referenced above, investment in lucrative, long-term strategies requires a minimum of two years before return is fully realized and, in some programs, just starts to flow. Exploring how a CEO might secure that investment would spark an interesting conversation.

On the same subject of investing in fundraising, can you provide a concrete example of a situation or opportunity in which you decided to invest in fundraising? How did you assess the value of that investment at the end of two years, and at the end of five years?

Similarly, what was the most recent occurrence in which you turned down a request from your Chief Development Officer to invest in fundraising? Why, and how would you assess that decision today?

- **How a CEO Candidate Will Contribute Directly to Fundraising Success:** While the CEO is central in motivating both professional staff and leadership volunteers, he also contributes directly to the fundraising bottom line. These questions explore the degree to which candidates are both willing to engage in fundraising and able to do a good job.

  For which parts of the spectrum in raising money are you ideally suited? Reference both your experience and personal preferences.

  Please describe a successful negotiation for a significant gift in which you were directly involved in making the ask. [supplementary if warranted] *What support did you request from fundraising staff and/or the Board in order to achieve this win?*

  In the past two years as a CEO, what would you say is your most disappointing major ask? Why? [supplementary] *If you had it to do over again, what would you have done differently in order to achieve a better result?*

CEOs are actually the chief fundraiser, whether they realize it or not. They should be available to meet with donors individually and in groups and be there when their fundraisers need them. Training is the key; it's not hard when you know what you're doing.

Please think about your proudest achievement in cultivating the interest of someone who eventually became a major donor. What role did you play in bringing this partnership about?

Please describe a recent situation where you rescued a relationship that was souring or had been severed altogether?

What was your role as CEO in the most recent donor recognition event where you currently work (recently worked)? [supplementary if warranted] *What role would you assign yourself today in a similar event that is recognizing donors?*

- **Supporting the Board in Their Fundraising Work:** Board members are key players on the interview panel. Interviewers whose Boards are under-performing in fundraising might be reluctant to ask questions that are too revealing. Or, if the Board has never assessed its own performance objectively, interviewers may simply not know what skills they need in a CEO that would help them do a better job. Even a top-flight Board in fundraising can still improve on its performance with the right support and leadership from the CEO.

Coaching a reluctant Board to raise money is perhaps the most challenging part of a Chief Executive Officer's job. Good interview questions reveal how candidates manage this delicate dance. At the same time, well structured questions give interviewers insight into how CEO candidates handle matters beyond fundraising as well. Phrased skillfully, questions unearth enlightening information while positioning Board-level fundraising in a constructive manner.

What do you feel are the three most important Board responsibilities in fundraising and why? [supplementary] *Describe the tenets of a board evaluation program relative to these responsibilities you just referenced.*

Please talk about your interpretation of the role of Board members in fundraising when there is a full complement of professional staff whose job it is to raise money.

While we would prefer that all Board members make generous, regular gifts to our organization, some members are reluctant to contribute, citing their volunteer time as a substitute for giving. What is your position concerning 100% of Board members giving to their not-for-profit? Why? How have you worked with your current or a recent Board to achieve that objective?

A few members of the Board are very active in fundraising but they shoulder a disproportionate load and are at risk of burning out. How have you helped your current or a recent Board share the responsibility for fundraising more equitably?

Though well connected, some members are reluctant to use their social or business network to expand our pool of donors and prospects. How have you helped Board members overcome their hesitation on this issue?

Describe a situation with a Board of Directors in which you played an instrumental role in moving members from reluctant and under-performing to goal-oriented and successful?

In your current not-for-profit, how would you describe your working relationship with the Chair of the Board on fundraising matters? [supplementary] *Specifically, how have you and your Chair worked together to achieve a fundraising goal?*

Similarly, how have you and the Chair worked together to overcome a problem related to fundraising? Please provide a specific, recent example.

Please describe a successful major gift ask involving a member of the Board where you were instrumental in coaching or supporting the volunteer.

What has been your least successful situation concerning fundraising in the past two years that involved you and the Board or a member of the Board?

- **On Managing Fundraising Staff:** While it is not compulsory for CEOs to be experienced fundraisers, it is essential that they know enough about raising money to manage for optimum results. They also need to project an attitude about fundraising that conveys the right message to Development professionals and all staff. These sample questions explore the critical relationship between the CEO and the Chief Development Officer. You may also wish to review the sample questions in Chapter 8, especially those related to hiring the Chief Development Officer. Slightly revised, some of them may be valuable depending upon the opportunities and issues with which your not-for-profit is currently contending.

Please describe the working relationship you have with your Chief Development Officer, including what you feel is its most important advantage for fundraising. [supplementary] *How, in your view, could the relationship be improved?*

I believe that the Board's job is fiduciary responsibility – strategic direction, hiring the CEO, etc. We shouldn't be expected to be donors and fundraisers as well. I see that as a conflict with our overseeing role.

Learning to work with Boards of Directors has been my biggest challenge…and achievement. They don't like staff telling them what to do, even when they are not fulfilling their fundraising responsibilities.

On what performance criteria do you currently evaluate your Chief Development Officer? (See Chapter 11, section on "Tenure-Extending Performance Evaluations", for the criteria that are and are not measurably useful.)

The Chief Financial Officer of our not-for-profit, who is well respected by the Board, and our Chief Development Officer do not agree regarding restricted versus unrestricted fundraising. We understand that restricted fundraising could be more lucrative but respect our long-standing CFO's position that as much money as possible should be raised unrestricted. What is your position on this issue and how would you work with the CFO and CDO to resolve the matter.[2]

Describe how you built cohesion in the organization where you currently work between goal-oriented fundraisers who are focused on making a profit and other staff who have a more not-for-profit, less bottom-line sensibility.

- **Fundraising Planning, Budgeting and Goal-Setting:** *From what you know about our organization, how would you articulate our most compelling case to donors at this time?* It is the quality and appealing nature of the case which largely determines fundraising success. This question affords the not-for-profit a valuable opportunity for an objective assessment of the case from an experienced leader. Even CEOs lose their objectivity once they are on the job. This is the best moment to get a truly valuable assessment.

  Please describe a situation where you have approved investing in fundraising beyond current budget limits. Why did you make this choice, and what was the outcome? Cost and investment are two different things. Do not let your preconceptions as Board members cloud your judgment. The answer to this question concerning investment offers insight into the candidate's leadership style well beyond how she manages fundraising.

  How did you establish the fundraising goal for the most recent fiscal year where you currently work? What did you review with your Chief Development Officer to assure yourself that the goal was both ambitious and reachable? Applying a percentage increase to last year's performance concedes a lesser level of understanding of how to budget fundraising. Forecasting based on patterns in donor behavior, combined with lessons learned from last year's fundraising efforts, is more reliable. [supplementary] *How close did you come to realizing that goal?*

  [supplementary if significantly over or under] *How have you adjusted your budget-setting process to ensure that more accurate or realistic goals are set in the*

[2] Restricted versus unrestricted fundraising is not simply a matter of preference. Restricted fundraising, i.e., asking for gifts for a specific, measurable project, program or area of service, is much more lucrative. See Chapter 4.

future? This is really the key issue. Anyone can be a good CEO when things are unfolding as planned. It is when things go wrong that a great CEO demonstrates his talent.

Where you currently work, what information do you request from your Chief Development Officer when reviewing interim progress on fundraising? If the answer is limited to revenue year-to-date or revenue now compared with the same time last year, this has value but is not nearly as revealing as statistics on donor retention and change in average gift value. Also, financial statistics against budget, especially when they are off the mark (in either direction) are not particularly useful unless accompanied by some kind of analysis explaining the discrepancy.

- **Avoiding Crises/Crisis Intervention:** *Please describe a recent situation in which you used or responded to the media in order to mediate or avert a negative situation at your not-for-profit.* For the person who becomes your candidate of choice, this would be an interesting question to ask of referees as well. [supplementary] *After the fact, how would you assess your performance? What would you have done differently if you had it to do over again?*

  What is the most significant fundraising-related problem you have had to face in your career as a CEO? How did you handle it? [supplementary] *What do you know now that you did not know then?*

- **Public Profile and Community Leadership:** *When was the last time you made a speech in your role as CEO of (current employer)? Who was the audience and what was the theme of your presentation?*

  If a fundraising conference were looking for a keynote speaker or session leader, what would you want to highlight from your unique perspective as a CEO to whom fundraisers report?

Reference-Checking as It Relates to CEO Candidates and Fundraising

No one wants their CEO to play a prominent role in fundraising more than the Chief Development Officer; so it is a good idea to include a reference from your candidate's current or most recent head of fundraising. This is the person who can speak to the candidate's skill in raising money and relating to donors. If questions are phrased well, there should be no concern about seeking a reference from someone who reports or reported to your candidate. Here are some examples:

While many Development professionals complain about lack of involvement of Board members in fundraising, I have seen the opposite. Sometimes an active, engaged fundraising Board is intimidating for a Development Director who is used to controlling the agenda. It takes a unique skill set to work with – and keep up with -- a high performance Board.

It's a good idea to ask finalist candidates if they would be willing to provide copies of performance reviews from previous employers. Employees have the right to request them and many do so.

Our CEO has no fundraising experience but insists on micromanaging our office. Some of the things she dictates are way out there, leaving me and my colleagues flabbergasted.

What would you say is/was your CEO's (former CEO's) single greatest advantage to fundraising in your organization?

How would you say your CEO's approach to fundraising changed, if at all, during the period in which you worked together?

In what kind of situations with donors does/did your CEO excel? Probe for skill in negotiating gifts with donors, hosting donors at special events, etc., where the candidate would be using his influence as the most senior member of the staff.

Can you describe a particularly critical gift negotiation in which your CEO played a central role? How would you assess his/her performance after the fact?

How would you assess your CEO at influencing the Board on carrying out their fundraising responsibilities? Can you give me a specific example where she made a positive difference with leadership volunteers?

What way(s) of interacting with your CEO have you found most successful in order to achieve your objectives related to fundraising?

What have you learned from your CEO that will serve you well in your future career?

The Inescapable Truth

> In 2012, after eight years as President, James Spaniolo announced his retirement from the University of Texas at Arlington. In an interview in which he reflected on his role and accomplishments, he said that he spent about 30% of his time fundraising, but that it should have been even more. "I don't think there [was] any day when [I wasn't] thinking about it", he mused.[3]

Today, anyone aspiring to the role of Chief Executive Officer in any not-for-profit, regardless of its size, should expect to spend a lot of his time raising money. Then he should expect to spend even more time making sure that his Development staff and Board accomplish their fundraising goals.

There is no escaping it. CEOs are fundraisers.

---

[3] "Retiring UT-Arlington President Reflects on Fundraising, Growth, Athletics", Ralph K.M. Haurwitz, statesman.com, August 11, 2012.

Hiring the Board

There are over 1.2 million charitable organizations in the United States; almost 90,000 in Canada. Though they deal with issues as diverse as life itself, they all have one thing in common – they were started by volunteers.

One in four Americans and almost one in two Canadians volunteer and the amount of time they dedicate to their communities is astounding. In 2011, Americans who volunteered contributed 8.1 billion hours of volunteer service; Canadians 2.1 billion.[4]

Among these exceptional citizens are volunteer Board members who shoulder the ultimate responsibility for the welfare of the not-for-profit sector. They occupy a place at the top of the commitment ladder and they are very important to fundraising. During the most recent recession, my firm surveyed 25,000 donors about how they were managing their philanthropy amidst a deep financial crisis. In particular, we wanted to know what not-for-profits could do to make sure they stayed on donors' priority lists for funding if they had to cut back on giving overall. Donors suggested structuring campaigns that featured matching gift opportunities, gearing communications to show how not-for-profits were improving the lives of people affected by the economy, and altering fundraising and other events to reflect a tone of restraint. But, as helpful as these suggestions were, they ran a distant second to donors' most important observation: "If a leadership volunteer asks me to give, it will be almost impossible to say no."

With the extraordinary power they wield through the influence that comes with the title, you would think that Board members would be itching to use it to ensure the financial health of their not-for-profits. But, for the most part, they aren't. While four out of five leadership volunteers admit they have responsibility for fundraising, they rate their Boards' collective performance at a lackluster 4.7 on a one to seven scale[5] on this statement: My board makes a significant contribution to the bottom line through fundraising. When asked to rate their personal contribution to fundraising as Board members on the same seven-point scale, they are just as critical, giving themselves a score of 4.6.

Members of our board must give quite generously to qualify for Board positions. It cuts out many fine candidates, especially younger up-and-comers who would roll up their sleeves and raise money. I wonder if this policy is helping or hurting us?

My Board does not tend to value my opinions. However, they're happy to pay good money to an outside consultant who tells them exactly the same thing. (Sigh.)

---

[4] *Volunteering in the United States - 2011;* Bureau of Labor Statistics, US Department of Labor, February, 2012 and *Volunteering in Canada*, Statistics Canada, 2010

[5] On the 7-point scale, 1 represented "not at all effective" and 7 represented "highly effective" in reference to the Board's performance in fundraising. A score of 5.2 or higher would be considered marginally effective; 5.7 or higher very effective.

Dissatisfaction with their performance in fundraising is not limited to Board members themselves. Only 30% of Chief Executives we surveyed said they were moderately to fully satisfied with their Boards' efforts in raising money. The majority of CEOs (55%) also said that convincing Board members to fulfill their fundraising duties was the least rewarding aspect of their jobs.

Volunteers tend to think that some Board members are influential – those who head major corporations or who are at the top of the social ladder in their communities. But donors think that *all* Board members are influential simply because they serve. To donors, giving one's time and taking responsibility at the highest level of a charitable organization are the most laudable of human activities.

Reawakening the Giant

There was a time when leadership volunteers did it all, including raising all the money, and that time was not so long ago. They were good at it, too. Between 1956 and 1972, total charitable giving was consistently at or above 2.0% of GDP.[6] During this period, professionalized, mass market fundraising was gaining momentum but the old-style, volunteer-led approach was still prominent. Between 1973 and 1996, a period which saw exponential growth in volume-based fundraising operated by paid staff, vendors and consultants, GDP actually fell below 2.0%.

Early on, mass marketing appeared to have endless capacity for growth, signalling to Board members that they could pull back without jeopardizing the bottom line. Leadership volunteers began seeing themselves as overseers of fundraising executed by staff rather than as front-line fundraisers themselves. It became acceptable to elect members to the Board who had no track record in raising money and who, in fact, agreed to serve on condition that they did not have to fundraise. Over time, responsibility transitioned from leadership volunteers to paid staff in the mistaken belief that success in raising money is a product of labor alone. But it is not. Fundraising success is primarily a product of influence – plus labor – and influence cannot be transferred to paid staff.

Professional staff took the fundraising programs and tactics that they could execute themselves as far as they could go; some might say too far. The very success of staff-led, volume-based fundraising made it possible for far more charities to enter the game. That increased competition which, in turn, forced individual players to drive those programs more aggressively in an effort to meet ever-increasing goals. As a result, over-solicitation caused donor attrition to soar while stifling the contribution values of donors who continued to give.

---

[6] *Giving USA: The Annual Report on Philanthropy for the year 2011.* Chicago, IL, Giving USA Foundation, 2012.

What is missing today in most not-for-profits is a balanced approach to raising money. If leadership volunteers had stayed in the game, their organizations would be enjoying the superior results that a volunteer/staff team approach can generate. But it is not too late. Applying a donor-centered approach to selecting, orienting and supporting volunteers will help rebuild their confidence and their resolve. With skilled professionals at their side, Boards can once again become the fundraising powerhouse they used to be in the days when they did it all.

Hiring Board Members Who Will Raise Money

"Hiring" is the operative word. So many things would improve if not-for-profits approached the task of filling positions on the Board in the same way that they approach hiring staff. Not only would it be easier to find a full complement of Board members, but leadership volunteers willing to serve would also be ready to deliver tangible results as soon as they were elected.

Candidates for Board positions are often presented with a rosy and unrealistic picture of fundraising in the hope that glossing over their responsibilities for raising money (and for giving) will improve the chances of someone agreeing to serve. This is a risky approach to take. Candidates interpret statements like "We expect our members to contribute to fundraising" in a myriad ways. They are justified in feeling duped when told after instead of before their election that they are expected to give generously and engage in fundraising in specific ways. Vague references to fundraising can also drive some candidates away. Not knowing what "contributing to fundraising" means, they imagine themselves in a donor's home or office, stumbling alone through a request for a major gift, fearful of being asked a question they cannot answer. Who would want to put themselves in that situation?

Basic Requirements of Serving on the Board

Our research found that very little seems to be expected of Board members and the expectations that do exist do not necessarily produce results. 69% of leadership volunteers surveyed were required to attend a minimum number of Board meetings per year; 60% were expected to sit on one or more Committees of the Board. These requirements concern themselves with process; they deal with the semblance of productivity without actually ensuring that something meaningful happens. Useful requirements, especially as they relate to fundraising, focus on the objectives that Board members are expected to meet and the concrete tasks they need to carry out in order to be successful.

Boards often don't understand that they can delegate work but not responsibility. The Board remains responsible for the financial security of their not-for-profit in the long run.

Basic requirements for serving on a Board, according to Board members:

69% Attending minimum number of Board meetings
61% Participation in one or more committees
48% Attending special functions
38% Making gifts to the organization at any level
38% Participation in raising money
12% Making gifts to the organization at a specific level

47% of Boards surveyed expect their members to attend special functions such as donor recognition events. Here, once again, the requirement is focused on showing up as opposed to accomplishing an objective during and after those events take place.

Only one in three Board members is expected to make regular charitable contributions to the organization he serves; even fewer (12%) are required to give at or above a certain minimum amount. The statistics tell the story – a debate still lingers regarding whether Board members should be expected to make charitable contributions to their own organizations.

Board Members Who Don't Give

A Board of Directors is a not-for-profit's public persona. Its members lead by example. Board members who are unwilling to give philanthropically to their own institutions, no matter what the reason, send these loud-and-clear messages to donors:

- *Even though I am responsible for the financial security of my not-for-profit, I do not feel I should personally contribute to its bottom line...but I think you should;*

- *I think that volunteering my time is a sufficient contribution to my not-for-profit. Even though you are likely volunteering your time somewhere as well, I think you should give to my organization;*

- *I think it is the responsibility of other colleagues on the Board, not me, to shoulder the load when it comes to giving to my organization;*

- *Even though we genuinely want your money, fundraising is not really all that important in my organization because not all Board members give;*

- *We are about to launch the biggest campaign we have ever run and we want you, our donors, to give like you've never given before...even though I don't plan to step up to the plate myself;*

- *I don't give to my own organization because my philanthropic budget is fully committed elsewhere; however, I expect you to prioritize my cause.*

When and how Board members are asked to give matters; and, if it is done right, it results in 100% of members contributing and doing so generously. How and when candidates should be informed of giving expectations is referenced later in this chapter.

The Perk that Boards Deny Themselves

The most important contribution a Board of Directors makes to fundraising is ensuring that their not-for-profit operates to a specific goal-oriented strategy, three years in duration. (One year is too short to be strategic; anything beyond three years is too speculative.) This is the document from which fundraisers develop their selling case to donors. The fundraising case derives its emotional appeal from imagining what could be accomplished if the objectives in the plan were realized. The plan's forecasts for organizational growth through programs' expansion and new initiatives give fundraisers the other thing they need – the intellectual, evidence-based case that justifies donors' philanthropic investment. A strategic business case of this kind is also essential for reasons apart from fundraising. It stipulates the measurable objectives that the Board and CEO have committed to reach, making evaluation of their own and their staff's performance possible.

Developing the strategic plan is the responsibility of the Board, but it is also their privilege. Nothing the Board does will ever be more interesting or more potentially important to bettering society (the ultimate objective of all not-for-profits). It is noteworthy, then, that only 24% of Boards surveyed felt it was their responsibility to create this plan or at least approve it. 20% felt that doing so was the responsibility of the CEO and 34% said fundraisers should be determining the case. This surprising finding underscored a fundamental misunderstanding at the very top. A majority of decision-makers believe that fundraisers can somehow concoct a case for donors disconnected from the overall strategy, or raise money by endlessly selling the brand. National donor attrition statistics underscore how wrong this assumption is. Donors will make their first gift to a charity based on its well-known name or appealing mission. But after they have transitioned from outside observer to inside investor, they need more and better information in order to sustain their interest. It is because most do not get it that 65% of donors who make that first tentative gift never make a second.

Fundraising Expectations Should Align with Board Members' Talents

47% of Board members surveyed said they were expected to "participate in raising money", but no specifics were offered to illustrate that responsibility. Only 9% were assigned a specific fundraising goal to achieve but, again, how members were expected to reach that goal was seldom delineated.

In a donor-centered environment, fundraising work done by the Board is very specific, in terms of both what members do and the amount of work they undertake in order to reach the goal. Board members concentrate their time where

---

Negative attributes of Board members according to fundraisers:

34% Refuse to make gifts to the not-for-profit they serve
31% Unwilling to participate in fundraising
24% Set unrealistic fundraising goals
18% Cross the line into staff work
17% Make short rather than long-term decisions

Reasons connected with fundraising that cause **10%** of Board members to leave before end of term:

47% Requirement for Board to give / give at certain levels
29% Differences in views of how money should be raised
26% Requirement for Board to ask others to give
24% Philosophical differences with fundraising staff

Our Board is hard-working and effective, but they would benefit from having more direct interaction with donors. I've tried to get our CEO to let us plan a reception for donors and the Board attached to a weekend Board meeting, but so far I've been unsuccessful.

their influence as leadership volunteers can improve the chances of success. That sometimes means doing the challenging, adrenalin-pumping work of closing major gifts, but it does not mean only that. Influence can be applied in so many ways that benefit fundraising and many of them do not involve asking for gifts.

Here are the areas where leadership volunteers shine and why they are so effective when they undertake this work:

1. **Saying Thank You**

    In *Donor-Centered Fundraising*, I described how Board members at the Paraplegic Association called a test group of donors within 48 hours of the receipt of their first-time, modest gifts. Their only job was to say thank you, which they did something like this:

    > Hello. I am Sally Jones, a volunteer on the Board of the Paraplegic Association. I've just been informed that you have made a first gift to our organization and I wanted to call you myself just to say how very much we appreciate your support.

    When these test donors and all other donors who gave in the same appeal were asked to give again, the test group returned second gifts that averaged 39% higher in value than donors in the control group. For two years, I tracked the performance of the test group against the control group. After six more solicitations, the test group was still performing considerably better, even though they only received that one brief call from a Board member. Their gift values were 42% higher than the control group.[7]

    While these personal thank-you calls by Board members averaged only 45 seconds in length, and while many messages were left on voicemail, they were still very effective in retaining donors longer and increasing the value of subsequent gifts – the two things that all fundraising is trying to achieve. And, nowhere in this test were Board members required to solicit; in fact, doing so would have severely compromised the efficacy of the test which was measuring whether Board members could influence the giving behavior of donors in ways other than asking for money. Many test donors specifically mentioned how impressed they were that a member of the Board would take the time to call and how such a gesture elevated their trust in the charity. Trust and fundraising profit are linked. Once donors transition from being interested in a not-for-profit to trusting that organization, they start giving at a level much more indicative of their real capability and they settle in for the long haul.

---

[7] *Donor-Centered Fundraising*, Penelope Burk, Cygnus Applied Research, Inc., Chicago, IL, 2003.

In a similar way, personal thank-you notes from Board members, written by hand, make donors' hearts soar and influence their future giving. They do not have to be long; as a matter of fact, short notes on small note cards or undersized personal stationery containing just one or two sentences are more powerful and are appreciated by donors because a Board member took the time to write them.

2. Being Great Hosts

Throughout a donor's relationship with a not-for-profit, Board members have opportunities to use their influence to extend loyalty and raise gift values. At donor recognition or similar events, it is the welcoming handshakes and genuine interest expressed by Board members that make donors sit up and take notice. We have often surveyed donors about their experiences as guests at charities' special events. Many have said that if they see Board members clustered together talking with each other, it sets the wrong tone and makes donors wonder why they came. On the other hand, if a Board member approaches them with a smile and an outstretched hand as they enter the room, their hesitation disappears.

Basic good manners and a little advance planning is all it takes for Board members to be influential relationship stewards at these events. With the help of staff, Board members should each be assigned a few donors whom they will look after during the evening. They need enough information in advance about their donors to initiate a conversation but not so much that they come across like Homeland Security. Their job is to put donors at ease and facilitate two of the things that donors love about successful events: meeting the people behind the organization and meeting other donors who support the same cause.

3. Contributing to Prospect Research

When I visited my 93-year old mother recently, I could tell she was irritated about something. It wasn't long before she showed me a letter she had just received from the Hospital that had treated my father during the last year of his life. This was the same Hospital in which my eldest sister had trained to become a nurse some thirty years before, so the family had strong ties to and affection for this institution.

It was a fairly typical appeal letter, one that might be sent to a mid-level donor. It started politely with "Dear Mrs. Diletti", acknowledging my mother's previous gift of $5,000 in the first sentence. I was not sure why mum was showing it to me.

"Look who it's from", she said, pointing to the signature at the bottom. The name, which appeared over the title, Chair of the Board of Directors, seemed familiar.

In the last not-for-profit where I worked, the Board was always declaring that they wanted more fundraising – as long as they themselves didn't have to get involved.

"That's Ron Maxwell", my mother continued. "Your Dad taught him to sail and he used to crew on Wednesday night races. I sold them their first house when they moved here from London. They spent Christmas with us the first two years that they lived here."

"Oh, yes, now I remember."

"Well, obviously <u>he</u> doesn't. 'Dear Mrs. Diletti'...What was he thinking? The whole letter reads like he doesn't even know who I am."

"I'm sure it wasn't intentional, mum. These letters are turned out by the thousands."

"But he signed it."

"I doubt it. It's probably an electronic signature. It's amazing what technology can do these days."

"It's more amazing what good manners can do these days", mum retorted, not missing a beat.

And then she grew quiet for awhile, after which she said, "Well, I'm going to make the same contribution again because the letter says they really need the money. And, well, they were awfully good to your father."

My curiosity overcame me and I said, "What would you have given if Ron had sent you a personal letter or called you?"

"Oh, several times that I'm sure, depending on why they needed the money."

Now it was my turn to sit in silence for awhile. I had mixed emotions as I thought about how easy it would have been to ask members of the Board to glance down the list of names of donors who were about to be asked for their annual fund contributions. On one hand, I was disappointed that something so simple and so obvious was missed in favor of expediency or "doing it the way it's always been done". On the other hand, I silently thanked the hospital's Development Office for keeping my inheritance intact.

The databases of most not-for-profits are full of donors that no one in the organization knows much about. These are the new donors, most of whom have made first gifts that were far less generous than they could have been. Along with them are donors who have been giving for awhile but whose contribution values are barely rising, if at all. And, then, there are even more donors who used to give but no longer contribute. Collectively, these donors are minimally profitable at best and many lose money for the charity. But all of them have one thing in common. They had an important reason for giving initially.

Many of my company's research studies have confirmed that, while donors may give modestly at first, they do not give indiscriminately. They don't wake up one morning, decide they are feeling philanthropic, and give to the next organization that comes along. Because donors choose their charities purposefully and because most donors could give more than they are currently contributing, not-for-profits have a goldmine in their databases just waiting to be discovered.

Endless generic appeals or pleas to come back will not get fundraisers anywhere near the potential that resides inside their databases. If their giving has stagnated, it is a signal that donors need their enthusiasm reignited, but in a different way, and no one does that better than Board members. It is a boon to fundraising when Board members bring their own contacts to the table. But leadership volunteers can be equally if not more influential with donors who are sourced through typical acquisition programs. The number of current or lapsed donors that your volunteers may know personally is not so important. What is important is that they are given the opportunity to advise fundraisers of those connections.

4. **Opening the Door**

The hardest job in fundraising is not closing the sale; it's opening the door.

This means getting the appointment, whether that be an in-person meeting or a phone call. Because they are relationship managers, professional fundraisers are outstanding once they are in the room. But most of them are poor cold-callers, largely because their job as the people paid to raise money denies them the influence that gets a call returned or an appointment set.

Here is where Board members have a much better chance of success. In typical fundraising, Board members pass names of people they know to fundraisers who are then expected to contact them for a gift. It would work much better if fundraisers passed names of donors who had already started to give to Board members who then opened the door with supporters they know. Influencing philanthropy at a whole new level would become possible.

5. **Producing Fundraising Events**

Most fundraising events have inherent weaknesses: they are high cost and high risk; they contribute to fatigue among faithful donors who are called into action yet again; they devour an enormous amount of staff time that could be more profitably utilized; and they inadvertently minimize giving from otherwise generous major gifts donors. So why would any not-for-profit want to run them?

Our school does have a Board but the order priests who run the school make all the decisions. Regarding fundraising they quite often say, "God will provide", which is the same as letting everyone off the hook. I'm looking heavenward, but so far…

There are tremendous benefits to fundraising events if they are conceived and executed to capitalize on their intrinsic benefits. This means looking well beyond the event itself and assessing its value in ways like these:

- *brand awareness and reputation:* An event with reach – one that touches a large number of people – can often achieve this. Run-a-thons, walk-a-thons and the like are good examples because they attract large numbers of participants and even larger numbers of sponsors who contribute to support their friends and relatives. They are visible, reminding participants, donors and onlookers that not-for-profits are working in their community.

- *donor acquisition:* Good events don't simply lean on existing supporters for one more thing. They reach out to potential supporters who are under-represented through other acquisition strategies. Cygnus' 2012 study on community-based fundraising events[8] found that event participants don't just take part because of their interest in the sport or activity; the cause is very important in their decision to become involved. So, too, with the people who sponsor event participants. While sponsors' primary motivation is to support their friends and relatives who are running in the marathon, 50% said the cause is also a deciding factor. Even more exciting, willingness to give directly among event sponsors after a sponsorship experience is high when compared with success rates in converting non-donors to donors through traditional acquisition methods.

- *volunteer development:* Events offer Boards an opportunity to observe future members in action. For not-for-profits who recruit leadership volunteers from their Committee system, events showcase members' creativity, commitment and willingness to put in the time.

No one joins a Board so that they can sit in more meetings and take on more work after their regular business day is done. They join to meet other people, to expand their networks and to have fun. A creative event, run well and profitably, takes a lot of work, but it can still be really fun. Successful events give Board members a sense of satisfaction and build their confidence for other fundraising work.

---

[8] *The Cygnus Donor Survey...Where Philanthropy Is Headed in 2012*, Penelope Burk, Cygnus Applied Research, Inc., Chicago, Il., April, 2012

How to Find Great Fundraising Volunteers

Four Strikes, I'm Out

When I first moved to a new city, I was eager to volunteer as a way of meeting new friends and establishing myself in the community. I called the main office number of a not-for-profit organization that I had long admired. I told the receptionist that I was interested in learning more about volunteering on the Board and asked if I could be referred to the Chair or Head of the Nominating Committee. For some reason, this request was viewed suspiciously. In between putting me on hold while she took other calls, I was asked what my precise reason was for wanting to speak with a Board member (I thought I had already explained myself sufficiently) and, in the end, was told that no one has direct access to the Board. I was asked for my name and number, which I provided. No one ever called me back.

I was undeterred, chalking up the experience to a poorly informed receptionist who was having a bad day. I called a second worthy cause but had a terrible time trying to navigate their voicemail. I did not know how to get to the right person because the system worked only by name, not by title. Twice I got booted back to the general mailbox where I was reluctant to leave a message, given my prior experience. What should I do? The decision was soon made for me when the voicemail system suddenly said, "good bye" in that irritating polite-but-firm tone and hung up on me. I wondered what happened to donors who call in to make a gift, then I scratched this charity off my list.

In my third attempt, I took a different tack. I went to the website of a local not-for-profit hoping to find a list of its Board members or at least one member and contact information. No luck. But I did find a reference to a Volunteer Coordinator. I sent her an email reiterating my interest in a Board position. She responded right away with an urgent request that I volunteer at their walk-a-thon scheduled for this coming weekend. I replied to say, regrettably, that I was already committed but asked that she forward my request to someone on the Board. I never heard back.

I wondered whether I should have made more effort to make my interest known, but my initial experiences with these three not-for-profits made me cautious. First impressions matter, I think, and negative ones are a warning sign that I should move on or risk a prolonged bad experience.

In spite of the fact that my radar was now up, I made one last attempt. While having lunch one day with my insurance agent, we fell into conversation about family, career and life in general. I told her about my interest in serving on a Board and the poor experiences I had had. She said she had a client who was on the Board of our town's regional theatre. I was quite excited, having taken arts courses in college and being an avid theatre-goer. My agent said she would connect the two of us, and

> All I need to keep me motivated as a Board member is a sincere "thank you". While most of my volunteer experiences have been rewarding, I have been serving on one board for ten years and not once have they thanked me for the extensive effort I have made. I'm burned out as a result.

she did. I received a call one day from a member of the theatre's Board who told me, very politely, that the Board does not recruit members. Rather, positions are filled by leaders in the community well known to other Board members. Embarrassed, I apologized for wasting her time.

59% of volunteers surveyed by my firm agreed that their Boards have difficulty finding candidates who are willing to raise money. The problem can be traced back in many cases to how prospective members are sourced. Only 70% of respondents said their Boards have a Nominating Committee. Among the 30% who do not, 63% admitted having difficulty finding candidates willing to be involved in fundraising. Taking Board membership seriously by charging a committee with responsibility for sourcing prospective members is an obvious first step.

Nominating Committees With a Purpose

The Nominating Committee is the Board's equivalent of an HR Department. Like all other committees of the Board, the Nominating Committee's job is to be a productive and efficient resource for the Board while never usurping its authority. Specifically, the Nominating Committee is charged with identifying prospective Board members, vetting them for the attributes and skills that the Board is seeking, and recommending qualified candidates for election. The Board as a whole retains decision-making authority about who does and does not get on the slate for nomination, and the not-for-profit's members ultimately decide who is elected. The Nominating Committee is only authorized to do the legwork, but it is vitally important legwork and interesting, too.

If He's Breathing, He Can Serve

The Nominating Committee needs to vet candidates for their suitability, but first they need to be found. This requires marketing and/or community outreach, not all of which has to be done by the Nominating Committee. Some tasks may be better handled by staff within parameters set by the Board. But, no matter who makes it happen, taking an active approach to building a pipeline of good Board prospects is better than settling for whoever is available. It also does justice to the many people out there who are seeking rewarding volunteer experiences but are unsure of how to best connect with organizations they admire.

Our research with Board members suggests that a strategic approach to finding candidates is not the norm. Only 42% of Boards with Nominating Committees vet candidates for leadership volunteer positions year-round. 54% said their Nominating Committees are active only for a limited period of time prior to the

Annual General Meeting.

Given how difficult it is for many Boards to just fill the slate, you may feel that being able to choose the best board members from a pool of vetted, qualified candidates is a pipedream. Or, this selective, strategic approach may be contrary to the sensibilities of some who feel that not-for-profits should be grateful for any offer of volunteer service. Of course every Board should be relieved to reach its membership quota and grateful for offers of service, but setting its sights that low will not help their not-for-profit succeed. The Board's objective is not filling the chairs around the table; it is assembling a team that produces results.

Redefining the Nominating Committee's job from short-term to strategic is an excellent first step. This means letting go of the notion that the Nominating Committee functions for only a short time during the fiscal year in order to come up with the slate of candidates for the next annual general meeting. In a high functioning Board, the Nominating Committee's job is to help build a better Board over time – one that is qualified to make strategic decisions and carry out its work at an ever-increasing level of productivity. This only makes sense. Since the CEO and his Development staff are expected to raise more money every year, the Board must also demonstrate progressive performance in the tasks for which it is uniquely suited.

53% of Boards surveyed said lack of diversity in age and/or ethnicity was among their primary issues concerning Board membership. And, 60% said they had difficulty attracting leadership volunteers with specific skills. A multi-tiered approach to volunteer recruitment is called for, not just to find enough candidates but to find the right ones.

The Marketing Side of Board Recruitment

Not-for-profits have many ready resources and easy ways to help build their pipeline of potential leadership volunteers:

Make it easy for people seeking leadership volunteer opportunities to find you

A special landing page on your website designed to showcase Board recruitment is an obvious asset. Cygnus' 2012 national study of donors found that, today, 62% of donors go to not-for-profit websites to learn more before making a gift or renewing their support. They are doing their homework, sometimes prompted by an email or direct mail appeal, but other times simply because this is how donors manage their philanthropy today. Donors and potential donors appear to be more diligent now

Our visionary founder has left the Board. New members seem more business-minded but they are not nearly as driven. We don't seem to be doing any better.

How donors determine which not-for-profits to support:

71% Information from appeals and communication materials
62% Conduct research through charity's website
55% Information from media
43% Word-of-mouth
33% Follow recommendations of friends or family
32% Consult charity ratings guides

and more proactive than before. Since there is a strong connection between giving and volunteering, Boards should make good use of their not-for-profits' website as a primary recruitment tool.

Content on this dedicated landing page should showcase current Board members, what they do for a living and feature something personal, like quotes from members about what they get out of serving. The Board's recent accomplishments should be noted and, perhaps most important, what the Board has done in the past year together that was fun. Not-for-profits with a policy of promoting Board candidates through the Committee system might describe some of the interesting work that their Committee members do. A short video from the Chair of the Board about the experience or interests of candidates that would complement the current Board's talents would be particularly advantageous. This is useful on two fronts – it is a practical and non-critical way to communicate the Board's selective approach to recruitment and the video is a way to showcase the Chair as a warm and interesting person that Board members are eager to work for (assuming this is the case, of course).

If the Board is attempting to broaden its membership, the landing page is an ideal space to describe the characteristics and specialized skills it is seeking. For example, when trying to attract more younger members, a testimonial from a current young Board or Committee member about the Board's openness to what young people have to say would be beneficial. If a not-for-profit is trying to build representation from a particular ethnic community, then a link to more information translated into their native language says that the Board is both serious and considerate.

Concerning fundraising specifically, the Board of Directors' landing page could showcase one or more key, recent accomplishments that leadership volunteers have orchestrated or contributed to in meaningful ways. And, these accomplishments should not be limited only to how volunteers have closed major gifts or opened doors with prominent philanthropists, though these achievements are singularly important. Most ways in which Board members can contribute meaningfully to fundraising, (see earlier in this chapter and Chapter 12), would not intimidate any volunteer, including those who do not see themselves as influential in fundraising.

Visitors to the Board of Directors' page should be able to send an email directly to the Chair of the Nominating Committee in order to make their interest in volunteering known or to request additional information. From this landing page, there should also be quick links to the latest audited statement, a summary of the not-for-profit's strategic plan for programs and services, a profile of the CEO, and any other background information that current members say would have been valuable when they were considering serving on the Board.

Overall, if copy and photos on your Board landing page underscore pride in achievement and an upbeat demeanor, anyone who is researching volunteer opportunities and happens upon your site will be very impressed.

Welcome Direct Inquiries

Developing and implementing a staff plan that facilitates inquiries from potential volunteers is easy. Potential Board members should not be grilled by the receptionist – or ignored. The person who answers the phone should be well briefed on how to handle inquiry calls about volunteering on the Board or a Committee. Whoever monitors messages in the general mail box should know to whom inquiries of this nature should be referred. An email to the Chair of the Nominating Committee confirming that an inquiry has been made will help prevent unsolicited inquiries from falling through the cracks.

Boards that have a waiting list of superb candidates can be as exclusive as they like. All other Boards need to be conscious of the image they are presenting, whether directly by Board members themselves or indirectly by staff. Unsolicited inquiries should always be followed up. Yes, some potential volunteers may be unsuitable, but the vetting process described later in this chapter will unearth the kind of candidate your Board needs at this time while ensuring that everyone is handled in a respectful manner.

Use Your Senior Staff

I know Boards that build a strict wall between themselves and their staff regarding volunteer recruitment. They seem to fear that the CEO or Development Director would gain some kind of advantage or control over the Board if candidates favored by staff were to be considered for membership. This is a sign of an organization in trouble, one that has lost sight of what a collaborative approach can achieve. No one connects with more members of the community in the context of the not-for-profit than its CEO; the Development Director is similarly well connected from a fundraising perspective.

In negatively-charged environments, the Nominating Committee can be a level-headed asset. Staying focused on the skills that the Board needs in its candidates and distancing themselves from internal politics facilitates the recruitment of good people who are not partisan. As this more positively-motivated group grows in number, they will influence the whole Board, helping them overcome an unhealthy "us versus them" mentality.

Regardless of the existing culture, any not-for-profit Board should welcome recommendations from staff. The Board's own recruitment process, entrusted to its Nominating Committee, will ensure that the best candidates emerge for the right reasons.

It would be more productive and it would save a lot of time if I could have a direct relationship with the Board's Fundraising Committee rather than every word having to go through my Executive Director.

I am grateful to my boss for helping me understand the important role that volunteers play in making a not-for-profit successful. He taught me how to interact with them to improve results which has been instrumental in the promotions and success that I have had in my career.

Use the Media Creatively

Advertise where your talent lives. Tell your story in local community papers and on community television. Going to the people is much more productive than simply hoping they will come to you. If you are trying to diversify your membership in terms of language and culture, then advertise in media that publish in other languages serving non-native English populations. Or, interview staff members or donors of different ethnic backgrounds about why they work for or give to your not-for-profit, and use them to open doors with leaders in those communities.

Industry media is also valuable in reaching potential volunteers. If a Board needs marketing expertise, there are dozens of professional associations, each with industry publications that cater to their members. National Boards that are recruiting members from all over the country might consider advertising in or submitting a feature story to the editors of airline magazines. The people who read them are corporate players, mobile, and a captive audience while up in the air – and they don't need one more article on how to pack their bags. Instead, not-for-profits could give them something interesting and meaningful in their communities to come home to. Many industry magazines and newsletters will include your notice free. Others will be intrigued by your story and you may end up with considerably more exposure than a simple public service notice would yield.

Use Your Corporate Network

The CEOs or Vice Presidents of your corporate donors or sponsors may not be available to sit on your Board, but approaching them for a recommendation from their middle management ranks produces results. Corporate CEOs with an appreciation for what community engagement can achieve for their company, as well as for not-for-profits, will be motivated to nominate someone from their ranks. Staff on an accelerated track to senior management or who are being groomed for top executive positions will welcome opportunities to demonstrate their community commitment to their bosses.

Corporations are also a great place to find motivated Board members under the age of forty. In addition to bringing their creative energy and fresh ideas to the Board table, younger volunteers are the gateway to a large and relatively untapped younger donor pool.

Develop Your Board Chair's Public Profile

In the same way that the CEO is pivotal to the success of the staff team, the Chair is integral to the cohesion and productivity of the Board of Directors. While the dynamics of the relationship are somewhat different, Board members still report to the Chair and they are very much influenced by that individual's style and management skill. So, when a not-for-profit is fortunate enough to have an appealing

Chair – someone who is dynamic or warm or an excellent speaker (or all those things) – he is a decided asset in volunteer recruitment.

Give this exceptional leader a public forum for showcasing your not-for-profit and recruiting potential Board members. Have him speak at service clubs and business associations; feature her on community television; showcase him at fundraising and other events that your organization hosts. Citizens looking for a high-quality volunteer experience will migrate to your dynamic Chair, but only if you give her the means to connect with the community.

Recruit from Other Boards

Do not overlook high performing volunteers just because they are already serving on other Boards. Some volunteers who manage their time exceptionally well serve on more than one Board simultaneously and they may be willing to consider yours. However, be sure that their dual responsibility would not put them in a conflict of interest, especially regarding fundraising. If it does, they are still a very valuable resource, but perhaps not at this moment. Meet with those individuals now, find out whether they would join your Board when their current terms expire, then be prepared to wait your turn. Whoever heads the Nominating Committee a few years from now will be very grateful for your forward-thinking effort.

Use Social Media

As the technology of choice for younger donors and volunteers, social media should be part of a Board's volunteer recruitment strategy. Its advantage as a two-way communications tool offers opportunities to start a discussion about the merits of volunteering for your not-for-profit. Its networking asset automatically multiplies your efforts to find and cultivate volunteers with particular skills. Cygnus' 2011 North American donor survey found that among respondents who followed one or more charities through social media, 19% became volunteers or reached out to offer their volunteer services.[9]

Source Candidates from Your Committees

This is the best way to recruit leadership volunteers. If you have a policy to promote high performing Committee members to positions on the Board (or at least a preference for that way of recruiting), you gain several advantages. While they are serving as Committee members, you will be able to tell whether your volunteers follow through on their commitments, whether they are active participants in fundraising and whether they are a pleasure to work with. Equally beneficial, recruiting only from your Committee structure sends a message to the volunteer community that

I've had all kinds of experiences with Boards regarding involvement in fundraising. Sadly, sometimes you just have to wait out the Chair's two-year term.

---

[9] *The Cygnus Donor Survey: Where Philanthropy is Headed in 2011*, Penelope Burk, Cygnus Applied Research, Inc., Chicago, IL, April 2011.

you are strategic and that it is not easy to win a position on your Board of Directors. Anything that is hard to obtain is automatically more desirable. Being both selective and demanding will actually increase, not reduce, the number of potential volunteers who are interested in serving on your Board.

How to Vet Candidates for Board Positions

Interviewing potential Board members is different from interviewing candidates for paid staff positions. Regardless, the process should still be thorough and consistent candidate-to-candidate so that qualifications and other attributes can be objectively compared. The Nominating Committee will still look to the Board for recommendations of good candidates but, with a multi-tiered marketing strategy in place, the Committee can ensure diversification in the Board's membership.

With a process now in place for potential Board members to make themselves known, people who inquire about volunteer opportunities should feel glad they made the call. A quick referral to someone on the Nominating Committee or to a staff member with an excellent customer service manner will set a great first impression. Organizations with voicemail instead of receptionists should include, *"to inquire about volunteer positions on our Board and Committees, please press X"* as part of their outgoing message. Those calls should route through to someone in either donor relations or major gifts. It is possible, even likely, that some people inquiring about Board positions may already be donors. They deserve the attention that these specialized staff members provide. For inquiries made after hours, the voicemail message should reassure callers that they can leave their name and number and that their calls will be returned the next day.

Gathered online or over the phone, this preliminary information will be helpful to the Nominating Committee:

- name and contact information;
- best time for the potential volunteer to be contacted and how;
- what prompted the individual to inquire about volunteering (this helps the Nominating Committee assess which of its marketing approaches are working. It needs to be asked up front, before the applicant forgets. Use a drop-down menu to make answering easy.);
- an open box for other information or questions.

Avoid falling into the trap of gathering too much information too soon. It can be off-putting to the potential volunteer and it can actually over-prepare the interviewer from the Nominating Committee, depriving him of the joy of discovery that makes good conversation flow. That said, if the potential volunteer is a donor, especially a major donor, the Development Director may know a fair bit about her and any non-confidential information could be valuable to the interviewer.

Interviewing Candidates

Like great hosts, great interviewers are more interested in the person they are speaking with than in talking about themselves. In a first phone call or meeting over coffee, the Nominating Committee member should be looking to answer these two questions, "Does this person have a skill or asset to offer that the Board needs?" and "Would this individual be compatible with the team?" Compatibility does not mean compliance, by the way. Individuals can have quite different opinions on issues and vote differently on motions without behaving in ways that cause fellow Board members to grit their teeth.

The answers to the following questions provide useful insight about the person who may one day be sitting on your Board:

- *What is it about our not-for-profit that interests you?* A personal connection to the cause is highly meaningful (though not always desirable). If this person goes on to serve, never again will his perspective be as objective. Be sure to capitalize on this opportunity.

- *What do you hope to gain or accomplish through volunteering?* Whether it is making new social or business connections, learning new things or giving back, the answer will give you an opportunity to say how volunteering with your not-for-profit will help the prospective candidate achieve her personal or career goals. Cite real examples of how serving on your Board has been advantageous to other Board members' careers or has helped make the transition to a new city easier. If you are part of a multi-level not-for-profit, discuss how volunteering for the local affiliate could lead to being appointed to the national Board at some stage.

- *What do you do for a living?* (if unknown) or *Tell me more about the work you do.* This question and the next two give the interviewer insight into the skills and advantages that this individual could bring to the Board.

- *What are your interests or hobbies?* She might play tennis, for example, and be a member of the Racquet Club which speaks to an interesting network and a source for a quiet reference later on.

- *Where/how have you volunteered in the recent past?* Experienced volunteers can be a boon if they already understand the culture of decision-making

It's just as important to check into potential volunteers' backgrounds as it is to check the qualifications of staff candidates, especially when it comes to fundraising willingness and results.

I'm very willing to teach my Board the mechanics of fundraising. I just can't teach them to have passion and be willing to interact with people. They have to want to do that.

It is challenging, to say the least, when Board members fly in from out of town twice a year to attend meetings but think they know all the answers when it comes to fundraising.

in not-for-profit organizations. The answer to this question may lead to another reference source, too, especially concerning whether the candidate delivers results.

- *Are you currently available to serve?* Especially if the Nominating Committee has pursued this person, her volunteer time may already be fully committed. This should not color the interviewer's thinking. "We need you now" can be flattering, but only if the volunteer is actually available on short notice. It is more important to get good candidates thinking about how attractive it would be to serve on your Board, regardless of when that might be.

Break Down Your Own Barriers

In return, interviewers should be prepared to provide clear information on basic requirements such as the Board meetings schedule and minimum attendance requirements. On the latter issue, Boards of Directors have an opportunity to modernize their thinking in order to attract the kind of volunteer they need. The Nominating Committee can help the Board do this by questioning whether certain rules or ingrained practices actually serve or inhibit their recruitment needs.

For example, meeting attendance requirements should take into account the pressure on volunteers who are running hard in the shadow of a severe recession. If a busy mid-level manager who travels on business half the month is told, "We require our members to attend at least 80% of Board meetings each year," the Nominating Committee will lose this otherwise valuable candidate. On the other hand, if the same candidate is provided with information in a different way, one which acknowledges his busy schedule and offers a solution, the problem is eliminated:

> The Board meets monthly on the third Wednesday of the month, eight times a year from September to May. We do not meet in January. We know you travel frequently, as do several other members. We use technologies like Skype, conference calling and web conferencing so that you can actively participate in meetings no matter where you are. We also organize the agenda so that when you are out of town you can attend just for the critical parts of a meeting, particularly when we discuss and vote on motions. We try to respect our Board members' time, especially when they are on the road or away on vacation.

This accommodating approach acknowledges the global reality of life in the 21st century and the technological advances that make community engagement still possible. A barrier to serve is eliminated and the candidate is left with another positive impression – one that is respectful of Board members while still focused on the thing that really matters, getting the job done.

Other practical issues that interviewers from the Nominating Committee should address with candidates include:

- **whether Board members are recruited directly or indirectly through the Committee system.** If the latter, candidates should be offered a brief description of the not-for-profit's Committees – not the dreary definitions from the organization's by-laws, but upbeat one-line descriptions plus one or two sentences about what each Committee has accomplished in the past year. This should fit on a single page – brevity is critical. Candidates should know that the interviewer will connect them with the Chair of any Committee in which they might be interested.

- **the Board's policy regarding members' philanthropic gifts to the organization.** It is better to introduce this subject early, once it becomes apparent that the candidate is genuinely interested in serving. Our research has found that it is more the element of surprise, not so much a philosophical resistance, that makes some Board members dig in their heels and refuse to give. But, if someone is determined that he will not give philanthropically, it is best to know this early on and cut your losses. You need 100% of your members contributing money as well as time, and you do not need one adamant member signalling that it is OK to let other members carry the load.

- **what is expected of Board members regarding raising money.** While a detailed job description for fundraising is not necessary at this point, saying something like this is helpful to candidates:

  > Our Board has identified ten ways in which its members can contribute meaningfully to fundraising. One of them, for example, involves identifying people in their own personal or business networks who might be interested in becoming donors and opening the door. Would you be in a position to do that with, say, five people you know? [Pause and wait for the answer.] Or, would you be willing to call donors who have just made a gift to thank them for their contributions? You don't need to know these donors personally, but we have found that being thanked by a Board member goes a long way in making donors want to give again later. Could you see yourself doing that?

  It is easy to warm to this second task so, if a candidate does not seem keen, think twice about welcoming her onto the Board, or give her an opportunity to serve on the Fundraising Committee until she develops more confidence.

  Avoid downplaying the importance of fundraising, something that interviewers often do for fear that candidates will refuse to serve. Statements like "It will hardly take any time at all" are untrue and, to many candidates, insulting. Your Board needs willing participants who will put in the time.

Most of my board members have been around for a long time. They're comfortable and want to maintain the status quo. My staff, particularly the younger members, are well educated and energetic; they want to pull the organization forward. They are like two ships passing in the night.

Here is a more constructive way to reference Board responsibilities in fundraising:

Our board is quite proud of its track record in fundraising, even though we are a group that would not define itself as particularly well connected. We raise a lot of money and we have fun doing it. Our confidence and our enthusiasm come from:

- a superb case that donors find irresistible;
- a fundraising staff and a CEO who make our job easier by handling the details and supporting us whenever we need them;
- leadership from longer serving board members who have experience selling our not-for-profit to donors;
- training from experts – we bring in the best to share their expertise on current fundraising trends and strategies that will help us raise more money faster while taking our busy schedules into account.

Checking Volunteer Candidates' References

Asking potential Board members for references may seem unusual and the Nominating Committee may be reluctant; but they feel more awkward about this than candidates who see reference-checking as the logical end-function of the nominations process. Checking references sends a powerful message about the care with which your not-for-profit selects its most important volunteers.

Reference checking should give you information that you would be less likely to get from candidates themselves, especially:

- whether they engage actively and constructively in discussions at Board meetings;
- whether they take on work willingly;
- whether they follow through on their agreed commitments.

What if you unearth information that makes you reluctant to put a candidate's name forward for consideration? In a difficult situation like this, your multi-faceted nominations process will come to your aid. If the Nominating Committee is doing its job diligently all year round, you will have more candidates for Board positions than can be included on the slate. You might consider offering Committee positions to some where you will be able to observe their strengths and weaknesses first-hand.

Sell Yourself

If you convey these messages about your Board through your recruitment strategy and directly in conversations with candidates, your volunteer opportunities will be hard to resist:

- we like and respect our fellow leadership volunteers;
- we accomplish important things when we meet;
- we rise to the challenge, whether that be for fundraising or for any other purpose;
- there is mutual respect between Board and Staff;
- we have a lot of fun.

If you would not currently define your Board in these ways, now is the time to begin that conversation. If you create a better climate and volunteer experience for the members you already have, they will stay to the end of their terms and work more productively. They will also be your best ambassadors. Retention and job satisfaction are not just staff issues.

> There is so much more money out there that donors want to give but are holding back. They are waiting for the right approach by the right person for the right reason. For not-for-profits that have figured out who does what best and are as optimistic as donors about what philanthropy can achieve, the future is very bright.

Nothing about fundraising can be done alone; you always need to depend on others. So, it is very important to respect both the skills and the opinions of the people around you.

PART III
Holding Onto the Team You Build

Chapter 10:

Bright, Shiny and New: How to Maximize the Value of New Staff and Volunteers

I was scheduled to have lunch with someone to discuss her new position as Planned Gifts Officer for a mid-sized not-for-profit. This was her first job in fundraising, but she had had a long and successful career in the corporate sector and her skills and experience were very compatible. She was also a graduate of both elementary and advanced planned giving courses, making her a stand-out candidate for this exciting position. It was the charity's first foray into planned giving and my acquaintance had the enviable opportunity of starting the program from scratch.

But, as she arrived at the restaurant, she seemed worried and distracted – not the demeanor I expected in someone who had just landed such a great new job. It wasn't long before she told me what was bothering her. "I thought everything had been agreed to", she said, "but in our last meeting two weeks ago, I learned that I would be expected to sign an employment contract. I just received it yesterday and was surprised to see that they are only committing to hiring me for two years."

I tried to cheer her up by focusing on the creative opportunity that lay ahead and the strong likelihood that she would be very successful. She thought about my encouraging comments for a minute and her face brightened. "You know, you're right. In two years I will be able to get this program up and running, I'll build up my credentials in the planned giving field, and I'll prove that I can transition from the corporate world to the not-for-profit sector. Maybe a two-year contract is a good thing after all. With that experience behind me, I can start looking for a better job in a bigger not-for-profit in about eighteen months."

The first few months on the job can be a heady time. Full of energy and not (yet) shackled by the organizational culture, new employees bring a can-do attitude to work that has the potential to energize the entire team. They have uncluttered opinions and different ideas; they offer new solutions to problems and even question long-held practices and beliefs. At the senior level, new directors have the ear of the CEO and the Board and the benefit of the doubt from staff in a way that they will not enjoy later. In these precious first few months, new directors and managers have greater leeway to effect change in every direction.

It takes a fair bit of time to see whether a new employee can actually raise funds and build relationships with donors. They also need time initially to plan and orient themselves to their new organization and responsibilities.

How managers supervise new staff and how new managers handle the staff they inherit are important factors in building and sustaining a high performance fundraising team. The choices they make, the expectations they establish and the way they choose to engage set the stage for outstanding productivity and long-term loyalty – or disillusionment and early departure or dismissal. And, new leadership volunteers bring their own version of that "new car smell" to their Boards. They pay attention closely; they speak up when they don't understand, and they ask questions about things that other members take for granted. Their early service can set up a volunteer experience that will be fondly remembered long after their terms have expired. Or it can be unfulfilling, leading to peripheral involvement, poor attendance and early resignation "for personal reasons".

Employment Agreements

Employment agreements[1] are important for many reasons, not the least of which is that they bring the job negotiation to a close, articulating how each party will serve and benefit from the other. Through their language and tone, employment agreements also reflect the strategic demeanor of the new business partnership, reflecting the respect and consideration that employer and employee have for each other.

An employment agreement addresses the obvious issues such as start date, salary and payment schedule, probationary term, benefits (including when they become active), vacation provision, allowable business expenses and how they are reimbursed, and to whom the staff member reports. You should consult your HR Department or lawyer about appropriate wording and other inclusions that may be standard for your organization.

An employment agreement for a fundraiser should also include clauses about:

- confidentiality of information about donors, prospects and former donors;
- confidentiality regarding financial information concerning the not-for-profit;
- ownership of proposals, reports and any other documentation produced by the fundraiser;
- the not-for-profit's policy regarding the storage of files and data at the employee's home and/or in a personal computer or device owned by the employee;

---

[1] Information on employment contracts, Board member agreements, probation and other matters in this chapter is meant to help employers use these tools to further development and retention of good employees and volunteers while limiting employers' exposure to poor hires. This is not legal advice. Laws differ between Canada and the United States and between states or provinces on such matters.

- the not-for-profit's policy regarding ownership and use of laptops, iPads, smart phones and other transportable devices provided to the employee. This clause should also make reference to personal versus business calls, and how reimbursement of those expenses will be handled.

An employment agreement also typically includes clauses or appendices related to work expectations, outcomes and supervision such as:

- specific goals to be reached in order to successfully pass probation;
- criteria and methodology for the initial performance review.

An employment agreement is best presented to the preferred candidate in draft form even if the employer is certain that both parties have discussed and agreed to everything in the document. The final stage of negotiation, which includes review and acceptance of the employment agreement, is particularly sensitive. If the agreement is presented as a proposal rather than as a written directive, it sends a message that the employer respects the finalist's equal status at this stage of the game. This is an important and meaningful gesture when hiring within an industry that has a supply/demand imbalance. It is wise to assume that, even though the negotiation has come this far, the prospective employee may still be negotiating with other not-for-profits for equally enticing positions.

Do Limited-Term Contracts for Fundraisers Help or Hurt Employers?

Most managers we surveyed agreed with the underlying message in the story that introduced this chapter – that putting professional fundraisers on time-limited contracts risks their premature resignation. The not-for-profit, not the employee, loses out in the long run. 54% of Directors of Development and 65% of fundraising program managers said that limited-term contracts contribute to too rapid staff turnover; only 7% of managers felt that staff retention was improved by the use of contracts that stipulate an end date.

Though opinions on limiting the employment term of fundraisers were very one sided, our research did uncover some support among Development professionals who run one-person-shops. 50% said that limited-term employment contracts afforded them some level of financial security if they are laid off before their terms expire.

Fundraisers are particularly reticent about contracts that tie a limited employment term to a financial goal. The fact is that no fundraiser is unilaterally responsible for fundraising success. Reaching a goal requires, first of all, that it be realistically

Oddly, our attractiveness to fundraisers lies in the fact that we have not developed our potential for raising money. It's fertile ground here which is very attractive to fundraisers who want to make a dramatic impact.

achievable within the stated timeframe and, second, that management and the Board make decisions that enable success. Chapter 4 explained how many not-for-profit decision-makers continue to hold beliefs about raising money that are uninformed or outdated, ensuring fundraising under-performance. It is illogical to demand that a professional fundraiser reach a goal and do so by using inferior strategies. It is also self-defeating. Sooner or later, the staff member will leave or be dismissed and management will once again have to shoulder the cost of a premature rehire.

Limiting the term of employment is ill advised, especially if this is not common practice with non-fundraising staff in the organization. On a practical level, if a fundraiser is contracted for a specific period, she is going to start looking for another job as the end of the contract period approaches. No matter how well she has performed, she cannot be sure that she will be re-hired when her contract expires.

What about Contracts for Leadership Volunteers?

Many not-for-profit consultants and authors who specialize in volunteer management recommend that new Board members sign written agreements that stipulate their responsibilities as well as the support they can expect to receive. Written agreements remind leadership volunteers and not-for-profits that they both have measurable expectations of each other. They also set a purposeful tone for debate and decision-making, making Board meetings more productive.

Readers can consult several resources for examples of Board member agreements[2] covering a wide range of issues. The following information will help shape clauses related specifically to fundraising responsibilities.

- **General conflict of interest:** While this should be covered by the Nominating Committee early in discussions with prospective Board members, conflict of interest as it relates to fundraising should also be defined in the written agreement. It takes both time and intestinal fortitude to raise money, making fundraising the most challenging job for most Board members. When a member exempts himself from fundraising because of a pre-existing commitment to raise money for another organization, it is unfair to the rest of the volunteer team. It is especially serious if a member with volunteer or professional commitments to fundraising elsewhere occupies

---

[2] CompassPoint Nonprofit Services (http://www.compasspoint.org) published their sample Board Member Agreement in 2003. An adaptation by Blue Avocado (http://www.blueavocado.org) was published in 2009. Author and consultant, Kim Klein's version of an Agreement for Members of the Board is referenced in her article, "Recruiting Better Board Members", Grassroots Fundraising Journal, (undated).

an executive position or is the Chair of the Board. Unable to lead by example, his conflict of interest frustrates other members or sends a signal to the Board that raising money for this organization is optional. Including a general conflict of interest clause in Board member agreements makes it clear that exemptions related to fundraising are not permitted.

After I left my job as Development Director at a private school, the Board abolished the position. That speaks volumes about what I was up against.

- **Specific conflict of interest:** On occasion, a Board member may have good reason to declare herself in conflict concerning a particular donor, prospective donor or fundraising issue. The agreement should describe how and when a member should make that conflict known.

- **Fundraising responsibilities:** "I will actively participate in one or more fundraising activities" is typical of references in Board member agreements but not helpful to either members or their not-for-profits. Vague statements such as these omit both the specific actions that are needed in order to raise money and the measurable requirements for success. Table 28 in Chapter 12 lists the ten fundraising activities at which leadership volunteers excel and puts measures of performance against those activities. This is the core of a plan for fundraising at a leadership level and it can and should be included in Board member agreements.

- **Rights of Board members concerning fundraising:** Agreements are not agreements but edicts if they lay out what not-for-profits expect from leadership volunteers without referencing how they will support members in return. This includes the right to receive timely information concerning progress or problems, accurate and timely financial information, confirmation of liability insurance and the like. Clauses on rights and obligations should also spell out the discrete responsibilities of leadership volunteers and staff on fundraising matters. The specific duties that professional fundraisers will undertake to support Board-led fundraising should be referenced to emphasize that Board members have dependable resources to increase their chances of success.

A clause like this would do more to boost fundraising results than anything else:

> As a member of the Board charged with fundraising responsibilities, I will never be asked to raise unrestricted funds. Additionally, the specific program, project or initiative for which I am asked to fundraise will always be a strategic and measurable priority for the Board and the not-for-profit.

It is odd that, as a collective decision-making body, the Board and CEO are quick to insist that as much money as possible be raised unrestricted. However, as soon as individual Board members find themselves on the front

When I started this job, the Chairman of the Board told me that if I asked him to fundraise or asked any Board member to give, he would quit. I wish I had asked him for a gift right then and there!

lines having to justify their own asks to donors, they see how this unreasonable position restricts their ability to raise money. When Cygnus conducts confidential research with our clients' Board members, "being unable to tell donors why my organization needs the money" is the number one reason why leadership volunteers underperform.

- **Giving requirements:** References to Board members' charitable gifts to their not-for-profits are too often expressed vaguely and seldom put in writing when clear direction would be much more useful to everyone. "I will make an annual financial contribution at a level that is meaningful to me" is certainly better than no reference at all, and it implies that a token gift offered to meet the literal obligation to give is unacceptable. But more productive and more respectful of Board members as donors would be something like:

> As a member of the Board that is responsible for fundraising success, I will give generously within my own means on an annual basis. I make this commitment in respect of other donors who are also asked to support my not-for-profit as generously as possible. Additionally, I will give generously and regularly in respect of my fellow Board members, all of whom commit to do the same for the financial well-being of the not-for-profit and as a public show of strength during fundraising campaigns.

Board members have the right to enjoy the same respectful consideration when being asked to give that would be afforded any other donor, including the right to have their giving information held in the strictest confidence.

While serving on Boards, I have seen and heard things that made me cringe concerning giving by Board members, things which external donors would never endure. I have witnessed Board members who have not yet given being criticized during meetings; others have been questioned in front of their peers for not meeting the minimum gift expectation, even though it had never been stipulated; and, perhaps most humiliating of all, I have heard the Chair exempt a Board member from giving by revealing during a meeting that he knew the individual had just lost her job.

When Board members are expected not only to give but also to figure out when, how and how much, everyone loses. No experienced professional fundraiser would leave that much to chance when dealing with an external donor; so why is this commonplace with leadership volunteers where the full participation of all members at a generous level is so important to fundraising success? Securing Board members' gifts is the responsibility of the Chair of the Board, the Chair of the Nominating Committee and the CEO, with support from the Director of Development. As would be the case with any other donor, prospect research should be used to help set an appropriate gift range for the ask. This should include taking into account valuable information gained during the search and nominating process. The Chair, perhaps accompanied by the CEO, should ask for the gift in an appropriate, private setting, deploying the same respectful approach that all donors deserve. Board members should be offered every convenience to enable generous giving such as monthly installments and they should be given the opportunity to designate their gifts to a program or priority project that is meaningful to the volunteer. All solicitors, including the Director of Development, should be charged with ensuring the confidentiality of Board members' gift information. Finally, Board member donors should receive regular, personal reports on how their gifts are being used and the results that are being achieved.

Our business has seasonal peaks and valleys. We have to evaluate how an employee will perform in peak periods when there is no margin for error or failure, so short probation periods generally don't work for us.

In every way, save the up-front expectation that they will give, Board members should experience the same respectful approach and enjoy the same rights as any other donor. Besides solidifying the relationship between member and Board in a positive way, it is simply smart fundraising because this approach will raise more money.

When Should Members Be Asked to Sign Agreements?

Draft or sample agreements for Board members should be provided to potential candidates before they agree to stand for election – not so early in the discussion that doing so jars the negotiation, but early enough that candidates can assess the volunteer opportunity within a full understanding of their rights and obligations as Board members.

Probation

Probation is a trial period during which the employer assesses and evaluates the employee to determine whether she is suitable for long term employment.[3] 75% of respondents in non-management positions in our survey and 66% of those managing one-person-shops were placed on probation at the start of their current jobs. Views of managers in our survey towards probation were largely positive. 85% of Development Directors agreed that probationary periods offer valuable insight

---

[3] *Probationary Employees: What Employers Need to Know*, Barry W. Kwasniewski, Charity Law Bulletin No. 168, June 24, 2009.

Fundraising is a long-term process. A 90-day probation period is too short to highlight strengths and expose weaknesses. It can weed out the utterly clueless or those who have lied about past accomplishments, however.

What cannot be fairly measured through probation, according to fundraisers:

22% Relationship-building with donors
22% Likelihood of reaching fundraising goals
8% Ability to handle big events
7% Integration / relationship with team

on many fronts, including whether new employees are likely to stay in their jobs for an acceptable period of time.

Given the connection between probation and staff retention, it is interesting that the majority of, but not all, not-for-profits take advantage of this important hiring tool. Among those who do not, half said that probation is simply not policy within their organizations and 15% felt they could fire employees at will, making probation redundant. On that issue, employers should be careful. With some exceptions, probation does provide employers with protection if they choose to fire an employee without cause during that period.

Respondents agreed that almost every aspect of performance can be adequately assessed during a typical probationary period (with "typical" defined as three to six months). But there is an exception. Developing relationships with donors requires more time than any reasonable period of probation affords, though only one in five Development Directors noted this in our study. Where building relationships with donors is central to success, major gifts officers require eighteen months to two years to demonstrate their skill and produce meaningful results.

How Long Should Probation Continue?

There are no fixed limits to probationary periods, though the end of probation often coincides with the point at which employment benefits become active. Seniority and sophistication of the job also impact the length of probation. Staff hired for jobs that are less complex and with no management responsibilities tend to have shorter probationary periods than staff hired for more senior, demanding positions. But this assumes that the more multi-faceted the job and the higher it sits on the seniority ladder, the longer staff need to master their responsibilities. Our research found that this is not the case. There is an inverse relationship between seniority and time required to get up to speed. Junior, non-management fundraisers said they needed ten to twelve months of orientation, training and close supervision before feeling that they were performing at full capacity, whereas management-level fundraisers taking responsibility for the entire Development department required only three to six. This is because experience is generalized to some degree, especially in the fundraising industry which operates in a similar fashion regardless of the purpose or location of the not-for-profit.

Why Some Employees Do Not Pass Probation

Managers in our study said that one out of two employees who do not pass probation is dismissed for reasons connected with resistance to authority (being unresponsive or resistant to direction), or incompatibility with colleagues or supervisors. This is understandable as these issues are difficult to assess during the interview process. To do a better job in the future at weeding out these candidates before they are hired, have staff interview finalists. They observe candidates from a collegial rather than an employer/employee perspective and they may recognize communications or compatibility issues not obvious to managers. And of course, purposeful reference-checking is an employer's best ally, (See Chapter 8).

According to survey respondents, 25% of dismissals during probation can be attributed to lack of industry knowledge. These incidents can be reduced substantially by phrasing interview questions related to fundraising knowledge and experience in ways that make generalized or contrived responses impossible. If firing due to lack of knowledge is the result of taking a chance on someone without direct fundraising experience but with assumed transferrable skills, then handling orientation and early training with that in mind will reduce premature dismissals.

Fair and Useful Performance Objectives for Probationary Employees

The most important determinant of length of probation is the amount of time required for productivity to be fairly measured. When drafting employment agreements and articulating probation period objectives, employers should ask themselves, "What can I reasonably expect my new hire to accomplish in the short term that is both measurable and beneficial to our fundraising operation?" This requires translating the tasks that comprise typical job descriptions into tangible outcomes in order to make performance evaluation possible. The example in Table 20 expands the job duties of a probationary Manager of Donor Relations on the left to include more useful productivity measures on the right.

Table 20: Typical Versus Meaningful Performance Measures for a Manager of Donor Relations by the End of the Probationary Period

Job Duties	Measurable Performance Indicators
Inaugurate newsletter for mid-level donors and send first two issues in June and September.	Stabilize donor retention in mid-level giving which has fallen from 46% to 39% in the past two years. Test a communications strategy that prevents further erosion of mid-level donors (i.e., retention does not fall below 39%).
Review and improve communication program to online donors.	Improve average annual contribution among donors in the online giving program (annual fund) from $175 to $210 by crafting more vivid emails, introducing real time reporting and innovating other communications strategies.
Update thank-you letters to annual fund donors.	Improve first-gift-to-second-ask retention from 35% to 39% and average value of second gift from $76 to $85 by improving acknowledgement processes for first-time donors. This will involve reducing turnaround time from three weeks to ten days and testing a minimum of five new thank-you letters based on the "20 Characteristics of Great Thank-You Letters" published in *Donor-Centered Fundraising*.
Review and update communications program to recurring (monthly) donors.	Redesign and test a communications program to recurring (monthly) donors to achieve: improvement in renewal rate from 45% to 60% when credit card requires reactivation; improvement in rate of transfer of recurring donors to major gifts prospects from 1.5% to 2.5%.

After six months, learning accelerates and the new employee is able to take on more tasks. By that time, he or she understands how the organization works and can make decisions in context.

Information in the left-hand column of Table 20 is typical of how expectations are expressed to probationary employees – as things to be done rather than as objectives to be achieved. The inherent contradiction is that if the left-hand column were the performance guide, the new Donor Relations Manager would pass her probation by simply demonstrating that the work had been accomplished, whether or not fundraising improved. Expressing work by objectives ensures that the true measures of management skill are put to the test, making assessment of performance meaningful. The Donor Relations Manager must be able to solve problems and introduce new ideas in order to impact the bottom line, and she must understand and use donor and financial data to guide her actions. The added bonus of this objectives-based approach is that it gives the Donor Relations Manager considerable leeway in making the job her own. She is expected to reach goals but how she does so is not imposed upon her. This is a strong statement of confidence in the new employee and confidence in management to make excellent hires.

Measurable indicators can be identified for every position, even front-line fundraising jobs where the employee has far less leeway for independent decision-making. Table 21 offers an example for an annual fund associate in his first fundraising job.

Table 21: Typical versus Meaningful Performance Measures for an Annual Fund Associate by the End of a 12-Month Probationary Period

Job Duties	Measurable Performance Indicators
Draft communications emails for online donors.	What email length sells best? Objective: draft and test 1-, 2-, 3- and 4-paragraph copy lengths to determine whether length affects open rates, read rates and click-thrus.
Source premiums (token gifts) for direct mail appeals.	Find and brand an original premium that speaks to our not-for-profit's mission. Objective: to replace non-associated address labels and fridge magnets with something that builds awareness while incurring no loss of revenue among premium donors.
Monitor social media comments.	Develop a social media conversation. Objective: to boost conversion of followers to donors from 3% to 5% in one year.

Choosing outcomes-based over task-based performance assessment is a definite hiring advantage in an industry searching for more skilled practitioners. "We want you to bring the full weight of your experience and creativity to this position to help us accomplish ambitious goals" is a much more enticing message to candidates than, "We know what needs to be done and we just want you to execute it." Especially for not-for-profits that are less competitive on salary, offering a more fulfilling career experience is a trump card that anyone can play.

Nothing Works Every Time

If negative interpersonal behaviors show themselves during probation, it is almost certain they will magnify once the employee wins permanent status. If a new member of the staff struggles to meet goals that planning and experience tell you can and should be achieved, you can expect under-performance to continue post-probation. Take action early and decisively to eliminate poor performers from your staff team.

Even when best practices are deployed, employers are still bound to hire staff from time to time who under-perform and/or are not well suited for the job. Even the most seasoned employers make mistakes now and then, so be ready to forgive yourself or the person responsible for the hire so that you can move on as quickly as possible. You have tools at your disposal to overcome the problem. Using them while taking time to reflect on what went awry will set you up for a better experience the next time. Learn from it and share your new knowledge with others in your not-for-profit who hire and supervise staff. You will be respected for your candor and your staff and colleagues will rally around you.

Apprenticeship: The Solution to a Hidden Problem

The compartmentalized nature of fundraising means that the programs that raise money are isolated from one another and even actively competing for donors and gifts. By default, so are the people who manage and work in those programs. Each method for raising money is expected to be independently profitable, whether or not donor trends, technological advancements and other matters make continuous upward movement of net revenue possible. This fractured approach to Development also flies in the face of the real objective of all fundraising – to move as many donors as possible as quickly as possible to a state of giving generously within their own means. Only when this superior objective is in play does a Development operation have the chance to increase fundraising profit reliably and indefinitely.

With that in mind, the fundraising industry may be unwittingly compromising its own ability to succeed. By leaning heavily on direct marketing for profit, it must choose approaches to raising money that are antithetical to relationship-building where more profit can be realized. Mechanical and volume-based by definition, direct marketing programs and the fundraisers who work in them deploy aggressive tactics, solicit frequently and minimize donor communication in order to ensure profit in the short-term. Donor attrition is extraordinarily high in these programs; but staff who run them cannot stop long enough to consider why supporters who

Look closely for transferable skills and carefully focus on them during initial probation. Helping non-fundraising staff or junior fundraisers understand the big picture and how their jobs fit within the overall mission gives them a sense of pride and enthusiasm for their work.

singled out their organizations from so many competitors would then fall away so soon. Of necessity, when donors are giving through direct marketing programs they are file numbers, gift amounts and gift frequency statistics.

Discrete sensibilities are required for direct marketing and relationship fundraising. This forces Development operations to bear the cost of finding, training and developing two different kinds of fundraiser instead of being able to rely on volume-based programs to be the training ground for more senior Development positions. This wouldn't be so bad if direct marketing staff were staying put, but they are not. They are leaving after two to three years on the job because they see no possibility for career growth if they stay. This is so unfortunate because the business of fundraising is actually very diverse with lush opportunities for a lifetime career, but not if its practitioners feel they have been slotted into too narrow a definition of what it means to be a fundraiser.

Reward and Punishment

Every not-for-profit wants its fundraising operation to be more profitable. Getting there will not be accomplished by endlessly growing the number of donors but by stewarding existing supporters from entry-level contributions to major and planned gifts. But that cannot happen until the mindset in fundraising is altered to encourage that upward flow. Managers of entry-level programs need to be rewarded for delivering donors to their colleagues in major and planned gifts. Right now, they would be punished for doing so because this would cause profit in their own programs to fall. So they hoard high-performing donors instead of offering them up. These same managers also need to be rewarded for investing in the orientation and training of junior fundraisers and preparing them to take on more demanding roles outside their departments.

The ultimate return on investment in fundraising is realized when donors are retained longer. The ultimate return on investment in human capital is realized when staff stay longer – not in the same job because that is an unrealistic expectation, but in the same not-for-profit because that means everyone wins.

A Collaborative and More Profitable Alternative

Adopting apprenticeship as a core principle of fundraiser training would be a boon to every multi-faceted Development office. Typical orientation and training teaches an employee to execute the functions of her current job description. Apprenticeship shows her where her role fits into the bigger picture and how doing her current job well will open up more career opportunities.

Apprenticeship addresses so many weaknesses in current fundraising configuration that it is surprising it is not standard practice as it is in other industries. Take cosmetology, for example. The hairdressing business knows that many things can be learned in a classroom, but until those scissors are poised over a real person's head, it's just theory with no consequences. Only when the hairdresser makes contact with the customer can his skill be truly measured.

Anyone wanting to become a licensed cosmetologist must first graduate from high school and then take one to two years of classroom training before becoming an apprentice hairdresser. Apprenticeship then requires about three thousand hours of on-the-job training after which candidates can sit the state licensing exam. All this for a profession where the fallout (no pun intended) from a less capable practitioner is arguably less serious than it is in fundraising. After all, hair grows back. But, when a fundraiser loses a donor, he loses the incalculable future value of the gifts that his organization will now never receive.

In order for an apprenticeship program to work in Development, fundraising managers will need to abandon their territorial approach to staffing and chief Development officers will need to make that sacrifice worthwhile.

No one wants to invest time and money in new staff only to have them quickly promoted into someone else's program. Orientation, training and on-the-job experience all translate into transferrable skills. In other words, the director of corporate sponsorship becomes the direct beneficiary of the investment made by the fundraising events manager in training when the latter's employee is promoted to sponsorship associate. But there is no benefit to the events manager who must start all over finding, orienting and training a new person. No wonder they guard their staff closely and dissuade them from applying for internal promotions.

When staffing is donor-centered, promoting from within is not just preferred; it is policy. Assuming the best possible hires were made in the first place, managers look to the junior pool to fill their staffing needs. That puts baseline fundraising programs, where most new fundraisers get into the business, at a disadvantage. Promoting from within means that time spent hiring and training by direct marketing and events managers will be disproportionate and the length of time they enjoy their fully trained and productive staff will continue to be limited. Consequently, managers who hire and train more frequently need to have their budgets and job descriptions adjusted to take the inherent time and cost into account. This adjustment will yield a hidden bonus. Since hiring frequently makes these managers more skilled at this job, they could play an HR advisory role for

Training and orientation need to progress beyond a duty-specific focus into general orientation about fundraising in the big picture, including its ethics, principles and methodologies. AFP's courses as well as local and state conferences are excellent adjuncts to our orientation program.

Reasons why staff are dismissed during probation:

49% Resistance to supervision
47% Incompatibility
25% Insufficient industry knowledge
19% Inability to adapt to new environment

the entire Development Department. For operations large enough to warrant it, a director of fundraising talent could alleviate the expense for all program managers while lessening the amount of time in which they are diverted from their primary work.

Apprenticeship as a Retention Strategy for Young Fundraisers

A donor-centered apprenticeship program for young fundraisers is aimed directly at extending new employees' tenure beyond the typically short stays confirmed by our research. The financial benefit is obvious – not-for-profits will realize a better return on the investment that they make in hiring, training and supervising. In addition, apprenticeship better qualifies junior employees to compete for internal promotions, lessening the instances of staff having to leave to gain meaningful career experience. Apprenticeship is a practical and productive hedge against rapid turnover in an industry where practitioners have the upper hand. It also fills the void between landing one's first job in fundraising and qualifying to write the CFRE exam. Certification is a smart and valuable addition to the profession and it is entirely appropriate that fundraisers who earn this designation have a minimum of five years of practical experience behind them. Apprenticeship is the bridge between classroom learning and professional certification.

Apprenticeship is different from orientation. Apprenticeship guides junior employees systematically through the full range of fundraising programs rather than focusing on a single job. Apprenticeship extends tenure because it shows young fundraisers where their careers could take them if they stay in the organization. For employers, apprenticeship discovers talent early. For example, someone hired to write copy for direct marketing appeals may also show exceptional ability in writing copy for the planned gifts officer, but only if given the opportunity. Apprenticeship encourages learning, growth and exploration for the triple purposes of uncovering talent, fast-tracking experience and furthering staff retention.

Shaping an Apprenticeship Program

One approach to designing an apprenticeship program involves placing the new employee in a rotation through the Development Department until she has worked in all programs and/or units. (Fundraising in a particular faculty or school is quite different from being a member of the team in the central advancement office, for example.) After this period of apprenticeship, the new hire takes on a specific job description. Another version, one likely more acceptable to the manager who hired the new staff, would see the recruit working part-time in the job for which he was initially hired and part-time in an apprenticeship rotation through other fundraising programs or departments. In either case, the onus is on the assigned supervisor in each rotation segment to orient and train the apprentice and assess her performance on the job.

The manager who hired the employee may feel shortchanged if he loses his recruit for half the day. There are remedies and many are explored in more detail in Chapter 12. Four hours of work in the morning is generally more productive than the same length of time in the afternoon, so the hiring manager should have that advantage. Parkinson's Law is as true today as it was fifty years ago – that work expands to fill the time available for its completion.[4] And, time diverted from work into meetings for any staff member, whether an apprentice or not, is more often time wasted than time well spent.

Having been observed and evaluated by each program or unit manager, the apprentice will eventually complete her tour of duty. Imagine these managers coming together to discuss her aptitudes and how she has grown into increasingly challenging assignments. Everyone knows her; everyone is seeking to maximize her value; she belongs to the entire Development operation, not just to one program. What a feeling to be valued to that degree. That alone would make someone want to stay.

A Donor-Centered Apprenticeship Program

An apprenticeship program that is "donor-centered" is exactly what its name implies. It is designed with the fundamental objective of all fundraising as its core premise, which is to retain donors as long as possible by guiding them through introductory, volume-based solicitation tactics into major and planned gifts programs. When being donor-centered is the objective and when everyone works together towards that goal, it impacts how the whole staff thinks. If a young fundraiser is hired to write copy for direct marketing programs, he will approach that work differently if he has been through a donor-centered apprenticeship program. As he rotates through the relationship-based approaches to raising money, he will be more inclined to write copy for donors as they really are – caring, thinking, human beings who respond generously when treated well. Back in the direct marketing program, it will now be impossible for him to see donors only as bits of data. He will realize that they are the same caring, thinking people who are simply not yet giving at a level that is causing them to be noticed. Now he will be asking himself two questions:

We're known in the fundraising industry for being a place where employees can grow, be mentored and access professional development. We also have a strong focus on certification. As a result, we have great staff retention.

---

[4] First articulated by Cyril Northcote Parkinson in a humorous essay published in The Economist in 1955.

My advice to other managers is: learn how to make your expectations known right from the start and be prepared to step in right away when you see things start to slip.

- What could I do to trigger a more generous response from donors in this program right now?
- What should I stop doing or minimize in order to prevent them from leaving prematurely?

Even though this junior employee has a narrow job description and no decision-making power, he actually has considerable influence over whether donors stay or go by how he does his work. His new understanding of donor psychology and the long term goal of fundraising learned first-hand through apprenticeship expands his creative potential and guides his approach to the job. Drafting thank you letters for donors in direct marketing programs is an important example. On the surface, this job function appears to have limited scope and impact. But my research over a decade has proven that this is not the case. Exceptional thank-you letters, composed with care and creativity, produce improved retention rates and higher average gift values among donors who receive them.

Apprenticeship and Employee Retention

Apprenticeship does more than just add value to young employees' entry-level jobs. It gives them a reason to stay. 41% of fundraisers under the age of 30 said they left their last not-for-profit to take a more senior position elsewhere; 38% said they left to work in an organization that had more opportunities for career advancement. This is crippling to a not-for-profit that invests in young fundraisers only to lose them within twelve to eighteen months. But young workers lose too when they leave too soon. They miss the opportunity to show their boss and their not-for-profit how much more they could have contributed; they risk being labelled a "job-hopper", something that becomes increasingly problematic the more they rack up short job stays; and they miss the opportunity to win internal promotions – a critically important measure of achievement in business.

In a not-for-profit with an apprenticeship program, supervisors and managers ask themselves, "How soon could this talented employee be ready for more demanding responsibilities?" This is very different from traditional management thinking which tends to favor, "How long can I keep this employee doing the same job?" Managers we surveyed expressed frustration at their young employees' insistence on moving up the career ladder early, especially because this was not the pace at which their own careers had progressed. But since the not-for-profit sector continues to grow and, with it, the demand for experienced fundraisers, managers should be welcoming, not resisting, their young fundraisers' ambitious career intentions. Apprenticeship, combined with a policy of promoting internally, gives managers an edge on the only question that is actually on the table – whether young employees will leave in order to build their careers, or whether they will find opportunities for upward mobility where they are currently employed.

Transitioning in Mid-Career

The Executive Manager of Direct Marketing of a prominent national charity and I were meeting to plan next steps. We were on the verge of launching a series of tests to answer the question, "How could online giving and direct mail be adjusted to deliver more and better cultivated prospects sooner to the major gifts team?" Just getting to this point had required several months of program analysis and consultation and some very skillful management of the direct marketing team.

A sharp knock broke our concentration and there in the doorway was the organization's new CEO who had been on the job for just over a month. I had not met him before but I could see instantly why the Board had made such an effort to lure him away from the corporate sector. Most recently he had been President of a manufacturing company destined for the Fortune 500 ranks. He was very well known in the business world plus he was a prominent donor and volunteer.

The CEO was certainly a force to be reckoned with – his personality took over the room as he entered. Extending one hand to me and acknowledging his manager with the other, he said: "I heard you two were meeting and I wanted to know more about what you're up to."

The manager looked at me as if to say, "You go ahead." I referenced the research we had already done which showed a strong interest among direct mail and online donors in closer relationships and how we had identified a significant capacity for more generous giving. As I started to described the tests we were about to conduct, the CEO interrupted.

"Sorry, I'm a bit short on time today. From my experience, I know that if you can get people together into a well-planned event like a high-level auction, the guests really get caught up in the action – especially if there's an open bar. I have served on the Boards of several organizations that have done this and I've seen for myself that these events really work."

Looking directly at me, he continued, "As a consultant dealing with lots of charities, you must be aware of what's happening out there that is new and exciting – something that we could do here that could become an annual event that we could brand. I'm willing to invest in the right concept. I want to present some ideas to the Board next week. Can you put together a briefing and get it to me by Friday?"

"Uh-oh", I thought to myself. A little knowledge and a lot of power is a dangerous combination.

Working in not-for-profits gives no one an excuse to be less professional. In fact, fundraisers must be more professional and work twice as hard to get half as far as their for-profit colleagues.

The problem with transitioning programs and services staff into fundraising is that they bring their preconceptions and outmoded ways of operating with them. They need lots of retraining and it's not always a worthwhile investment.

All the knowledge of fundraising that a newly transitioned CEO or Development Director could acquire will have little meaning if he does not know the most important thing of all – that the best fundraising strategies are designed and executed to sustain the loyalty of donors who are already contributing, to maximize their generosity, and to inspire them to give more generously sooner. All top decision-makers, whether newly minted from the corporate sector or lifelong third-sector workers, need to grasp this fundamental truth about how to raise money reliably and sustainably in any economy. This is especially so for CEOs and Development Directors whose job it is to expose the industry to more profitable ways of raising money.

With this core fundraising principle guiding their thinking, transitioning managers and directors have a context in which to demonstrate the value of their business experience. They are more inclined to listen and ask questions than to suggest ideas that are off-strategy; they are able to assess staff performance in the context of what really matters in fundraising; and they are motivated to keep the Board focused on moving donors up the giving ladder in ways that they do best.

Orientation for Board Members

Not-for-profits do not expect their new employees to produce results without first receiving orientation to the job plus training, supervision and performance evaluation. But these considerations are rare for leadership volunteers. 58% of Board members surveyed said no orientation program existed when they joined the Board.

In cases where in-person orientation was offered to new Board members, the program commonly covered an introduction to the by-laws of the not-for-profit, especially as they related to Board membership (such as meeting attendance requirements, understanding voting procedures, etc.). Also typically addressed were the structure and reporting relationship to the Board of the various committees, the history of the not-for-profit and, where such existed, the organization's strategic plan. But practical, hands-on matters that new members have to deal with in their first meeting, such as interpreting the financial statements, were rarely included as topics for orientation.

While only a minority of Board members had experienced an in-person approach to orientation, a larger number (62%) received some kind of Board package or manual to review on their own. They rated this resource at a positive 5.2 on a 1 to 7 scale for its helpfulness in orienting members to their responsibilities. Respondents who offered lower scores pointed to content that was too general or theoretical, often unrelated to the charity on whose Board they were serving. Criticism was also levelled at content that was too elementary or unsophisticated. But respondents' chief complaint was simply that they preferred a more experiential style of learning over reviewing a package of background material.

Less Is More in Donor-Centered Volunteer Orientation

A donor-centered approach to orientation acknowledges that leadership volunteers are donors as well as Board members and that their most demanding job is to engage with other donors and raise money. Donor-centered orientation acknowledges that Board members are running flat out in both their professional and personal lives while attempting to make a worthwhile contribution to society through volunteering. Donor-centered orientation also takes advantage of the multi-dimensional nature of today's learning tools while reversing the tendency to overload volunteers with information that our research has found they rarely access. Donor-centered orientation is designed around this question: "What information is essential to fundraising success at the leadership level and how should it be made available to Board members?"

Board members need three things as they join the Board. Anything else that they or their not-for-profits feel is important can be accessed online through a private website portal. Overloading leadership volunteers with more information than they need is counter-productive. For busy people, volume means avoidance. On the other hand, taking a minimalist approach and letting volunteers direct their own supplementary learning will increase the likelihood that they will seek out more information.

At the outset, Board members need:

- **the selling case for fundraising**. Our research with Board members who raise money for the annual fund found that the number one reason why they underperform is lack of clarity about what they are selling and why.

    Written as an emotionally compelling and intellectually satisfying narrative, the selling case should be no longer than two paragraphs in length. Supplementary information, if necessary, can be accessible through the Board members' portal on your website. The two-paragraph case should be the not-for-profit's top priority for funding and it should include a rationale, supported by evidence, that meaningful results will be achieved if the required funding level is reached.

My very first job in the not-for-profit sector was managing volunteers. It was invaluable in teaching me how to manage both donors and staff.

- **business cards** featuring both their volunteer and professional coordinates on the front. Influence is Board members' most critical asset for fundraising so they should be equipped with this practical networking tool. Consider having individual Board members' answer to this question printed on the back: "What does this not-for-profit mean to me?"

- **a fully annotated profile of members of the Board.** This is more than a contact list; it is a background document aimed at helping new Board members get to know their colleagues. Networking for business or social reasons is a factor that motivates people to serve. Not-for-profits that actively help Board members expand their circle of friends and colleagues contribute to coalescing the Board, especially around their obligations in fundraising. The process of compiling this profile will also be helpful to fundraising staff. The more they know about their own Board members, the more they can facilitate meaningful connections between them and donors.

  Besides the obvious contact details, it would be interesting for new members to have a brief account of fellow volunteers' career highlights, to know something about their families, their hobbies and other personal interests; to learn about Board members' special achievements and awards, and to know if any members sit on corporate Boards or hold other prominent business or community positions.

- **a staff list.** Not the full staff list that is often provided on a reporting grid, but a streamlined, annotated list of people essential to Board members' fundraising work. This practical resource directs Board members efficiently to the person(s) who can provide information, solve problems and, in essence, help them meet their fundraising goals. The very existence of this document tells Board members that they are not out there on their own which raises their level of confidence. Greater confidence means volunteers are more willing to make the ask which, in turn, leads to higher levels of success. Table 22 illustrates. Note that the support functions and the people available to provide those resources are tied to the specific fundraising activities at which Board members excel, (See Chapter 12, Table 28).

Table 22: Board Members' Support Team for Fundraising

Fundraising Resource	Who to Contact
Accessing names of active donors with compatible characteristics for cultivation activities such as making thank-you calls, writing thank-you notes, cultivation calls to begin upgrading donors to major gifts: • living within 2 miles of Board member's home; • working in same/similar field as Board member; • attending same church/synagogue; • being members of same athletic or other membership club.	Gary Manchester, Manager Data Analysis, X 355 (email address)
Obtaining additional background information on Board member-identified prospects.	Jeannie Walters, Director, Prospect Research, X361 (email address)
Obtaining proposal summaries on projects available for funding: • related to medical research; • related to patient / family services; • related to capital projects	Yvonne Adams, Grants Manager, X380 (email address) Miles Brown, Grants Associate, X382 (email address) Brian Orrenthal, Campaign Director, X400 (email address)
Obtaining annual fundraising dinner tickets for sale and/or getting tips on selling tickets from experienced volunteers.	Claire deVries, Event Committee Chair, (555) 555-5555 (day) (555) 555-5555 (evening) (email address)
Strategizing major gift asks.	Eleanor Lamarche, VP Development, X300 (email address)

Some well-resourced Development offices have a staff member assigned to the Board who, among other duties, acts as liaison between volunteers and staff on functions described in Table 22. But for Fundraising operations that do not have that luxury, providing clear and concise directions to Board members in this manner accomplishes several things. It focuses volunteers' attention on fundraising; it breaks down the job into achievable components; it reminds them that staff are ready and available to support them; it offloads the detail work, maximizing the value of time that Board members devote to raising money.

Dedicated Online Fundraising Resources for Board Members

A password-protected resource on your website can house anything else that Board members need to support their work in fundraising as well as other obligations. Following the model of the Career Landing Page described in Chapter 6, Board information online should be vibrant, appealingly designed and diverse in the media used to express it. Table 23 offers some examples of content on such a landing page and the format that would increase the likelihood that Board members will access it:

Table 23: Board-Dedicated Website Content that Supports Fundraising

Content	Format/Source
History of the not-for-profit.	Video: 2-3 minutes narrated by a founding member, a noted historian or an actor.
Not-for-profit's bylaws.	Text: with tenets related to fundraising and fiscal management highlighted and annotated.
About the Fundraising Committee.	Text: focuses on the role of the Fundraising Committee and how it differs from that of the Board. Video: 1-2 minute highlights from the most recent event under the auspices of the Fundraising Committee.
Rules of order for Board meetings.	Video: via links to YouTube which offers several short and informative videos.[5] Text: concise, user-friendly and limited to the top 5-7 rules that are used most often when running meetings. (One Board member might be charged with the task of being a reliable resource for the more obscure rules.)[6]
Recent accomplishments by the Board.	Video: 1-2 minutes, narrated by the Chair, on what the Board accomplished in the past year, with particular emphasis on achievements in fundraising.
Selling case for fundraising.	Video: 2-minute visual account of the program, service or project that is the Board's (and the not-for-profit's) primary focus for fundraising, narrated by the programs director, physician, artistic director, etc., most directly connected with the issue or opportunity. (A second video describing an alternative funding priority could be included, but offering more than two options diffuses fundraising efforts, taking longer to reach goal and raising concerns among donors about strategy and commitment.)
Fundraising Q&A for Board members.	Text: "top ten" questions that donors and prospective donors ask and how to answer them – compiled by leadership volunteers and the Director of Development who have encountered these questions previously.
Fundraising progress chart.	Link: to a separate password-protected site where individual Board members' personal gifts and accomplishments in fundraising are charted, the latter on a points system. (See "Time and Productivity in Board-Related Fundraising", Chapter 12, Table 28.)

"I'm So Glad I Joined this Board"

If new members are saying this to themselves after their first meeting, then the Board has done its job well in volunteer orientation. Members who are fully engaged and appreciated by their peers feel a heightened sense of responsibility to the team. They are more eager to contribute and they definitely do not want to let their fellow Board members down. This is the attitude that progressive Boards strive to instil in their new members – in fact in all members – so that they take on the challenging job of raising money willingly.

Two simple things will help new Board members feel fully engaged and appreciated.

1. Pair new members with partners – experienced Board members who will support new recruits for the first meeting or two until they are contributing independently.

---

[5] The best ones being by Susan Leahy, including "Robert's Rules of Order – Mastering the 3 Most Important Motions", narrated by Susan Leahy from robertsrulesmadesimple.com. www.youtube.com/watch?v=eYwKX_P8YkU

[6] A version of "Robert's Rules of Order", updated for 21st-century meetings by Dave Rosenberg, can be found at www.daverosenberg.net/articles/RulesOfOrder.htm

2. As the last item on the agenda, hold a reception in honor of new members to draw them into the group from the start. This says we respect what you have to offer, we are here to support you, and we expect you to be an active member of the team. Delegates who attend conferences say that the time they spend networking in the halls in between sessions is more valuable than the workshops they attend. So it is with Board meetings. Building social networking opportunities into Board meetings strengthens the sense of commitment to the group.

The Orient-ation Express

Orientation for volunteers concentrates learning so that new members have both the knowledge and the confidence to start producing as early as possible. But piling on the knowledge does not mean piling on the paper. Gone is the Board Orientation Manual in the four-inch binder. In today's world in which everything moves at lightning speed and everyone is drowning in a sea of information, you can show your appreciation for your leadership volunteers by remembering that less is more.

> In any job, be it paid or volunteer, your new staff or Board member will only ever have one first day. Make it count. Let your new recruit see the best you have to offer and, most important, show him how thrilled you are that he has joined your team. Assume the best and that's exactly what you will get.

Development staff would be much more motivated -- and successful -- if the Board would just strive to meet its own fundraising goals.

Chapter 11:
How to Hold onto Good Staff

In order to land my first official job in fundraising, I had to move from Ohio to a small university in Iowa. I had planned to stay just one year to get enough experience to qualify me for jobs closer to home.

My main job as Associate Director of University Advancement was to write appeal letters and other correspondence. About eight months into that first year, my Director approached me about writing for and editing the alumni magazine. I was thrilled. I remember calling home that night and saying, "If they were looking for a way to keep me longer than a year, they've found it."

That early acknowledgement from my Director that I was producing quality work convinced me to stay. I knew she had seen my potential and had faith in my abilities. I also realized that she had been paying attention to who I was and what I was good at all along and looking out for creative opportunities for me to grow professionally. The alumni magazine job was a much better match for my skills and I ended up staying at the university for three years, not one. I would have stayed even longer, but family matters necessitated a move back home.

The experience I gained in Iowa prepared me well for my next, more senior position. I will always be grateful to my first Director for showing me early in my career that fundraising is a broad profession and that there is a place for me in this field.

Hiring the right staff and guiding their orientation and early training is just the start. Now the even more challenging task begins. Holding onto the great people you have found and helping them become increasingly productive is the job of everyone who manages staff or leads a team of volunteers.

Managing a Donor-Centered Development Department

31% of fundraisers who were planning to leave their jobs at the time we conducted our research cited concerns over how money was raised. An "old-school culture", marked by chasing immediate, short-term revenue at the expense of more lucrative, long term funding solutions, was identified as a particular problem. Responses were similar when we asked fundraisers to tell us why they left their last position. 36% identified that same old-school approach to raising money in the face of changing donor trends and more progressive approaches.

I left a not-for-profit because their idea of fundraising was "begging" for support instead of "partnering" to achieve a mutually beneficial goal. Today, five years later, they are still at the same inadequate funding level.

Development professionals are right to red-flag this issue. One out of every two donors could give more generously right now – some much more generously – and donors themselves have defined the concept of Donor-Centered Fundraising (Chapter 4) as the approach that would unleash their giving at a whole new level. So, if decision-makers adjust their fundraising to become donor-centered, it will be well worth the effort. They will raise more money and retain Development staff longer.

The Difference Between Typical and Donor-Centered Development Departments

A donor-centered Development Department functions differently from the norm. It still utilizes all the fundraising programs that would be found in a typical fundraising operation, including everything from direct marketing to planned giving. However, programs are shaped and resourced to maximize their potential and to avoid the things that donors say inhibit their giving.

In a typical Development operation, each fundraising program that asks donors to give is expected to make money and do so independent of each other program running in the department. Further, all fundraising programs are separately evaluated for their success in achieving that goal on a progressive scale, as are the people who manage and run them. Surrounding these central programs that ask for money are secondary activities that come under the heading "donor relations". They include donor communication, donor recognition and anything else touching donors that is not intended primarily as another gift request. There is general agreement in the fundraising industry that donor relations is important but little real understanding about what it can actually accomplish. This is because fundraisers erroneously think that if they are engaged in work that might not be bringing in money immediately, the usefulness of that work cannot be measured. As a result, there is no consistency to donor relations and definitely no standards regarding what is and is not a worthwhile investment of time, talent and budget.

Most typical Development Departments are bottom-heavy. The majority of fundraising staff and the largest portion of the Development budget are assigned to building volume of donors and attempting to secure repeat, but relatively modest gifts. At the top of a typical fundraising operation are major and planned gifts programs that tend to be under-resourced relative to potential, especially in light of their superior ability to generate profit. To illustrate just how much potential is being missed, in a study that my firm conducted in 2010, 32% of American donors and 21% of Canadian donors who have made a will, but have not yet assigned a bequest to any charity, would strongly consider doing so if asked by a qualified not-for-profit representative.[1] Staffing is the single largest expense in fundraising, as it is in all other areas of not-for-profit service. The imbalance of staffing relative to fundraising program potential has a profound impact on the fundraising budget. Resource allocation in a typical fundraising operation is highest in programs generating the weakest return.

In a donor-centered Development operation, profit, not just revenue, is the primary objective. It is understood that some fundraising programs (major and planned gifts) are much better at making profit than others (events and direct marketing), so time, talent and budget are strategically invested in the former to generate the highest possible net return. Programs that fall into the other group are appreciated for the short-term revenue they generate, but valued much more for the important role they play in influencing profit in major and planned gifts. The primary purpose of entry-level fundraising programs in a donor-centered department is to acquire the best, not the most, donors and then instill in as many of them as possible an early desire to give generously.

To achieve that goal, donor-centered Development Departments recognize the central importance of donor relations. Stewardship, donor communication and donor recognition activities are well resourced but they are also very specific. Donor-centered fundraisers design donor relations to provide the three things that donors themselves say are essential to their desire to stay loyal and give more generously, (See Chapter 4).

In a donor-centered Development operation, investment is highest in the programs that generate the most profitable return and in the strategies that move donors forward.

Managing the Transition from Typical to Donor-Centered Fundraising

Even though a donor-centered Development Department raises more money, the lure of greater profit alone is not enough to inspire change in an industry that is designed for a different time and a different donor sensibility. While this is unfortunate, inability to adapt in order to capture a bigger prize is exclusive neither to fundraising nor to not-for-profits. An entire industry of change management specialists exists to help the corporate sector grapple with working differently in order to sustain or grow market share in a changing world.

> *If you always do what is best for your donor and build an honest and respectful relationship, the money will always be there – and usually more than you expected.*

---

[1] *The Cygnus Donor Survey: Where Philanthropy Is Headed in 2010*, Penelope Burk, Cygnus Applied Research, Inc., Chicago, IL, August 2010.

Adopting donor-centered fundraising affects everyone in the department. Table 24 provides several examples of how work priorities and objectives become oriented differently when typical fundraising gives way to a donor-centered approach.

Table 24: Work Objectives in Typical versus Donor-Centered Fundraising

Program	Typical Fundraising	Donor-Centered Fundraising
Direct mail acquisition.	Acquire as many new donors as possible with every appeal.	Acquire a strategic, controlled number of new donors at any one time. The number is determined by staffing and budget resources available to ensure that all new donors receive donor-centered stewardship to maximize retention and gift value going forward.
Post-gift communication with new donors.	Withhold from donors who give modestly so that the immediate net value of their gifts can be maximized.	Provide to all donors, regardless of gift value, in the knowledge that meaningful information on gifts-at-work is what inspires donors to give again and give more generously. This strategy is also essential because donor attrition is the highest (now 65%) between initial acquisition and the first renewal appeal. Early, meaningful communication mitigates this problem.
Renewal of generous donors in the online giving program.	Keep those donors focused on giving online in order to maximize the profit margin in the online giving program.	Cultivate these donors' interest in giving even more generously, applying effective stewardship practices and proactively transferring donors who show potential to major gifts officers, even though this reduces revenue in online giving. The online giving manager is rewarded, not penalized, for a drop in revenue when that drop is caused by transferring high value donors to major gifts.
Communicating with recurring/ monthly donors.	Minimize contact with recurring/ monthly donors to maximize profit in this program and because donors who give through automatic deduction do so because they do not want to be contacted.	Keep recurring/monthly donors informed about progress being achieved with their contributions in the knowledge that, without compelling information, donors will not be inspired to give even more generously. Recurring donors do not want to be solicited frequently, but Cygnus' research has confirmed that they still want to receive information about what is being accomplished with their gifts.
Recognition of donors who include a bequest in their wills.	Withhold recognition until donor is deceased to ensure that recognition is not offered to any donor who might rescind his bequest commitment.	Recognize donors while they are still living because waiting until they are dead is both cynical and counter-productive. Committing a bequest is not the "end of the line" in philanthropy but merely a gift transaction choice at a particular point in time. Donor-centered recognition inspires even the most generous donors to make additional cash contributions and/or deferred gift commitments after making an initial bequest.

It is the responsibility of management – both managers of individual fundraising programs and Development Department directors – to help non-management staff learn the difference between these two fundraising philosophies and guide them through the transition. This requires skill and patience; it cannot happen overnight. Keep in mind that managers and non-managers have quite different perspectives on the same issues, largely because managers have the power to decide what will and will not happen whereas front-line staff do not. A new concept or a different procedure can be an exciting challenge for top management but not necessarily for their staff who are tasked with carrying out a different plan. Non-management employees working in programs that are targeted for change know only that their work life tomorrow will not be the same as it was yesterday. They will be second-guessing things and questioning their ability to succeed in a differently configured job. They will feel like their world has been turned upside-down.

Stronger than Stats

There was a time when I thought that irrefutable evidence that one approach raises more money than another was all it took to convince fundraisers to adjust their practices. But it is not. Evidence can be just as likely to cause fundraisers with entrenched views to dig in their heels. When two professionals have differing opinions on an issue, they can disagree without consequence as long as one viewpoint carries as much weight as another. But, when evidence from research and testing is introduced, it turns the debate into opinion versus proof. This is enough to start some fundraisers along the road to change. Just as often, though, it serves to shut the conversation down, not to alter practitioners' points of view.

Today I am more realistic. The impact of change on certain members of the Development team is deep and wide. Leading the transition from typical to donor-centered fundraising means unearthing the concerns of staff as they see them and understanding what they are being asked to give up in order to realize the department-wide goal of securing more profit.

Implications of Change on Direct Marketing Staff

Several years ago, our research with one particular client uncovered huge potential for new revenue and my Vice President and I were very excited to report our findings. This amazing organization, founded by a handful of single-minded volunteers, had grown to become a shining example of success in its field. It attracted financial support from all over the country and was internationally recognized for its innovative approach. The charity operated entirely on private sector support, and, for the twenty years of its existence, all its revenue had been realized through direct mail. The program had been started by one member of the pioneering volunteer group who figured out how to raise money this way through trial and error, gradually building up direct mail to a multi-million dollar enterprise. This one man's commitment, ingenuity and sheer hard work was behind our client's every achievement.

Cygnus' job was to recommend enhancements to the existing communications strategy with direct-mail donors. But our surveying uncovered substantial major gifts potential being missed due to the limitations inherent in volume-based appeals. Our report identified close to $10 million that was immediately available through the establishment of a major gifts program, and substantially more within five years.

I once had a boss who used to say, "Less with data; more with donors". Data analysis is essential but I was immersed in it to such an extent that I was afraid to get out there and connect with donors. Once I learned to balance research and preparation with building relationships, my fear subsided and I never looked back.

There was a buzz in the room as we reported our findings. It was not lost on the CEO what this windfall could mean in making his and his Board's dreams come true.

The whole staff was giddy with excitement, except for the manager of the direct mail program. He listened in silence from the back as we presented our findings and our forecasts. During the conversation that followed, he quietly left the room.

If direct mail had never been invented, a significant percentage of not-for-profit organizations would not exist today. For decades, direct mail has been the fundraising program through which the largest volume of gifts is transacted. And, while some other programs raise more money, direct mail has been largely responsible for connecting potential donors with organizations they admire and turning their initial interest into action. Without direct mail, online giving would be only half as successful as it is today and, more important, far, far fewer Americans and Canadians would be making charitable gifts of any kind to any charity.

Professional fundraisers who manage and run direct mail programs are routinely relied upon to find new donors, to maintain a base level of reliable revenue, and to come up with a quick injection of cash whenever their organizations run into trouble. Whether they are praised openly for these accomplishments or not, fundraisers who work in direct mail know how important their work is to the fiscal security of the not-for-profits that employ them. No matter the criticisms about over-solicitation and low gift value, direct mail is predictably reliable and the people who operate this program are justifiably proud of the contribution they make to fundraising.

Understanding this history, it is easy to see why shifting the spotlight from direct mail to major gifts would, at the least, leave direct marketers feeling unappreciated. It is also easy to see why they would feel like their program had been raided and their best donors confiscated when major gifts prospects are taken from the direct marketing donor pool. For fundraisers whose success has always been measured by volume of donors giving and gross revenue raised, the loss of one's best donors to another staff member who did nothing to find them in the first place, or to steward their early giving, is a hard pill to swallow. That loss causes an immediate and significant drop in direct-mail revenue. Building direct-mail revenue back up can only happen from the bottom – by acquiring more new donors whose initial gifts will be modest while the cost to find them will be significant. It will take a long time to get revenue in the direct-mail program back to what it once was. Meanwhile, the pressure will still be on direct marketers to keep the money coming in now while the major gifts officers get to build relationships slowly with their donors on the promise of more money....some day.

Reward, Don't Punish, Progressive Behavior

It is a fact that donor attrition is extraordinarily high in direct mail and, unless someone steps in and takes high performing direct-mail donors by the hand, they won't be performing for long. It is also a fact that the potential value of donors' major gifts is far beyond that which can be realized as long as they remain in the direct-mail program. So, not using direct mail as a prospect strategy for major gifts is a waste of the resources already invested in these donors' initial acquisition and early retention.

It is easy to understand what prevents a smooth transition of donors from direct mail to major gifts – there is no benefit to the direct-mail manager or her staff for giving them up. It is up to the Development Director, then, to ensure that direct marketers are rewarded for actively building the major gifts pipeline. Consider these strategies:

1. **Prioritize the Department-Wide Goal**

   A siloed approach to fundraising in which staff focus only on the single program goal for which they are responsible reinforces a territorial, competitive attitude that misses opportunities to maximize individual donor value. Meetings and written reports should showcase how the entire staff team has collaborated to progress closer to the department-wide goal.

2. **Reward Achievements in Donor Movement**

   Success in direct marketing programs needs to be defined more broadly than simply raising more money. In fact, because the priority is the movement of donors up to major gifts, direct marketing revenue must be allowed to fall from time to time without negative repercussions on staff. By consistently reinforcing this new priority in reporting meetings, managers will help fundraisers adopt a broader definition of their own achievement:

   > *"Max and his team have brought direct mail to a new level of success. Not only is donor retention up among direct-mail donors who have been giving for two years or longer, but last month Max and Jennifer identified 35 top performing direct-mail donors eligible for transfer to the major gifts prospect pool."*

3. **Give the Direct Mail Manager Authority in Defining Readiness for Major Gift Cultivation**

   When considering which direct-mail donors might be ready for major gift cultivation, the obvious profile is donors who have been giving the longest

My Director of Development can be over-confident at times. She sets expectations too high and, when her department falls short, she tends not to own the choices she made. We're working on this.

and are the most generous contributors. But other characteristics can also signal readiness. They include donors who make very modest gifts whenever they contribute but who respond to multiple appeals in a year. Donors who include personal notes along with their mailed contributions are also sometimes signaling greater interest. The direct marketing manager is best positioned to recognize the signs exhibited by donors wanting closer relationships. If given the time and resources to test responsiveness within various donor profiles, she is more likely to become a proactive partner in donor movement instead of feeling that she needs to prevent her donors from being co-opted.

4. **Reward Early Movement, not Just Movement**

Gifts officers often require six to eighteen months to close the first major gift with a prospect. Only minutes of that time is spent actually asking for the money, but months go into bringing the donor up to speed on the charity's goals, finding out what interests the donor, shaping and reshaping a proposal and preparing to make the ask. Because major gifts revenue is directly related to time spent cultivating relationships, the interesting question is, "Could the cultivation time required before asking for a gift be shortened?" What if it took only three to nine months instead of six to eighteen to close? Could gifts officers raise twice the money in the same period of time? Having more active major donors means investing more time in their post-gift stewardship, but no Development Director with even a basic understanding of investment/return would begrudge that.

Direct marketing managers hold the key that unlocks donors' eagerness to give more generously sooner. By applying donor-centered strategies in gift acknowledgement, communication and donor recognition early, direct marketers will create better informed donors from the start, reducing gifts officers' cultivation time prior to making the ask.

5. **Remember Who Made Success Possible**

Relationship databases make it possible for fundraisers to see a multi-year history on a single donor. The value of this picture, however, is in understanding not only how far a donor has come but how she became one in the first place. When reporting on closing a major gift, make sure that the team who introduced the donor to your not-for-profit is credited for all that they did to instill early commitment and grow initial interest. In a donor-centered fundraising operation, every donor – regardless of who is primarily responsible for building the relationship now – continues to belong to everyone in the department.

6. **Be Prepared to Give Donors Back**

We're conditioned in fundraising to think that every goal must be bigger than the last and that donors should only move up the giving ladder. But there are times when it makes more sense to move a donor down a rung. This is especially so when a major gifts prospect is not responding well to cultivation or when the gifts officer is simply overloaded with more donors than he can handle. (See "How Many Prospects Can a Gifts Officer Manage?" later in this chapter.) In circumstances like these, the worst thing that can happen is that no one solicits the donor. This misses revenue but, more important, breaks the communications cycle, leaving the donor at risk of drifting away entirely.

7. **Adopt Smarter Job Titles**

Fundraisers' titles are generally tied to process when they should relate to objectives. Titling staff after specific fundraising programs perpetuates territorial instead of progressive thinking and behavior. And, when a fundraising program's popularity wanes due to technological advances or simply changing donor preference, it leaves fundraisers who are titled after that program feeling less valuable. Professional fundraisers should have titles that put the donor front and center while better defining the purpose of their work. Manager of New Donor Relationships is far superior to Manager of Direct Mail Acquisition, and Manager of Donor Transition is better than....well... there is no equivalent that I know of, which only illustrates the problem.

Are You in Sync with Your Supplier?

Vendors who specialize in designing and executing volume-based appeals are a major force in the fundraising industry. Not-for-profits that use these profit-making companies must take them into account if they hope to be successful at orchestrating change.

Review your contract and make sure that future agreements reward vendors for what makes more money for you as well as them. When contracts are structured to compensate based on volume, vendors are understandably motivated to solicit as many donors as possible as often as possible. But this leads to over-solicitation, now the number one reason why donors stop giving. In volume-based compensation agreements, the loss of donors hurts both you and your vendor, but it hurts you more. When donors stop giving, you lose everything that they could have done for you in the long term, not just the immediate next direct marketing gift.

My CEO felt threatened and started to treat me differently when he saw donors begin to call me instead of him.

I accepted a major gifts position with no experience going in. No one has mentored me and I feel like I'm treading water. I also don't feel I'm marketable anywhere else because I'm struggling here.

Since meaningful communication offered to donors early improves both their retention and gift values, the right vendor could help you improve information flow to donors. Communication is a field that is evolving as fast as technology is changing. It requires specialized skills and considerable experience to capture the attention of donors when so many other priorities are distracting them. Vendors could become an essential resource to their clients by growing their expertise in donor communication. Their skills would be especially valuable to clients who cannot resource communication in-house at a level that would produce measurable results for fundraising.

Be careful what you outsource, however. Certain donor-centered strategies are best handled internally. This is especially true for personalized gift acknowledgement, such as calling donors to thank them for gifts just received. I was disheartened to learn recently that some not-for-profits are paying vendors to say thank you to their donors. Donors would be horrified if they knew. I also have to wonder about professional fundraisers who are that disconnected from their own donors that they think doing this is OK. Good grief. Besides displaying appallingly bad manners, these practitioners have no idea what they are missing. They are off-loading the priceless opportunity of getting to know their donors, of opening up conversations that could lead to more generous gifts, and of simply reminding themselves what philanthropy – and fundraising – are all about.

Success in Major Gifts Fundraising

Nowhere does staff retention have a greater impact on the bottom line than in major gifts.[2] The revenue that a single gifts officer can raise relative to cost is substantial and the influence that these crucial fundraisers have on donors cannot be overstated. Staff who build high-value relationships have specialized skills; they are hard to find and they require a unique kind of support. But, unlike managing direct marketers where the main challenge is helping them adapt to a different fundraising culture, the central issue in managing major gifts officers is time.

In Chapter 3, I noted that major gifts staff in our study stayed 3.8 years, on average, in their most recent jobs. It takes time to steward a prospective major gift donor from initial interest to gift commitment and more time to secure subsequent major gifts. Since time per gifts officer is finite, managers' central preoccupation should be ensuring its best use. This means examining gifts officers' traditional approaches to major gifts fundraising for their return relative to time invested. Most important,

---

[2] In this section, references to major gifts and major gifts officers assume the wider fundraising arena and profession encompassing both major and planned gifts and/or officers.

though, it means looking inward. Meetings, reporting and simply getting to the office consume time, so your question to yourself as a manager should be: "Do the requirements I place on my staff further or impede fundraising growth?"

How Many Prospects Can a Gifts Officer Manage?

There are so many components to a gifts officer's job but size of portfolio is one of the things I am asked about most often. In practice, portfolio size varies drastically, with gifts officers reporting anywhere from thirty to one hundred fifty active prospects and donors, though larger contingents are much more common. A good deal of uncertainty and anxiety surrounds this issue, as the size of one's donor/prospect file is a common measure in performance evaluations. The appropriate number, however, is "It depends."

Every donor is an individual who responds differently to fundraisers' stewardship efforts. It can take a talented gifts officer two days of work, spread over a period of time, to land a seven-figure gift from one donor; it can take the same gifts officer two months of tough slogging over several years to negotiate a similar gift value from another. Does the term, "high maintenance donor" ring a bell?

Process or Outcome?

Once assigned a volume of donors to steward, the gifts officer is expected to orchestrate the forward movement of every prospect under his care. But this is a process goal when a goal that focuses on outcomes would be much more appropriate and would raise more money. At the time prospects are assigned, both gifts officer and manager hope that all donors on the list will be productive, but no one really knows. Even prospect lists developed with the assistance of wealth screening cannot guarantee superior results. This is because no amount of cross-referencing the behavior and philanthropic performance of a donor can answer the critical question, "Regardless of what he might have previously done elsewhere, will this donor give generously to you?"

On that point, the best wealth-screening device fundraisers can ever access already belongs to them. And since they pay for it handsomely, they should use it more often and more creatively for its real value. That device is direct marketing. Its acquisition strategies find the donors who are interested in their cause; its renewal programs separate the tentative from the serious. Most gifts officers do not need to look beyond this unique and proprietary resource for a volume of major donor prospects that would keep them occupied indefinitely. This has been confirmed in several Cygnus studies, most recently in 2011 where 58% of donors who were

When I helped a donor establish an in-memoriam scholarship fund I felt that I was genuinely contributing to helping the family heal from their loss. It was both satisfying and humbling.

I know I made the right decision by continuing to send my gifts officers out to meet with donors during the recession – not to ask in all cases, but to keep in touch and show them we care. My job has been to keep tight control on the budget in the meantime as we all look forward to an improved fundraising climate.

making major gifts valued at $10,000 or more to one or more charities were simultaneously making modest contributions through direct mail to others. Donor-centered acknowledgement and communication is the screening device that all not-for-profits have at their disposal. Donors who respond to a donor-centered approach with loyal and more generous giving are signaling their interest in closer relationships.

It matters far less how many prospects a gifts officer has than how much money she raises. In fact, the prospect list can, in itself, contribute to fundraising under-performance. If a gifts officer has a list of, say, one hundred fifty donors for whom she is responsible, she will be expected to account for what she has done to move everyone on that list forward. Meaningful stewardship will work its magic on some donors better than on others, but the gifts officer will still put in time with the full list, whether productive or not. When responsible for a large pool of major gift donors and prospects, the gifts officer cannot be faulted if all available time is expended simply handling the volume. This approach leaves too little time for the more delicate, sophisticated and time-consuming work required to move best prospects towards the ask. At this level of fundraising, volume should definitely not be trumping profit.

Even a more realistic approach to handling a large pool of donors has a troubling downside. If the gifts officer has free rein to focus his time and talent on only the prospects who are more responsive to his stewardship efforts, then the rest of his list goes under-developed. These donors, who were put on the major gifts prospect list in the first place because of assumed potential, are now quarantined for all intents and purposes. Neither another gifts officer nor the annual fund can touch them because that might jeopardize the big gift – even though the officer responsible for the file does not have the time to develop the relationship himself.

Size of the prospect list and compatibility is yet another issue. All donors and gifts officers have unique personalities and the fit between them is that delicious intangible. When donor and gifts officer click, money gets raised; when they don't, progress stalls. When responsible for a large prospect pool, it may be some time before the officer comes to the conclusion that it might be the poor fit that is inhibiting the relationship.

In all these examples, the problem is not with the quality of the work that the gifts officer is doing day-to-day but with the size of the list itself. A prospect list that is too large to cover or which, in attempting to cover it, leaves too little time to close gifts with priority donors, adds another level of stress to an already challenging job.

This negatively affects the staff member's performance overall and contributes to her premature resignation.

Fundraising by Absolutes

In determining the ideal number of prospects, it is sensible to start with the things over which staff have no control, then develop a strategy within the parameters they dictate. Number one is time. No matter the volume of prospects, there are still only twenty-four hours on the clock and far fewer in which major gifts officers can produce good work. If four hours a day of productive work directly related to securing major gifts is reasonable (see Chapter 12, Time and Productivity), and if there are two hundred forty work days in a year, then most of the information needed to answer the question about the optimum size of a prospect pool already exists. Additionally, time and attention required per donor increase the closer the relationship progresses towards the ask. It takes longer to prepare a draft proposal to present in a critical meeting than it does to gather background information on a new prospect.

What are the steps required to progress from identifying a prospect to getting a "yes"? How much time does it take to get through each step? How much time is required after "yes" to steward this relationship to the next ask? This is a Gifts Officer's maximum requirement of time per donor, knowing that some prospects will progress quickly through some steps or skip steps altogether. The other question that needs to be answered is one that fundraisers find very tough to face: "At what point should I let a prospect go?" Fundraisers never like to give up on a donor and they are certainly reluctant to do so after investing time and effort in major gifts stewardship. Gifts officers' colleagues and managers are an invaluable resource when facing tough decisions on whether to keep fishing or cut bait. There is always hope, of course, but highly valuable gifts officers must be selective about where they put their time because their number one responsibility remains reaching their goal.

The Right Number of Prospects

For a new major gifts officer, the ideal number of prospects starts with one, leaving all others in the full donor pool, available to other staff and for other appeals. Once that prospect has been moved to her first natural resting stop (a point at which more attention would be premature or counter-productive), then another name can be pulled from the database. At some point, the Gifts Officer will know that adding any more names to the active file would jeopardize time needed for meaningful work with existing prospects, work designed to yield major gifts at the

It's not just about donor relationships; the relationship you establish with your staff is just as important. Develop your team, invest in them, respect them, push them to excel. Create an environment that rewards success and they will respond with their best work, and with loyalty.

Trust your intuition and don't be afraid to reach for the stars. Anything is possible.

earliest opportunity. The gifts officer will have to justify this to her boss in very tangible terms based on measurable progress per prospect, proximity to making the ask and anticipated ask value.

For gifts officers who already have donor lists that are too long, some will be eager to put prospects back into the pool; others may resist. Even though they have not received the time and attention required to effect measurable progress, these donors still represent revenue in theory, so it is difficult for fundraisers to let them go. When this situation exists, it is the responsibility of the Manager to make sure that work being done to simply satisfy a contact requirement is not jeopardizing time required for other work that is legitimately closing the sale.

In the end, the number of prospects that is reasonable will vary from one gifts officer to another, based on the investment/return assessment of each prospective donor. There is nothing wrong with that. I would be thrilled to have a gifts officer with only five active prospects if each were on track for a gift of $1 million or more. Expenses all in, that would represent a cost per dollar raised of about 4%. How could anyone argue with that kind of return?

Managing Yourself in a One-Person Development Shop

When you are the only fundraiser responsible for the entire Development operation, you run a small business. You are the boss, the planner, the marketing and branding specialist, the donor acquisition associate, the fundraising events coordinator, the major gifts officer, the data manager, the meetings secretary, the sounding board for the CEO and the cheerleader/cajoler of the leadership volunteer team. Your job description is impossible; yet somehow you keep breathing – and smiling. Whether you possess an unusually high level of tolerance for stress or are simply crazy, it appears that you are attracted to work environments in which you do absolutely everything. Among all the professional fundraisers we surveyed, sole practitioners appeared to enjoy the highest level of job satisfaction.

Michael Gerber understands this type of business personality. He wrote the bestselling business book, The E-Myth[3] (E stands for entrepreneur, not email) and he has clear-headed advice for small business owners who are attempting to get a foothold in a highly competitive world. Many of his insights about how entrepreneurs can corral their raw energy and determination more strategically are applicable to small fundraising shops, especially those with only one professional

---

[3] *The E-Myth Revisited: Why Most Small Businesses Don't Work and What to Do About It*, Michael E. Gerber, HarperCollins Publishers, Inc., 1995.

employee. Gerber suggests that sole practitioners are actually three people in one: the entrepreneur with the ideas, the manager who puts strategy and order to those ideas and the technician who carries out the work. All three are required to run a business (and a Development office) successfully. But when only one person plays all three roles, the sole practitioner must be able to move seamlessly from one to the next. The key to survival is recognizing when you should be firing up your imagination (entrepreneur), when you should be putting your head down and getting the work done (technician), and when it's time to oversee and assess your own work (manager). While you do have a CEO, she is multi-tasking as much as you are. As the only paid fundraiser on staff, you are reporting to yourself most of the time.

The sheer scope of the job means that no one is challenged more on the issue of time and productivity than a one-person-shop fundraiser. Sole practitioners are always pulled by the immediate reality of the direct-mail appeal that must launch next week or the golf tournament that happens on Saturday, because no one else is there to make sure these things will get done right and on time. Sole practitioners draw much of their job satisfaction from the kind of direct-action fundraising that defines small shops. But depending on short-term revenue is like suffering from an addiction. You chase whatever will keep your not-for-profit afloat for just a little while longer. The difference between one-person-shop fundraisers who get by and those who excel is how they balance the technician in themselves with the manager, while still leaving room for the entrepreneur.

In Chapter 6, I argued against a mindset defined by the declaration, "We can't hire any more staff." Revenue and, especially, fundraising profit are a product of time invested. But many one-person-shop fundraisers live by their own version of that mantra – "I prefer to work alone." If you feel this way, you are cheating your not-for-profit out of revenue it should be earning and you are not facing the fact that you cannot sustain the required pace indefinitely. 60% of respondents who were planning to leave their one-person fundraising shops said that the breadth of their responsibilities made it impossible to achieve fundraising goals. It may be time to find the strategic manager within you who can drive fundraising forward. The same applies to sole practitioners who are pleading for more staff. It may be time to get up off your knees and put a cost/benefit argument in front of your decision-makers.

Think about what you could accomplish with twenty hours of uninterrupted time, then claim it. Take the first hour of each work day for a month and devote it to managing the forward movement of your Development department. Let nothing pre-empt or invade that hour and stop when the hour is up. Do not worry if, initially, you feel you are wasting this time. If you have difficulty concentrating – if the technician in you

I learned to focus on doing a few things really well…and saying "no" to everything else. The quality of my work has improved exponentially as a result.

keeps barging into your consciousness to drag you back to your to-do list – do not become frustrated. Keep bringing yourself back to the strategic question with which you are contending. You will soon find yourself producing good work and, then, looking forward to that hour. In a month you will be well on your way to having an irrefutable case for staff expansion. These practical activities will help you get there:

- Conduct a time study on yourself for a period of two weeks to a month. How much time do you spend doing work that could be done by a more junior fundraiser or by someone with no fundraising credentials at all? I have found this information to be very compelling for CEOs and Boards. They instantly understand how diverting a professional fundraiser's time to administrative and support tasks wastes specialized talent as well as time.

- Analyze fundraising events ruthlessly for the staff time devoted to their planning and execution. Make sure you include the amount of time you devote to supporting the Committee responsible for the event. Develop a job description for staffing each event with as much or more time than you give it now so that certain aspects can become more profitable. Express the cost of a contract event planner or temporary staff person as an investment in the event's enhanced ability to generate revenue.

- Think about one of your most generous donors. Chart a history of that donor's value to your not-for-profit, from the time she made her first contribution to her most recent gift. How long did it take for her to evolve to her current level of generosity? Who and what were instrumental in stewarding this donor's contributions? Talk to the donor about the people and the funding opportunities that influenced her to keep giving. Estimate the time invested in this donor relative to the total value of her lifetime contributions. How much of that time has been expended in just the last year? When you see these questions translated into time and revenue, it will be easy to forecast major gifts revenue from real-life experience; and the cost/benefit outcome will be exhilarating.

As you build a new revenue forecast and calculate the investment in staff and other expenses that will be needed to secure more profit, build in time and money for training, especially your own. Moving from sole practitioner where you did it all to managing someone else is a transition into a whole new way of working. For your own sake and that of the person or people you will be supervising, learn and then practice the art of managing other people. And, if you discover that this is not the kind of role you want to play, that is absolutely fine. Just make sure you don't play it anyway. The remainder of this book should help you make that decision.

Managing Young Fundraisers

At the age of 21 I was hired by a prominent regional theatre company as "chief assistant to the assistant chief of public relations". Only the gofer[4] was lower on the seniority ladder. Early on I showed a talent for drafting marketing copy and was gradually given more and more assignments crafting brochures, drafting press releases, and the like. While never officially told that this was my job, over time I and most others on staff came to understand that I was the go-to person whenever new promotional copy or editing was required.

Somehow, though, that understanding failed to permeate top management. As the deadline approached for launching the next season and its flagship full-color, multi-page season ticket brochure, I found myself out of the loop. The General Manager and Artistic Director along with an outside consultant spent many hours hunched over copy re-writes and design drafts while I sulked in my cubicle.

The brochure eventually went to print and, a few weeks later, 30,000 copies arrived at the office. I pulled one from the tower of boxes and headed back to my office to read the end product. I took five steps and stopped dead in my tracks. In glorious gold 24-point type, the front cover read:

THEATRE ABC'S 1972/73 SEASON – BOLD AND BRILLANT

There is nothing that a writer or editor fears more than a mistake discovered too late. It elicits a nauseating feeling of embarrassment combined with panic. I was feeling it now as my heart rate went into overdrive. And then I remembered that I didn't write this thing and scurried to my office to read the rest of it.

There were seven spelling and grammatical errors and I highlighted each by circling it with a very red pen. With a feeling of muted triumph, I marched my young-and-stupid self into the General Manager's office. "Your brochure just arrived", I said, as I dropped it casually on his desk. "You might not want to rush it into the mail."

The consultant and the Artistic Director were quickly summoned to a long meeting behind closed doors. I went back to my press release, feeling vindicated.

The next morning, I was called into the General Manager's office…and fired.

There are vast differences between the world of work into which today's young fundraisers are emerging and the world that launched the careers of their managers and directors. Yet employers have a hard time relating to their young employees

---

[4] An affectionate term used in the arts for a "jack-of-all-trades" member of the crew whose job it is to do whatever is required.

How managers define advantageous characteristics of young fundraisers:

20% At ease with modern technology
12% Positive outlook / enthusiasm
9% Understand new media strategies
8% Driven
7% Welcoming to other cultures

outside the context of their own experience. That is nothing new, of course, since each generation cannot comprehend the next. But are young workers really dangerously deficient in skills essential to fundraising success or are managers failing to utilize young talent in ways that could raise more money?

Senior directors and managers were asked to identify particularly promising attributes or characteristics of employees under thirty years of age that are having or could have a beneficial impact on the fundraising industry. By far the most common observation concerned young workers' ease in using technology (20%).[5] 10% singled out their understanding of social media and how quickly young fundraisers adjust to rapidly changing trends. 13% cited young fundraisers' enthusiasm, their positive outlook and sheer energy as decided assets. 8% noted their inclusive world view.

Social Media Experts

Given the speed at which today's hot innovation becomes yesterday's old news, I don't blame managers for hesitating to invest in new technologies and social media. But if decision-makers are waiting for the communications industry to settle down first, that is not going to happen. The pace at which technology is changing is the story and there are compelling reasons for Development operations to resource their social media presence immediately and fully.

Donor acquisition is weakening in traditional fundraising but could renew itself through social media. Donors are no longer passively accepting the argument for giving that charities make in direct mail appeals, telephone scripts and emails. Instead, they are counting on their own common sense and their ability to do basic research to make independent choices about the organizations that they will support. Charities' websites are by far the most popular source of information but content is still wholly dictated by not-for-profits hosting the sites. But, social media is where the conversation happens. Here, donors can interact with charity representatives and with other followers of the cause while not-for-profits gain invaluable first-hand views from their supporters.

Social media is on its way to becoming an important donor acquisition tool, especially as it pertains to young donors. About 16% of followers of charities' social media accounts are what is known in the industry as "mass influencers". According

---

[5] This was an open-ended question in which no-answer options were provided. In open-ended questions, it is considered very noteworthy if 15% or more of respondents answer in the same way.

to a study by Forrester Research,[6] mass influencers are responsible for 80% of the brand impressions in online social settings. They stand out both in terms of the number of followers, friends and connections they have and the frequency of their contacts. Our own research has found that mass influencers are more willing to actively fundraise through their networks and to volunteer. They are an opportunity waiting to be developed but not-for-profits must harness their energy and support their efforts.

Online fundraising and other modern technologies will overtake traditional mass marketing techniques in the not-too-distant future, so charities need to be ready now for inevitable change. Only 27% of donors under the age of 35 made any charitable contributions via direct mail in 2010, compared with 65% of donors over 65 years of age.[7] As they age and become able to give more generously, young donors are not going to revert to the gift transaction methods popular with their parents and grandparents; they are going to stay with the technologies that are part of their everyday lives. If charities are to have any hope of sustaining donor volume now and building revenue in the future, they must resource social media and other technologies as they emerge.

Social media is also a hiring advantage. In Chapter 6, I encouraged not-for-profits to develop a Career Landing Page on their websites to attract good candidates. Promoting your organization as a great place to work via social media spreads the word farther while enhancing the qualitative experience. Through social media, candidates can speak directly with current staff and get first-hand testimonials about what it is like to work in your shop.

All this is to say that big opportunities will be won or lost through a not-for-profit's adoption of or resistance to social media. The people who understand it and use it as their everyday means of communication are the ones who should be designing your program and building its capacity. They are your young fundraisers and they have much to offer in this environment.

The Profit Potential of Diversity

It is easy to see how young workers are a unique asset in keeping not-for-profits abreast of new media; but their potential for furthering diversity in fundraising may not be appreciated to the same extent. The fundraising industry's youngest

In my department, the younger fundraisers do a lot of talking, going off to conferences and generally being in "learning mode" while the rest of us do the work. There's some resentment around here.

---

[6] *Tapping the Entire Online Peer Influence Pyramid*, Augie Ray with Josh Bernoff et al., Forrester Research, February 2010, www.forrester.com

[7] *The Cygnus Donor Survey: Where Philanthropy is Headed in 2011*, Penelope Burk, Cygnus Applied Research, Inc., Chicago, IL, April 2011

practitioners were born into a global communications network, educated in classrooms that mirror the world's ethnic complexity, and shaped by friendships and relationships that were more likely than ever before to reach across cultural barriers. In many ways, this generation has evolved beyond fighting for equality and acceptance into simply living an ethnically diverse existence. As they move from front-line to management positions they will (hopefully) be more likely to hire people for their talent, skill and experience than for the color of their skin or their native language.

This is a boon to a fundraising industry that is predominantly of white, European descent today while the population of the United States and Canada is rapidly diversifying. Philanthropic desire may be a universal concept, but that doesn't mean that all cultures respond to a common approach to fundraising. Our industry is definitely recognizing the need for greater diversity within its professional ranks but young fundraisers may be able to speed up the transition.

Employers can use their young workers now to help them achieve their diversity goals. Consider these examples:

- include young employees on hiring Committees, even if they are in non-management roles;

- encourage young staff to promote fundraising as a career and their not-for-profit as a destination to their personal and social media networks;

- use young workers to attract young donors to the Board and to volunteer Committees;

- assign "diversity projects" to young workers aimed at building donor support within different ethnic cultures. Budget this effort realistically to improve the potential for success.

Young workers' inclusive attitude and the ease with which they assemble and work within diverse teams make them invaluable in helping reshape fundraising to better reflect tomorrow's giving population. And, employers need to help them help the industry now. The 2011 US Census noted that more than half of babies born in 2010 were minorities.

When I was your age, I walked six miles to school every day…in four feet of snow…in my bare feet…uphill…both ways.

Our research findings on young workers were not entirely one-sided. Management-level respondents voiced their opinions concerning trends among employees under thirty that they thought were detrimental to fundraising success. 22% identified short job stays, but how respondents articulated the issue was as telling as the statistic. Most used charged language such as "constantly changing jobs", "no sense of loyalty", or "focused only on what is good for them with no consideration for the organization or the team". 10% acknowledged that young workers today are generally well educated in the formal sense but lack real-world knowledge and 10% said that their young recruits expect instant results. Some noted that they lack the requisite patience for building relationships with donors and, in their haste, sometimes use tactics that are overly aggressive.

Sometimes, direct supervisors were harsher in their criticisms than Directors of Development who may not have day-to-day contact with young workers. For instance, 14% of managers of specific fundraising programs felt that young workers displayed an attitude of entitlement whereas only 7% of Development Directors made this observation.

14% of seasoned managers said that young fundraisers expect to be promoted very quickly. I was intrigued by the strength of this criticism as it revealed a lack of awareness among managers concerning population statistics and generational shift. The exceptionally large baby boom cohort has controlled jobs at the top for two decades. Behind it, a statistically smaller generation has not had the opportunity to climb the seniority ladder at the same pace. But 49% of today's senior-level fundraisers will retire or leave the fundraising business for another field within the next few years. Add to that the extraordinary pressure on workers in an industry suffering from a shortage of trained practitioners and it seems that Gen X and Gen Y fundraisers will soon be getting what they wished for. It is in everyone's best interests to welcome, not squelch, young workers' eagerness to accelerate their careers because rapid promotion will be a necessity. As a matter of fact, the job shift is well underway. Managers in our study lamented the ease with which young fundraisers are able to land mid-level and even director-level positions in other not-for-profits after barely a year or two of experience. Their frustration stems from the impact that these rapid moves are having on their own bottom line, but a better understanding of the big picture might cause managers to adopt a different attitude.

Climbing the seniority ladder too soon can be detrimental to upwardly mobile fundraisers. Management is entirely different from front-line fundraising and charities don't always make wise decisions when hiring. They are as desperate to fill Development jobs as young fundraisers are eager to win them and the urgent need to get someone into the position can cloud an employer's judgment. Once the new fundraiser is hired, however, the onus is entirely on her to deliver, whether or not she actually has the requisite skills. And this is where things often go wrong.

Characteristics of young fundraisers that could adversely impact the industry:

22% Lack of job loyalty
11% Expect early promotion
10% Expect results too soon
9% Poor work ethic
8% Attitude of entitlement
8% Lack of dedication

Lacking the career experience necessary to handle challenging situations and the life experience to influence the Board and CEO, under-qualified fundraisers stumble and are soon fired. Many leave the industry at this point, when a different approach might have guaranteed a better result.

It is simply not relevant for today's employers to use the benchmarks and timetable of their own career progression when supervising young fundraisers. Expecting them to stay longer without showing them the benefits of doing so is unrealistic, especially when they are being actively recruited for more senior jobs. Rather, employers should address the issue openly and directly – staff will be tempted into positions beyond their ability, so they must become better prepared now, while in a genuinely supportive environment. Employers who guide and promote their young staff win in two ways: they reap the financial benefits of promoting staff internally and they create a hedge against losing them prematurely. Now when their fundraisers are approached by other not-for-profits, they will be weighing the risk of leaving against the known benefits of staying. The choice is still theirs in the end, of course, but employers can rest easy in the knowledge that they have done everything they can to hold onto their blossoming young staff.

Young Fundraisers and Job Tenure

With job stays frustratingly short among young fundraisers, I was interested in learning more about why they switch jobs frequently. 41% left their last job for a position with greater responsibility – generally one in which they were visibly moving up the seniority ladder. 38% left to work for a not-for-profit with more opportunities for career advancement. This latter choice generally meant opting for an organization that deployed a more sophisticated array of fundraising techniques and/or had a larger staff contingent.

It is interesting to note, however, that fundraisers under thirty years of age were less likely to leave a job for higher pay elsewhere (38%) than were their older counterparts (48%). This offers an important advantage to employers struggling to keep up with salary expectations within the industry.

The Case for Accelerating Young Fundraisers' Careers

Young people enter the workforce today having earned one or two university degrees, being technologically advanced and completely at ease in a world that moves incredibly fast. They master the limited requirements of their entry-level positions quickly and soon approach their bosses for more variety in their work and greater responsibility. But, their enthusiasm is sometimes dampened by managers who, ironically, have too much to do themselves and too little time in which to do it. As a result, the benefits of retaining eager, motivated and now experienced young staff members are sacrificed because of the time it takes to orient, train and supervise them in their new jobs and hire their replacements.

Managers are right, however, to wonder whether their young fundraisers are as ready for the future as they think they are. No, they don't know anywhere near what their bosses know; and, yes, it's so easy for young workers to be confident about their abilities when they have never been tested in a crisis. Still, managers cannot criticize young workers for having been brought up in an overly protective environment, and then keep them in a similarly protected state on the job. The fundraising industry needs to train its young practitioners well, then throw them into the fray so that they can fall down early, pick themselves back up, and become the next generation of Development leaders as soon as possible.

Tenure-Extending Performance Evaluations

94% of professional fundraisers we surveyed work in jobs where their performance is evaluated (85% of one-shop fundraisers). Most evaluations happen annually, but 10% of respondents have semi-annual performance reviews. The majority of respondents are somewhat satisfied with the way in which their performance is assessed, scoring the process at 5.0 on a 7-point scale. For respondents who were less satisfied, their chief complaint was that there is no tangible reward for high evaluation scores. For instance, raises are based on cost-of-living increases or granted to all staff across the board regardless of variation in performance.

According to management-level respondents, these attributes make a performance evaluation tool effective:

77%	it includes a self-evaluation component for the employee;
71%	it acts as a planning tool for the next year, guiding work objectives and identifying training needs;
56%	it is balanced – showcasing achievements as well as identifying areas requiring improvement;
56%	it is specific about the criteria on which staff performance is assessed;
51%	it is concise, allowing performance evaluations to be completed within a reasonable period of time. (Where managers had criticisms about their own performance management tool, they most often cited the sheer volume of criteria to be assessed that caused the evaluation to drag on.)

Performance evaluations? Ha! My boss gives us instant feedback whenever she's unhappy with something we've done.

What Should Performance Reviews Be Assessing?

One of the most important findings from the nine research studies that contributed to this project was revealed while investigating criteria for performance evaluation of professional fundraisers. It appears that, from the CEO to the Development Director to managers of specific fundraising programs, those responsible for ensuring fundraising success are focusing on the wrong measures when assessing staff performance. Table 25 illustrates.

Table 25: Performance Evaluation Measures Favored by CEOs, Directors and Managers

Criteria	CEOs Assessing Directors of Development	Directors of Development Assessing Fundraising Managers	Fundraising Managers Assessing Non-Management Staff
Increase in # of active donors.	58%	62%	51%
Gross revenue raised.	57%	60%	52%
Improvement in donor retention.	53%	47%	57%
Net revenue raised.	45%	26%	21%
Reduction in cost per dollar raised.	40%	25%	18%
Improvement in average gift value among retained donors.	37%	37%	19%

The information in Table 25 is troubling. I might have expected CEOs without fundraising experience to be unclear about how profit is made; but even Directors of Development are depending on the wrong measures as a gauge of staff performance.

Gross revenue is not a reliable indicator of success or even of fundraising progress. Development operations disproportionately weighted in mass marketing programs and fundraising events can experience a rise in gross revenue while net return stays the same or, worse, falls. Not-for-profits can only spend the net revenue that is raised, so focusing on gross revenue and evaluating performance on that basis is unreliable at best and, in some cases, is misleading.

Most not-for-profits represented in the research studies we conducted have in their databases thousands or hundreds of thousands of donors who have already chosen them for support. These organizations do not actually need more new donors; their focus should be on improving the average gift value of the donors they already have because that will make their operations more profitable. Increasing the number of active donors should only be a priority for a relatively small minority of not-for-profits who are at one of these two stages:

- they are new players in fundraising and still building an initial base of support;

- they are already performing above the norm in donor retention and improvement in average gift value and have the resources to grow the number of active donors.

Reduction in cost per dollar raised is an interesting issue on several fronts. Cygnus has tracked donors' opinions on fundraising cost for fifteen years. While this issue preoccupies not-for-profits, especially their Boards and CEOs, it has not been a demonstrative factor for donors in driving their giving choices – that is until the recent recession. Cost per dollar raised then moved from insignificant to the second most influential factor in their decision-making. In early 2009, one out of three donors cited concern over fundraising cost as an issue with which they now contend and which they did not consider five years previously.

There are three ways in which decision-makers think the cost of fundraising can be lowered, but only one of them works.

1. **Cutting the Development Department's budget arbitrarily to reduce the cost of raising money.** This serves only to limit resources required to make fundraising more profitable. What do not tend to get cut back are expenses related to soliciting donors – i.e., costs underwriting strategies that raise immediate, short-term revenue. Most often compromised are resources necessary for donor retention and raising future gift values such as post-gift communication. These investment funds are necessary for growing the margin between gross and net revenue, in other words, increasing profit. Cutting budget funds alone is not the answer.

2. **Laying off staff or instituting a hiring freeze.** As staffing costs comprise the largest portion of the budget, it appears on the surface to be a responsible move to cut where costs are highest. But, as fundraising success is related to time and talent invested, and the most profitable activities in fundraising require that investment first in order to realize a later return, under-resourcing staff time relative to potential is akin to refusing to make more money.

3. **Reducing fundraising cost by correcting the imbalance between quantitative (mass marketing, some events) and qualitative (major/planned gifts) fundraising.** This is a strategic and effective way to lower overall cost per dollar raised. Being more successful in major and planned gifts fundraising requires holding onto donors long enough to interest them in more generous giving. This, in turn, requires investment in donor-centered strategies in order to turn early interest into committed loyalty. As performance improves at the top, a more controlled approach to marketing-based

My not-for-profit lacks a big picture philosophy for fundraising. Over its long, 105-year history, it has focused on fundraising tactics that produce short-term revenue only. They also put a lot of energy into sticking donors in giving clubs with contrived benefits for every giving level. Surely, there's a better way.

fundraising at the bottom becomes possible. Reduction in cost per dollar raised is a by-product of this approach. Change does not happen overnight; but in time the cost of fundraising comes down when the Development portfolio is more balanced. At some point, a more attractive revenue/cost ratio becomes a marketable advantage to donors.

Gratifying Performance Reviews

If you have developed a Donor-Centered Fundraising Plan (Chapter 5), then you already have the guiding principles and measures of success that form the basis of meaningful performance reviews. In addition, if you have hired staff using the methods advocated in Chapters 6, 7 and 8, and if you have adjusted orientation and probation on the model described in Chapter 10, performance evaluations will be experiences that both you and your staff will enjoy. That is because they will not be forums for correction or discipline but creative one-on-one conversations that spur staff onto greater heights while reminding you of the amazing team that you are privileged to lead.

I get a knot in my stomach when studying the bulk of expert advice on performance evaluations because it is geared to overcoming mistakes: mistakes in hiring the wrong person to begin with; mistakes in poor or insufficient training of new staff; mistakes in not dealing with problems right away; and mistakes of omission – particularly leaving staff in the dark about performance expectations. If you find yourself laboring over a negative performance review and wondering how you are going to handle the meeting, ask yourself whether the problems you are now facing could have been addressed and eliminated before now or avoided altogether. The answer will be "yes" in almost every case, and you will be a factor in what went wrong.

There is no end to the advice on performance evaluations available online, from your HR Department if you have one, and from professionals who specialize in performance matters. Here are my ten best rules for productive performance assessments, honed through trial and error and motivated by the desire to turn staff evaluations into useful undertakings that contribute to retention and higher productivity.

1. **No negative surprises.** Nothing regarding negative performance should be brought up for the first time in a performance evaluation by the evaluator. A negative surprise during an annual review speaks to a weakness in supervision because a better opportunity to deal with the problem was missed at the time the issue arose. If, however, the matter was dealt with immediately and successfully, it no longer needs addressing in a formal performance

review, except in the positive context of how the employee has overcome the problem.

If you ask your employee to look back on the previous year and reflect on what he did exceptionally well and where he could have performed better, that is constructive; if you look back on your employee's last year and point out where he excelled and under-performed, that is far less productive. Both praise and criticism should be offered at the time they are deserved in order to be meaningful.

2. **Evaluation criteria must be measurable.** Being a product of numbers of donors, giving frequency and gift values, most criteria for evaluating a fund-raiser's performance are highly measurable. But analysis is required in order to establish goals and benchmarks that are both measurable and reliable as standards of performance.

Be careful about using benchmarks from other organizations, even ones with similar mandates, or about setting common goals across all staff without regard to the donors for whom they are responsible. When setting performance criteria for major gifts officers, there are so many variables – differences in the makeup of prospect lists, length of time officers have been on the job, cases being offered as funding opportunities and other factors. Each officer's fundraising goal needs to be forecast independently on the basis of her unique donor pool and fundraising conditions. This means that financial goals officer-to-officer will not be the same, but they will be fair and achievable because good science went into their estimation.

It is easier to develop performance criteria for staff who work in volume-based fundraising programs because the complexities of building relationships with individual donors are not a factor. Here, though, measuring the right things in the right way is the issue. For example, donor retention is commonly measured by calculating a single overall net annual figure which takes into account the number of donors who gave last year and did or did not give again this year, while adding in the number of new donors who gave this year for the first time. But that is a misleading measure when the objective of all fundraising is to hold onto donors indefinitely or at least long enough to secure significantly generous gifts. A calculation based on giving in a single year does not reveal the length of time that donors are staying loyal or, to put it more vividly, how soon they are falling away. Donor retention and attrition should be measured by following a set group of donors from the moment they are acquired through several successive campaigns. The period of time required for an accurate assessment of retention/attrition is at least three years and as much as five, depending upon solicitation frequency.

I wish I had resigned from my last job instead of having to say I was fired. Even though I worked there for 10 years, was promoted and constantly received great evaluations. The politics of the moment ruined my career.

People have to be one foot out the door and with another job offer before money for a raise magically appears.

3. **Evaluation criteria must be provided up front.** This seems obvious, but some respondents in our studies pointed out that the annual performance review marked the occasion when they were first informed about the criteria by which their performance was being assessed. This speaks to a management style oriented to tripping staff up rather than supervising and mentoring them in ways that leverage their success.

4. **Goals must be achievable.** Fundraising goals must be based on real data, not numbers pulled out of the air or calculated to plug an anticipated budget shortfall (see Chapter 5).

5. **The staff member's self-assessment is often more valuable than the manager's.** I find that my employees are generally more critical of their own performance than am I, which is partly why I like to have my staff member speak first. It sometimes means that I am agreeing with what my employee has identified as an area requiring improvement, far less traumatic than having me bring it up first. This allows us both to shift the conversation quickly to what will be done to overcome the problem. At other times I am able to reassure my employee that my assessment is more positive than his own, allaying his concerns.

6. **Listening more than talking improves the quality of the performance evaluation.** Performance reviews are nerve-wracking experiences, not just for the person being assessed but for the evaluator as well. Some people talk more when they are nervous as a means of lessening stress. But the more the supervisor talks, the more the employee takes the cue that she should not. The annual performance review meeting could be the highest quality one-on-one time that employer and employee have all year, so make it count by listening – actively – as much as you can.

7. **Translating weaknesses into training opportunities is a constructive way to improve performance.** Everyone has performance weaknesses or simply gaps in their learning. Once identified, the solution may be in altering how you and your employee interact with each other but it may also be found in education. As part of the performance review, have your employee identify and rate training opportunities that would help her overcome a problem or enhance her knowledge. This process should include a timeline by which the training will happen, after which monitoring its impact on performance should become a new criterion for the next review.

8. **The employee in the context of the team is a vital measure of staff performance.** Regardless of her level of seniority, the person being evaluated is a member of a team. Even one-person-shop fundraisers are part of a Development team of fundraiser, CEO and leadership volunteers. How your staff

member under review has eased the load of a co-worker or helped the boss initiate change by exhibiting a positive attitude are attributes worth noting in performance reviews. These are important signs of an employee on track for promotion. On the other hand, an attitude or an action that has negatively impacted others is equally important to document in performance evaluations. Behavioral issues are often difficult to correct. They must be dealt with as they occur and close supervision is required to ensure they are not repeated, (See Chapter 14).

9. **Unearthing your employee's career ambitions impacts staff retention.** This question is commonly asked in interviews: "Where do you see yourself in five years?" But it is much more meaningful when asked of an employee after she has had time on the job. "Where do you see yourself in this not-for-profit in five years?" is both revealing and intriguing to employers who are more interested in keeping a high performing employee on staff than in keeping her in the job she has now. This question opens the door to the most meaningful discussion of all, providing the boss with clues about training, promotions, lateral moves, job reconfigurations, exchanges – even whole new positions – in order to capitalize on changing fundraising and donor priorities. Great bosses recognize the ever-increasing capability of great staff (and their ever-increasing attractiveness to competitors) and they are motivated to provide more exciting opportunities for career advancement than their staff will find by going elsewhere.

10. **Every staff evaluation is a review of the supervisor's performance, too.** As an employer, you are a contradiction – you exude the confidence required of any leader while examining the efficacy of your every decision, because responsibility ultimately rests with you. Premature resignations, behavioral problems, under-performance, miscalculations – they all lead back to you in one way or another. Performance evaluations invite self-assessment on a very human level. Give yourself some time at the end of every review to ask the obvious questions – "What did I do to help this employee grow in the last year?" "What could I have done better or differently to avoid a problem or overcome one sooner?" "How am I a better manager today than I was a year ago?"

I consciously work at appreciating all my co-workers, regardless of their level of seniority. I want them all to know that I value them.

My best advice to other fundraising leaders is this: be honest, communicate thoroughly, deal with problems early, and take responsibility for the morale in the office.

Fundraising managers know they must compete vigorously for new talent — but they may be less aware that they are also competing every day for the talent they already have on staff. As a manager, if you hire well, compensate fairly and creatively, offer enticing career-building opportunities, and run an innovative and modern Development operation, you give yourself the best chance of extending the tenure of your staff. Other not-for-profits will always be trying to lure away members of your team. Your job is to give your fundraisers every reason to stay.

Chapter 12:
Time and Productivity

I was eagerly anticipating a first in-person meeting with a potential new client. I informed my contact that my flight would not be landing till about 5:30 p.m. and suggested several options when we could get together the next day. She emailed back to say that, since their office was only a ten-minute cab ride from the airport, she would be happy to meet with me at 6:30 p.m. on the day I arrived.

When we met, I thanked her for inconveniencing herself in order to accommodate me. "Please don't apologize", she quickly responded. "I'm here every night till at least 8:00."

"Why is that?" I asked.

"It's the way it works around here", she said, swiveling her chair around and pointing to her computer screen. "Everything on my appointment calendar in red is an internal meeting." She studied her schedule for a moment, then added, "Today was a pretty good day, though. There were only three."

"When do you get your work done?" I asked.

"Before 9:00, after 5:00 and on the weekends", she replied as she slowly revolved back round to face me. She seemed to be taking in the full implication of what she had just said for the first time.

"Anyway, enough of all that. I've been looking forward to meeting with you and getting your advice. We're experiencing an unusually high turnover rate, particularly among middle-management fundraisers. We're hoping you can help us fix that problem."

She pulled a pad of paper towards her, and picked up her pen, preparing to take notes. Her earnest, exhausted face was framed in the light from her computer screen behind her. The light glowed red.

Seven hours a day; thirty-five hours a week; one hundred forty hours a month; one thousand eight hundred twenty hours a year – that is the value of one major gifts officer translated into time. Now deduct vacation time, statutory holidays, sick days, personal appointments and emergencies – approximately twenty-five days or one hundred seventy-five hours a year if you grant only a minimum allowance of two weeks for

No matter how successful I am, I have to top it the next time. There is no time to recoup; I have to be at peak performance at all times.

vacation. This reduces time on the job to one thousand six hundred forty-five hours. Now think about the amount of time staff spend in meetings where work is being discussed, planned and assessed but not actually getting done. According to the National Statistics Council,[1] 37% of employee time is spent in meetings. Let's cut that back to 30% on the assumption that you run a more efficient shop. Now each member of your staff has one thousand one hundred fifty-two hours per year available to carry out her job. But, don't forget reporting – everything from monthly progress reports on each gift officer's full list of prospects, to individual post-meeting updates on specific donors, to completing the travel requisition form so that your employee can meet with a donor in Atlanta, and the expense reconciliation report so that she can be reimbursed for meals and cab fare when she gets back to the office. How about a conservative 10% for this function, which is equivalent to one hundred sixty-five hours per year? Now your gifts officers are down to nine hundred eighty-seven hours of time devoted to raising money, which is the equivalent of twenty-eight weeks per year or just over six months. Of course, this assumes that staff never look at email, never get interrupted by a co-worker and never take a trip to the washroom.

But, everyone eats lunch at their desks, you say, and staff put in lots of overtime. Meetings with donors and special events in the evening keep fundraisers on the job two nights a week, often more. Our own research concurs. 93% of professional fundraisers we surveyed work overtime, with management-level respondents putting in the most time beyond a regular workday. On average, Directors of Development work nine to twelve hours overtime per week while managers of fundraising programs work five to eight.

Why Fundraisers Can't Get Their Work Done in a Thirty-Five Hour Week

Not surprising, excessive overtime is a factor in premature staff turnover. 25% of respondents in our study left their last positions due to the breadth of responsibilities they shouldered that made it impossible to fulfill their duties within a regular work week. 30% said they left their most recent jobs due to expectations for raising money within unreasonably short timeframes. This caused them to work significant overtime in an effort to reach the goal by a predetermined, often arbitrary, deadline.

These two reasons for necessitating overtime were prominent among survey respondents:

---

1 *Meetings in America: A Study of Trends, Costs, and Attitudes toward Business Travel and Teleconferencing, and Their Impact on Productivity,* a Verizon Conferencing White Paper, prepared by Infocom, a division of NFO Worldwide, Inc., Greenwich, CT, 1998

1. **The duties assigned combined with the timeline for meeting goals cannot be accomplished without significant overtime.** If the job description is so all encompassing that expectations cannot realistically be met in a regular work day, then the employee has been set up for failure. Either she works a standard number of hours per day that makes it possible to refresh, but risks underperforming, or she works overtime in the attempt to cover all her responsibilities. The latter is unsustainable. A snowballing combination of exhaustion and decreasing productivity sets in as overtime extends, resulting in a below-par performance evaluation. This breeds dissatisfaction and loss of confidence leading to a desire to leave. In the end, the employer pays a heavy price.

2. **An overtime culture.** In some Development Departments, there is an unspoken rule that only the slackers leave at 5:00, so no one wants to be the first to turn out the light. In extreme cases, some survey respondents revealed that no one in their department feels he can leave before the boss does – and she *never* leaves at 5:00. When staff put in a regular work day and are criticized outright for doing so or, more commonly, subjected to off-hand remarks about not being a team player, it is generally indicative of a management problem.

It is not unusual for fundraising managers and directors to have job descriptions and work expectations that are impossible to satisfy in a thirty-five-hour week, but senior decision-makers are no more productive than their staff after working for eight straight hours. The solutions to genuinely impossible workloads involve:

- allocating certain responsibilities in whole or in part to staff with lesser seniority. There is a bonus to delegation. How junior and intermediate staff execute assignments gives management concrete evidence about their readiness for more senior positions.

- analyzing the amount of time spent on tasks not related to strategic direction and mentoring or managing direct reports, then being ruthless about reducing or eliminating the things that get in the way of genuine progress.

- adopting a donor-centered approach to fundraising management. This means eliminating fundraising practices which are no longer (or which never were) effective in building donor loyalty and gift value. Focusing front-line fundraisers' job descriptions on effective strategies has implications on workloads all the way up the chain of command.

I feel harried instead of capable; unprepared instead of on point… and I hate that feeling. Time to think is just not in my job description.

It starts with strategy and executing a plan, of course, but it's more than that. It's about paying attention to the details and, definitely learning from your mistakes.

Management-specific issues related to confidence and style also contribute to an overtime culture in some organizations. If the boss does not control his own time well, he can unwittingly or even deliberately hide that deficiency if all his reports are expected to linger past 5:00 too. Managing by martyrdom is another negative tactic used to gain sympathy while masking the manager's own poor time-management skills. But most common is expecting reports to work overtime alongside the manager (or even after the manager has left) as a reminder of who wields the power. This is unfortunate because managers who do this misunderstand a critical tenet of management. Power is inherent in the position and, therefore, never has to be exerted. (See Chapter 14, Donor-Centered Leadership).

Maximizing Workplace Productivity

From my earlier calculation, it appears that fundraisers have less than 50% of their work day available for raising money. But does it have to be this way? Managers hold the key that can unlock more productive time and lock out time-wasting activities.

Stop Meeting about Getting Work Done and Just Get the Work Done Instead

Jason Fried, who found that staff get important work done anywhere but in the office (see Chapter 7), also noted that "people have traded in their work day for work moments".[2] Constant interruptions mean that employees – and employers – cannot devote the concentrated time required to accomplish meaningful work. And, he points to meetings and to the people who schedule them, as the primary culprits. Fried has a number of opinions on meetings, one of the most provocative being to simply cancel the next scheduled one. "You will discover that everything is just fine and the meeting that never happened never needed to happen anyway."

Readers will be familiar with many of these facts about meetings but it is still worth reminding managers, who are far more likely to be the ones doing the scheduling, that all meetings have the potential for improving productivity but their inherent qualities make them more likely to drain it:

- a one-hour meeting that ten people attend consumes ten hours, not one, of staff time;
- preparation for meetings is crucial to productivity, both during the meetings themselves and afterwards, so meeting preparation time must be factored into the amount of time that meetings consume;

---

[2] *Why Work Doesn't Happen at Work*, Jason Fried, Ted Talk, October, 2010, http://www.ted.com/talks/jason_fried_why_work_doesn_t_happen_at_work.html

- in-person meetings require the most time for preparation, holding meetings and follow-up;[3]

- recurring meetings (i.e., meetings that happen on a pre-determined schedule) are less productive than one-time meetings convened for a specific purpose.[4]

Meetings That Move Donor-Centered Fundraising Forward

Meetings have a role to play in helping Development operations transition from typical to donor-centered fundraising. With the upward movement of donors a core objective of donor-centered fundraising, meetings between direct marketing and major gifts staff held to hand off donors who are ready for relationship fundraising are vital. Innovations in acknowledgement, communication and recognition designed to develop early loyalty among new donors is another essential topic of donor-centered meetings. But reinforcement of new measures of success is, perhaps, the most important justification for meetings in a donor-centered Development office. Imagine a meeting in which a major gifts officer, who recently closed a leadership gift with a donor, takes staff through the evolution of this important philanthropist, including how he was initially drawn to the not-for-profit through its direct mail program. Bringing everyone together for this success story reminds staff that the million-dollar gift is as much an achievement of the direct mail team as the major gifts staff. Both worked collaboratively to find the donor, sustain his interest, and capitalize on his desire to accomplish something exceptional.

Meetings convened to praise accomplishments, celebrate goals and appreciate individual workers, teams or departments, are always worthwhile. Make the meetings as exhilarating as the achievements themselves and you will motivate the entire staff to reach even greater heights. Keep them short and hold them at times when energy and productivity tend to wane, like late in the afternoon. (More meetings are held in the early morning depriving most workers of their most productive time of the day for accomplishing tasks that require contemplation and creativity.)

Table 26 illustrates the characteristics of worthwhile and time-wasting meetings.

"How do we move forward?" and "What have you learned?" are far more productive approaches when mistakes are made than placing blame and getting angry.

---

[3] *Meetings in America: A Study of Trends, Costs, and Attitudes toward Business Travel and Teleconferencing, and Their Impact on Productivity*, a Verizon Conferencing White Paper, prepared by Infocom, a division of NFO Worldwide, Inc., Greenwich, CT, 1998.

[4] Ibid.

Table 26: Signs of Productive versus Time-Wasting Meetings

Clues that Staff Are Meeting for the Sake of Meeting	Characteristics of Meetings that Get Things Done and Inspire Staff
The agenda always looks the same – same topics, same order, focused on process (Report from the CEO, Report from the Manager of Direct Marketing, etc.).	The agenda has a single purpose, stated in terms of objective(s) to be achieved (e.g., Meeting to consider the impact of the 3-month social media experiment on donor acquisition).
The agenda is too all encompassing.	The agenda is limited to a single issue requiring input and decision-making so work can move forward.
Attendees are expected to report on what they are doing or did in the last week, last month, etc.	Attendees bring situations or problems forward that could benefit from input from the others in the room. Except in exceptional circumstances to showcase a particular achievement, staff are not meeting to report on what they did but on what they are trying to accomplish.
Some staff in the meeting are not integral to the topic(s) being discussed.	Only staff integral to the topic(s) are in the meeting.
There is a "new business" item on the agenda, giving official sanction to wasting time.	An issue with which one or more staff is contending is what prompts the meeting in the first place, not the other way around.
Meetings happen on a regular schedule, and, at the end of each meeting, a date/time for the next one is set.	Meetings happen only when necessary to move business forward. A follow-up meeting is not scheduled until the previous meeting's objective has been met or in case the objective cannot be met, requiring further input. (If the latter happens more than once, the problem cannot be solved in a meeting of these same staff members.)
At the end of the meeting, there are no clear decisions about what will happen with the information shared and/or attendees have conflicting views about what is to be done.	All attendees can iterate what was accomplished in the meeting and how/by when each of them will use the shared information to move business forward.

If a regularly scheduled meeting is the only time that staff get up to speed and give input, then you may be running too much of a top-down department. Staff should feel empowered to hold their own small group meetings when necessary to make decisions and discuss problems. They do not need to involve everyone and their single-issue nature makes them more focused, productive and a better use of time.

The Tendency Towards Over-Reporting

It is easy for management to introduce a new report but much harder for staff to get one eliminated. Completing recurring progress reports was the most common complaint from major gifts officers concerning things that compromise their time for raising money. Some reporting is essential, but managers would do well to review the number and variety of progress reports their staff are expected to complete, asking themselves the following questions to determine whether reports should be preserved on the current schedule, completed less often, shortened or eliminated altogether:

- **"What was the key piece of actionable information gleaned from the last report completed by my staff?"** If you cannot remember without looking it up, the report itself may not have been designed to throw a light on accomplishments or on problems that management needs to deal with. More likely, however, you may have become immune to your own report. It's not only your staff who groan when they have to fill it out; you may not be using its information or even reading it. This situation may call for a shorter, crisper format. Whittle your report down to its absolutely essential information, capture it in a table or graph that compares current information with the same quarter last year (or other suitable timeframe) and let your staff get back to work.

- **"What information is essential to assessing performance?"** Connected with the last point, this question focuses on what you need to know in order to evaluate the quality of work your staff team is producing. For example, major gifts officers evolve through about twenty steps from identifying a prospect to asking for the gift; then there are several more steps after getting the gift (or after being turned down) required to steward donors and prospects to the next ask. But must staff report on every step? What about identifying the three or four definitive markers of progress and modifying your reporting requirements to reflect only those essential benchmarks?[5]

- **"Is the frequency at which I require my staff to complete this report providing me with meaningful information in each edition?"** It may be more meaningful to report progress with donors and prospects quarterly than monthly or on a schedule that reflects typical donor movement and decision-making. To reassure yourself, look at the information in your most recent report and compare it with information from reports submitted three months ago. Could you have eliminated the two reports in between and still been adequately informed as a manager?

- **"Can I reduce the reporting burden caused by others' requirements?"** Managing up is all part of the game. If you have honed your reporting requirements to the point your staff now save time while you feel adequately informed, you have valuable new knowledge to offer your colleagues and the people to whom you report. All the way to the top, everyone suffers from lost time due to over-reporting.

- **"As I introduce a new report, which one will I eliminate?"** More reporting inevitably means less productivity. More useful reporting is what you should be striving for. If you have a new and better kind of report, great – but the deal you should make with yourself is that you have to take at least one other report off the list before introducing another.

The bureaucracy here is what slows us down. There are too many people not central to fundraising mucking about with my staff and making it hard to develop a team.

---

[5] Inspired by a conversation with Michael VanderHoef, President, Virginia Mason Foundation, Seattle.

Managing Time to Avoid Having Time Manage You

There are plenty of inviting distractions in today's workplace that tempt anyone who has difficulty staying focused. Email, social media, open meetings and interruptions cut deeply into time that would be otherwise spent productively raising money. Your best defense is hiring to intentionally weed out candidates at the start who suffer from poor time management and an inability to prioritize. Chapter 8 includes interview questions about handling a challenging workload, shouldering multiple responsibilities, meeting deadlines and delivering as part of a team. Resumes that feature a string of short job stays are a strong indicator of a candidate who cannot stay focused. Your second line of defense when hiring is reference checking. Well-phrased questions to referees will confirm your positive assessment or allay any suspicions you have.

That said, you may be contending now with an employee who does not manage time well but in many other ways is a valuable member of the team. I have found the following to be effective:

- reframe work deliverables in smaller units that can be completed more quickly. This provides the employee with a sense of accomplishment sooner and more often while making it easier for you to gauge improvement. Set a deadline by which you expect your employee to be working to the old supervision schedule so that you are not labored with stepped-up supervision indefinitely;

- identify the tasks or areas of work that capture the extended attention of the employee. This will undoubtedly be the work he prefers to do. Assign this work as a reward for handling other less popular tasks efficiently and with high quality. Withholding the pleasurable assignments too long will be counter-productive, however. You might consider scheduling pleasurable work in the afternoon, while tougher work is assigned to the morning when your staff member has more energy;

- turn wasted time on the internet or in social media to productive time spent conducting research or managing an interactive social media forum. Sometimes the solution is to alter the job description to accommodate an existing skill, but only if it genuinely adds value to your Development operation.

Managing Management Time

Directors of Development we surveyed work, on average, between nine and twelve hours of unpaid overtime each week. 36% of director-level fundraisers who were planning to leave their current jobs at the time they took part in our survey said that their job descriptions were so all encompassing that they had too little time to focus on reaching fundraising goals.

With so many management as well as fundraising responsibilities, Development chiefs could spend their valuable time in any number of ways. But, in a donor-centered environment, leaders deliberately concentrate their time where greatest net return can be achieved. Table 27 summarizes several issues explored in the book from the perspective of how time focused in one way or another produces a better or poorer result.

Table 27: Where to Concentrate Management Time for Best Results

Emphasis Here Is a Good Investment of Time Yielding High Productivity Benefit	Emphasis Here Drains Time Resulting in Little or No Productivity Benefit
Managing the fundraising strategy - enables concrete work objectives for each staff member to be expressed on a clear timeline; - defines productivity by results achieved that relate directly to ensuring higher profit.	Managing staff in the absence of strategy - redirects management time to HR issues (vacations, sick time, absenteeism, personal issues); - prevents staff from learning to manage their own time effectively in order to meet goals.
Hiring strategically, including taking enough time to hire well - instilling a policy of internal promotion; - attracting unsolicited candidates by showcasing your not-for-profit in ways that drive fundraisers to your door; - using your staff as your hiring ambassadors; - advertising more creatively.	Hiring quickly, settling for whoever can fill the position soonest - favoring external hires over internal promotions; - advertising positions within formats that make your ad look like every other not-for-profit's search; - reserving hiring as a management-only function rather than using your staff team to broaden and deepen the prospect pool.
Paying well, including offering innovative benefits that help staff save time and live a more balanced and fulfilling life - attracts better skilled candidates; - ensures longer tenure.	Paying as little as possible and offering no benefits on the assumption that people work in the third sector because it is a more meaningful career experience - prioritizes short-term cost saving over long-term revenue generation; - causes drawn out hiring process when preferred candidates opt for better paying jobs; - risks early attrition among staff who can secure higher-paying jobs with relatively little difficulty.
Convening meetings only for a specific purpose - to set goals, learn something new, solve a problem or reward staff for achievements; - including only those directly concerned with the issue for which the meeting was called.	Convening meetings on a pre-determined schedule - focused on reporting activity since the last meeting; - all encompassing agendas making meetings too long and requiring too many staff to attend; - to satisfy the manager's need to be informed.
Conducting forward-looking evaluations - aimed at evaluating future potential rather than past performance; - focused on furthering staff loyalty and unearthing latent talent and interests; - forums for setting future goals and determining requirements for promotions.	Doing retrospective evaluations - forums for assessing a staff member's performance over the previous year; - focus on articulating where employees performed well and poorly when this would be better handled at the time performance issues (positive or negative) arise.

Emphasis Here Is a Good Investment of Time Yielding High Productivity Benefit	Emphasis Here Drains Time Resulting in Little or No Productivity Benefit
Eliminating problem employees quickly - keeps management time and innovation focused on staff who are motivated to excel and who work cooperatively with others.	**Focusing more time and attention on problem employees in the hope of overcoming deficiencies** - drains management time and confidence; - inflicts problem employees on co-workers for extended periods of time, leading to premature departure of good workers.
Incorporating management learning and experience across the full staff complement - defining limited-term projects that expose junior employees to controlled opportunities for managing staff so that management potential can be observed in a protected environment; - showcases potential for promotion to junior, mid-level employees.	**Concentrating management roles and issues among a handful of highly experienced staff** - overloads most senior staff with too much work related to management while denying more junior staff essential management training under the supervision of experienced managers.
Apprenticeship for junior employees - exposes junior staff to the full array of job possibilities, making internal promotion equally or more attractive to leaving in order to gain career experience; - allows managers to observe potential beyond current job description early and plan training accordingly.	**No apprenticeship** - prevents junior staff from understanding how they could grow their careers without leaving; - exacerbates the siloed nature of fundraising programs.

Email: The Scourge That Haunts Us All

Nowhere does Parkinson's Law manifest itself more insidiously than with email, its ability to suck up time being legendary. But, ignoring it is impossible. In a full screen view of your in-box, there is bound to be one email that is genuinely important, requiring prompt attention.

Assigning certain times of the day to reviewing and responding to emails is an obvious first line of defense. Disconnecting email while working on a project is another. This prevents that tempting pop-up in the bottom right hand corner of your screen from luring you back into email purgatory. Still, those emails will be piling up whether you control how you handle them or not. Maybe an old-fashioned approach is the answer.

Thirty-five years ago I attended a half-day seminar on managing time by managing mail (the old-fashioned kind – this was long before email was in common use.) The advice offered then was logical and beautiful in its simplicity; and, as great advice tends to be, it applies just as well today to handling electronic mail.

Any communication (phone message, note, traditional mail, email) falls into one of four categories and each category has a built-in course of action:

1. it is junk, unimportant to you or to anyone else on staff – throw it out or delete it immediately. Then block the sender;

2. it is not junk but it is also not your concern – delegate it to another member of the staff. In the case of email, if the appropriate staff have been copied, on the email you received, just delete it;

3. it does concern you and you are able to handle the request efficiently. Deal with it immediately. The person who requested your assistance or input will be grateful and you will experience a sense of accomplishment, putting you in a positive frame of mind for tackling more ambitious work;

4. it does concern you but responding will require some thought and take time. Refer it to your forward file.

Staff need room to develop. Subordinates need the opportunity to learn and grow from their mistakes. Too much micromanagement makes everyone uncomfortable and unhappy.

When I took the course, the forward file consisted of forty-three file folders – one for each month and thirty-one more representing the days of the month. They were not kept in the filing cabinet, but in the deep desk drawer, making them instantly accessible. (This system is easily transferable to electronic format.) Requests for information or work assignments that fall into Category 4 are assigned as they are received to the month and day when you have time available for their attention. Once assigned, they are off your mind until the file for today's date works its way to the front of the drawer and its contents become your to-do list for the day.

Urgent requests that take time require an immediate decision to be made. There are rare instances when it is worth reorganizing your own schedule to deal with an exceptional opportunity. Information that grant monies may be available from a newly uncovered source if a proposal is in by Friday, or learning that a long-time donor has suddenly been hospitalized – well, this is why you are so good at what you do. When the stakes are high, you are the person for the job. But urgent requests, from someone whose demands on your time are always urgent, speak to that individual's inability to manage his own time and how he justifies that deficiency by taking you off your game. You can let colleagues or reports who do this know that your time is currently fully booked but that you will deal with their request by a specific date or time.

It is somewhat more challenging when the urgent request comes from the boss. However, this clear but respectful response might work: "I am working on X time-sensitive project at the moment but your request appears to be a priority as well. Could you let me know which one I should defer?" That puts responsibility back in the hands of the person who created the conflict while it is now on record that another project will be delayed and why.

As the boss, my #1 rule for myself concerning staff meetings is to take the cotton out of my ears and put it into my mouth.

Let Your Door Do the Talking

The real value of email in today's communications mix is that it cannot interrupt you unless you let it. One cannot say the same thing about the boss or colleague who habitually plants herself in your doorway until you pay attention. An "open-door policy" is an invitation to staff to waste your time or, more serious, an indication that you define your own time as unimportant. Let staff know that, when your door is closed, no one can intrude (except, perhaps, your Executive Assistant, who will be expected to learn the difference between a worthwhile interruption and just an interruption). Balance between being accessible and inaccessible is the key. Your door should be neither open nor closed habitually.

If you do not have a door, sit with your back to the opening of your cubicle or space. Turn around at times when you are open to interacting with passers-by. Sometimes, solutions are simple.

How Board Members Can Put Their Time to Best Use in Fundraising

In Chapter 9, Hiring the People Who Lead, I described the fundraising tasks at which members of the Board excel, especially in light of their extraordinary influence with donors. It is the job of CEOs and Directors of Development to encourage their volunteers to turn their influence into results, while taking these realities into account:

- Board members' volunteer status makes it somewhat trickier to demand action and accountability in fundraising;

- their part-time status requires a thoughtful approach to assigning tasks and setting expectations for productivity;

- fear of fundraising is pervasive in some Boards, making them reluctant to step out of the shadows.

That said, Board members can produce extraordinary results if they are well supported by staff and led by an excellent Chair. Their collective admiration for your not-for-profit, their dedication to voluntarism, and their sense of good-natured competition work in your favor. If you help direct their time in the best ways, your Board is bound to take fundraising to a new level of success.

How Much Is Good Enough?

If a Board member agrees to call donors to thank them for gifts just received, what number of calls would be considered adequate, exemplary or insufficient? If someone is willing to ask for major gifts, how many asks in a year would she need to make to have fulfilled that commitment? How many hours should a volunteer contribute to organizing and running a fundraising event?

Your version of the Donor-Centered Fundraising Plan described in Chapter 5 is a good place to start in defining Board members' responsibilities in quantifiable terms. Add to that a sense of what is reasonable in order to find the balance between "ambitious yet achievable", plus experience gained through doing. Soon a plan for making the best use of volunteer time in fundraising – one that is both realistic and rewarding – will emerge. Table 28 provides an example.

Table 28: Time and Productivity in Board-Related Fundraising

Fundraising Activity	Productivity Level / Rating						
	Unengaged	>	Minimal Input	>	Good	>	Excellent
offering names of personal/business contacts which are added to prospect lists and moved into active cultivation;	0	1	2	3-4	5-6	7-8	9-10
augmenting information on current donors, especially identifying best volunteer contact;	0	1	2-3	4-5	6-10	11-15	16-20
making the initial contact with a donor or prospect, in essence the "cold call" that results in a first meeting;	0	0	1	2	3	4	5
being the primary volunteer member of the team making major gift asks;	0	0	1	2	3	4	5
writing personal, hand-written thank you letters to donors where personal connection exists;	0	1	2-3	4-5	6-10	11-15	16-20
making thank-you calls to new donors as soon as first gifts are received;	0	1	2-3	4-5	6-10	11-15	16-20
making thank-you calls to donors with a prior history of giving, with whom volunteer has personal connection;	0	1	2	3-4	5-6	7-8	9-10
taking responsibility for 4 donors/guests at each special event (assuming four events over the course of the year);	0	0	0	1	2	3	4
contributing to fundraising events in ways that raise money or offset expenses, such as selling tickets, acquiring auction items, obtaining in-kind services/commodities, volunteering during events (time contributed in hours);	0	1-2	3-4	5-7	8-10	11-15	16-20
training and development: participating in Board-prescribed training – during Board meetings, onsite outside Board meetings, and/or offsite focused on enhancing skill in making asks (training hours with 10 considered exemplary).	0	0	1-2	3-4	5-6	7-8	9-10
Total Potential Rating per Level of Engagement	**0**	**6-7**	**16-21**	**31-39**	**49-65**	**76-95**	**105-124**

Evaluating the Board for Their Contribution to Fundraising

In the above example, a Board member could be rated anywhere from 0 to 124 for a year's contribution to fundraising and her performance might be measured in this way:

- 100-124 – Board member is performing at the highest level;

- 60-99 – Board member's contribution to fundraising is good or acceptable;

- 30-59 – Board member is contributing but year-end evaluation would seek to find ways for improvement in fundraising;

- 29 or less – Board member is under-performing in fundraising and this would be taken into account when the Nominating Committee is considering which Board members are asked to stand for re-election or asked to consider an executive position.

Evaluating their performance is the only way that Boards know whether they are doing good work and accomplishing things that are meaningful to their not-for-profits. So it is surprising that only 18% of Board members surveyed by Cygnus in 2012 said their Board's performance in fundraising was assessed in any kind of objective manner. Among the minority of respondents whose Boards do evaluate their performance, reaching a pre-set fundraising goal was the most common and, often, the only criterion. Having a goal without defining the quantifiable tasks by which the goal will be met, though, often results in a few motivated Board members shouldering all responsibility for raising money. With the details of the job left to their imagination, other Board members remain on the sidelines hoping they won't be called upon to deliver.

The variety of tasks described in Chapter 9 and in Table 28 in Chapter 12 affords Board members the opportunity to contribute according to their talents and preferences. Ideally, Board members would be expected to take on increasingly sophisticated work the longer they serve, and the training offered to volunteers would assist them in tackling the tasks they find more challenging. Note that everything in Table 28 is actionable, leading directly or indirectly to improvement in fundraising. Credit is not given for simply showing up. Being on the Special Events Committee or attending a minimum number of Board meetings does not, on its own, translate into results.

Why Overtime Is Time Wasted

Overtime is commonplace, but is it productive? Research extending back over one hundred years is remarkably consistent in its conclusion that working beyond a standard thirty-five-hour week is counter-productive. Perhaps the best-known research was done by Henry Ford who was understandably motivated to squeeze as many hours out of his assembly line workers as possible. After a dozen years of research he conceded that, beyond eight hours, productivity decreased to the point that extending the work day was counter-productive. This prompted Ford to cut shifts from nine to eight hours (and double his workers' pay, incidentally). As a result, business boomed and Ford rose to number one in the industry. It is not just that Ford's research on overtime found productivity in the ninth and tenth hours to be less than optimal; net productivity was actually discovered to be greater in eight hours than in ten. Errors and sub-standard performance after eight hours required work to be redone, insurance and warranty claims to rise and customers to be lost.

You may think that this has nothing to do with fundraising. But, research on overtime with knowledge workers has come to the same conclusion. Many studies with military officers, emergency room physicians and scientists concur that chronic overtime does not add to profitability; in fact, it compromises the bottom line. There are exceptions, however. Occasional, short-term sprints to a goal that require concentrated overtime can be productive, but not at the level that the number of hours devoted to overtime work suggests. It appears that putting in a sixty-hour week in order to meet a deadline produces a result that is only 25%, not 50%, more productive.[6]

Flexible Work Schedules

> Like most higher education institutes, my university has suffered budget cuts. Staff haven't had raises in two years, and funding for travel to conferences and other perks have been cut as well. But I am still happy where I work because of the flexibility I am given and my wonderful boss. I am a new mom. My daughter is 18 months old. I am allowed to work from home on occasion if she is ill, and I have enough personal leave built in that I can take a day off to take her to the zoo or another special outing from time to time. I can't tell you how much this means to me. Like so many women, I feel torn between needing to work, liking my job and wanting to be home with my young child. In my current role, I have the flexibility to balance the demands of parenthood while still pursuing my professional goals.

Working beyond eight hours a day is counter-productive but gifts officers are expected to bring their A Game to an 8:00 p.m. meeting with a donor. In this frequently occurring situation, mangers have two advantages they can offer their staff to ensure that goals are reached – flexible work schedules and productive work environments.

As an employer, I am more interested in seeing my staff get the job done than putting in exactly 37.5 hours a week. When I give employees the freedom to come and go, without having to account for every minute of their time, they always give me far more time in the end.

---

[6] *Why We Have to Go Back to a 40-Hour Work Week to Keep Our Sanity*, Sara Robinson, published on AlterNet (http://www.alternet.org), March 2012.

We have initiated a flex schedule during summer months to give staff the experience of managing their own work schedules. They are still accountable for required hours and productivity, but I'm seeing a lot of staff shifting to longer days and a 4-day work week…and they love it!

An astounding 66% of respondents in our study who were planning to stay indefinitely in their current organizations cited the flexibility of their employers in accommodating non-traditional work schedules as a key reason for their job satisfaction. In most cases, flexibility involved more than simply not expecting their fundraisers to be at their desks at 9:00 a.m. if they had been working a donor recognition event the night before. Respondents referenced their appreciation for employers who were open to job-sharing and time off to deal with personal or family matters, but especially open to giving fundraisers more control over their own timetables. In our research on meaningful benefits that impact staff retention (Chapter 7), the benefits connected to alleviating time constraints were most coveted by respondents.

Unlimited Time Off

The ultimate in management flexibility regarding work schedules is captured in a concept called "unlimited time off". It is a hiring and staff retention advantage being used increasingly by businesses that are competing for scarce talent in highly competitive industries. Fundraising fits that description, especially when considering the level of competition among not-for-profits for trained, experienced major and planned gifts officers.

Netflix is a pioneer of this concept, which, as its name implies, offers employees as much time off as they wish for whatever purpose they choose. The Social Media Group, a Toronto-based niche social marketing company, has further refined the concept. Knowing that they could not compete on salary with their much larger and better resourced competitors, SMG opted instead for creating an innovative approach to work and an environment that would lure the best in the business. All employees can take as much time off as they want, for whatever purpose they choose, anytime in the year. Time off is not monitored by a manager or supervisor; it is, however, recorded for research purposes by a non-management colleague in order to answer the question, "How much time off do employees tend to take if no limit is imposed?"

The Social Media Group has three conditions attached to unlimited time off:

- employees are responsible for their own mental health (I would add "physical health" to this condition);
- employees are responsible to their co-workers;
- employees are responsible to their clients (read "donors" in the case of Development operations).

These are smart conditions as they speak to the ultimate objective that everyone on staff, whether manager or worker, is trying to reach. No one can be consistently productive with the hours they spend on the job if they are exhausted, sick or under severe stress caused by something going on outside the office. In the case of physical illness, no employee should feel she has the right to pass on the flu to everyone else on the team. Working through the pain by showing up at the office anyway is not heroism; it is disrespect. Not-for-profits have a right to expect that the people they hire to raise money will be firing on all cylinders. Staff cannot perform at peak efficiency and creativity unless they are empowered to deal – guilt-free – with personal and other issues that are holding them back. Unlimited time off takes away the fear of penalty (yet another stress) from employees so that they can deliver optimum return on their employers' investment in talent.

My boss makes me think, and he has faith in my decisions.

Being responsible to one's co-workers means that an employee cannot decide to take a month-long trip-of-a-lifetime just as his team is preparing to launch a major campaign. Unlimited time off does not give anyone the right to compromise the success of the project, let alone unfairly heap work on colleagues.

Thoughtfulness of others and careful planning are the hallmarks of a policy of unlimited time off as is the transfer of responsibility for their actions from supervisors to workers themselves. This is a highly beneficial by-product of this different way of operating. Workers who make decisions about their own work/life issues are more conscious of each other, keenly aware that every decision they make affects everyone else on the team. Equally valuable, supervisors and managers are relieved of the time-consuming and thankless job of managing their staff's affairs, leaving them with more time to do the job that only they can do. The job of management is to keep the entire staff team focused on the goal at hand, guiding workers creatively, empathetically and, sometimes, invisibly to ensure that the goal is reached.

Being responsible to clients, customers and, in the case of fundraising, donors, is the third condition to which employees who enjoy unlimited time off must adhere. And nowhere is this more appropriate or important than in Development. Fundraisers must be available at all times of the day and evening, including on weekends, for one-on-one meetings with donors, fundraising and donor recognition events, Board and Committee meetings. Offering flexible work schedules to staff is a good start, but actually shifting responsibility for creating and managing those schedules to employees themselves is much better. Only the front-line fundraiser is in a position to know whether she can still come into the office and draft a critical grant proposal the morning after the Golf Tournament Dinner where guests lingered till 1:00 a.m.

I love people and believe that everyone has some special talent. The team is the thing for me.

Hire the Staff You Can Trust

Unlimited time off only works if you are confident in your own ability as a manager – confident enough to trust the people who work for you. Trust is also inherent in progressive strategies such as working from home, having flexible work hours, and other matters that grant staff the freedom to create a personal work environment that accommodates their individual lives. Employees do not have the opportunity to earn their managers' trust if their not-for-profits have rigid policies about work hours or work location or if benefits are very tightly defined. It is only when the reins are loosened that workers demonstrate whether they can be trusted.

Management that exercises power over staff by controlling where, when and how they get their work done is a poor substitute for management that inspires staff to excel. You are justified in thinking, however, that trust has to be earned and that this level of freedom may not work for everyone, or for every job. For example, the office receptionist needs to be at his desk during regular business hours, but, even with this position, a job-sharing option would give two people greater control over their work schedules for half the week, rather than no control at all. Most other Development jobs are well suited to a flexible schedule.

If you adopt a policy of unlimited time off and someone abuses the privilege, it is possible that you hired the wrong person in the first place. So, during your search process, ask specific questions and pay close attention to these things that give you insight into your candidate's maturity and trustworthiness:

- Review your candidate's resume for frequent, short tenures. Short job stays suggest that the candidate is good at winning over employers in interviews, but easily lured away to other opportunities. Loyalty is a feature of staff who work in companies offering flexible schedules – loyalty to their fellow workers, to their donors and to their boss. They are loyal because they are personally responsible, not merely carrying out the orders of a manager who assumes responsibility for everyone else's actions.

- Ask direct questions about how the candidate handled a schedule of demanding hours in her last job. If she was expected to be available for fundraising-related meetings or events in the evening or on weekends, how did she refresh herself for work during the day? Resist using theoretical language when asking these questions; rather, ask for specific examples from her current or most recent job.

- Ask for examples of recent situations where the candidate managed time effectively in order to achieve something important. Fundraisers' job descriptions can be all-encompassing. Supervisors, volunteers and donors expect fundraisers to be "at their service" while still reaching ambitious targets. During interviews, it is important to find out how your candidate manages multiple priorities and whether he falls into the trap of time managing him.

The Social Media Group's research on unlimited time off found that their employees took, all told, an average of three weeks off a year. Some employees' performance reviews noted they were not taking enough time off. Taking more vacation or personal time the next year in order to improve their on-the-job performance was noted in their file as something requiring attention.

Staff who are trusted by their employers, and given the tools to manage their time in ways that work best for them individually, come to work because they want to be there, work productively because they are healthy and focused, and stay loyal because they appreciate how privileged they are.

The After-Five Job Your Fundraisers Do for Free

Networking is a key component of sales, especially when the product you are selling is philanthropy. And, the one thing your fundraising staff are not doing while sitting in the office is networking.

I am a proponent of leaving the office at 5:00 (off-hour work appointments notwithstanding), and not just for the obvious benefits of avoiding burnout and re-energizing for the next day, though these are substantial. Offices are not environments that are especially conducive to thinking, innovating new ideas or solving problems. Offices are places where staff are under pressure to get something done, usually by a deadline. This is why solutions tend to present themselves when you are taking a walk or washing the dishes; why ideas seem to come to you in your sleep and why your imagination gets fired up anywhere but in the office. I doubt whether anyone fully turns off his business brain at 5:00. But getting out of the office takes the self-imposed and management-imposed blinders off. A different environment allows one to think creatively and solve problems.

But the world after 5:00 offers fundraisers, and especially the not-for-profits they work for, something even better. This is the time when workers should be doing the things that interest them, learning, investigating, and pursuing their dreams. This is how they meet new people, make new friends and broaden their social networks. It won't be long before your employee who joins the Historical Society meets someone who can open a door with a top prospect at your college. Before you know it, your gifts officer who gets involved in her local community theatre

I give my staff additional time off when they have been achieving or exceeding the goals we set. This both improves the quality of their performance and inspires them to stay loyal.

Do everything while also maintaining a sense of humor, joy and wonder. Easy!

meets someone whose child was a patient in your hospital. So much is possible that will never happen as long as your staff are sitting in their office cubicles.

Most important, however, the things your staff do after five o'clock are what make them interesting. Their fuller, more engaged lives make them better conversationalists, giving donors more reasons to want to spend time with them. New connections emerge that were never there before. Your staff become better fundraisers – and it doesn't cost you a cent.

Managing a fundraising operation is very different from working on the front lines. It is also very demanding – and exhausting. If your staff are leaving at 5:00 but you are still at your desk well into the evening, you are depriving your team of a leader who can function at optimum productivity every day. Turn out the light, walk out of the office, and start living the life that you have earned.

Chapter 13:

I'm Leaving

There she is – that staff member who is officially in line for your job. She's watching you get older; she's monitoring your every move; she's adding up your mistakes. She's so cool about it all, too, just biding her time till you leave... or get pushed out...or drop dead on the job. Perhaps she's even nudging things along a little. After all, that banana peel on the floor beside your desk didn't just materialize out of nowhere. Better watch out.

Succession – A Leader's Ultimate Gift

You might be surprised at the number of managers who see the absence of a succession plan as confirmation that they are irreplaceable. 78% of Development Directors and 63% of CEOs we surveyed had no succession plan in place. Asked why, 57% said no one else on staff could do their job. And, yet, I have never heard of a not-for-profit that disintegrated on the spot when its CEO or Director of Development left. I have known many, however, that have been left in limbo after a sudden departure while a protracted search unfolds and even more where a less-than-ready chief executive replaces a high performer. This is the point of succession planning: it enables a smooth hand-off from one decision-maker to the next, ensuring that the not-for-profit does not stumble or regress. In fact, when done right, succession planning guarantees that the new CEO or Director will build on her predecessor's accomplishments.

Not having a succession plan for the CEO, the Director of Development and other pivotal positions is not just short-sighted; it is foolish. Not-for-profits contend with enough crises inflicted upon them by factors they cannot control; they don't need to create their own. Succession is central to the quality of organizational performance. Ensuring smooth transition from one leader to the next is entirely within the control of those who make key hiring decisions.

I can certainly see, though, why succession planning as it is commonly configured is more off-putting than reassuring to incumbents. Typical succession planning has three flaws:

1. **It starts too late.** If you were a CEO or Development Director who had been doing a good job for some time, then out of the blue your Board or boss brought up the subject of succession planning, would you not be suspicious about what motivated this sudden interest? Succession planning should begin immediately after the incumbent passes probation and definitely within her first

I want my staff to stay loyal and so I lead by example by being loyal to them.

year of employment. There is also a statistical justification for beginning the process as soon as the new hire has settled into the job. In the past decade, the median tenure of a CEO in Fortune 500 companies has fallen from 9.5 to 3.5 years.[1] Short job stays hold progress back, but they are nothing short of crippling at the top where critical decisions are made. 36% of organizations represented in our CEO study have had three or more Chief Executive Officers in the past ten years.

2. **It is unilaterally managed by the person or group ultimately responsible for hiring the successor, whereas its central advocate and orchestrator should be the incumbent.** No one is in a better position than the incumbent to understand the knowledge, skills and experience that are required in a successor. And no one is closer to the people in the pool of likely successors. Having the CEO lead the effort of identifying potential candidates for his position does not deprive the Board of its right – and obligation – to choose the next leader. The same applies to the Director of Development and the right and obligation of the CEO to make the ultimate hiring decision. But it does make the job a lot easier and the eventual decision more likely to be the right one.

3. **It identifies a single candidate for succession, whereas multiple candidates would serve the process much better.** A vibrant succession process identifies not one, but several possible candidates for each key leadership job. Candidates get on the list because they exhibit some of the skills essential for assuming a leadership role. Training, opportunity and mentoring help develop others. In the case of the top Development job, these skills include leadership ability, fundraising knowledge at a senior level, a track record of handling challenging assignments including orchestrating change, and a reputation for innovative decision-making. Because developing leadership skills takes time, some staff on track for key positions will leave to pursue their careers elsewhere; others will be added as their capabilities develop; still others may stay in their organization but be removed from the list. Someone right for a leadership job today may not be the best candidate five years from now when the environment and the not-for-profit's priorities are quite different. The pool is not static.

Time is the essential ingredient of a succession plan that works – time to observe the growing capabilities of those being groomed for higher positions, and time to see how they adapt to big challenges like a faltering economy or changing donor preferences.

---

[1] *The Art and Science of Finding the Right CEO*, A.G. Lafley, with foreword by Noel M. Tichy, Harvard Business Review, October 2011.

Succession Planning Starts at the Bottom

A policy that mandates succession planning, complementing a policy for promoting internally, is the strongest expression of faith that an organization can make in its people. It is also a hedge against premature staff turnover. In Chapter 6, I explained how promoting from within is the best possible hiring policy, reducing the cost of staff turnover while giving employees a powerful reason to stay loyal. The approach to succession described here extends that philosophy right to the top...but also to the bottom.

When better succession planning is the goal, hiring even the most junior, non-management staff member is a strategic investment in leadership. Luckily, there appears to be an eager body of fundraising professionals just waiting to prove that they have what it takes. While the majority of Chief Development Officers felt no one in their organizations could take on their jobs, their reports disagreed. 67% of respondents we surveyed said they were ready now or could be ready within a year to assume their boss's position.

Succession Planning for Leadership Volunteers

In most Boards with which I have worked, it is understood that the Vice Chair will become the Chair when the incumbent's term ends. While it is usually not expressed in this way, the promotion of Vice Chair to Chair is more an anointment than an election.

The productivity of the Board as a whole is largely a result of the Chair's strategic ability and delicate persuasiveness, and not everyone has these skills. So, it should not be acceptable for a member to become the Vice Chair simply because he has served on the Board longer than other members or because she was first to put up her hand in the meeting that chose the executive. Candidates for the position of Vice Chair should be required to demonstrate their potential long before they become the Chair-in-waiting.

Signs of leadership potential in Board members:

- taking on responsibility for Committee management which includes ensuring that specific, achievable goals are in place and that these goals are met;
- engaging in productive discussion and debate at Board meetings in order to move business forward;
- reaching fundraising goals, including willingness to ask for gifts.

I downplay the titles and emphasize the group. I can see what a difference that makes.

Why their Chief Fundraiser resigned prematurely, according to CEOs:

49% Inability to meet fundraising goals
44% Higher salary elsewhere
31% Appeal of competitors
28% Personal reasons
21% Philosophical differences
21% Inability to influence Board on fundraising matters

Over-engagement may be a sign that a Board member is not suitable as a candidate for Chair. Some leadership volunteers put extraordinary amounts of time into the not-for-profits they serve. They have a much more in-depth knowledge of the organization than do other volunteers. As workers, they are a godsend because they can always be counted upon to come through even when those around them drop the ball. It seems logical that they should be rewarded for their exemplary performance by being voted in as Chair. But superb Board Chairs are not the ones who do all the work. Their job is to get everyone else on the Board to do the work. Managing is difficult at the best of times; leading a team of volunteers whose paychecks and careers are not on the line if they don't come through is nothing short of an art.

I'm Leaving

The story that introduces Chapter 1 illustrates the anxiety that employers feel when a high performing staff member resigns. "I'm leaving" doesn't always mean that, however, so the next time you are faced with this worst of all possible news, remember – it's not over till it's over.

In a Development Department, about one employee in three changes jobs each year. Even though staff turnover is a constant reality, it is still a shock to an employer when a valuable member of the team announces that he is leaving for another position. In that deer-in-the-headlights moment, you need to pull yourself together and find out why. If you run a great shop and are an excellent manager (see Chapter 11,12 and 14), your employee is taking a big risk by going. Work environments designed to further staff retention are not the norm. You have every right to ask why your employee is leaving and you should listen closely to what she says. Forget, for the moment, about the work that lies ahead of you in order to replace this top performer. Instead, find out what it would take to get her to stay.

Is Money Always the Reason?

If your employee is thinking of leaving or is in active negotiation with another not-for-profit and comes to you to discuss her options, you have an opportunity, but only if you have thought through your own options beforehand. At the moment your high performer says, "I don't really want to go but I have been offered a very attractive salary somewhere else," he has thrown down the gauntlet. If this comes as a surprise or if you interpret it as holding you to ransom, you will not be in the right frame of mind to negotiate. So, before you face this issue – or face it again – create your game plan.

Among survey respondents in every job category, "to obtain a higher salary" was the top reason why they left their last jobs (47%). Among those seriously considering a change at the time they participated in the study, 64% were motivated, at least in part, by the prospect of earning more money elsewhere. Certainly, securing a higher salary is not always the impetus for leaving, but it is prevalent enough in fundraising that it cannot be ignored, (See Chapter 7).

Salary is not a prominent factor all the time, however. Once fundraisers have settled in, job satisfaction becomes more important. Even if they suspect or know outright that they could command a higher wage if they go elsewhere, salary takes a back seat until they are seriously pursuing another job (or being pursued). The exception involves fundraisers who are working for wages well below the industry average. Development professionals have ready access to national and regional salary scales and they have well developed professional networks. Salary is never off the minds of practitioners who know they are being short-changed.

55% of management-level respondents in our survey said they would sometimes match the salary being offered by another employer if it would cause a high performing employee to stay; but 40% say they would never do this. One in three employers willing to raise their fundraisers' pay in order to get them to stay said they were willing to match any other offer; 45% would offer only up to 10% more.

The illustrations in Chapter 3 expose the hidden costs of replacing high performing fundraisers. They are meant to put salary and salary raises into perspective for managers who are trying to decide whether to negotiate or let their staff member go. In one scenario, I estimated that it would cost almost $1 Million to replace Keith, the Director of Integrated Marketing at a national disease charity. Keith was earning $90,000 a year managing a Department of eighteen staff when he was approached with another job offer at a 40% increase in pay. On the surface, this seems like an impossible gap to breach, but 40% is $36,000, or $3,000 a month in a department raising over half a million dollars every 30 days. Compared with the cost of diverting his manager's time to rehiring and retraining, let alone that of his colleagues and reports who will have to shoulder a bigger load during the transition, $36,000 is not a bad investment in the face of the alternative – a $952,000 productivity gap.

Negotiating the Benefits of Staying

If your employee is hesitating over whether to go or stay, and if you want to keep this high performer, you have competitive advantages to offer. Even though Keith is excited about this new opportunity, he will also be weighing the risks:

A lot of fundraisers are "development gypsies" who are great when they're on the job, but will move on to the next not-for-profit for even the slightest increase in pay.

- Keith has been in his current position for only two years and would not want to be seen as a job-hopper.

- His current job is Keith's first management position and in two years he has barely scratched the surface of what he needs to learn about managing staff. The job on offer is more demanding, with a larger staff. Is he really ready for this challenge?

- The CEO heading the not-for-profit that is courting him is new to fundraising and new to the not-for-profit sector, whereas his current boss is a fundraising expert renowned for her outstanding management abilities. Does the new CEO understand changing donor trends and its impact on direct marketing or will he expect rabbits to be pulled out of hats?

It is unrealistic to expect Keith to stay indefinitely. But he is objective enough to realize that he may be leaving too soon. In one way, the competitor has offered his current employer insight into what would motivate Keith to stay. Both parties win if Keith's current employer offers incentives to stay that address the risks inherent in leaving, and positions that offer within a particular timeframe. This might include:

- a strategic management training program that would roll out over the next two years designed to better prepare Keith for a more demanding management role in a larger Development operation in the future;

- the opportunity to demonstrate substantial growth in the program he currently manages. At this point, Keith shows potential but has not really had the time to prove what he can accomplish;

- a budget for innovation in direct marketing, specifically directed at transitioning more donors into online giving, something that Keith has been saying is possible.

Staff Retention Is a Long-Term Strategy

37% of respondents left their last job for a more senior position; 23% left to work in a Development operation where they would learn a new skill; 36% left to get away from the old-school fundraising culture of "we have to have the money now". Employers cannot always resolve problems or put new job strategies in play quickly enough to retain a fundraiser who has started to look elsewhere. The best strategies to extend the tenure of your high-performing staff are those that are put in place the day you hire them.

If you run a fundraising operation that features the advantages referenced in this book and if you are an excellent manager (see Chapter 14), you will extend the tenure of your top performers. It is unlikely that you will keep them indefinitely, but doubling someone's tenure from two to four years cuts replacement costs in half while giving you a more senior, better qualified, "older and wiser" member of the team in those third and fourth years.

Losing Your Top Performer

Losing any hard-working employee is difficult, but losing your very best performer is extremely frustrating. But employees who have high standards, who focus on getting the job done, who produce results better than others and who never cause their managers to lose a moment's sleep, are also the ones who are most resolute when they do decide to go. These staff don't leave over a dispute about how money should be raised or because too much is expected of them with too few resources. They leave because they simply feel they have taken their careers as far as they can go where they work now. Only 7% of these strategic high performers said they could have been persuaded to stay once they made the decision to go.

Managers who want their future stars to stay longer can put steps in place that will extend their tenure. Exemplary performers distinguish themselves early – during probation. Feeling grateful (and relieved) for having someone on staff who delivers with minimal supervision is not enough. As the person responsible for the bottom line in your Development operation, you should recognize the value of investing in these performers. Instead of leaving them out there in the knowledge that they will come through for you, do the opposite. It will be the best investment in management time and resources you ever make.

- Give your top producers ambitious, time-limited projects even when their length of time on the job and specific work experience make you wonder whether they will be able to handle the responsibility. In almost every instance, they will blow you away.

- Reclassify their jobs so that you can raise their pay.

- Promote them as a priority. Avoid promotion based on length of stay alone; always reward results achieved with greater responsibility and higher pay.

- Reward them with atypical benefits that acknowledge their high-level performance (see Chapter 7 and "Unlimited Time Off" in Chapter 12).

- Invest in their management training early, before they are responsible for other staff on a permanent basis. Not every exemplary performer on the front lines adapts well to managing others so you should find out early where your stars do and do not shine.

- For high performers who are less suitable for promotion into management positions, make sure you initiate creative and tangible ways to reward their

I've been in this job for 8 years, carefully nurturing our fundraising. We're now on the cusp of seeing this investment pay off. There's no way I'm leaving now!

The best boss I ever had gave me the tools I needed to get the job done and then let me get on with it. He inspired me to push myself to accomplish more than I ever thought I could. His guidance helped me avoid the big mistakes and reach for the stars.

achievements as front-line practitioners. Allowing the Peter Principle to prevail would be the worst possible outcome for both your star fundraiser and your entire Development operation.

When the Decision Is Firm

Try not to take your staff member's resignation personally even though you might quietly be thinking, "Am I responsible for my employee's departure in some way?" Separate his decision to go from yourself as the employer who has invested so much time and effort in guiding his growth. Treat this critical moment as you would a conversation between two colleagues who are discussing the interesting topic of what motivates staff to stay or go. Ask him about the job he is going to, its focus and responsibilities. Then, ask this key question:

"Have you formally accepted an offer – in other words, signed a contract?"

If the answer is "yes", your employee's response to the following questions will be valuable in helping you make management, team or departmental adjustments that extend the tenure of other high performing staff.

- *What was it about the job you have now or about working here that made you open to the possibility of going elsewhere?* The response may be vague. Your employee will not want to hurt your feelings or he may not have analyzed his own reasons for leaving that closely. He may tell you that he was perfectly happy in his current position with no plans to leave but was approached by a recruiter or another not-for-profit. If the latter, ask these two questions:

- *What was it about the conversation you had initially that shifted your thinking from "how quickly can I get the recruiter off the line" to "this is intriguing"?*

- *If you look a year into your new job, what do you think you will have learned or experienced there that you don't think you will have the opportunity to learn or experience here over the next year?*

In the unlikely possibility that your departing employee who has already formally committed to his new job lets you know that he is open to negotiating salary or other conditions that would persuade him to stay, do not bite. He has just revealed why it's OK to let him go.

It's Also Not Over Under It's Over

Always keep the door open for a top performer. Her new job might turn out to be a disappointment and she may want to come back. He will no doubt evolve into an even more desirable employee after spending two or three years learning a new skill. So, by all means tell your departing stars that you wish them well and hope they will return one day – but do more than that. Put it in writing and add "re-engaging former employees" to your list of best hiring strategies. Make sure you keep track of where they go – even if it is out-of-state. They are now your alumni, and no one knows how to stay connected with and engage alumni better than a professional fundraiser. You may have lost this battle, but "strategic selection" works both ways.

Exit Interviews

Exit interviews are valuable at the best of times, but they are especially important when one or more of these conditions is present:

- good staff are frequently resigning prematurely – sooner than the average tenures noted in Chapter 3 or sooner than historic averages in your not-for-profit;
- when staff say they are leaving, they are resolute. Offers of better pay or benefits or improved working conditions cannot change their minds;
- one or more positions is chronically vacant in the Development Department;
- managers spend a disproportionate amount of their time hiring, not to expand but just to replace staff who have left;
- there is a reluctance among departing staff to give liberal notice; they are eager to get out as soon as possible;
- there has been an exodus of staff in a relatively short period of time.

These are signs of weak management. Even if good staff are leaving because of a difficult co-worker, the problem still lies with management who failed to deal with the situation appropriately. Exit interviews cannot resolve management problems but they can bring them to light, an important first step.

An exit interview is a survey conducted with departing employees. The value of information gleaned through exit interviews increases as time passes and more employees add to the body of knowledge. Just as in any other kind of research study, questions posed in exit interviews need to be standardized to enable an apples-to-apples comparison. However, that does not mean that questions should be the same across all facets of the not-for-profit. Fundraising is a specialized field. Its very nature as a profit-generating operation plus the supply/demand inequity in the industry mean that interview questions need to be configured to reflect the unique circumstances and requirements inherent in raising money.

Factors that make exit interviews a negative experience:

61% Doubts that any action will result
32% Questions too generic
24% Doubts about confidentiality
21% Questions seen to cover up negative aspects of organization

Only 31% of respondents we surveyed participated in an exit interview before leaving their last position. While 68% were not offered the opportunity, only 1% of those who were offered one turned it down.

Among those who experienced an exit interview, two out of three departing staff found it to be worthwhile, though reasons varied substantially depending upon seniority. Table 29 illustrates.

Table 29: What Respondents Valued About Exit Interviews (by Job Category)

Response	Directors of Development	Fundraising Program Managers	Non-Management Fundraisers	One-Person-Shop Fundraisers
Interviewer was genuinely interested in my views.	36%	62%	61%	60%
Concluded job on a positive note.	51%	54%	39%	50%
Provided opportunity to communicate information important to CEO/Board for planning purposes.	52%	5%	13%	10%
Provided confidential forum to discuss negative reasons contributing to resignation.	25%	45%	22%	35%
Helped me gain an objective perspective about my role and accomplishments.	28%	23%	44%	35%

37% of respondents who participated in an exit interview said the experience was not worthwhile. By a wide margin, respondents in all four categories said their primary concern was that the observations they made and advice they gave in the interview would not lead to any positive change. The questions themselves were also noted by 32% of dissatisfied respondents as "too general or too generic to apply to fundraising".

Collecting and Using Information from Exit Surveys

All employees, regardless of why they are leaving, should be offered an exit interview. In fact, I prefer a process that includes a confidential survey with an option, at the departing employee's discretion, for a follow-up interview. If a sensitive issue played a role in someone's decision to go, especially one that involves the boss, the staff member may not trust the process. One in five respondents who said their exit interview was not worthwhile felt that the interviewer purposefully directed questions away from issues that would bring known problems out into the open.

Most departing employees are not contending with sensitive issues related to personnel, but, for those who are, confidentiality of exit interview information is a central concern. This is where a Department of Human Resources is valuable, not only because HR staff are expert in employment matters but also because they are outside the Development Department. Web-based exit interviews, facilitated by a third party, are an excellent alternative for smaller not-for-profits that do not have the benefit of their own HR Department. They offer the combination of expert consultation, data compilation, objectivity and confidentiality, reassuring to departing employees otherwise reluctant to put sensitive information on the record.

Exit interviews play a role in helping employees end their jobs on a positive note, but their real value is the information they generate for planning and training purposes going forward. Managing is an extraordinarily difficult job. Offered constructively, exit interview and exit survey information can help a new manager grow and an experienced one develop skills needed for the top not-for-profit jobs.

A very enticing job presented itself to me a few months ago. I thought about the learning curve required to master the job description. I then realized how much more fulfilling it would be to stay where I am.

Think about your top performer – the one you definitely do not want to lose. Imagine her hovering in your doorway now, trying to find the words to tell you she is leaving. Ask yourself what allowances you would make in order to keep her on the job for one more year. Knowing that she will leave twelve months from now, would you finally assign her that meaty project that you know she would handle so well? Would you ask her to identify a likely successor and create a mentoring plan? Would you start interacting with her differently, bouncing off ideas…seeking her advice? Imagining that you have only one more year with your best fundraiser will change you. You will manage differently; you will focus more on the things that really matter. You will become a better leader. Twelve months from now, that is why she will want to stay.

Chapter 14:
Donor-Centered Leadership

When certain people walk into a room, they make heads turn. There is something about them that draws others towards them. They are important.

And then there are those other people. They turn heads whenever they walk into a room, too, but for a different reason. They make everyone else feel important.

These are the genuine leaders...and they are rare.

The data is impossible to ignore – there are big changes underway in philanthropy. Some reflect the simple reality that we all age in one direction but others signal a giving population walking away from unpopular fundraising tactics. Donors of the 1920s, '30s and '40s, with their keen sense of responsibility and trusting view of not-for-profits have been overtaken by a more independent, analytical and prove-it-to-me first generation; and they will soon be displaced by another even more complex, more diverse, and certainly far less well understood demographic.

Still, the number of charitable organizations grows unabated and along with it the expectation that fundraisers will somehow raise more money this year than they did last. The good news is that, despite the breathtaking generosity of donors so far, it appears there is more money out there. In each of the last four years in which my firm has conducted its North-America-wide survey of people who give, almost one in two respondents reported she could still contribute more – under the right circumstances. Those circumstances are encapsulated in the definition of donor-centered fundraising described in Chapter 4.

Giving donors what they say they need is half the battle; making sure they are not subjected to the things that drive them away is the other. It is the job of decision-makers to recognize and respond more quickly to changing donor trends and to examine practices that give fundraising a bad name. There is so much about the art and science of raising of money that is respectful, subtle and brilliant as well as highly profitable. But to the public, fundraising is what they see, and what they see are dumbed-down appeals, rampant over-solicitation and uninformative and sporadic communications. Ironically, the things about fundraising that compromise its public credibility make far less money for not-for-profits while alerting donors to high cost per dollar raised.

For two reasons, Development professionals cannot be expected to address the deficiencies of the industry alone. First, in an effort to cater to employers' insistence on short-term revenue, fundraisers are running flat out executing costly appeals when they should be devoting their time and resources to raising money more strategically. Second, the Development industry includes many practitioners and for-profit enterprises that do very well by the system as it is currently configured. They exert a great deal of influence on fundraisers, on their membership associations and on educators because they offer relief to those who cry, "We have to have the money now."

The power to effect meaningful change and, in doing so, unleash philanthropy at a whole new level, lies in the hands of those who bear the ultimate responsibility for the welfare of not-for-profit organizations: Boards, Chief Executive Officers and Chief Development Officers. All it takes is leadership.

Leader is Not a Title

Why is it that some people excel as leaders while others who occupy the top jobs are not leaders at all? What is the difference between being in charge and being a leader?

Leadership is not the purview of workers who are older or who have progressed up the seniority ladder; leadership can be found anywhere along the seniority spectrum. Anyone can lead from her first day in her first front-line job. But, when leadership is present in the person at the top – the CEO, the Director of Development, the Chair of the Board – anything is possible.

What differentiates leadership from management? An entire field of study and expert consultation concerns itself with this intriguing question, but the difference between the two can be easily summarized. This excerpt, which draws from the work of renowned German-American psychologist, Kurt Zadek Lewin, recognized by many as the founder of social psychology, explains the difference well:

> Leadership and management are both important, but they seek to do different things...Every organization structures itself to accomplish its goals in a way that is in tune with or responsive to its environment. Once the efficiency of the organization is established, people go about simply maintaining the system, assuming that the environment will stay the same. Management is the main focus because it keeps the

organization going well with little change. But…the environment for any organization is always changing. There are always shifts in consumer tastes, social attitudes, society's culture, technology, historic events, and so on…Organizations tend not to spot these changes quickly, often because of a management orientation which is focused more on "looking in" instead of "looking out". Over time, the organization can become less and less in tune with or responsive to its environment…Leaders seek to bring their organizations more in line with the realities of their environment, which often necessitates changing the very structures, resources and relationships… which they have worked so long and so hard to manage. And yet, as they do, leaders can bring renewed vitality to their people.[1]

Don't ask anyone on staff, no matter their position, to do something that you wouldn't do. Whether taking out the garbage or writing reports – get in there and show your people that you are part of the team.

Leadership is evident in the evolution of fundraising in America. In his autobiography, published in 1791, Benjamin Franklin documented his winning strategy for raising money. Modern-day major gifts fundraising is built on his philosophy. In the early 1900s, Charles Sumner Ward and Lyman L. Pierce, campaign directors for the YMCA, developed a fundraising strategy that became the foundation for today's capital campaigns, which raise more cash in less time than any other method.

Leadership in fundraising is required today once again in order to bring about a more equitable balance between high volume and high quality fundraising. These changes in the giving marketplace, many of which I have written about earlier in this book, are both a warning to the fundraising industry to question the virtue of some of its tactics and an invitation to the industry's leaders to step up.

- Donors are supporting fewer causes while the net number of not-for-profits continues to increase, jeopardizing the future of mass marketing as it is currently configured;

- In an effort to increase the net value of their contributions "on the ground", donors are abandoning fundraising approaches deemed unnecessarily costly. Over-solicitation is the number one trigger to donors' perception of high cost fundraising;

- Donors expect charities to produce measurable results with the money they give and to communicate those results from the start of the giving relationship, regardless of the value of their early contributions;

- Donors are abandoning causes sooner when dissatisfied, as witnessed by the rise in first-gift-to-second-ask attrition from 50% to 65% in only a decade;

- Donors are less compliant today about transacting their gifts, preferring to

---

[1] From *Leadership Vs. Management*, an article by Peter Coutts, St. Andrew's Presbyterian Church, Calgary, AB, October 2000, in which Mr. Coutts cites several authorities on the subject, including Lewin. http://www.coutts. name/Other%20Documents/%25PDF-Lead%20vs%20Manage.pdf

be offered a menu of options for giving. They are less willing to blindly follow fundraisers' instructions;

- In increasing numbers, donors are avoiding fundraising solicitations altogether, preferring instead to decide independently whom they will support, when and how. This suggests that fundraisers should be shifting from being the "gatekeepers" of philanthropy to adopting a more customer-service approach to stewarding donors and their giving;

- A significant number of donors is willing to give more generously sooner, but the current fundraising system is not structured to capitalize on that opportunity;

- Young donors are the most willing to support new causes, to increase their giving during poor economic times, to rally their network on behalf of charities they admire and to volunteer, but too little attention is being paid to them because the value of their gifts is still modest when compared with that of older donors.

To address these issues, the not-for-profit sector needs Directors of Development, CEOs and Boards who fully understand the current fundraising system but who refuse to let that system dictate what they can and cannot accomplish. These exceptional leaders have the vision and the ability to not simply shift resources from one area of fundraising to another, but to re-engineer Development strategies in order to make more money. Re-engineering means improving and prioritizing strategies and tactics where profit potential is greatest, while eliminating the fundraising system's inherent deficiencies.

Donor-centered fundraising raises more money precisely because it takes advantage of a new donor environment defined by these changes. But it is the job of fundraising leaders to translate this philosophy and its customer-service approach to raising money into efficient strategies inside diverse Development operations. Chief Executive Officers and Chief Development Officers are capable of modernizing a lumbering, expensive fundraising system that is bleeding donors and responding too slowly to the next generation of philanthropists. Our industry's leaders have the power to make the fundraising system leaner, more responsive to donors, and quicker to capitalize on innovation. They can guide fundraising in a different and better direction – if they want to.

Behind them, it will take the efforts of dedicated managers to ensure that changes stick, preventing fundraising from slipping back into yesterday's tactics. Both leaders and managers are essential in order to meet this challenge.

Leadership in Real Life

Leadership is a vast and much-studied subject and its tenets are vital to business success. Yet, for all its importance, leadership remains the most elusive of concepts. The following stories transpose leadership principles from the classroom to the Development Departments, Executive Offices and Boardrooms in which you live.

Anything Is Possible if You Can Manage People

I started directing when I was a teenager and my early films were not very good. Over time I began to realize that you have to cast great actors and then let them own their roles. What I had been doing, because I was an actor myself, was making puppets out of everyone. My actors would try their best but they didn't have ownership; they were just imitating what they thought I wanted them to do.

As I gained more experience, I began to develop an approach to directing that I call, "the six-of-one theory", which is that if one of the other five key artists on the film besides the director – the actors, editors, cinematographers, production designers, and certainly the writers – has an idea that they really believe in on some organic level and if it still achieves what we need, or gains something extra, I always go with it because they own it, and on some intangible level I know it's going to be so much better.

Frankly, if I felt that the way to make a great film was to tell everyone to shut up and do what I say, then that's what I would do. But when I began to create an environment where people could speak, could contribute, my films improved exponentially. So there was a real, objective value in creating that environment.[2]

People who excel at managing other people have several characteristics that distinguish them from less capable managers, but one stands out above all others. They derive their job satisfaction indirectly from the staff that they manage. They are the movie directors of the business world.

These exceptional managers focus their own talent and time on identifying staff with the potential and the desire to succeed, and then making sure that they do. Managers who excel take the time to train and mentor staff; they assign their reports ambitious projects that showcase their abilities but also challenge them in areas where growth and experience would be beneficial.

Great managers believe that the measure of their own success lies in the achievements of their staff, so they love to showcase employees and their victories to their

What I was taught early in life has served me well in management – all people want and deserve to be treated with respect. With training and guidance, most people can rise to just about any challenge.

Listen and watch – and don't get sucked into the details.

---

[2] Edited from the television production, *Iconoclasts, Ron Howard and Steve Nash*, Season 5, Episode 5, Sundance/ Grey Goose – Radical Media Production, October 2010.

We have been instructed by the CEO to remove our Board members from the annual fund prospect list. No one is allowed to ask them for money.

As a leader, you have to delegate and let your people sink or swim. Sometimes, no matter how good you are at managing, some people are going to fail. It's not your fault; you can't save everyone.

own bosses or to their Boards. Praise for a member of their staff from a donor, a board member or a colleague is treasured by exceptional managers because it is simultaneously an acknowledgement of their own ability.

Directors of Development we surveyed were asked to think about the best boss they ever had in their careers and identify the characteristics that made this exceptional person stand out. 68% noted that their exceptional bosses asked for and valued input from their staff; reports' views were not discounted because they held less senior positions. 65% appreciated how cherished bosses allowed and encouraged their staff to work independently. Great leaders involve themselves only when necessary. They know that managing every decision serves only to stymie creativity while robbing staff of the self-confidence needed to exercise good judgment. When they do step in, however, great bosses bring their considerable influence and experience to bear to solve a problem or capitalize on a significant opportunity. Their very involvement underscores the issue's importance.

Are you a leader?

- Do you get a bigger thrill out of accomplishing something yourself or out of guiding and supporting your staff in reaching their goals?

- Do you treat your staff in the same manner as you treat your boss?

- When was the last time you sought the advice of someone in your industry under thirty years of age?

- In staff meetings, do you talk more than 10% of the time?

- Are you confident that every staff member in your Department or not-for-profit knows the goals to be achieved in the next three years, expressed in measurable terms?

The Achilles Heel of Fundraising

While conducting the research for this book I stumbled across an intriguing example of what can be accomplished when innovation and leadership come together.

In less than a decade, a West Coast hospital evolved from laboring under significant financial and quality of care issues to becoming one of the top ten hospitals in the country. The hospital transformed itself by adapting the Toyota Production System (TPS)[3] to healthcare and adopting it as their core operating philosophy.

Witnessing his hospital's transformation and realizing that many of the tenets of TPS could be applied to fundraising, the Hospital Foundation's President examined his

---

[3] TPS transformed the Japanese automobile industry in the mid-1900s. Its core philosophy focuses on eliminating waste, ensuring that workers are not overburdened, and standardizing production practices.

major gifts program through the lens of the Toyota Production System. He observed the sequence of steps that Gifts Officers undertake to secure generous gifts, noting that they were very successful at initial research, interacting with donors, shaping proposals and closing the sale. They were less successful at getting the initial appointment, however, and spent a disproportionate amount of their time stuck at this step. (This is not surprising as the qualities that attract fundraisers to major gifts work are more compatible with relationship building than with cold calling.)

One of the principles of TPS involves identifying and then eliminating waste, including wasted time. The Foundation President stepped in with an innovative solution. He outsourced the cold calling part of major gifts fundraising to people expert in opening doors. This relieved his staff of a responsibility that was draining valuable time and eroding their confidence. As a result, revenue rose dramatically.

Take a holistic approach. Revel in your co-workers' and your reports' own career ambitions. It's not just about you.

Inertia sets in when a certain way of doing things is assumed to be the only way. From inside a long-standing, integrated fundraising system, even recognizing that a problem exists can be difficult. Here is where innovative leaders shine. Innovative leaders in fundraising are different because their thinking is not bound by the system that is already in place; it neither clouds their judgment nor limits their search for a solution.

Leaders expose problems before non-leaders realize they exist; and, after they do, they move beyond the boundaries of their own industry to find solutions that have worked in other environments. But, most of all, leaders recognize that people are the critical catalyst to success and that they are more important than the system. Their first course of action when solving a problem is to bring the system in line with their people's strengths, not to change the people in order to adhere to an intransigent system.

Are you a leader?

- When was the last time you learned something new about fundraising that excited you enough to make a change? (While being a well-defined system, fundraising must be liquid enough to move with the times. Leaders who rely on what they learned years or even decades ago take their cues and draw conclusions from information that is out of date.)

- When was the last time you adopted an idea offered by a member of your staff?

- When was the last time you innovated an approach to raising money that defied traditional thinking?

Midas as Manager

Early in my career I had a boss who was an award-winning fundraiser. She started as a Fundraising Events Coordinator, where she seemed to have the Midas touch. She could take an event that was languishing, quickly identify where it was going wrong, reconfigure it like she was moulding clay, and jettison its profit into the stratosphere. She wasn't a behind-the-scenes person in the way professional fundraisers often are, taking a back seat while volunteers enjoyed the limelight. On the contrary, she was the focal point of every event she managed – and no one objected. Very attractive and with a personality larger than life, she commanded the attention of organizers and donors alike whenever she entered the room. She was very good... and she was driven.

It wasn't long before she was being offered increasingly challenging roles, both in the organization where her fundraising career began and in other not-for-profits. She was as natural at building relationships with major donors as she had been at orchestrating winning events. Donors loved her; they made time to see her; they introduced her to other donors. Wherever she went as her career progressed, she excelled. As she chalked up the fundraising wins she also piled up the professional awards, from Young Fundraiser of the Year to Most Accomplished Senior Development Professional.

As my boss climbed the career ladder, she worked for increasingly prestigious organizations, reaching for and surpassing ever-bigger goals. She also worked with larger staff contingents or, at least, she was surrounded by an increasing number of colleagues as she continued her upward trajectory. She tended to work solo and co-workers tended to let her. It was never really discussed outright, but everyone seemed to concede her unusual ability. It was all very cordial, but she was somewhat distanced from other fundraisers, her eye always being on the prize.

Her accomplishments were rewarded with higher pay, more prestigious titles and greater responsibility and eventually she landed one of the most coveted jobs in the city: VP of Advancement for a thriving college. In the top position she was often in the news and lauded by the President and Board of Trustees for landing seven- and eight-figure gifts.

But behind the scenes things were less rosy. There were rumblings among major gifts officers whose cultivated prospects were being transferred to the VP just as they became ready for a big ask. Meetings that used to be collaborative exchanges of ideas became competitions – competitions that the VP always won. With her rarified prospect list and direct access to the President and the Board, she outshone everyone else in the Department. And just in case anyone missed the point, a monthly tally of monies raised per staff member was sent to the President and the Board, with the VP's gold-star performance heading the list.

The VP began complaining about a lack of initiative and enthusiasm among the staff. She convened meetings in which she walked staff through some of her more impressive successes in the hope that this would send everyone back to their desks determined to do better. It did not. Instead, senior fundraisers began to leave – just a few at first but soon there were many unfilled positions and fewer experienced fundraisers willing to apply for jobs at the college. The VP took on more and more work herself in an effort to meet ambitious targets, but eventually it all caught up with her. She convened a meeting of the staff one day and announced that she had accepted a job in a larger institution in another state.

There will never be enough money, so I set benchmarks and celebrate every big or small success. If I didn't, I would go mad.

Before leaving she was interviewed by the local media and asked what had triggered her decision to go. "Working at the College has been a great experience", she said, "but no one person can raise money at this level and do so sustainably on his or her own. I'm looking forward to working with a team that is as motivated to succeed as I am."

The temptation in fundraising to ignore the Peter Principle can be overwhelming. It seems so logical that the individual with the greatest talent and track record for raising money should be the one to show everyone else how it's done. And, surely, the person who raises the most money should be rewarded with the top management job. But if that were true in other vocations, every opera diva would be an artistic director, every top neurosurgeon a hospital CEO. Closing the sale and motivating a team to excel are two entirely different skills. Sometimes they are embodied in the same individual, but more often they are not.

There is a difference between leadership and power. The title of CEO or Director or Manager imbues its holder with power automatically. But "Leader" can only be bestowed upon you by the people you lead. If a manager exerts his power in order to achieve results, it might work for a while or sporadically, but eventually this poor substitute for leadership translates into high staff turnover and underperformance among those who stay. If you practice leadership, however, staff stay loyal; they come to work each morning wanting to excel, both for their own sense of satisfaction and as a tribute to their leader.

Are you a leader?

- When was the last time a member of your staff said she was proud to work for you?

- When was the last time a staff member said, unprompted, to someone else that she was proud to work for you?

- When was the last time you complained about a staff member or your staff team to a friend or colleague?

Bosses who are mentors are life-long assets. My best boss saw potential in me before I did. He opened doors to key promotions and, later, served as a reference in job searches.

I constantly have to remind myself that not everyone can work at my pace or be as motivated as I am by what I believe is important.

Between the Lines

I was very excited on the morning that my CEO and I were scheduled to meet with the Administrative Director of a prominent charitable foundation. This was an exploratory meeting, the kind seldom granted by this particular foundation, to discuss the possibility of a three-year, $750,000 grant to test a new national program. But, just before we were to leave for the meeting, I was told by his secretary that my boss had double-booked appointments and would not be attending. As it was too late to find a member of the Board to accompany me, I went to the meeting alone.

I could tell that the foundation executive was not pleased that my CEO had bowed out at the last minute. He was gracious, however, and our meeting proceeded with me unfolding our plans for this new and important program. In the subtle ways that people in his position do, the Director signaled interest or steered me in a different direction with the slightest change of inflection in his voice or shift in posture. (No one communicates like someone who stands guard over other people's money.) I understood what I should and should not include in our proposal and was very grateful for this opportunity to gather inside information. I left the meeting excited by the possibility of an important win. Lingering in the back of my mind, however, was the unintended slight.

I worked hard on the proposal. Our CEO was very busy and out of town a lot. Not wanting to miss the deadline, I consulted the Head of Programs and Services, the CFO, and social workers on the front lines and got great information. I remember that, when it was ready, I drove sixty miles to the home of the Chair of the Board so that he could sign the submission personally.

Two months later, I heard from the foundation that we had been awarded a one-time grant of $50,000. While this was nowhere near the value sought in our proposal, at least we got something, and the door was now open for a bigger submission down the road.

At the next staff meeting, our CEO announced that we had won this grant. In front of all my colleagues, he said how disappointed he was that I was unable to secure the full amount. "We won't be able to do much with only $50,000 and, of course, it means yet another delay in starting such an important program. This is going to affect a lot of people."

I sat there, feeling my cheeks turn red from embarrassment. The room was thick with discomfort.

Our research study asked both Directors of Development and Fundraising Program Managers to identify the characteristics or behaviors of their bosses that are detrimental to fundraising. Happily, both groups were more likely to say that their bosses displayed no weaknesses in that regard. Among those who did identify deficiencies, though, "being unrealistic about the time required to make fundraising successful" was most commonly referenced. It is not surprising to see this response from Development Directors in reference to their CEOs, many of whom do not know how to make more profit sustainably. However, Fundraising Program Managers were referring to their Directors of Development, who should have a more sophisticated understanding. This unexpected finding may be attributable to the ever-present tension in fundraising where managers do want as much money raised as possible but, in the end, push for asks to be made quickly or follow up appeals to be sent prematurely in order to meet year-end and interim goals.

One in five Development Directors felt that their performance in fundraising was not assessed objectively against consistent, meaningful measures by their CEOs. This concern appears to be justified. More than half of CEOs surveyed about how they measure their chief fundraiser's performance cited reliance on criteria that are not reliable indicators of fundraising profit (see Chapter 11, Table 25). Development Directors with concerns about their CEOs also referenced poor budgeting choices, especially failing to resource new or exploratory strategies that could grow revenue exponentially. Attempting to improve fundraising performance by cutting cost is common among decision-makers who do not apply an investment/return rationale to budgeting. While CEOs are the ultimate decision-makers regarding operating expenses, fundraisers must accept part of the responsibility when their bosses make poor choices regarding the fundraising budget. It is the job of Development professionals to bring recommendations based on evidence through testing to the budgeting process. Our research found fundraisers' skills to be lacking when it comes to positioning evidence-based arguments and managing up.

One-person-shop fundraisers responded differently to the question about management weakness in reference to fundraising. One out of four referenced their boss's reluctance or outright unwillingness to ask donors for gifts. As a management issue, this was interpreted by sole practitioners as a refusal to acknowledge that CEOs and Boards must step up when there is only one fundraiser on staff.

Are you a leader?

- When was the last time you praised a staff member privately for her effort or accomplishment, outside a performance evaluation meeting?
- When was the last time you praised a staff member in front of other staff?
- When was the last time your praise of a member of your staff was entered into the minutes of a meeting of your Board of Directors?

I have a charismatic boss. People from every walk of life want to meet with her – such a fundraising asset that I and my colleagues really value.

No one comes to work with the intention of doing a bad job. Treat your staff with kindness and respect.

My boss is the most curious person I have ever known. He is fascinated by new approaches, always thinking and innovating – what a joy.

- When questioned by your boss about a problem in your Department, when was the last time you blamed a member of your staff for the mistake?
- When was the last time you criticized a staff member for poor performance in front of other staff?

Baptism By Fire

In my first fundraising job, I worked for an Executive Director who was a very emotional person and who seemed to be having a lot of personal problems. He had been with the organization for over twenty years, gradually migrating upwards until he earned the top job, regrettably more due to longevity than to ability. The staff sensed that they were working for a weak Executive Director and were surprisingly vocal (with each other) about their opinions concerning his leadership style. They seemed to divide into two groups: those who recognized his history and loyalty and were concerned for his welfare, and those who were frustrated by his distracted behavior and questionable leadership. This latter group wanted him out. As time went on, the gossip and expressions of dissatisfaction became more vocal. Staff spoke to the Executive Director in angry tones in staff meetings and the ED was at a loss as to how to handle it.

Being the new person on staff, I was relieved to be able to take a neutral position. However, the beleaguered Executive Director sensed that, and would often spend long periods of time in my office telling me about his personal and management problems and asking my advice. With no management experience of my own, I was not very helpful to him and these one-to-one sessions did nothing to ingratiate me with the other staff. A few months later, when things were becoming unbearable for everyone, a few people from the Board showed up, had a lengthy closed-door meeting in the Executive Director's office, and the next day he was gone.

A search for a new Executive Director ensued. Several people from within the organization applied for the job but someone from outside was hired. Things went well for the first six months or so, but then the whispering in the hallways began anew. This time, though, complaints were about overwork, too much demand for accountability, lack of appreciation, etc. Surprisingly, a few staff who had been so negative about the previous Executive Director were now wistfully recalling the good old days. I went home every night with a headache.

57% of managers we surveyed had no training whatsoever in the management of staff before assuming their first leadership role. They learned on the job through trial and error at the expense of the people they led. On the job is where they should be implementing the skills they have already developed, not trying things out for the first time.

When comparing classroom learning with learning on the job, the latter is generally more powerful. In the School of Hard Knocks the arena is real; decisions have consequences. But when it comes to managing people, the impact of poor management on staff can be devastating, breeding self-doubt and anxiety that survive long past the negative job experience. Management skills need to be learned in the classroom, in a case-based format that exposes poor performers' lack of suitability for management before they are vested with authority over others. Staff management can be learned, but that doesn't mean that anyone can manage staff well.

Are you a leader?

- What formal training did you have in the management of staff before assuming your first management role?

- Since you first became a manager, what has been the progression of your formal leadership training?

- Do you tend to favor some employees over others?

- When was the last time you took a course or attended a seminar concerned with fundraising? (If it is longer than three years ago, you are at risk of thinking there is nothing more to learn.)

- When was the last time you helped a member of your staff who needed to leave do so with dignity?

The Art of Leadership

I was in animated conversation with a room full of fundraisers. I had just presented data on donors' take-it-or-leave-it attitude towards having their names published in a newsletter or annual report as a way of recognizing their support. Delegates in the seminar were reluctant to believe that something which they had been doing for so long, which took a fair bit of time to orchestrate, and which cost money, too, could be that unpopular.

"It's not that they don't like it", I said. "It's just that it's not very effective."

"What do they want then?", someone asked.

"They don't want anything...or they don't know what they want", I said, "until they get it."

By the quizzical looks on the faces of delegates in the front row, I could tell I wasn't getting through. I tried a different approach.

To become a stand-out boss you need to master these three things: knowing the difference between important and urgent, an ability to speak with anyone, and discretion.

Different personalities, different life goals, different expectations – managing that complexity is the essence of leadership.

It's not about me and how I want the job to be done. It's about my ability to listen to my staff's ideas and to give them the leeway and support to do the job their way... as long as we get to the same goal in the end.

"What if you worked for an organization which, every year on the anniversary of your employment, sent you a letter of congratulations from the CEO and a box of chocolates? Do you think that would be nice?"

Everyone nodded in agreement.

"Now, no matter how many years you continue to work there, you get the same letter of congratulations from the CEO, though a different box of chocolates, hopefully." (Everyone laughed.) "Would you still think that was a thoughtful gesture?"

Almost everyone agreed that this was still a nice thing to do.

"Now let's imagine that you work for another organization, one that doesn't send its staff letters and chocolates on their anniversaries. Instead, let's imagine that it's 7:30 at night and you are the only one left in the office. It's already dark outside. This is the third night in a row that you have worked late because you are about to launch the annual fund campaign. Your concentration is broken when you hear footsteps coming down the hall. You hold your breath and wait, wondering who is there. The footsteps stop and a face peers around your doorframe. You relax and smile when you realize it is your CEO.

"I saw the light was still on at the end of the hall - again", he says. "Three nights in a row now, isn't it?"

You nod. "How does he know that?", you think to yourself.

"How is the campaign prep coming along?"

You start to tell him, thinking he wants an impromptu report.

"That's OK. I just wanted to make sure you're alright. So, why don't you pack up here for the night. It's late and I think things will keep till tomorrow, don't you?" He doesn't wait for an answer. "Come on, I'll walk you to your car and you can tell me what's going on in your life that's fun."

I paused to let the story sink in. "So", I said, "which organization would you rather work for?"

I looked at the delegates in the first row and I had my answer. Their eyes were glistening.

Chief Development Officers we surveyed felt that great bosses create an environment in which employees feel free to ask questions, present concerns and challenge the status quo, and 64% identified this quality as a particular strength. 58% said that exceptional bosses actually expect more from staff than do less capable employers, and that employees rise to the challenge for outstanding bosses because they express confidence in their staff to deliver when it counts.

Exceptional bosses see the value in each member of their staff; they do not play favorites. They do, however, interact differently with one report or the next in the knowledge that everyone learns and responds to direction differently. Great managers do not expect staff to adapt to their singular personality or management style; they are the ones who adapt in order to get the best possible performance from their diverse staff cohort.

While great bosses are known for their equitable treatment of staff, they do not allow any one member to derail the agenda or compromise the productivity of the team. When contending with a poor performer, stronger and weaker bosses take two different paths. Less capable managers focus time and energy on the under-achiever in an effort to effect improvement. But, managers who excel keep their time and attention squarely focused on the high achievers, giving them all the tools and support they need in the knowledge that these are the staff who will reach ambitious goals sooner – and then do it again. Great managers know that spending time disproportionately on poor performers may only move them from poor to acceptable whereas focusing on high achievers will guide those staff from excellent to exceptional.

Are you a leader?

- When was the last time you asked your employee about his family?
- When was the last time you convened a meeting of your staff just to celebrate reaching a goal, without another agenda?
- When was the last time you assigned an ambitious project to a junior employee?
- When was the last time you walked an employee to her car?

Not-for-Profit Just Means "No"

In my first management job in fundraising, I had an office with a south-facing window. In the afternoons, the sun would pour in and heat the room like a furnace. So, I ordered a set of thermal window blinds. After considerable comparison shopping and haggling, I was able to get the price down to $450.00. I got my blinds and the bill came in eventually and was placed among the other accounts payable to be signed off by the treasurer. When he saw it, I thought he was going to expire on the spot. "What! $450.00 for window blinds? How do you justify this expense?!!" I calmly explained why I needed them, noting that the temperature in my office sometimes climbed to 85 degrees, making it impossible to think. "But, $450.00," he said again, convinced that repeating the price in a louder voice would trump my irritatingly logical argument. "I can't sign off on this. It will have to go to the Board."

And, so it did. My window blinds were the subject of a thirty-minute debate at the next Board meeting. Could they be returned? (No, they were made to order for an off-sized window.) Should the cost be deducted from my paycheck? (At that point the Chair of Fundraising intervened, worried that this might trigger my resignation.) Due to the time consumed in the Board meeting by my window blinds, two other agenda items had to be deferred including "Board Members' Contributions to the Annual Fund Campaign".

I was told in no uncertain terms that this kind of purchase was unacceptable, and to never do it again. "After all, we're a charity!" Whether for-profit or not-for-profit, I thought to myself, the window still faces south, the sun still shines and I'm still sweating. The lesson I learned, though, had nothing to do with frugality, and everything to do with denial based solely on the fact that I worked in the not-for-profit sector. The cost of the blinds mattered, but the cost in lost productivity didn't. The cause, being charitable, was all-important, but cause and effect were irrelevant.

I had the opportunity to apply an investment/return assessment to those window blinds recently. I worked for this organization for four years, then moved across the country to take another position. While I have been gone from that city for twenty-eight years now, I return every once in a while for a visit. On my last trip, I happened to find myself in the neighborhood of my former office. Nostalgia overtook me and I took a detour along my old route to work. Approaching the building, I looked up to the third floor and there, still hanging on the south-facing window, were my thermal window blinds.

Four hundred fifty dollars divided by thirty-two years – so far, the comfort and sanity of who-knows-how-many-people who have occupied that office have been preserved for the grand sum of fourteen dollars and six cents per year.

Are you a leader?

- When was the last time you made a decision about fundraising based on real evidence gained through research and supported by controlled testing with your own donors?

- When was the last time you refused to invest in a time-saving product or approach before conducting a cost/benefit analysis?

- When was the last time you allowed your Board to cross the line into direct staff management?

- When was the last time you said "no" just because you could?

The Boss from Hell

I once worked for a boss who was notorious for the awful way she treated staff. She yelled, slammed doors, threw things and loudly berated people in the hallways. Even worse was her insensitivity to human issues in our small social service agency.

She called one of my colleagues at home and berated her for leaving the office early without letting anyone know. My colleague happened to be in end-stage cancer, which my boss knew. She passed away four days later. Many times after my colleague died, my boss made reference to how her work had been slipping and that she should have resigned months earlier.

I was not exempted from my boss's horrible treatment of staff. She demanded that I plan and host a baby shower for a co-worker, even though she knew I had just suffered a miscarriage. My due date would have coincided with the party. My boss really knew how to take the Human out of Human Services.

I was never comfortable in a senior leadership role. I have spent too many sleepless nights worrying about how my decisions will impact people's lives.

If you have never worked with an abusive boss, co-worker or employee, you are very fortunate. Chronically disruptive and abusive employees and bosses are extraordinarily damaging and they are never worth retaining. They operate outside the accepted social code of behavior. They gain control over others by behaving without constraint while everyone around them reels under their emotional outbursts and vitriolic criticism.

Colleagues and employers become unwitting enablers of abusive workers. Employers are reluctant or outright afraid to confront an angry staff member in the heat of the moment. When the outburst subsides, they rationalize excuses and hope that it won't happen again. Seeing that management is not taking action, co-workers and reports do their best to stay out of the line of fire while they start looking for other jobs.

Abusive fundraisers use their skill at raising money like a weapon. They work relentlessly at building relationships with important donors and leadership volunteers where they never show their darker side. Employers and colleagues assume they will not be believed if they take their complaints to a higher authority. Directors and CEOs responsible for the bottom line believe it when their abusive fundraiser insists that major donors will pull their support if she is fired.

If you manage an abusive employee, you must take action. Do not be cowed by the person or by the realization that you cannot manage this situation to a positive outcome. The abuser is counting on you to feel too embarrassed or ashamed to act. Refuse to be intimidated anymore. Take this issue to someone in authority today and seek outside expert help if you need it. This is an emergency and you are responsible for the welfare of your other staff.

If you work for an abusive boss and you see no avenue open to deal definitively with the problem, get out. If you stay, your self-confidence will erode and the stress will make you physically ill. Worst of all, you will start to believe that the abuser may be right. Victims of abusive people carry the scars long after the perpetrator is gone. Don't let this happen to you. You deserve much better.

Are you a leader?

- When was the last time you chalked up an employee's unacceptable behavior to "having a bad day?"

- When was the last time you failed to deal with an abusive employee's behavior towards others at the time it happened in the hope that it would not be repeated?

- When was the last time you failed to deal with a disruptive employee after multiple complaints from other staff?

- When was the last time you were reluctant to fire a disruptive or abusive employee because she raises more money than other gifts officers?

- When was the last time you did nothing after being advised not to fire an abusive employee for fear of a lawsuit?

- When was the last time you felt frightened or intimidated by an employee... or your boss?

The People Who Serve

In a multi-level organization that is structured nationally, regionally and locally, working in the middle layer is by far the most difficult job. You don't have the clout that the national office wields and you must work without the persuasive, on-the-ground case of the local affiliates. In that middle layer, you walk a thin line while trying to be measurably beneficial to your more powerful cousins.

In my early career, I greatly admired Frank, an Executive Director of one such middle-layer agency. While I basked in my considerably easier job as Executive Director of one of his local affiliates, Frank worked much harder to make visible progress. Frank's quiet demeanor conveyed to his more outgoing and driven local agency Execs that he was there to help but not to get in their way. Frank had an uncanny ability to pull together this collection of disparate personalities for the benefit of the cause as a whole. He was an effective catalyst to so many important accomplishments while never taking credit personally for any of them.

Unfortunately, some members of his Board failed to appreciate Frank's special qualities, openly questioning his leadership in monthly meetings. Worse still, the Chair of the Board was Frank's strongest critic and he gathered around him a group of other members that the rest of the Board was reluctant to challenge. Over the course of two years, this clique piled on the pressure until, exhausted and demoralized, Frank finally resigned. An emergency Board meeting was called during which the Chair suggested he would be willing to make a sacrifice. He offered to step into the role of Executive Director immediately, thus relieving the Board of a lengthy and expensive search. Of course, he would need to be compensated somewhat better than his predecessor but, otherwise, he was ready to give his all to the organization. Board members who sensed that this was not the right course of action to take failed to object. Having spent the previous two years perfecting a talent for side-stepping their responsibilities, the Board did exactly what the powerful inner circle told them to do.

My own Board of Directors was well aware of what had been unfolding during that twenty-four month period. (It's impossible to keep anything secret inside a multi-level charity.) So, the atmosphere was tense as my leadership volunteers gathered for their first scheduled meeting following the "coup" at the regional office.

Immediately after bringing the meeting to order, my Chair said that he wished to address what had unfolded at the regional office.

"I want this Board to reassure our own Executive Director that what happened to the ED of the regional office will never happen to her, or to any future Executive Director of this not-for-profit."

Everyone nodded in agreement. Continuing, my Board Chair said:

"To that effect, the Executive Committee has drafted a motion for your consideration. It reads as follows:

> "Be it resolved that no member of the Board may apply for any paid staff position without first resigning from his or her position on the Board and on any Committee of the Board, and without a period of at least two years having elapsed between resigning and applying for a position on staff."

Will someone second this motion?

Almost every hand ascended.

"Stephen, thank you. Any discussion?"

There was none.

"I am calling the vote then. All in favor?"

As all hands rose in unison, several board members looked at me, smiling and nodding as if to add their personal reassurance to the motion they were passing. I became intensely preoccupied with a scratch on the table so that my wonderful Board would not see the tears welling up in my eyes. I was overwhelmed with admiration for these eighteen volunteers and enveloped in sorrow for Frank.

The most important lesson I have learned in my career is how to take criticism – from donors, from my boss, and even from people outside the fundraising industry. I've learned not to take it personally.

Are you a leader?

- When was the last time you used your slot on the agenda to thank your Board for their time and thoughtful contributions to your not-for-profit?
- What role have you played in helping your Board evolve from hesitant or minimally engaged in fundraising to demonstrably productive?
- When was the last time you were successful in changing the views of your Board on a philosophical issue about fundraising that was critical to the bottom line?
- When did you last take a willing but inexperienced Board member from inactivity to confidently asking donors for gifts?
- When was the last time praised your Board to your staff?

It All Comes Down to This

In Chapter 3, I addressed the financial implications of losing and replacing high performing fundraisers by calculating the real cost (both up front and hidden) when someone leaves. While it was possible to put a price on the premature turnover of junior, front-line employees, experienced major gifts officers and managers of fundraising programs, the same cannot be said for Directors of Development. The strategic choices they make, the management styles they exhibit, the influence they exert on their CEOs and Boards, have fundraising implications that are so deep and wide as to make quantifying the cost of their replacement impossible. However, superb Development Directors who are especially skilled at inspiring staff to excel can guide teams in surpassing even the most ambitious goals. It can also be said that weaker directors, those who are less skilled at managing people, can quite quickly jeopardize their entire fundraising operations.

There are some people who come by their extraordinary ability to manage other people naturally. They can be spotted long before they hold management-level positions because they display leadership characteristics even when they are working on the front lines. They give credit to others, they are supportive and encouraging, they refrain from gossiping or holding grudges, they see the value in each member of the team as well as in the collective unit – all this while excelling at their own jobs. Natural leaders are held in high esteem by co-workers and managers alike and when they have job successes or when they are promoted, no one else on staff is resentful. Natural managers are prodigies and, as such, are quite rare.

Most excellent managers are not instinctively capable, however. They are great because they have learned how to manage other people well.

Day and Night Management

My fundraising career spans over twenty-five years, but I felt both the strongest desire to stay *and* the most desperate need to leave while working for the same not-for-profit organization.

I was young, and it was only my second job in fundraising, but I still knew enough to know that I had lucked out. The Director of my Development Department was more than just a boss; he was a teacher and mentor in the most valuable ways. First, he knew the fundraising business inside out, having worked his way up from the bottom over his thirty-year career. While I stewarded donors, he stewarded me, helping me grow by giving me increasing responsibility and letting me try new things. He didn't throw me out there to sink or swim, though; he taught me how to think through an idea before I executed it and how to avoid making big mistakes. Whenever he had either criticism or praise, it was always offered constructively.

I guess the best thing I can say about this all-around wonderful boss was that he trusted me. As a result, he always expected the best from me, not the worst, and that attitude made me want to excel, both for my organization and for him. "Your success is my success", he would often say.

His analysis and budgeting skills were second-to-none, so our fundraising goals were always built on real data, supported by experience and economic trends. Goals were ambitious, but I and my colleagues knew we could reach them with our boss's guidance and support. It was an extraordinary environment in which to work and I loved getting up each morning, knowing that I was going to this great job.

I had been there for three wonderful years when my boss announced that he had accepted another position. I wanted to follow him and so did many other staff. But, he counseled me that I could learn more by staying and that this organization would need me now more than ever.

I lasted eighteen months and often wonder how I stuck it out that long. My new boss was a completely different personality and, initially, I had a lot of sympathy for her because of the big shoes she had to fill. But, unlike her predecessor, her door was almost always closed. Staff had to make appointments to see her and I always felt I was intruding on her much more important work. It wasn't long before the atmosphere changed from buoyant and collaborative to stressful and competitive. Whatever we achieved never seemed to be enough. Fundraising wins were expected, not celebrated; problems were criticized, not analyzed. Even when we met or exceeded a goal, it was quickly raised, depriving me and my colleagues of any sense of accomplishment.

One by one, staff members left and the once cohesive team that had accomplished so much became just a memory. I started waking up in the middle of the night, worrying about things that I used to look forward to under my old boss. By the end of the first year, our revenue was down 15% and three positions were vacant. It hadn't taken long for word to get around that this was no longer a great place to work. Excellent candidates were staying away in droves.

It turned out that my old boss was right – I did learn a lot by staying. I learned that the senior Director of Development can make or break an entire fundraising operation by the leadership style he (or she) adopts and the management choices he makes.

I am now a Director of Development myself. Whenever I am faced with a difficult problem, I think about both of these influential bosses. The first one's guidance and training allows me to see that almost anything can be achieved and tells me how to manage my staff for optimum results. The second one reminds me of what can happen if I ever forget that my own success is tied to how I treat the people who rely on me to lead.

Chapter 15:
You

In an operating theatre, Dr. Grant is up to his elbows in someone's intestines. Dr. Grant saves lives and makes a very comfortable living doing so.

The first time he thought about becoming a doctor was in high school. A guest speaker, a heart specialist, had come to his private school on Career Day to talk about what it takes to get to the top of his profession. Dr. Grant was enthralled. His young imagination took flight and he was hooked. Career Day took place in the school's new auditorium (part of a recent campus-wide expansion) and generous corporate sponsorship covered the cost of the event. You raised the money for both.

Dr. Grant applied himself in high school, helped substantially by access to state-of-the-art labs and excellent teachers. Your fundraising made them possible. He applied and was accepted to a prestigious university. While the fees were substantial, they represented only a portion of what his education actually cost. The rest was quietly subsidized by donors whose generosity and foresight reached back over two hundred years. Their willingness to give was a product of your encouragement; their action a result of your diligence. Dr. Grant's university education was made easier along the way by several scholarships. You raised that money, too.

Through his undergraduate and graduate degrees, internship and residency, you were there, working invisibly alongside him to help Dr. Grant accomplish his goal. Your fundraising built the residence he slept in, the library he studied in, the classroom he learned in and the campus hospital in which he practiced.

Twenty years later, here he is in Operating Theatre Six in the Northeast Wing of a world-class hospital, deep into his work. You raised the money for Theatre Six as well as Theatres One through Five. You raised the money to build the Northeast Wing and, come to think of it, the entire hospital.

On the table lies the unconscious but soon-to-be-grateful patient. She has been through a lot lately, but conclusive evidence from a CT scan has put her here today. Her life will be saved. You raised the money that paid for this equipment. Surrounding Dr. Grant is a plethora of machines, devices and tools keeping his patient alive and making his work possible – all thanks to your fundraising efforts.

Surgery goes well and Dr. Grant transfers responsibility to his five-member team, all of whom got to where they are today because of donors – and you. He's thinking ahead to tonight and a well-earned diversion. He's going to see a new play that's generating a lot of buzz. Tickets were very hard to get.

When he sinks into the unexpectedly comfortable seat (donor's name on the back – you did that) in the newly refurbished historical theatre (you again), he'll read the house program while he waits for the curtain to rise. You found the sponsors for this publication, sold the ads, and negotiated the printing at cost.

The play will not disappoint. Shouts of "bravo" and three curtain calls will bring the newly discovered playwright and his director to the stage. The director will make an impassioned, off-the cuff speech about encouraging young talent; the playwright will talk about his inspiration and the intricacy of his dialogue. No one will mention the equally intricate grant application you wrote that raised the money that launched the New Playwrights Development Program that brought these two artists together that made tonight possible.

When the evening is finally over, Dr. Grant will step out of the theatre into a night that will be colder than expected. He will turn up the collar of his coat and quicken has pace towards his car. Without noticing, he will pass under a sign that reads, "Global Environment Association, Foundation Office".

Three stories up, a light will still be burning.

Acknowledgements

I will always be grateful for the wisdom of research study respondents that is reflected in the statistical data and some of the stories in this book. It is very clear that it was gained through hard-earned experience. I especially appreciated respondents' willingness to share highly personal and often difficult information about their careers and the time they took from their busy lives to devote to this project.

I had a research question on my mind five years ago but no preconceptions about what I would uncover or what my findings would mean when I first embarked upon this project. It was the respondents who pointed me in the right direction all the way through this five-year journey. Thank you to 6,728 Professional Fundraisers, Chief Executive Officers and Board Members as well as 5,768 Donors for their collective contribution to this book.

Due to the sensitive nature of the subject matter in this book, the names of survey respondents have been withheld. But readers might be interested in this demographic picture of the people who contributed.

Table A: Profile of Professional Fundraisers

Characteristic	Directors of Development	Fundraising Program Managers	Non-Management Fundraisers	One-Person-Shop Fundraisers
Gender - Male - Female	29% 71%	17% 83%	18% 82%	17% 83%
Age - Under 35 - 35 to 55 - 56 or older	6% 66% 28%	17% 62% 21%	29% 49% 22%	11% 65% 24%
Education - Secondary/College/ Some University - Undergrad Degree - Some Post-Grad or Post-Grad Degree - Doctoral Degree	7% 39% 48% 6%	11% 44% 41% 4%	12% 49% 38% 1%	9% 41% 48% 2%
Religious Conviction - actively religious - not at all religious - spiritual/somewhere in between	35% 20% 45%	30% 25% 45%	38% 16% 46%	37% 21% 42%
Has Responsibility for Financially Supporting Family Members	69%	61%	53%	67%
Ethnic Background - Caucasian - All Other	95% 5%	95% 5%	87% 13%	95% 5%
% Respondents Who Speak a Language in Addition to English	15%	16%	19%	10%
Nationality - American - Canadian	84% 16%	77% 23%	88% 12%	81% 19%

Table B: Fundraising-Related Education and Certification of Professional Fundraisers

Characteristic	Directors of Development	Fundraising Program Managers	Non-Management Fundraisers	One-Person-Shop Fundraisers
Highest Level of Fundraising Education				
- Masters Degree in Fundraising Mgmt	4%	3%	5%	5%
- Undergrad Degree in Fundraising	1%	1%	0%	0%
- College Certificate in Fundraising	6%	5%	4%	6%
- Some Fundraising Courses through Continuing Education	23%	17%	14%	23%
- Fundraising Workshops	51%	57%	60%	51%
- Other/None	15%	17%	17%	15%
Certification				
- ACFRE	1%	0%	0%	1%
- CFRE	28%	16%	11%	23%

Table C: Types of Not-for-Profits in Which Respondents Worked When Participating in This Research

Characteristic	Directors of Development	Fundraising Program Managers	Non-Management Fundraisers	One-Person-Shop Fundraisers
Education Institutions	42%	51%	56%	21%
Arts and Culture	8%	5%	2%	9%
Environment Organizations	2%	2%	4%	3%
Hospitals and other related Health Services	15%	16%	18%	19%
Disease Charities and other Health Agencies	4%	7%	2%	8%
Scientific/Research Institutions	2%	1%	.5%	0%
Federated Charities/United Way and Other	0%	1%	.5%	0%
Animal Welfare Organizations	1%	0%	1%	0%
Social/Community Services	19%	12%	8%	32%
International/Relief Organizations	3%	2%	2%	2%
Religious Institutions	1%	2%	2%	2%
Political and Other	3%	2%	4%	3%

Table D: Number of Years that Professional Fundraisers Have Worked in the Fundraising Industry

# Years Worked in Fundraising	Directors of Development	Fundraising Program Managers	Non-Management Fundraisers	One-Person-Shop Fundraisers
5 and under	6%	12%	20%	26%
6 to 10	16%	32%	35%	29%
11 to 15	22%	21%	20%	18%
16 to 20	23%	18%	10%	10%
21 to 30	28%	14%	8%	23%
more than 30	5%	3%	1%	-

Table E: Profile of Chief Executive Officers Who Participated in the Study

Characteristic	Chief Executive Officers
Gender - Male - Female	 34% 66%
Age - Under 35 - 35 to 55 - 56 or older	 1% 55% 44%
Education - Secondary/College/Some University - Undergrad Degree - Some Post-Grad or Post-Grad Degree - Doctoral Degree	 4% 42% 44% 10%
Nationality - American - Canadian	 81% 19%

Table F: Profile of Donors Who Have Been Assigned a Gifts Officer for Stewardship of Their Philanthropy

Characteristics	American Donors	Canadian Donors
Gender - Male - Female	 58% 42%	 60% 40%
Age - under 35 - 35 to 64 - 65 or older	 3% 56% 41%	 5% 64% 31%
Religious Conviction - actively religious - not at all religious - spiritual/somewhere in between	 58% 14% 28%	 27% 32% 40%
Household Income - Under $70,000 - $70,000 to $129,999 - $130,000 to $199,999 - $200,000 or more	 11% 26% 22% 41%	 21% 34% 20% 25%
Occupation - Retired - Homemaker - Professional/Academic - Executive/Owner/Entrepreneur - Tradesperson/Clerical - Student - Sales/Marketing/Retail - On Disability/Unemployed	 37% 3% 39% 16% 1% 0.1% 2.9% 1%	 32% 2% 35% 20% 3% 1% 5% 2%
Education - Secondary/Some College - Undergraduate Degree - Post Graduate/Doctoral Degree	 4% 23% 73%	 22% 33% 46%

Table G: Profile of Leadership Volunteers Serving on Boards of Directors

Characteristics	American Board Members	Canadian Board Members
Gender		
- Male	43%	49%
- Female	57%	51%
Age		
- under 35	4%	6%
- 35 to 64	63%	64%
- 65 or older	33%	30%
Religious Conviction		
- actively religious	33%	30%
- not at all religious	27%	25%
- spiritual/somewhere in between	40%	45%
Household Income		
- Under $70,000	19%	27%
- $70,000 to $129,999	33%	41%
- $130,000 to $199,999	22%	17%
- $200,000 or more	26%	15%
Education		
- Secondary/Some College	7%	17%
- Undergraduate Degree	29%	35%
- Post Graduate/Doctoral Degree	64%	48%
Annual Gift Level		
- $10,000 or more	31%	14%
- Less than $10,000	69%	86%

Initial Advisors

Before beginning the research, I had intriguing conversations with fundraising and management consultants, business executives, HR Experts and not-for-profit CEOs that brought to light issues they were experiencing related to staff turnover. These conversations were very important in crafting relevant research questions. My thanks to:

Allan Arlett
Marilyn Bancel
Margot Biggin
Ken Burnett
Pamela Cook
Patrick Corrigan
Jean Crawford
James Daniel
Edith Falk

Arthur Filip
Deb Greenfield
Scott Haldane
Aleah Horstman
Lyn McKay
Katheryn Northington
Candice Palson
Ivana Pelnar-Zaiko
Vit Vaculik

Expert Resources

These institutions and the work that they publish were vital sources of information supporting *Donor-Centered Leadership*. The following organizations make a continuing and invaluable contribution to the fundraising industry. My thanks to:

- **The Association of Fundraising Professionals** for their annual AFP Compensation and Benefits Study as well as other research, and especially to Reed Stockman who led me to historical information on fundraising
- **Giving USA Foundation** for Giving USA: The Annual Report on Philanthropy
- **The National Center for Charitable Statistics**
- **The School of Philanthropy, Indiana University-Purdue University**
- **Statistics Canada**
- **Target Analytics, a Blackbaud Company** for their quarterly Index of National Fundraising Performance figures
- **US Bureau of Labor Statistics**

Innovative Sources

The thing I enjoy most about conducting research is uncovering information that is so different from what I expected to find and, simultaneously, so fundamentally logical.

An article in the October 2011 issue of the Harvard Business Review described A.G. Lafley's approach to succession planning. Lafley is the retired CEO of Procter & Gamble. Among other significant career accomplishments, he has turned succession planning into an art. My references to the subject in Chapter 13 draw upon his sage advice.

While attending the 2011 AHP Conference (Association of Healthcare Philanthropy), I happened to overhear a conversation among fundraisers concerning a workshop they had just attended. Michael VanDerhoef, President of Virginia Mason Foundation in Seattle, had just explained how he had reengineered his Foundation's approach to major gifts fundraising based, in part, on the principles of the Toyota Production System. Several months later, I was fortunate to spend two hours with Michael and they were two of the most interesting hours I have ever spent in fundraising. Some of my thinking in Chapter 12 and a story in Chapter 13 were influenced by what I learned from Michael, a true innovator in the Development world.

No Detail Too Insignificant...

Ingrid Lawrie's keen eye and sophisticated hand weave their way through this entire book. From her office in the UK, Ingrid has done a magnificent job as our Editor-in-Chief. Thank you.

Doing the Impossible

In Altona, Manitoba, a small town outside Winnipeg, Friesens Corporation pulls rabbits out of hats for authors like me who spend years writing books, then expect their printer to turn around a finished product in a matter of days. Thank you, Friesens (again) for being unflappable as well as amazing.

Behind Every Author...

While my name goes on the cover, so many others behind the scenes have made Donor-Centered Leadership possible.

Haihong Wang, PhD, is the research and quality control expert behind all Cygnus studies. I am so grateful to you, Hai, for your ability to juggle multiple studies simultaneously while cheerfully catering to my constant requests for "just one more cross-tabulation". Thank you for ensuring that our research is published at the highest possible standard.

Starting in 2008, **Carolyn Veldstra**, PhD (ABD), assisted by **Sarah Rietkoetter**, co-ordinated the first series of research studies with professional fundraisers. They also led the effort in finding Development professionals who were willing to take part in our lengthy research studies, no mean feat considering the work and time pressures that weigh heavily on fundraisers' shoulders. Your work in the first two years laid the groundwork for the entire project. Thank you both.

Pat Sinka and, more recently, **Peter Aloian** are responsible for our lifeline – our mailing list from which we draw research subjects and through which we connect to the not-for-profit sector. Their tireless work and diligent attention to detail makes it possible for Cygnus to communicate with our marketplace. Thank you both for your vital contribution to the company's success.

While there were hundreds of research questions in the study, there were literally thousands of open-ended comments. **Gwen Cottle** and **Joy Uson** read and categorized them all, the best of which appear in the margins of this book. They were supported by **Niall McGregor**, **Lauren Stephens** and **Thomas Vaculik**. Their analytical skill and creativity resulted in two books inside one – the quotes in the margins tell the story on a whole other level. Thank you to this wonderful team.

Scott Koblyk, Director, Client Services, is one of the reasons why our clients' research studies with donors produce such interesting information. Scott, your thoughtful work made me know that all was well back at the shop while I focused on writing the book. Thanks for your talent and for your quirky sense of humor.

Our Essential Bridge

As I travel around North America, every conference organizer and speaking engagement host sings the praises of **Theresa Horak**, our Manager of Customer Relations and the public voice of Cygnus Applied Research. Theresa is our lifeline to clients, customers, the media and friends, making my company look good every day of the year. Theresa's creative hand shapes our marketing and the widespread industry and mainstream media coverage that our research enjoys is due to her influence. Thank you, Theresa, for making it such a pleasure for the rest of us to work in this company.

"Art is Not a Thing; It Is a Way"

We are lucky at Cygnus; we have an artist on staff. **Amanda Diletti-Goral** takes words and makes them sing, takes ideas and makes them breathe. Amanda's talent for design lives on every page of this book as well as its cover. She designs our website, our research study publications and our marketing materials, too. It is not easy to corral research information and narrative into a format that makes it visually appealing, but Amanda does it with flair. Thank you, Amanda, for your talent and your lovely demeanor.

The Show Must Go On

When people ask me how I can write a book and run a business at the same time, I am flattered but I know that I can't. Without **Jeff Dubberley**, hardly anything would get accomplished at Cygnus and what would get done would be nowhere as good. Jeff captains the Cygnus ship, managing the company's affairs, directing client services, and strategizing our future. His leadership keeps us headed in the right direction. In addition, his direct contributions to this book, from analytical computations to marketing copy, have added so much value to this publication. Without you, Jeff, I would have never survived this project. Thank you.

Great Beginnings

I'm one of those lucky people who didn't have to survive my childhood. Thanks to my mother, Jane, and my late father, Bill, for the lush adventure that was my formative years. You instilled in me a love of ideas and the confidence to pursue them. And, although I am sure you loved me best, thanks also for surrounding me with five great siblings – Phyllis, Annabelle, James, Nancy (En) and Robert.

Index

Other Publications by Penelope Burk

Donor-Centered Fundraising and *The Cygnus Donor Survey...Where Philanthropy Is Headed This Year* are available online at our website: www.cygresearch.com, (Bulk order discounts are available). For more information, please contact us at cygnus@cygresearch.com or (800) 263-0267.

In ***Donor-Centered Fundraising®*** Penelope demonstrates how not-for-profits can make much more money by becoming "donor-centered". The book examines typical practices in gift acknowledgement, communication and recognition, suggesting new approaches that reflect what donors say they need in order to stay loyal longer and give more generously. *Donor-Centered Fundraising®* is the companion publication to *Donor-Centered Leadership*. The product of six years of research with thousands of donors, fundraisers and not-for-profit leaders, *Donor-Centered Fundraising®* is the essential methodology for keeping donors long term and running a much more profitable Development operation.

Since 2009, Penelope has authored the annual ***Cygnus Donor Survey***, a compelling study showcasing the views of 25,000 North American donors. The survey charts where philanthropy is headed in the coming year, focusing especially on the trends and issues that fundraisers and donors are contending with right now. Its compelling narrative and easy-to-read charts and graphs provide professional fundraisers, executive staff, and leadership volunteers with clear recommendations on how not-for-profits can test new initiatives and improve overall fundraising performance immediately.

Donor-Centered Leadership

Where to Learn More

Cygnus Applied Research can help you leverage the principles of Donor-Centered Leadership in order to address the high turnover rate of staff and the financial toll it takes on not-for-profits. Penelope's webinars, seminars and client-specific training programs speak directly to decision-makers while also being an essential resource for fundraisers building their careers.

For more information about Donor-Centered training for Board members, staff leadership and fundraisers, or to learn more about our client services, please visit our website at www.cygresearch.com

Keynote Addresses

Penelope is a leading speaker at industry and business conferences. For a summary of her most-requested keynote topics, please go to: http://www.cygresearch.com/pb/spktopics.php

To inquire about Penelope's availability, please contact Theresa Horak, t.horak@cygresearch.com or (800) 263-0267.

 # About Cygnus Applied Research

Cygnus Applied Research, Inc. is known for its independent research on fundraising and donor behavior, and for helping not for profits take advantage of what our research has uncovered. With offices in the United States, Canada and the United Kingdom, Cygnus' team of senior consultants and researchers provides these specialized services:

- **Donor Surveys**… Designed to help you learn more about your supporters and what it will take for your donors to stay loyal longer and offer more generous gifts. Cygnus' questionnaires are insightful and strategic, our interviews are intriguing, our findings often surprising and always compelling.

- **Fundraising Data Analysis**… Some of the most actionable information about your donors and what they are likely to do next lies undiscovered inside your database. Cygnus is expert in analyzing fundraising data and translating statistical information into productive development strategies.

- **Donor-Centered Fundraising Plans**… Designed to suit your unique organizational needs and objectives, Cygnus' plans transition clients from typical fundraising to a donor-centered way of raising money through common sense strategies backed by evidence from clients' own donors and data.

For more information on our services, please visit our website at www.cygresearch.com or contact us directly at cygnus@cygresearch.com or (800) 263-0267.

NOTES

NOTES

NOTES

NOTES

NOTES

NOTES

NOTES

NOTES

NOTES

NOTES